Volume 12: Religious Freedom: Social-Scientific Approaches

Annual Review of the Sociology of Religion

Editors

Enzo Pace, Luigi Berzano and Giuseppe Giordan

Editorial Board

Peter Beyer (*University of Ottawa*)
Anthony Blasi (*Tennessee State University*)
Olga Breskaya (*University of Padova*)
Roberto Cipriani (*Università di Roma Tre*)
Xavier Costa (*Universidad de Valencia*)
Franco Garelli (*Università di Torino*)
Gustavo Guizzardi (*Università di Padova*)
Dick Houtman (*Erasmus University, Rotterdam*)
Solange Lefebvre (*Université de Montréal*)
Patrick Michel (*CNRS, Paris*)
Ari Pedro Oro (*Universidade Federal do Rio Grande do Sul*)
Adam Possamai (*University of Western Sydney*)
Ole Riis (*Agder University*)
Susumu Shimazono (*University of Tokyo*)
Jean- Paul Willaime (*EPHE, Sorbonne*)
Monika Wohlrab- Sahr (*University of Leipzig*)
Linda Woodhead (*Lancaster University*)
Fenggang Yang (*Purdue University*)
Sinisa Zrinscak (*University of Zagreb*)

VOLUME 12

The titles published in this series are listed at *brill.com/arsr*

Volume 12: Religious Freedom: Social-Scientific Approaches

Edited by

Olga Breskaya, Roger Finke and Giuseppe Giordan

BRILL

LEIDEN | BOSTON

The Library of Congress Cataloging-in-Publication Data is available online at https://catalog.loc.gov
LC record available at https://lccn.loc.gov/2021030329

Typeface for the Latin, Greek, and Cyrillic scripts: "Brill". See and download: brill.com/brill-typeface.

ISSN 1877-5233
ISBN 978-90-04-46803-0 (hardback)
ISBN 978-90-04-46808-5 (e-book)

Copyright 2021 by Olga Breskaya, Roger Finke and Giuseppe Giordan. Published by Koninklijke Brill NV, Leiden, The Netherlands.
Koninklijke Brill NV incorporates the imprints Brill, Brill Nijhoff, Brill Hotei, Brill Schöningh, Brill Fink, Brill mentis, Vandenhoeck & Ruprecht, Böhlau Verlag and V&R Unipress.
Koninklijke Brill NV reserves the right to protect this publication against unauthorized use. Requests for re-use and/or translations must be addressed to Koninklijke Brill NV via brill.com or copyright.com.

This book is printed on acid-free paper and produced in a sustainable manner.

Contents

List of Figures and Tables   VII
Notes on Contributors   VIII

Introduction. Religious Freedom: Social-Scientific Approaches   1
  Olga Breskaya, Roger Finke and Giuseppe Giordan

PART 1
Religious Freedom, Secularity and Secularism

1   How Does Secularity "Travel"?: Toward a Policy Mobilities Approach in the Study of Religious Freedoms   13
    Efe Peker

2   Religious Freedom, Legal Activism, and Muslim Personal Law in Contemporary India: A Sociological Exploration of Secularism   35
    Anindita Chakrabarti

3   Religious Freedom and Secularism in Post-Revolutionary Tunisia   59
    Anna Grasso

4   Religious Pluralism, Religious Freedom and the Secularization Process in the Greek Educational System   83
    Alexandros Sakellariou

PART 2
Multi-level Study of Religious Freedom

5   Regulating Sincerity: Religion, Law, Public Policy, and the Ambivalence of Religious Freedom in Pluralist Societies   105
    Zaheeda P. Alibhai

6   The Religionization in Alevi Culture: An Exploratory Study on Spiritual Leaders (*Dedes*)   123
    Nuran Erol Işık

7 One, Many or None: Religious Truth-Claims and Social Perception of Religious Freedom   151
   Olga Breskaya and Giuseppe Giordan

8 Religious Freedom in Prisons: A Case Study from the Czech Republic   175
   Jan Váně and Lukáš Dirga

PART 3
Politics and Policies on Religious Freedom

9 Organizations and Religious Restrictions: An International Overview of the Intersection of State and Non-Governmental Organizations and Religious Groups   197
   Dane R. Mataic and Kerby Goff

10 Religious Freedom between Politics and Policies: Social and Legal Conflicts over Catholic Religious Education in Italy, 1984–1992   220
    Guillaume Silhol

11 The Measure of CEDAW: Religion, Religious Freedom, and the Rights of Women   241
    Barbara R. Walters

12 Religious Freedom and the Religionization of World Politics: Views of EU Political and Religious Representatives   271
    Chrysa K. Almpani

Index   299

Figures and Tables

Figures

7.1 Means for 'Religious Diversity' (negative and positive attitudes)   163
9.1 Distribution of restrictions on organizations of minority religions by global region in 2014   201
9.2 Distribution of restrictions on organizations of minority religions by countries of particular concern   207
10.1 Articles dealing with IRC published in *La Repubblica* between 1984 and 1993   234
11.1 Gender Inequality Index (GII) by CEDAW OP state party and year   251
11.2 GIII by religion and year   258

Tables

6.1 Socio-demographic characteristics of *Dedes*   134
6.2 The key themes in participants' answers   144
7.1 The Astley-Francis Theology of Religions Index (AFTRI)   158
7.2 Dimensions of the concept 'Religious Diversity'   158
7.3 Means for dependent variable 'Religious Freedom'   160
7.4 Religious truth-claims AFTRI (frequencies (%))   162
7.5 Correlations (Pearson's r, 2-tailed) between AFTRI, SPRF and Religious Diversity   164
7.6 Regression analysis for Religious Freedom   166
9.1 Internal organizations and structure and government restrictions on minority religious organizations in 2014   204
9.2 Regression modeling the association between restrictions on religious minority organizations in 2014   205
10.1 Main judicial sentences concerning IRC between 1984 and 1992   231
11.1 GII by CEDAW OP state party and year   251
11.2 CEDAW OP party by entered reservations   254
11.3 Entered reservations by religion   255
11.4 CEDAW OP party by religion   256
11.5 Gender inequality index by religion and year   257
11.6 CEDAW OP party by religious freedom for predominantly Muslim nations   260
11.7 Legal status of underage marriage in predominantly Muslim countries by religious and secular freedom   261

Notes on Contributors

Zaheeda P. Alibhai
is a PhD candidate in Religious Studies with a specialization in Canadian Studies at the University of Ottawa. Her research investigates the critical intersections between religion, law, politics, media, human rights, science, and ethics in the study of identity, multiculturalism, and pluralism in Canadian and international contexts. She is the recipient of the Leading Women Building Communities Award from the Canadian Minister of the Status of Women. She has contributed to several volumes exploring the intersection between religion, public policy and pluralism. Her research is supported by the Social Sciences and Humanities Research Council of Canada (SSHRC).

Chrysa K. Almpani
graduate of the Department of International and European Studies (UoM), is currently a PhD Candidate in Sociology of Religion, Department of Ethics and Sociology, School of Theology, Aristotle University of Thessaloniki, Greece. She holds two MSc degrees in the fields of 'Economic and Regional Development' (Faculty of Economic and Political Sciences, AUTH) and 'Sociology of Religion' (see above). Her doctoral thesis, *Religion and International Relations in Second Modernity: Power, moral cosmopolitanism and the responsibility to protect,* has been awarded with a scholarship from the Hellenic Foundation of Research & Innovation (HFRI). She has been Research Associate at the Social Research Centre for Religion and Culture since 2017, while she previously worked as an asylum caseworker in the Hellenic Ministry of Migration Policy during the EU's Relocation Programme (2016–2017). She is also co-author of "Ateni-zo: A Non-formal Educational Guide on Human Trafficking" (Athens: Human Rights Defense Centre—KEPAD, 2014).

Olga Breskaya
is a postdoctorate researcher at the Department of Philosophy, Sociology, Education and Applied Psychology, University of Padova. She got her doctorate from the International Joint Ph.D. Programme "Human Rights, Society, and Multi-level Governance" at the University of Padova. Her research interest is focused on sociology of human rights and quantitative study of religious freedom. She serves as Board member of the International Sociological Association (Research Committee 22 Sociology of Religion, representative for Europe) from 2018 till 2022. Among her publications is Human Rights and Religion: A Sociological Perspective in the *Journal for the*

Scientific Study of Religion together with G. Giordan and J.T. Richardson 57 (3), 2018.

Anindita Chakrabarti

is an Associate Professor of Sociology at the Department of Humanities and Social Sciences, IIT Kanpur. Her research and teaching interests lie in the fields of sociology of religion, sociology of law (with a focus on personal law), economic sociology and urban sociology. She has been a visiting scholar at the University of California, Berkeley and a visiting fellow at CSSS (JNU), and at the Department of Sociology, Delhi University. In 2010 she won the Professor M. N. Srinivas Memorial Prize awarded by the Indian Sociological Society. Her monograph titled *Faith and Social Movements: Religious Reform in Contemporary India* (Cambridge University Press) was published in 2018 and co-edited volume titled *Religion and Secularities: Reconfiguring Islam in Contemporary India* (Orient Blackswan) in 2020. She has been a Senior Fellow at the Humanities Centre for Advanced Studies (HCAS) at Leipzig University (2016–20).

Lukáš Dirga

is Assistant Professor at the Department of Sociology of the University of West Bohemia in Pilsen and chief research coordinator at the Ministry of Justice of the Czech Republic. He concentrates on ethnographic research within the field of penitentiary sociology (sociology of prison life).

Roger Finke

is a Distinguished Professor of Sociology, Religious Studies, and International Affairs at the Pennsylvania State University and is the Founder of the Association of Religion Data Archives (www.theARDA.com). He has authored two award-winning books with Rodney Stark. His most recent books include *The Price of Freedom Denied* with Brian Grim (Cambridge University Press, 2011), *Places of Faith: A Road Trip Across America's Religious Landscape* with Christopher P. Scheitle (Oxford University Press, 2012) and *Faithful Measures: The Art and Science of Measuring Religion* with Christopher Bader (New York University Press, 2017)

Giuseppe Giordan

is Professor of Sociology at the University of Padova. He is Coordinator of the International Joint PhD programme on *Human Rights, Society and Multi-level Governance*, and Co-editor of the *Annual Review of the Sociology of Religion* (Brill). His sociological research focuses on spirituality, conversion, religious and cultural pluralism, and religious freedom. He recently edited volumes

Global Eastern Orthodoxy. Politics, Religion, and Human Rights with Siniša Zrinščak (Springer, 2020) and *Chinese Religions Going Global* with Nanlai Cao and Fenggang Yang (Brill, 2021).

Kerby Goff
is a Ph.D. candidate in Sociology at the Pennsylvania State University and a research assistant with the Association of Religion Data Archive. His research focuses on religion, culture, and women's social movement organizations.

Anna Grasso
is a postdoctoral researcher at the Institute of Political Studies of Aix-en-Provence (Sciences Po Aix). She holds a PhD in Political Science (2018) on the topic of politicization and trade unionism of Imams in contemporary Tunisia. Her research is mainly focused on religion and public policy, religious authority, as well as religion and political mobilisation in both France and Tunisia. She is currently codirecting a research project on the place of women in the mosque in France with regards to the issue of gender equality and inclusivity.

Nuran Erol Işık
is currently Professor of Sociology at Izmir University of Economics, İzmir (Turkey). Her publications cover themes and issues at the intersection of culture, media, and politics. In 1993, she completed her Ph.D. thesis on discourses in the *New York Times* at Michigan State University, Department of Sociology, and since then, has published on narratives of popular religion, rhetorical and discursive strategies of the media. She also participated in ethnographic field study projects in different regions of Turkey. Her most recent interests focus on narrative identity, storytelling practices in Turkish TV series, and the New Age culture in Turkish society.

Dane R. Mataic
is Assistant Professor of Sociology and Community Development at North Dakota State University. He is a senior research associate for the Association of Religion Data Archive and research associate for the Religion and State Project. His research focuses on the intersection of mobilization, international conflict, and social inequalities. Broadly, he applies organizational and community theories to address topics such as the spread of governmental policies that regulate religious organizations, the mobilization of religious members by American congregations, and the spread of religious bias and advocacy.

Efe Peker

is an Assistant Professor in Sociology at the University of Ottawa. He holds a joint-PhD in Sociology (Simon Fraser University) and in History (Université Paris 1 Panthéon-Sorbonne). He completed his Postdoctoral Fellowship (2017–19) in Sociology at McGill University, funded by the Social Sciences and Humanities Research Council of Canada. His research focuses on state-religion relations, secularity, and nationalist-populist politics in comparative-historical perspective, including North America, Europe, and Asia (with particular attention to Québec, France, Turkey, and India). His recent works were featured in *Social Policy & Society*, *Journal for the Scientific Study of Religion*, and *Social Science History*.

Alexandros Sakellariou

is teaching sociology at the Hellenic Open University since 2016 and is a senior researcher at Panteion University of Athens working in large-scale EU and national projects since 2011. He earned his PhD on Sociology of Religion from the Department of Sociology of Panteion University. His scientific interests include, among others, sociology of religion, sociology of youth, politics and religion, religious communities in Greek society, youth activism and civic participation, right-wing extremism, radicalisation, and qualitative research methods. He is a board member of the Hellenic League for Human Rights.

Guillaume Silhol

is an associate researcher in political sociology from the University of Aix-Marseille and Sciences Po Aix-en-Provence in France (Department of Political Science, CHERPA-MESOPOLHIS, UMR 7064). His research interests include the sociology of religion in the public sphere, the sociology of public policies and the historical sociology of the State in Southern Europe.

Jan Váně

is Associate Professor and Chairman of the Department of Sociology, University of West Bohemia in Pilsen. He concentrates on comparative research in the field of sociology of religion (individualization, religious cultural memory, transformation of religious communities); and problems of homelessness and social services provided to socially disadvantaged groups.

Barbara R. Walters

is Professor Emerita of Sociology, City University of New York, currently teaching the first Senior Seminar on CEDAW and the Rights of Women at CUNY Queens College. She completed the B.A. at Vanderbilt University and the

Ph.D. at the State University of New York at Stony Brook in 1978, where she was a NIMH Methodology Trainee and later a NIMH Post-Doctoral Fellow in Psychiatry. She is the author of *The Politics of Aesthetic Judgment*, *The Feast of Corpus Christi*, *Hiring the Best*, and numerous comparative historical articles that examine religion, liturgy, church-state politics, and the status of women.

Introduction. Religious Freedom: Social-Scientific Approaches

Olga Breskaya, Roger Finke and Giuseppe Giordan

Over the past three decades, issues related to religious freedom have increasingly come to the fore. The European Court of Human Rights ruled the landmark case on religious freedom, *Kokkinakis v. Greece*, in 1993, the U.S. passed the International Religious Freedom Act in 1998, and the King of Morocco hosted a major international conference in 2016 on promoting the rights of religious minorities in Muslim majority countries. The year 2020, marked by the global pandemic and limitations on religious gatherings in many countries around the world, raised new challenges for religious freedom showing its vulnerability and centrality for individuals, religious groups, civil society, the state, and the international community. At the background of these historical dynamics, interest in the concept of religious freedom grew in the social scientific community setting in motion disciplinary boundaries between law, political sciences, international relations, and sociology and opening new interdisciplinary debates on theory and method of religious freedom research.

Legal studies and political science, most notably international relations, completed much of the earliest research on religious freedom and human rights (Breskaya, Giordan, and Richardson 2018). The expertise needed to review the legal and government battles over religious freedoms seemed most appropriately suited for these disciplines. Legal scholars addressed the adjudication of legal cases and political scientists addressed the state-religion policies and political relationships (Sullivan 2005; Fox 2015; Cumper and Lewis 2019; Sandberg 2019). This emphasis on the judicial and the political, combined with the normative component of all human rights, served as initial obstacles to sociologists entering the discussion (Breskaya, Giordan, and Richardson 2018). To the extent that sociologists addressed the topic, they focused more narrowly on individual nations and religious groups (Beckford 1985; Finke 1990); or religious freedoms were a side conversation in a larger discussion on secularization and other theories (Dobbelaere 1981).

The most recent work, however, has demonstrated both a need for more sociological research on religious freedom and more interdisciplinary sharing in methods and theory. Like most human rights, religious freedom has become a global concern holding social implications that go far beyond the political arena.[1] At the institutional level, the rise and operation of social movements and religious organizations rely on the religious freedoms they are granted. At the individual level, the practice and profession of religion are dependent on these freedoms. Religious freedoms, however, have consequences that go far beyond religious institutions and individuals. These freedoms are often closely associated with other social institutions, social discrimination, social inequalities, social conflict, and other human rights.

Legal scholar Russell Sandberg (2014) has noted that until recently the dialogue between the disciplines was as an exception rather than a regular practice. In recent years, however, we have seen a sharp rise in interdisciplinary work. In the area of theory, James T. Richardson (2006) has drawn on a social constructionist approach that brings socio-legal and socio-religious analysis together to better understand judicial decisions on religious freedom in a religiously pluralistic context. The religious economy or rational choice theory has drawn on the work of sociologists and political scientists to help us understand both the origins and the consequences of religious freedom (Gill 2008; Finke 2013). This approach has highlighted the importance of religion and state relations, as well as a nation's governance. Secularization theories also continue to serve as a guide for research in multiple disciplines; highlighting how cultural secularity and a secular state have an impact on religious freedoms. Legal theorists have also entered these debates by arguing how "the case law provides qualifications to sociological theories of internal secularization" (Sandberg 2014, 118).

Interdisciplinary efforts are even more evident in the research methods used. The careful review and systematic evaluation of court cases and constitutions have become a method used by multiple disciplines. James Richardson's (2015) recent presidential address to the Society of the Scientific Study of Religion reviewed multiple court cases in Europe and the United States. Both legal scholars and social scientists have devoted data collections to coding measures of religious freedom in national constitutions and to coding measures on religious freedom court cases.[2] A recent law journal devoted an issue

---

1 To review the global documents by the UN and other sources prior to 2004, go to Lindholm et al. (2004).
2 The Religion and State Projects coding of constitutional clauses on religion is available on the ARDA: https://www.thearda.com/Archive/Files/Descriptions/RASCONS.asp. The International Center for Law and Religion Studies offers more written documentation on religion and national constitutions at: https://www.iclrs.org/law-and-religion-framework-overviews/. Wybraniec and Finke's (2001) coding of American court cases on religion is also available on the ARDA: https://www.thearda.com/Archive/Files/Descriptions/RELFREE1.asp.

to "Religious Freedom and the Common Good" where more than one-half of the contributors were social scientists.[3]

Scholars from multiple disciplines have also used case studies to address key issues related to religious freedom. Many of the earliest case studies centered on the treatment of religious minorities (Beckford 1985; Richardson 2004). These studies brought attention both to the freedoms denied to religious minorities and the global variation in the freedoms granted. More recently, political scientists and sociologists have used case studies of individual nations to uncover how the relationship between religion and state influences the religious freedoms granted (Kuru 2009; Yang 2012; Koesel 2014; Sarkissian 2015). When combined with studies of individual judicial systems and individual court decisions, case studies have told the story of religious freedom across the globe.

For the last 15 years, interdisciplinary research has also drawn on a wealth of quantitative cross-national collections. The Religion and State Project (Fox 2008), the Association of Religion Data Archives (Grim and Finke 2011), and the Pew Research Center (Majumdar and Villa 2020) have all conducted global data collections on more than 180 countries over multiple years. Although focused on the broader issues of religion and state relationships, societal discrimination, social hostilities, and other topics, they offer important evidence on the trends and national variation in religious freedom across the globe. Social scientists have used these collections for hundreds of new studies on religious freedom, and legal scholars, policymakers, and others have cited them as a new source of evidence.[4]

The interdisciplinary borrowing of methods and theory is on display in this volume. Authors use case studies, cross-national collections, and surveys to explore religious freedoms, and they rely on interdisciplinary theories to guide this research, including social constructionist, religious economies, secularization, and other theoretical approaches. Moreover, the diversity of the authors and the locations they are studying further enhances the richness of the discussion. When combined with multiple levels of analysis and the introduction of new measures, the authors offer new sociological insights on the study of religious freedom.

---

3   See the *University of St. Thomas Law Review,* Volume 15, Issue 3 (2019).
4   The Religion and State site (https://www.thearda.com/ras/publications/) lists 195 research publications using the Religion and State data collections alone. In addition, researchers, policymakers and the public can easily access the data and key findings from the Association of Religion Data Archives (www.theARDA.com) and the Pew Research Center (https://www.pewresearch.org/) websites.

We have organized the volume into three sections. The first section "Religious Freedom, Secularity and Secularism" presents theories and analysis on secular cultures, secular states, the secularization thesis, and political secularism. The four chapters in this section cover a broad range of examples exploring the relationship between religious freedom and secularism. Efe Peker's (McGill University) contribution, *"How Does Secularity "Travel"? Towards a Policy Mobilities Approach in the Study of Religious Freedoms,"* draws attention to the global spread of religious freedom policies over time and space. While theories of secularization fail to explain the diffusion and increase of policies on religion across nations, this chapter contends that a policy mobilities approach, which originated in geography, holds a vast potential for going beyond nationally bounded investigations of religious freedoms. By taking into account "the globally interconnected nature of historical and contemporary secularities," Peker proposes integrating a socio-religious analysis of secularity with the policy-mobility approach. After considering the impact of French *laïcité* on secular policies in the Canadian province of Québec and examining the burqa bans in France, Belgium, Bulgaria, Austria, and Denmark, the author concludes that the geographical and sociopolitical spread of secularity is not a "simple transfer" of policy from one country to the other. Rather than representing a "carbon copy" of the policies of other nations, the new policies are "mutations" that are shaped by local social and political movements and actors, the legal context, and techniques of learning from each other.

The second chapter *"Religious Freedom, Legal Activism, and Muslim Personal Law in Contemporary India: A Sociological Exploration of Secularism"* by Anindita Chakrabarti (Indian Institute of Technology, Kanpur) argues that understanding the concept of secularism requires paying careful attention to constitutional law, citizen' rights, and judicial intervention. By examining two landmark cases in the Indian Supreme Court related to the religion-specific personal law (Muslim Personal Law) and its recent reforms in India, she argues that secularism, religious freedom, and citizenship rights produce a common framework for the understanding of the adjudicated cases. Linking cultural sociological analysis of secularity and secularism and applying sociological ideas of Monika Wohlrab-Sahr and Marian Burchardt with the theoretical ideas of judicialization of religion developed by James T. Richardson, she emphasized that the "meaning of secular in the idea of secularism alters with different social and political contexts and histories of social conflict." She explains that secularism in India gets its current meaning through the adjudicated decisions on religious freedom.

The third contribution in this section *"Religious Freedom and Secularism in Post-revolutionary Tunisia"* by Anna Grasso (Sciences Po-Aix) offers an

INTRODUCTION—RELIGIOUS FREEDOM: SOCIAL-SCIENTIFIC APPROACHES   5

overview of how religion and state relations have changed in Tunisia since the 1950-s and provides explanations and evidence on how and why the changes occurred. She reviews the transformation from an authoritarian *laïcité*, where the state secularizes law and holds control over religion, to a complex relationship where a new Constitution introduces the principles of religious freedom and equality. In order to understand the socio-legal changes and the increasing religious violence during the five decades of analysis, the author introduces multiple socio-religious and socio-political theories. Relying on Karel Dobbelaere's functional differentiation, Ahmet Kuru's differentiation of passive and assertive forms of secularism, and Jean Baubérot's and Micheline Milot's analysis of secularization and *laïcité*, this chapter explains the ongoing tensions in the sphere of Tunisian politics and religion and seeks to understand the implications of recent changes. The author highlights how a combination of these theoretical approaches, and careful attention to the secular-religious divide, assists in understanding the process of internal secularization of the Islamist party Ennahda in Tunisian society.

Chapter four *"Religious Pluralism, Religious Freedom and the Secularization Process in the Greek Educational System"* by Alexandros Sakellariou (Hellenic Open University, Panteion University of Athens) offers a detailed analysis of recent debates on religious freedom in Greek schools. Relying on the sociological theories of religious pluralism, as developed by Nancy Ammerman, James Beckford, Enzo Pace and Giuseppe Giordan, and Fenggang Yang, the author argues that religious pluralism together with religious freedom "become crucial parameters of the secularization process of the Greek state and society." Sakellariou highlights that the distinctive Greek educational system is facing challenges from increasing cultural and religious diversity; however, he concludes "the road to the full implementation and respect of religious freedom and pluralism remains long." Recent data collections and research have clearly shown that the Greek Orthodox Church holds many privileges in Greece and that minority religions often face discrimination. This chapter offers helpful details on how privileges are given and how freedoms are denied in the educational context.

The second section of this volume "Multi-level Study of Religious Freedom" contains four chapters. Exploring multiple levels of analysis, including the individual and institutional, the authors highlight agency-oriented perspectives toward the study of religious freedom. In chapter five, Zaheeda P. Alibhai (University of Ottawa) integrates two sociological approaches in her study of legal cases on religious freedom, *"Regulating Sincerity: Religion, Law, Public Policy and the Ambivalence of Religious Freedom in Pluralist Societies."* The first approach borrows from the work of James Richardson to stress the impact of courts in producing the meaning of religious freedom. This approach helps to explain how the judicialization of religious freedom became instrumental in pluralistic Canadian society. The second approach builds on Meredith McGuire and Nancy Ammerman's work on "lived religion" or "everyday religion" and is applied to the habitual religious practices and subjective reasoning of the plaintiffs and their regulations. When applied to legal cases on wearing niqab by Muslim women, Alibhai explains that integrating the two perspectives uncovers an "interlocking system of power." On the one hand, the chapter demonstrates the importance of the judiciary and its power for ensuring the freedoms of minority religious groups and for defining what is included under the canopy of religion. On the other hand, this chapter uses insights from the "lived religion as practice" approach to understand why courts are so important for protecting religious freedoms of minorities.

Chapter six by Nuran Erol Işik (Izmir University of Economics) called *"The Religionization in Alevi Culture: An Exploratory Study on Spiritual Leaders (Dedes)"* addresses the important issue of how religions define themselves and how the courts can influence this process of identity formation. Based on phenomenological interviews with Alevi *dedes*, the author examines the concept of religious freedom through its relationship to religious agency and morality. The theoretical approach of 'religionization' developed by Markus Dressler was applied to critically address the issues of religious belonging and the process of reconfiguring cultural and religious identities in modern Alevism in Turkey. The structural level of analysis highlights the role of traditional religion in social life and social institutions, including the courts. With the focus on the mystical/spiritual leaders (*dedes*), the chapter explains the ambiguous process of identity formation through the tension between regulation and autonomy.

The seventh chapter *"One, Many or None. Religious Truth-Claims and Social Perception of Religious Freedom"* by Olga Breskaya and Giuseppe Giordan (University of Padova) analyzes the impact of religious truth-claims and religious pluralism on perceptions of religious freedom. Relying on a primary data collection of 1035 university students in Northern Italy, and applying theoretical perspectives of religious pluralism and theology of religions as developed by John Hick, Jeff Astley, and Leslie Francis, the chapter tests five hypotheses concerning the influence of pluralism on religious freedom. The authors find that students endorsed pluralistic religious truth-claims and that this endorsement was associated with the perceptions of religious freedom as individual autonomy. When entered into a regression equation, however, exclusivism, inclusivism, interreligious perspective, and atheism had significant statistical effects on the perceptions of religious freedom, while the measures of pluralistic truth-claims had no causal relations with the religious freedom measure.

The data revealed that positive attitudes toward religious diversity in society had a strong positive influence on the perceptions of religious freedom as a societal value, i.e. the role it performs in promoting interreligious dialogue and peaceful coexistence of religion. Negative attitudes toward religious diversity showed a negative impact on three out of five dimensions of religious freedom, specifically suggesting that neglecting religious diversity leads to disrespect to human rights meaning of religious freedom.

Chapter eight by Jan Váně and Lukáš Dirga (University of West Bohemia) titled *"Religious Freedom in Prisons. A Case Study from the Czech Republic"* offers interesting and sometimes unexpected examples of how religious freedoms are denied in prisons. The study initially draws on the theory of total institutions to study religious freedom in the prisons of the Czech Republic. The authors identify prisons as total institutions with a repressive, post-communist environment where the exercise of power relies on discipline and punishment. By interviewing prison chaplains, convicts, volunteers, psychologists, and other specialists working in the penitential system, the authors document the limitations of religious freedom. Drawing on these interviews and borrowing on the theoretical work of Michel Foucault, the authors reveal that religious freedoms are the victim of an ongoing power struggle and conflicting ideologies on how to work with convicts. Rather than treating this as a structural problem or as an explicit attempt to limit the religious freedom of convicts, the authors stress the importance of understanding relationships within the prison.

The third section of this volume "Politics and Policies on Religious Freedom" delves into the specifics of social, legal, and political aspects of domestic, international, and supranational policies of religious freedom. Chapter nine *"Organizations and Religious Restrictions: An International Overview of the Intersection of State and Non-Governmental Organizations and Religious Groups"* by Dane Mataic (North Dakota State University) and Kerby Goff (Pennsylvania State University) provides a theoretical and analytical overview of the restrictions placed on religious organizations. Although past quantitative research has given extensive attention to the religious freedoms of individuals, the authors find that freedoms of organizations have received far less attention. Using cross-national data from the Religion and State Project and other international sources, they explore how organizations are both targets and actors in the area of religious freedom. They find that an independent judiciary and open elections reduce restrictions on minority religious organizations, but international monitoring agencies have surprisingly little association with organizational religious freedoms and restrictions. Finally, they document the rise and spread of social movement organizations seeking to increase global religious freedom.

Chapter ten, by Guillaume Silhol (University of Aix-Marseille and Sciences Po Aix-en-Provence) titled *"Religious Freedom between Politics and Policies: Social and Legal Conflicts Over Catholic Religious Education in Italy, 1984–1992"* offers a detailed overview of the events surrounding the reform of Catholic Religious Education policies in Italy between 1984 and 1992. The author demonstrates that the courts, religious institutions, and the larger society went through a negotiation process to define religious freedom and to determine a process for implementing it, with the courts having a lasting impact. Building on the theoretical work of James Richardson and Damon Mayrl, the author highlights the importance of three processes: judicialization, politicization, and bureaucratization of religious education. Focusing on these three processes and the interaction between them, he explains the tensions around religious freedom in a particular context of public education and its polysemic nature.

Chapter eleven *"The Measure of CEDAW: Religion, Religious Freedom, and the Rights of Women"* by Barbara R. Walters (City University of New York) offers a cross-national analysis on 184 nation-state members of the United Nations, including 45 predominantly Muslim states, to explain a nation's commitment to the Convention for the Elimination of All Forms of Discrimination Against Women (CEDAW). Although she initially finds higher gender inequality and lower commitment to CEDAW in Muslim majority nations, additional analysis shows that most of the relationship is attributed to nineteen religiously repressive regimes. Her results point to the importance of considering how religion and religious freedom might influence nation-state support of an international treaty on gender equality (CEDAW). Walters also discusses the problem of the secular-religious divide embedded in CEDAW provisions and the challenges they pose for countries with a dominant religious culture.

Chapter twelve *"Religious Freedom and the Religionization of World Politics: Views of EU Political and Religious Representatives"* by Chrysa Almpani (Aristotle University of Thessaloniki) explores how the European Union (EU) representatives understand and interpret the relationship between religion and human rights. Semi-structured in-depth interviews with 30 political, religious, and policy leaders at the EU level highlight the importance of religion in the current international political agenda and "the need of 'inclusivity' of religious actors to the EU political dialogue." Relying on a broad range of sociological theories, including the work of Zygmunt Bauman and Ulrich Beck, Almpani argues that the role of faith-based organizations is becoming more prominent in peace-building processes and policy-making in conflict and post-conflict conditions. Representatives sought to understand religion as a "peacekeeping or war-triggering component." The interview data indicate that advancements in religious freedom and inclusion of religious actors are part of the EU international political agenda. Specifically, religious freedom-centered policies may advance the EU position as a global actor at the level of external relations with developing countries.

The chapters contribute theoretical perspectives, sociological concepts, and empirical analyses that highlight the development of religious freedom as an area of study in the social sciences. The volume also covers diverse geographical and geopolitical cases, including Austria, Belgium, Bulgaria, Canada, Czech Republic, Denmark, France, Greece, India, Italy, Tunisia, Turkey, and global data collections. Although covering a broad range of interdisciplinary perspectives, this volume tends to center on sociological theories, showing their importance in the study of religious freedom and empirical analysis of data. We emphasize that such sociological contributions not only enhance the discipline, but they promote stronger engagement with other disciples addressing religious freedom in the global world.

References

Beckford, James A. 1985. *Cult Controversies: The Societal Response to New Religious Movements*. London: Tavistock.

Breskaya, Olga, Giuseppe Giordan, and James T. Richardson. 2018. "Human Rights and Religion: A Sociological Perspective." *Journal for the Scientific Study of Religion* 57, no. 3: 419–31.

Cumper, Peter, and Tom Lewis. 2019. "Human Rights and Religious Litigation—Faith in the Law?" *Oxford Journal of Law and Religion* 8: 121–50.

Dobbelaere, Karel. 1981. "Secularization: A Multi-Dimensional Concept." *Current Sociology* 29 (2): 1–216.

Finke, Roger, and Rodney Stark 1992. *The Churching of America, 1776–1990: Winners and Losers in Our Religious Economy*. New Brunswick: Rutgers University Press.

Finke, Roger. 1990. "Religious Deregulation: Origins and Consequences." *Journal of Church and State* 32 (3): 609–26.

Finke, Roger. 2013. "Origins and Consequences of Religious Freedom: A Global Overview." *Sociology of Religion* 74: 297–313.

Fox, Jonathan. 2008. *A World Survey of Religion and the State*. New York: Cambridge University Press.

Fox, Jonathan. 2015. *Political Secularism, Religions, and the State. A Time Series Analysis of Worldwide Data*. New York: Cambridge University Press.

Gill, Anthony. 2008. *The Political Origins of Religious Liberty*. Cambridge: Cambridge University Press.

Grim, Brian, and Roger Finke. 2011. *The Price of Freedom Denied: Religious Persecution and Violence*. Cambridge, UK: Cambridge University Press.

Koesel, Karrie J. 2014. *Region and Authoritarianism: Cooperation, Conflict, and the Consequences*. New York, NY: Cambridge University Press.

Kuru, Ahmet T. 2009. *Secularism and State Policies toward Religion*. New York, NY: Cambridge University Press.

Lindholm, Tore, W. Cole Durham, and Bahia G. Tahzib-Lie. 2004. *Facilitating Freedom of Religion or Belief: A Deskbook*. Leiden, The Netherlands: Martinus Nijhoff Publishers.

Majumdar, Samirah and Virginia Villa. 2020. "In 2018, Government Restrictions on Religion Reach Highest Level Globally in More Than a Decade." Accessed on February 25th, 2021, https://www.pewforum.org/2020/11/10/in-2018-government-restrictions-on-religion-reach-highest-level-globally-in-more-than-a-decade/.

Richardson, James T. (ed.). 2004. *Regulating Religion: Case Studies from Around the Globe*. New York: Kluwer Academic/Plenum Publishers.

Richardson, James T. 2006. "The Sociology of Religious Freedom: A Structural and Socio-legal Analysis." *Sociology of Religion* 67 (3): 271–94.

Richardson, James T. 2015. "Managing Religion and the Judicialization of Religious Freedom." *Journal for the Scientific Study of Religion* 54 (1): 1–19.

Sandberg, Russell. 2014. *Religion, Law and Society*. Cambridge: Cambridge University Press.

Sandberg, Russell. 2019. "A System Theory Re-Construction of Law and Religion." *Oxford Journal of Law and Religion* 8: 447–72.

Sarkissian, Ani. 2015. *The Varieties of Religious Repression: Why Governments Restrict Religion*. Oxford, New York: Oxford University Press.

Sullivan, Winnifred F. 2005. *The Impossibility of Religious Freedom*. Princeton, NJ: Princeton University Press.

Wybraniec, John and Roger Finke. 2001. "Religious Regulation and the Courts: The Judiciary's Changing Role in Protecting Minority Religions from Majoritarian Rule." *Journal for the Scientific Study of Religion* 40 (3): 427–44.

Yang, Fenggang. 2012. *Religion in China: Survival and Revival under Communist Rule*. New York: Oxford University Press.

PART 1

*Religious Freedom,
Secularity and Secularism*

CHAPTER 1

How Does Secularity "Travel"?: Toward a Policy Mobilities Approach in the Study of Religious Freedoms

Efe Peker

1 Introduction

As secularity studies began expanding the focus beyond the North Atlantic world, there has been an increased interest in how secularity "travels" through global entanglements. This literature paid particular attention to the historical spread of secularity via European colonialism, engendering culturally specific ideational and institutional arrangements in the non-West (Burchardt, Wohlrab-Sahr, and Middell 2015, Taylor 2016, Künkler, Madeley, and Shankar 2018, Fitzgerald 2007). What remains underexamined is how contemporary secular policymaking and the political (re)configuration of religious freedoms also may be shaped, at least partially, through cross-national/regional interactions and influences, both within and outside the West.

This chapter lays out preliminary ideas on developing a policy mobilities perspective as a potentially fruitful research agenda to advance the study of secular flows across different socio-legal and socio-political contexts. Originated in the discipline of geography in dialogue with political science and sociology, the policy mobilities literature offers diverse methodological tools to study the movement, translation/mutation, and assemblages of various governmental policies transcending national/regional borders (Clarke et al. 2015, McCann and Ward 2013, Temenos and McCann 2013). The chapter explores the prospects of this outlook for the sociology of religion, particularly as a way to capture the dynamic and globally interconnected nature of historical as well as contemporary processes of secular policymaking, and what they may entail for the exercise of religious freedoms.

The discussion proceeds in four main parts. The following section overviews the current state of the secularization literature, especially the recent yet growing interest in investigating the exchanges and interactions in the making of secular arrangements around the world. The subsequent section summarizes the origins and current state of the policy mobilities scholarship. The third section considers the potentialities of this body of work for the analysis of policies toward religion, followed in the fourth section by the presentation of two exploratory case studies. The first study examines the potential impact of France's laïcité (state secularism) model on the Canadian province of Québec's changing secular policy agendas in the past decade, especially the restriction of religious symbols for government employees. The second study surveys the spread and variegation of laws against face covering in public spaces in five European Union countries (France, Belgium, Bulgaria, Austria, and Denmark), popularly known as the "burqa ban." The cases seek to illustrate the practical applicability of a policy mobilities approach as a methodological guide for data collection and a theoretical framework for analysis.

Based on evidence from these polities, the chapter argues for going beyond investigating religious freedoms as nationally bounded phenomena, which has been the dominant approach in the literature. The qualitative findings demonstrate that policymakers and related stakeholders not only find models and inspirations elsewhere, but they also may actively engage with their counterparts in other countries and regions to develop domestic agendas on religion and secularity. Emulation, however, does not lead to a carbon copy of policies, but rather engender variegations and mutations in line with the local social, political, and legal context. The concluding section further elaborates on these arguments and highlights the policy mobilities perspective as a promising research agenda in global secularity studies, particularly for the study of political processes that shape the framework for religious freedoms.

2 Secularization in Time and Space

As old as the discipline of sociology itself, the secularization debate seemingly reached an impasse by the late twentieth century. On one side of the standoff, the classical secularization paradigm of postwar sociology argued that forces of modernity would unavoidably trigger the decreased social significance and increased privatization of religion (Bruce 2002, Berger 1967). On the other side was the religious economies paradigm, which arose in the 1980s and used a neoclassical economic framework to claim that individual religiosity was livelier than ever, thus declaring the death of the secularization perspective (Stark and Finke 2000, Hadden 1987). Informed by both of these schools of thought, a new generation of scholarship in the last two decades brought about what I have elsewhere called a "spatiotemporal" turn to the debate (Peker 2020). Rather than fixating on whether religion has more or less social significance, the spatiotemporal outlook nuances the terms of the conversation with increased attention to place and time to highlight variations in geography, evolutions in time, and comparisons thereof. Attention to place matters, because the geographical scope of the original debate was restricted mostly to the Western world, and considering time is crucial, because although the question of secularity is essentially a historical one, systematic politico-historical accounts and comparisons were not widespread in either paradigm.

Addressing the issue, cross-religious and cross-regional inquiry of secularization as a time-sensitive topic became a promising avenue of research (Gorski 2003, Casanova 1994). Since the early 2000s, many qualitative case studies and comparative works emerged to contribute, directly or indirectly, to the spatiotemporal turn (Başkan 2014, Buckley 2016, Kuru 2009, Mayrl 2016, Smith 2003, Gill 2007, Grzymała-Busse 2015, Saeed 2017, Zubrzycki 2016). Other scholars have produced a wide-ranging series of quantitative global comparisons featuring religious indicators as well as policies and societal factors affecting religious freedoms (Fox 2020, Finke and Mataic 2019). To be sure, the works of these authors follow neither a particular theory nor set of methodological guidelines to study religion and secularity. What I call the spatiotemporal turn denotes a "family resemblance" (Wittgenstein 2009) of approaches — historically and geographically sensitive accounts that defy the homogeneous and teleological understanding of secularization.

Expanding the spatiotemporal reach of the debate also evoked interest in how secularization, an originally Western phenomenon, takes distinct shapes around the world. Hence the proliferation of concepts on the globally variegated nature of secularity: modes and varieties of secularism (Taylor 1998, Warner, VanAntwerpen, and Calhoun 2010), multiple secularities/secularisms (Stepan 2011, Wohlrab-Sahr and Burchardt 2012, Katznelson and Jones 2010), and multiple/alternative modernities (Eisenstadt 2000, Casanova 2011). Particularly, the literature focused on how colonialism and imperialism enabled secularity to "travel" beyond the West, where it took politically and culturally embedded forms through appropriation, contestation, meaning creation, and institution building (Burchardt, Wohlrab-Sahr, and Middell 2015, Taylor 2016, Künkler, Madeley, and Shankar 2018, Fitzgerald 2007, Cady and Hurd 2010, Akan 2017, Fabbe 2019).

A few examples should be helpful to illustrate this growing sensitivity to secular flows. Charles Taylor (2016, 13), for instance, in his essay "Can Secularism Travel?", underlined the need to better understand the "interactive context" caused by colonialism in the global spread of Western secularity, where local peoples and cultures had to reconcile two opposing dynamics: the desire to imitate the West and the desire not to be ruled by it. Künkler et al. (2018, 26), likewise, showed in their comparative-historical volume involving eleven cases in Asia, the Middle East, and North Africa that Western encounters constituted "the single most important factor in structuring later public conceptions of religion and its desired role in the public." Burchardt et al. (2015, 2) also devoted a book to comprehend "the *longue durée* of global interconnectedness and transnational exchanges of values and ideas" that has shaped secularity beyond the West, and created new politics and practices of secular translations. They also highlighted the contemporary entanglements of secularities through transnational migration, supranational organizations, and the changing place of religion in international politics and human rights regimes. Others have studied the external impact of the United States' foreign policy, especially since the 1998 International Religious Freedom Act, on the making of religious policy in various countries in the last two decades, including during Trump's presidency (Haynes 2020).

More specifically on contemporary policy diffusions, Mataic (2018) has recently shown how policies concerning religious freedoms/restrictions are spatially clustered, as national governments are likely to mimic neighboring countries in their regions. In addition to internal factors, such as the domestic religious economy or the type of government, his global quantitative study confirmed that geographical proximity is positively correlated with the mimetic diffusion of secular policies, whether they may be expanding or curtailing religious freedoms. Yet although we know that diffusion occurs, the literature still lacks a systematic framework for answering the question of "how" —that is, the analysis of the *particular mechanisms and processes* through which such secular diffusions happen in neighboring as well as distant polities. Research is needed on how ideas and visions of secularity and religious freedoms travel and transfer into actual policymaking, as well as the empirical examination of the concrete actors, societal groups, and institutions that facilitate secular flows. With a view to addressing this gap, I now turn to the policy mobilities literature.

3   Policy Mobilities Approach

Originated in the 2010s within critical policy studies in urban geography, policy mobilities (PM) research may at first glance seem far from the sociology of religion's abode. PM came to being as a challenge to the longstanding "policy transfer" perspective in political science, critiquing it for its rational-choice methodology that assumed a smooth and linear adoption of global "best practices" models by impartial experts (Peck 2011). Instead, PM scholars brought forth three key concepts: *mobilities*, *assemblages*, and *mutations*. Borrowed partly from sociology, the concept of *mobilities* underlines the complexity of power relations embedded in policy movement rather than following a simple A-to-B trajectory. PM scholarship pays particular attention to why governments and policy actors prioritize certain models over others, and how such policy *assemblages* get *mutated* and translated in the process of traveling. *Assemblages* highlight how policies amalgamate "parts of the near and far, of fixed and mobile pieces of expertise, regulation, institutional capacities, etc. that are brought together in particular ways and for particular interests and purposes" (McCann and Ward 2013, 328). *Mutation*, finally, takes interest in what happens to policies in the process of movement — because they "do not arrive at their destination in the same form as they appeared elsewhere" (Temenos and McCann 2013, 349). Informed by these organizing concepts, the PM approach seeks to "follow the policy," that is, the material construction of policies and policy imaginaries through various geographical flows and influences (Peck and Theodore 2012). According to Theodore (2019), PM research is particularly attentive to the investigation of the following elements:

- *Models:* how policies, programs, plans, and related ideas and discourses come to have extra-national/regional salience;
- *Connections:* how places and policy domains become interlinked through networks and epistemic communities;
- *Movement:* how policies are transformed and adapted through the circulation of expertise, ideas, and models;
- *Institutions and actors:* local and national governments; diverse institutional arrangements in sites of policy implementation; international organizations and bodies, various cross-border networks;
- *Techniques for learning:* such as study tours, conferences, best practices reports, and evaluation science.

With a distinctly urban focus, the policy domains examined via the PM approach have so far included diverse elements, such as financial instruments, education, redevelopment, climate policies, social welfare programs, and policing. Depending on the type of policy studied, the actors and sites investigated through a PM perspective may include elected officials, political parties, bureaucrats/civil servants, policy entrepreneurs and experts, consultancy firms, NGOs and pressure groups, transnational corporations, think tanks, research institutes, supra-national governmental and nongovernmental institutions, spiritual organizations and philanthropic foundations, university centers, scientific associations, professional societies, and training institutes, among others (McCann 2011).

Methodologically, policy mobilities research is based primarily on qualitative inquiry that features content analysis, semi-structured interviews, and ethnography (Baker and McGuirk 2017, Peck and Theodore 2012). Content analysis examines various documents (or "policy artifacts"), including parliamentary debates, government declarations, policy documents, related think tank reports, newspapers, web pages, etc. Interviews spotlight key policy figures, such as politicians, policy experts, and NGO representatives, among others. Ethnographic work, finally, takes place in sites where policy mobilization is facilitated — such as public meetings, conferences, site visits, seminars, and lectures. All in all, the PM perspective offers a dynamic theoretical framework as well as concrete methodological guidelines for the study of how policies and policy imaginaries travel across borders and take novel forms that are politically, culturally, and geographically specific.

4   Secular Policy Mobilities?

What would a PM approach look like in the study of secular flows? I argue that there are at least two immediate contributions that a PM perspective can bring to the sociology of religion. First, in the secularization canon, even in works that are concerned with what Taylor (2007) calls Secularity 1,[1] which take the state and state actors seriously in shaping public secularity and religious freedoms, the object of study is not commonly viewed from a distinctly policy standpoint. Although, at the end of the day, Secularity 1 is produced through a series of constitutional changes, laws, decrees, and regulations issued by public institutions; as secularization scholars we are not always knowledgeable about how the processes of policymaking at various governmental levels actually take place —let alone the mechanisms through which policies are mobilized across geographies. A PM outlook would primarily help go beyond viewing secularity and secular flows as a merely cultural phenomenon (which is arguably the dominant point of view in the literature) by urging us to familiarize ourselves with the concrete steps, interactions, and sites that advance the development of policies impacting religions and the exercise of religious freedoms.

Second, and relatedly, thinking through PM would allow sociologists of religion to spatiotemporally diversify the perception of secular flows. Space, because secular "travels" have so far been studied mostly as an itinerary that begins in the West and ends in the non-West. Intra-Western and intra-non-Western interactions have not received the same level of attention. Moreover,

---

[1] The differentiation of public life from religious norms and authority, including domains such as politics, the economy, law, education, civil society, etc.

the nation-state has traditionally been the sole unit of analysis, with little interest accorded to regional interactions or supranational influences. Time, because although historical processes of colonialism and imperialism as vectors of secular expansion have been examined, how *contemporary* secular policy imaginaries and frameworks are mobilized is yet to be explored. This is all the more relevant given that we are going through a historical period where twentieth century secular settlements are going through substantial transformations that impact the course of religious freedoms. These transformations are based on multiple phenomena, such as the "going public" of religions (Casanova 1994), globalization (Beyer 1994), transnational migration (Saunders, Fiddian-Qasmiyeh, and Snyder 2016), the problematization of Islam in Western societies (Roy 2019), and the rise of religious nationalisms and populisms around the world (Juergensmeyer 2010, DeHanas and Shterin 2020). A PM outlook would facilitate the capturing of the complexity and the multiplicity of secular (as well as anti-secular) flows in a larger spatial and temporal framework, with particular attention to the mobility, assemblages, and mutation of policies. With these goals in mind, I now present two exploratory case studies that exemplify contemporary intra-Western policy mobilities in an effort to concretize the theoretical discussion. Both cases pertain to the restriction of religious freedoms that disproportionately affects minority religions, which makes understanding the external influences and flows that may have shaped them all the more important.

5   Notes from Two Exploratory Case Studies

The first case involves the recent turn toward the French conception of laïcité in the Canadian province of Québec, and the second is on the propagation of laws against face coverings in several European Union countries, namely the "burqa bans." By definition, exploratory case studies do not feature a complete data collection process that offers fully formed theoretical insights. They should rather be seen as "a preliminary step of an overall causal or explanatory research design exploring a relatively new field of scientific investigation" (Steb 2009, 372). While criteria such as validity and reliability still apply, exploratory case studies stand out as being more intuitive, flexible, and fragmentary, rendering them particularly useful in generating pertinent research questions and hypotheses for inspiring future studies (Yin 2018). Operating in this framework, the studies I discuss below are works in progress that already show promising signs for the relevance of the policy mobilities framework for the sociology of religion. In both, I carry out a content analysis resting on various "policy artifacts" such as parliamentary debates, declarations of politicians and officials, diplomatic meetings, related national/supranational policy papers and reports, court decisions, and websites of civil society organizations.

6 Laïcité in Québec

In the first study, I investigate the potential impact of France's laïcité narratives[2] on Québec's changing secular policy agendas in the past decade, which directly concern the freedoms of religious minorities. The analysis scrutinizes the extent to which Québec's competing political actors' mobilized laïcité as a "best practices" model to inform and legitimize their agenda setting. Applying the policy mobilities perspective to the case of Québec, the study scrutinizes the province's restrictive legislative action, led by different political parties at different times, on religious garments. These include the 2013–2014 Charter of Values (*Parti Québécois*, PQ), the 2017 face covering ban (*Parti liberal du Québec*, PLQ), and the 2019 state secularism bill (*Coalition avenir Québec*, CAQ).

The 2013 Charter of Values (Bill 60) proposed to ban conspicuous religious signs for all public employees, but failed to become law as the PQ lost power in the 2014 provincial elections. The PLQ's 2017 law on religious neutrality (Bill 62) restricted face covering to effectively ban Muslim women wearing the burka or niqab from receiving public services such as transportation, unless they be prepared to reveal their face. The Québec Superior Court soon after suspended the application of the law due to its violation of freedoms enshrined in the Canadian and Québec charters of rights and freedoms. The CAQ's 2019 law on state secularism (Bill 21), finally, declared the Québec state *laïque* and banned religious symbols for all government employees in "positions of authority," which includes judges, prosecutors, police officers, prison guards, and schoolteachers, among others. Completing the task of Bill 62, it also banned face coverings for all government employees and recipients of public services. Except for the PLQ bill of 2017, these bills made direct references to the concept of laïcité.

What is interesting about this series of legislative action is that although the province went through a major secularization cycle in its Quiet Revolution during the 1960s, the French concept of laïcité was not deployed as a legal

---

2   In the comparative secularity literature, French laïcité is regarded as a firmer variety of secularism seeking to limit religions' public visibility and involvement, which is underpinned by a Republican ideology that evolved during the nineteenth-century struggles against the prevalence of the Catholic Church (Bowen 2007).

principle, social mobilization tool, or a provincial identity marker. It is only as late as the mid-1990s and early 2000s that laïcité began making its way into some official documents on education, immigration, intercultural relations, women's rights, as well as into larger public debates (Milot 2009, Mancilla 2011). Around the same time, France was dealing with its own "headscarf affair," which produced the 2004 ban on wearing ostentatious religious symbols in public schools, and later a ban on full face coverings in public in 2010 (Nilsson 2017). Evidence suggests that the French notion of laïcité, especially through the linguistic, epistemic, and cultural affiliations between the two polities, began gaining ground as a policy framework over the years to rationalize the restriction of religious garments (for a comparison between the veiling debates in France and Québec, see Laxer 2019).

In a 2004 report, for instance, Québec's Council of Intercultural Relations wrote that although the notion of laïcité has not been distinctly expressed in the province's history, "the adoption by France of a law prohibiting in the name of laïcité the wearing of conspicuous religious symbols has, however, led us, in recent months, to realize the importance of this definition." It added: "In France, laïcité is a value that is defended, while in Quebec, it is a practice that has not always borne its name" (CRI 2004, 6, 46). It is in this period that the debates on the reasonable accommodation of religious minorities in Québec created a "French temptation" among some provincial intellectuals, who saw France's law of 2004 as an inspirational model for diversity management (Bosset 2005, 90). Liberal scholars and those adhering to Canadian multiculturalism have consistently challenged this view. For instance, referring directly to France's law of 2004, the 2008 report penned by sociologist Gérard Bouchard and philosopher Charles Taylor argued that "this type of restrictive laïcité is not appropriate for Québec," characterizing it as "radical" (CCAPRCD 2008, 46, 66).

Especially among nationalist circles, the need for adopting laïcité in Québec was nevertheless voiced ever more strongly through a series of books, essays, and conferences (some examples are Beauchamp 2011, Lamonde 2010). In many of such initiatives, Koussens and Amiraux (2014) note, there has been a tendency to depict an oversimplified conception of French laïcité, often stripped of its political, legal, and historical context to be reduced to an abstract ideal that justifies the banning of religious garments and symbols, as in France's laws of 2004 and 2010. The PQ's legislative action involving *laïcité* shows clear indications of such French emulation. During the debates on her government's Charter of Values bill in September 2013, Québec Premier Pauline Marois stated the model she had in mind in unambiguous terms: "The best example, in my opinion, is France". In a diplomatic visit to Paris a few months later, she further uttered that French laïcité was a direct "inspiration" for her party's bill. She said, "there is a common inspiration" among the two nations "to highlight and bring forth the neutrality of the State." In his response, French Prime Minister Jean-Marc Ayrault underlined that France and Québec are united by language and values, and that "laïcité is at the heart of this process. It is what makes living together possible" (La Presse 13 December 2013).

What was proposed in the 2013 Charter, particularly the "general ban of the right to wear visible religious symbols was directly imported from the French legal system," thus representing a break with the Québécois and Canadian jurisprudence on religious freedoms (Lampron 2015, 142). Guillaume Rousseau, an advisor to the PQ who took active roles in the creation of the Charter, justified the bill on the grounds that Québec has followed "French civic republicanism" since at least a century for "rejecting religious intrusion into civil and political affairs" (Rousseau and McDonald 2014, 92–93). Although it failed to become law, the bill introduced laïcité for the first time in Québec's legislative agenda, as well as a far-reaching plan to restrict the wearing of religious symbols that disproportionately affects the province's Muslim, Sikh, and Jewish minority communities.

In 2019, when the concept returned in the CAQ's state secularism bill, the ruling party made visibly fewer references to France. Instead, they portrayed the concept as intrinsic to the province's national "history and values," as Premier François Legault clarified, because "this is how we live in Québec" (Journal de Québec 31 March 2019). During the parliamentary discussions, Minister of Immigration Simon Jolin-Barrette, the sponsor of the bill, insisted that "what we are doing is a Québec model of laïcité. What France does concerns them. Each state has the right to its own concept of laïcité" (ASSNAT 14 May 2019). Still, comparisons with France were prevalent throughout the legislative process. Favorable to the bill, the PQ's interim leader Pascal Bérubé drew parallels: "Laïcité is not premature for Québec. In France, it has been settled for a very long time, and in Quebec we are getting there" (ASSNAT 7 May 2019). PLQ deputy Paule Robitaille critiqued the bill on its French inspiration: "The Minister [Jolin-Barrette] and those who supported him during the consultations praised the French-style laïcité," which is "far from our legal culture, from our North American culture. Do you really think this is a model to follow?" (ASSNAT 4 June 2019). Sol Zanetti of socialist *Québec Solidaire* also described France as a bad model: "There are many who say 'look at other countries, look at France.'" He then cited a 2019 study that shows the long-term negative effects of the law of 2004 for French Muslim women, and added: "But things are not going well in France" (ASSNAT 30 May 2019).

Finally, an example of international collaboration between civil society organizations also should be highlighted. In early 2020, France's *Fédération*

Nationale de la Libre Pensée (FNLP, National Federation for Free Thought) came to the aid of *Le mouvement laïque Québecois* (MLQ, Quebec Secular Movement) to start a fundraising campaign in defense of Québec's 2019 laïcité bill, which is likely to be challenged in Canadian courts. Titled, "The Same Battle: In Québec as in France, Laïcité Needs You", the declaration introduced the Québec context and made a call for donations, because "the more countries that establish *laïcité* in their institutions, the more secularism in France will be protected" (FNLP 2020). Further research is undoubtedly needed to provide a more comprehensive picture of the French connection in the shaping of Québec's secular imaginaries in the twenty-first century, especially those concerning the public visibility of religions. The preliminary evidence attests however that for all actors involved, the case of France has been an ongoing reference point whether they are critical or in favor of mobilizing a laïcité-based policy program for Québec.

7 "Burqa Bans" in Europe

The second study involving policy mobilities surveys the spread of national legislation on face coverings in all public places across five European Union (EU) countries: France (2010), Belgium (2011), Bulgaria (2016), Austria (2017), and Denmark (2018). Yet the "burqa bans" go beyond these five: The Netherlands introduced one for certain public spaces in 2018, and many other EU countries have discussed, or are currently discussing, such a ban, including Germany, Finland, Latvia, and Luxembourg. Switzerland, Spain, and Italy already have local bans in place (for an EU-wide comparison, see Open Society 2018). From a policy mobilities perspective, the bans on face covering present an interesting puzzle due to the rapid propagation of laws based on similar language and arguments across the continent in less than a decade, especially when the number of women who actually wear the burqa or niqab in these countries is utterly insignificant (Ferrari and Pastorelli 2016, Lægaard 2015).

Moreover, the existence of supranational organizations that comprises these nations, such as the EU and the Council of Europe (CoE), adds another level to the analysis of mobilities and mutations. The center-right European People's Party (EPP), for instance, which is the European Parliament's biggest political group, made an official call in 2017 for an EU-wide ban on face coverings (Parliament Magazine 28 April 2017). The approbation of the bans in France and Belgium by the European Court of Human Rights (ECtHR, the international court of the CoE), likewise, encouraged more countries to deploy a similar policy (Leonen 2017). Promulgated under the Nicolas Sarkozy government, the 2010 French ban was challenged at ECtHR, which upheld the law in 2014, respecting the French government's right to implement "a certain idea of living together" (The Guardian 1 July 2014). In 2017, Belgium's 2011 law also was upheld by the ECtHR on the grounds that wearing the burqa was a "practice considered incompatible in Belgian society" (The Independent 11 July 2017).

Initial findings demonstrate inter-country emulations that served as "benchmarking" (McCann 2011, 116) to justify the effectuation of the bans on face coverings. Although France was the first country to legislate the matter in 2010, its parliamentary discussions made reference to other EU countries that had begun acting on the matter. The sponsor of the bill, Jean-Paul Garraud, declared that the proposed law was in line with "the evolution of legislation ... in other European countries, where there is a growing movement in favor of a ban, in Belgium as well as in Spain or the Netherlands" (Assemblée Nationale July 6, 2010). Other deputies referred to Belgium in particular, which had started its legislative process, as a direct influence: "our Belgian friends have already shown the way by unanimously adopting a similar text" (Assemblée Nationale July 7, 2010).

A year later, several deputies in the Belgian parliamentary discussions referred back to France as an inspiration: "France has also adopted such a ban and other European countries are preparing legislation to the same effect." Another deputy, after laying out the case for the ban, implied that there is no need for a longer discussion, because "these arguments were used in France during the vote to ban the burqa" (De Kamer 28 April 2011). "Just like France," one politician underlined, "the adoption of this bill is an outstanding message to the world about owning up to our values of women's dignity and liberty and Enlightenment" (cited in Burchardt, Yanasmayan, and Koenig 2017, 16). A parliamentary committee report in Bulgaria, the third country to legislate on the matter, noted that "similar restrictions had been imposed in six European countries," some national and some local. It added: "These are democracies such as France, Belgium, Germany, Switzerland, Italy, and the Netherlands. With this bill, our country will join a trend that is pan-European, and which aims to preserve the secular foundations of the countries in the European Union" (Parliamentary Committee 26 May 2016).

According to Burchardt et al. (2017), such cross-referencing between countries has led to a "standardization of justificatory repertoires" to introduce the bans on face coverings. These justifications include fighting Islamic radicalism, integration of immigrants for better "living together," public security and communication concerns, and promoting women's rights (Howard 2020, 37–49). A commonality of countries with a nationwide general ban is that the laws do not explicitly refer to the Muslim full veil, but frame the issue in general terms as restrictions on covering the face. Also, each of these laws introduces penalties for non-compliance, and while they make certain exceptions to the rule (such as for health and professional reasons), covering the face for religious reasons is never one such exception (Open Society 2018, 9). This has become particularly visible in the COVID-19 context, where Muslim women wearing the full veil in public have potentially become subject to a dual fine: one for covering their face for religious reasons, and another for not covering their face (with a mask) for sanitary reasons (*The Washington Post,* May 10, 2020).

Austria and Denmark were the fourth and fifth countries, respectively, to legislate face coverings. Article 1 of the Austrian ban in 2017 clarified that "the goals of this federal law are to promote integration by strengthening participation in society and ensuring peaceful coexistence in Austria" (Bundesrecht 2017). In the parliamentary debates, David Stögmüller from the Greens, who opposed the bill, rejected the government's argument that France could serve as an example, because "the judgments of the European Court of Human Rights in France cannot be transferred to Austria as there is secularity [laïcité] in their constitution ... that does not exist in Austria" (Donnerstag 1 June 2017). In the justification document of the Danish bill the following year, the integration argument was reiterated: "the Danish government takes the view that if one covers up their face it is a signal of not wanting to be a part of the Danish society" (Retsinformation April 11, 2018). Yet some opposing Danish deputies saw the Austrian example as a cautionary tale due to the ban's applicability issues. As one eco-socialist politician put it, "the Austrian police find the rules very difficult to administer," therefore, "the experience of Austria shows that it is difficult to legislate on certain types of clothing without having unintended consequences" (Folketinget April 19, 2018). Cross-referencing such as these can be found abundantly in all of these countries' legislative processes.

Another example can be given from the Dutch case. Although the Netherlands' 2018 nationwide ban is limited to certain public spaces (namely public transport, education, healthcare, and public government buildings), the Dutch parliamentary discussions demonstrate direct influences from previous European debates. Alexander van Hattem of the right-wing Party for Freedom declared, for instance, that "it is not without reason that more and more countries are imposing a burqa ban." After citing the examples of France, Belgium, Bulgaria, Austria, and Denmark, and countries with local bans, he added: "Several European countries have therefore been able to introduce a ban that applies to public spaces. That is therefore legally feasible" (Eerste Kamer 12 June 2018). Minister of the Interior Kajsa Ollongren justified the bill by referring to the falling number of women wearing the burqa or niqab in France after the 2010 ban. Questioned about the legality of restricting individual freedoms, the Minister pointed to the ECtHR decisions to validate the ban: "The European Court of Human Rights has allowed the ban on face-covering clothing in France and Belgium. In these countries it is a far-reaching ban, because it covers the entire public space. So I think we can say with confidence that it can indeed pass that test" (Eerste Kamer 12 June 2018). Another deputy seconded the Minister: "In those [ECtHR] judgments, it is striking that the Court attaches great importance to democracy and legal culture in the country concerned. There is a large margin of appreciation" (Eerste Kamer 12 June 2018). Similar to the Québec case, while more research is necessary to comprehend the subtleties, cross-country connections, and variegation of these mobilized policies in each of these countries, initial data suggests that cross-referencing has been a powerful tool in justifying or raising concerns about the proposed bans on face coverings. The ECtHR decisions on France (2014) and Belgium (2017), moreover, are interpreted by several states as a green light from a supranational body to implement similar policies in their national legislation without fear of an eventual legal challenge.

8 Discussion and Conclusions

This chapter contended that a policy mobilities perspective can indeed be a useful tool to account for the movement and mutations of policies toward religions across various geographies and political, social, and legal traditions. In conformity with the very nature of exploratory case studies, the examples of Québec and the multiple EU countries discussed above were not intended as a full-fledged investigation of these polities' changing secular trajectories, or a comprehensive account of cross-national influences that inspired and reshaped related policies. Further research is needed through interviews with policymakers, experts, and other stakeholders as well as the analysis of networks such as diplomatic meetings, conferences, study tours, lobby groups, NGOs, etc. to "follow the policy" as it moves from one place to another (Peck and Theodore 2012).

What the fragmentary findings do show, however, is that it would be utterly insufficient to analyze the shifting governmental approaches toward religions and religious freedoms as confined to national boundaries, which has been the dominant paradigm in the literature. Existing quantitative works and comparative studies on the course of secularity and religious freedoms in different countries can be accompanied and enriched by qualitative research that documents the interactions and influences between cases, rather than taking them as separate units. A PM perspective thus holds relevant for making sense of the evolving relationship between religion and the state, especially in the age of globalization where cross-national/regional emulation and exchanges are abundant (Beyer 1994). The exact ways in which policies that impact religious freedoms move, mutate, and create novel assemblages can be the subject of a new and fruitful research agenda in the sociology of religion, and the social sciences in general.

The exploration of Québec and the EU countries make it clear that politicians, intellectuals, and other stakeholders are keenly aware of the regional and global contexts in which they operate as well as the similar debates going on elsewhere. This is valid for those who are for or against the bills in question. Québec's gradual adoption of a laïcité framework, for instance, was justified with numerous references to the French example, including during a diplomatic visit to this country. Yet laïcité also was brought up by the opposition parties as a cautionary tale for minority rights, with allusions to the consequences of France's 2004 and 2010 laws. Similarly in the EU, policymakers introducing the bans on face coverings in France, Belgium, Bulgaria, Austria, Denmark, and the Netherlands repeatedly cited each other for benchmarking, with those in the latter four countries further emboldened by the ECtHR's favorable decisions on the first two. Opposition politicians also employed cross-referencing, yet for the purpose of questioning, the applicability and/or the net benefit of such restrictions for their countries.

Policy diffusions, however, do not seem to engender a simple transfer of "best practices." As the PM perspective predicts, it involves a careful interpretation of themes, ideas, and strategies deployed in other cases to be mobilized in novel ways domestically, filtered through the political agendas and contexts of various actors. As a province of Canada, Québec does not share the same political or constitutional history of laïcité as France, which prompted a distinct set of discourses and socio-legal frameworks of laïcité to enforce less comprehensive restrictions on religious signs (Laxer 2019). Although many of the justificatory repertoires were streamlined for the European burqa bans, each country stipulated different rules, spatial scopes, and fines and punishments across the EU (Open Society 2018). Mutations and new assemblages, therefore, are an integral part of secular policy mobilities.

The two exploratory case studies focused on intra-Western mobilities, yet a PM approach can be applied to the study of the policy interactions and inspirations between the West and the non-West as well as between non-Western cases themselves. And while the examples of Québec and the EU are from the contemporary era, there is no reason why a PM outlook would be incompatible with analyzing historical processes of policymaking concerning religious affairs and freedoms. As an example of a historical exchange between two non-Western cases, for instance, it has been suggested that the 27-day visit of Iran's Reza Pahlavi in Kemal Atatürk's Turkey in 1934 has had direct implications for the restrictive veiling practices that he initiated soon after returning home — although in more assertive ways (Chehabi 2003). As for the West's relations with the non-West, the PM outlook would be perfectly applicable for expanding the research agenda on the journeys of secularity through colonial and imperial entanglements, which the literature has already begun exploring (Künkler, Madeley, and Shankar 2018).

Finally, it should be noted that secular diffusions can be investigated in various geographical scales and levels of analysis. While Mataic (2018) has verified that proximity can be a significant variable for the mimetic spread of policies on religion (such as in the EU countries studied in this chapter), the France-Québec connection attests that cultural, epistemic, and linguistic ties may also be a factor facilitating the mobility of policies across distant lands and even continents. Moreover, the nation-state need not be the sole unit of analysis for the study of secular diffusions; as the Québec and ECtHR examples show, mobilities can also be mediated through provincial and supranational governments or institutions. The swift banning of the "burkini" (a Muslim swimsuit for women) in more than 30 French coastal towns in the summer of 2016, for instance, exemplifies that the mobilization of policies can occur at the municipal level as well (Almeida 2018). Overall, the sociology of religion would benefit from a PM perspective to further familiarize itself with the intricacies and various levels of policymaking. A PM outlook holds the potential to be an enriching contribution to the social scientific study of religion and religious freedoms — as a theoretical framework to study the *mobility, assemblages*, and *mutations* of policies toward religions across cases, as well as a methodological guide for qualitative data collection to advance the understanding of how secularity "travels."

References

Akan, Murat. 2017. *The Politics of Secularism: Religion, Diversity, and Institutional Change in France and Turkey*. New York: Columbia University Press.

Almeida, Dimitri. 2018. "Marianne at the Beach: The French Burkini Controversy and the Shifting Meanings of Republican Secularism." *Journal of Intercultural Studies* 39 (1): 20–34.

Assemblée Nationale. July 6, 2010. "XIIIe législature Session extraordinaire de 2009–2010, Compte rendu intégral, Troisième séance du mardi 6 juillet 2010." Accessed

June 19, 2020. http://www.assemblee-nationale.fr/13/cri/2009-2010-extra/20101010.asp.

Assemblée Nationale. July 7, 2010. "XIIIe législature, Compte rendu intégral, Première séance du mercredi 7 juillet 2010." Accessed June 20, 2020. http://www.assemblee-nationale.fr/13/cri/2009-2010-extra/20101011.asp.

ASSNAT. June 4, 2019. "Journal des débats de la Commission des institutions, Vol. 45 N° 44." Accessed June 11, 2020. http://www.assnat.qc.ca/fr/travaux-parlementaires/commissions/ci-42-1/journal-debats/CI-190604.html.

ASSNAT. May 7, 2019. "Journal des débats de la Commission des institutions, Vol. 45 N° 33." Accessed April 11, 2020. http://www.assnat.qc.ca/fr/travaux-parlementaires/commissions/ci-42-1/journal-debats/CI-190507.html.

ASSNAT. May 14, 2019. "Journal des débats de la Commission des institutions, Vol. 45 N° 38." Accessed June 19, 2020. http://www.assnat.qc.ca/fr/travaux-parlementaires/commissions/ci-42-1/journal-debats/CI-190514.html.

ASSNAT. May 30, 2019. "Journal des débats de la Commission des institutions, Vol. 45 N° 47." Accessed May 22, 2020. http://www.assnat.qc.ca/fr/travaux-parlementaires/assemblee-nationale/42-1/journal-debats/20190530/244591.html.

Baker, Tom, and Pauline McGuirk. 2017. "Assemblage Thinking as Methodology: Commitments and Practices for Critical Policy Research." *Territory, Politics, Governance* 5 (4): 425–42.

Başkan, Birol. 2014. *From Religious Empires to Secular States: State Secularization in Turkey, Iran, and Russia*. New York: Routledge.

Beauchamp, Caroline. 2011. *Pour un Québec laïque*. Laval: Presses de l'Université Laval.

Berger, Peter L. 1967. *The Sacred Canopy: Elements of a Sociological Theory of Religion*. New York: Doubleday & Company.

Beyer, Peter. 1994. *Religion and Globalization*. London: Sage.

Bosset, Pierre. 2005. "Le droit et la régulation de la diversité religieuse en France et au Québec: une même problématique, deux approches." *Bulletin d'histoire politique* 13 (3): 79–95.

Bowen, John R. 2007. *Why the French don't Like Headscarves: Islam, the State, and Public Space*. Princeton: Princeton University Press.

Bruce, Steve. 2002. *God is Dead: Secularization in the West*. Oxford: Blackwell Publishers.

Buckley, David T. 2016. *Faithful to Secularism: The Religious Politics of Democracy in Ireland, Senegal, and the Philippines*. New York: Columbia University Press.

Bundesrecht. 2017. "Anti-Gesichtsverhüllungsgesetz." Accessed April 21, 2020. https://www.ris.bka.gv.at/eli/bgbl/i/2017/68/P1/NOR40193538.

Burchardt, Marian, Monika Wohlrab-Sahr, and Matthias Middell, eds. 2015. *Multiple Secularities Beyond the West: Religion and Modernity in the Global Age*. Boston: De Gruyter.

Burchardt, Marian, Zeynep Yanasmayan, and Matthias Koenig. 2017. "The Judicial Politics of 'Burqa Bans' in Belgium and Spain: Socio-Legal Field Dynamics and the Standardization of Justificatory Repertoires." *MMG Working Paper* 17 (10): 7–34.

Cady, Linell E., and Elizabeth Shakman Hurd, eds. 2010. *Comparative Secularisms in a Global Age*. New York: Palgrave Macmillan.

Casanova, José. 1994. *Public Religions in the Modern World*. Chicago: University of Chicago Press.

Casanova, José. 2011. "Cosmopolitanism, the Clash of Civilizations and Multiple Modernities." *Current Sociology* 59 (2): 252–67.

CCAPRCD. 2008. *Building the Future: A Time for Reconciliation*. Québec: Gouvernement du Québec.

Chehabi, Houchang E. 2003. "The Banning of the Veil and its Consequences." In *The Making of Modern Iran: State and Society under Riza Shah, 1921-1941*, edited by Stephanie Cronin, 203–221. New York: Routledge.

Clarke, John, Dave Bainton, Noémi Lendvai, and Paul Stubbs. 2015. *Making Policy Move: Towards a Politics of Translation and Assemblage*. Bristol: Polity Press.

CRI. 2004. "Laïcité et diversité religieuse: l'approche québécoise." Accessed April 15, 2020. http://www.mifi.gouv.qc.ca/publications/fr/cri/diversite/Avis-laicite-diversite-religieuse.pdf.

DeHanas, Daniel Nilsson, and Marat Shterin, eds. 2020. *Religion and the Rise of Populism*. New York: Routledge.

De Kamer. April 28, 2011. "Séance plénière du jeudi 28 avril 2011 après-midi." Accessed April 21, 2020. https://www.dekamer.be/doc/PCRI/html/53/ip030x.html. Accessed April 21, 2020.

Donnerstag. June 1, 2017. "868. Sitzung des Bundesrates der Republik Österreich." Accessed September 10, 2020. https://www.parlament.gv.at/PAKT/VHG/BR/BRSITZ/BRSITZ_00868/fnameorig_672857.html.

Eerste Kamer. June 12, 2018. "Behandeling Gedeeltelijk verbod gezichtsbedekkende kleding." Accessed January 25, 2020. https://www.eerstekamer.nl/verslagdeel/20180612/gedeeltelijk_verbod.

Eisenstadt, Shmuel N. 2000. "Multiple Modernities." *Daedalus* 129 (1): 1–29.

Fabbe, Kristin E. 2019. *Disciples of the State?: Religion and State-Building in the Former Ottoman World*. Cambridge: Cambridge University Press.

Ferrari, Alessandro, and Sabrina Pastorelli, eds. 2016. *The Burqa Affair Across Europe: Between Public and Private Space*. London: Routledge.

Finke, Roger, and Dane R. Mataic. 2019. "Promises, Practices, and Consequences of Religious Freedom: A Global Overview." *University of St. Thomas Law Journal* 15 (3): 587–606.

Fitzgerald, Timothy, ed. 2007. *Religion and the Secular: Historical and Colonial Formations*. New York: Routledge.

FNLP. 2020. "Un même combat: Au Québec comme en France, la Laïcité a besoin de vous." Accessed April 14, 2020. https://www.fnlp.fr/2020/02/13/un-meme-combat-au-quebec-comme-en-france-la-laicite-a-besoin-de-vous-au-quebec-pour-linstituer-en-france-pour-la-defendre/.

Folketinget. April 19, 2018. "L 219 Forslag til lov om ændring af straffeloven (Tildækningsforbud)." Accessed April 3, 2020. https://www.ft.dk/samling/20171/lovforslag/L219/BEH1-85/forhandling.htm.

Fox, Jonathan. 2020. *Thou Shalt Have No Other Gods Before Me: Why Governments Discriminate against Minorities*. Cambridge: Cambridge University Press.

Gill, Anthony. 2007. *The Political Origins of Religious Liberty*. Cambridge: Cambridge University Press.

Gorski, Philip S. 2003. "Historicizing the Secularization Debate." In *Handbook for the Sociology of Religion*, edited by Michele Dillon, 110–22. New York: Cambridge University.

Grzymała-Busse, Anna. 2015. *Nations under God: How Churches Use Moral Authority to Influence Policy*. Princeton: Princeton University Press.

Hadden, Jeffrey K. 1987. "Toward Desacralizing Secularization Theory." *Social Forces* 65 (3): 587–611.

Haynes, Jeffrey. 2020. "Trump and the Politics of International Religious Freedom." *Religions* 11 (8): 385–405.

Howard, Erica. 2020. *Law and the Wearing of Religious Symbols in Europe*. New York: Routledge.

Journal de Québec. March 31, 2019. "Projet de loi sur la laïcité: « au Québec, c'est comme ça qu'on vit », dit François Legault." Accessed April 22, 2020. https://www.journaldequebec.com/2019/03/31/laicite-de-letat-legault-sadressera-aux-quebecois-en-fin-dapres-midi.

Juergensmeyer, Mark. 2010. "The Global Rise of Religious Nationalism." *Australian Journal of International Affairs* 64 (3): 262–73.

Katznelson, Ira, and Gareth Stedman Jones. 2010. "Introduction: Multiple Secularities." In *Religion and the Political Imagination*, edited by Ira Katznelson and Gareth Stedman Jones, 1–22. Cambridge: Cambridge University Press.

Koussens, David, and Valérie Amiraux. 2014. "Du mauvais usage de la laïcité française dans le débat public québécois." In *Penser la laïcité québécoise: Fondements et défense d'une laïcité ouverte au Québec*, edited by Sébastien Lévesque, 55–75. Québec: Les Presses de l'Université Laval.

Künkler, Mirjam, John Madeley, and Shylashri Shankar, eds. 2018. *A Secular Age Beyond the West: Religion, Law and the State in Asia, the Middle East and North Africa*. Cambridge: Cambridge University Press.

Kuru, Ahmet. 2009. *Secularism and State Policies Toward Religion: The United States, France and Turkey*. New York: Cambridge University Press.

Lægaard, Sune. 2015. "Burqa Ban, Freedom of Religion and 'Living Together'." *Human Rights Review* 16 (3): 203–19.

Lamonde, Yvan. 2010. *L'heure de vérité: la laïcité Québécoise à l'épreuve de l'histoire*. Montréal: Del Busso.

Lampron, Louis-Philippe. 2015. "The Quebec Charter of Values: Using the Concept of French Laïcité to Create a Clash with the Canadian Multiculturalism." In *Politics of Religion and Nationalism: Federalism, Consociatialism and Secession*, edited by Ferran Requejo and Klaus-Jürgen Nagel, 137–50. New York: Routledge.

La Presse, December 13, 2013. "La laïcité française, une «inspiration» pour Marois." Accessed April 21, 2020. https://www.lapresse.ca/actualites/politique/politique-quebecoise/201312/13/01-4720644-la-laicite-francaise-une-inspiration-pour-marois.php.

Laxer, Emily. 2019. *Unveiling the Nation: The Politics of Secularism in France and Quebec*. Montreal: McGill-Queen's Press.

Leonen, Titia. 2017. "In Search of an EU Approach to Headscarf Bans: Where to Go After Achbita and Bougnaoui?" *Review of European Administrative Law* 10 (2): 47–73.

Mancilla, Alma. 2011. "Religion dans l'espace public et régulation politique: le parcours de la notion de laïcité dans le discours étatique Québécois." *Recherches sociographiques* 52 (3): 789–810.

Mataic, Dane R. 2018. "Countries Mimicking Neighbors: The Spatial Diffusion of Governmental Restrictions on Religion." *Journal for the Scientific Study of Religion* 57 (2): 221–37.

Mayrl, Damon. 2016. *Secular Conversions: Secular Political Institutions and Religious Education in the United States and Australia, 1800–2000*. Cambridge: Cambridge University Press.

McCann, Eugene. 2011. "Urban Policy Mobilities and Global Circuits of Knowledge: Toward a Research Agenda." *Annals of the Association of American Geographers* 101 (1): 107–30.

McCann, Eugene, and Kevin Ward. 2013. "A Multi-Disciplinary Approach to Policy Transfer Research: Geographies, Assemblages, Mobilities and Mutations." *Policy Studies* 34 (1): 2–18.

Milot, Micheline. 2009. "L'émergence de la notion de laïcité au Québec. Résistances, polysémie et instrumentalisation." In *Appartenance religieuse, appartenance citoyenne. Un équilibre en tension*, edited by Paul Eid, Pierre Bosset, Micheline Milot and Sébastien Lebel-Grenier, 20–38. Québec: Presses de l'Université Laval.

Nilsson, Per-Erik. 2017. *Unveiling the French Republic: National Identity, Secularism, and Islam in Contemporary France*. Leiden: Brill.

Open Society. 2018. "Restrictions on Muslim Women's Dress in the 28 EU Member States." Accessed April 20, 2020. https://www.justiceinitiative.org/uploads/dffdb416-5d63-4001-911b-d3f46e159acc/restrictions-on-muslim-womens-dress-in-28-eu-member-states-20180709.pdf.

Parliamentary Committee. May 26, 2016. "Комисия по вероизповеданията и правата на човека [Commission on Religions and Human Rights]." Accessed October 11, 2020. https://parliament.bg/bg/parliamentarycommittees/members/2335/reports/ID/6208.

Parliament Magazine. April 28, 2017. "EPP and Ukip under fire for calls for EU-wide burka ban." Accessed February 10, 2021. https://www.theparliamentmagazine.eu/news/article/epp-and-ukip-under-fire-for-calls-for-euwide-burka-ban.

Peck, Jamie. 2011. "Geographies of Policy: From Transfer-Diffusion to Mobility-Mutation." *Progress in Human Geography* 35 (6): 773–97.

Peck, Jamie, and Nik Theodore. 2012. "Follow the Policy: A Distended Case Approach." *Environment and Planning A: Economy and Space* 44 (1): 21–30.

Peker, Efe. 2020. "Beyond Positivism: Building Turkish Laiklik in the Transition from the Empire to the Republic (1908–1938)." *Social Science History* 44 (2): 301–327.

Retsinformation. April 11, 2018. "Forslag til lov om ændring af straffeloven (Tildækningsforbud)." Accessed April 17, 2020. https://www.retsinformation.dk/eli/ft/201712L00219.

Rousseau, Guillaume, and James McDonald. 2014. "Legislating Secularism in Quebec." *Inroads* 35 (Summer): 92–6.

Roy, Olivier. 2019. *L'Europe est-elle chrétienne?* Paris: Seuil.

Saeed, Sadia. 2017. *Politics of Desecularization: Law and the Minority Question in Pakistan*. New York: Cambridge University Press.

Saunders, Jennifer B., Elena Fiddian-Qasmiyeh, and Susanna Snyder. 2016. *Intersections of Religion and Migration: Issues at the Global Crossroads*. New York: Palgrave Macmillan.

Smith, Christian, ed. 2003. *The Secular Revolution: Power, Interests, and Conflict in the Secularization of American Public Life*. Berkeley: University of California Press.

Stark, Rodney, and Roger Finke. 2000. *Acts of Faith: Explaining the Human Side of Religion*. Berkeley: University of California Press.

Steb, Christoph K. 2009. "Exploratory Case Study." In *Encyclopedia of Case Study Research*, edited by Albert J. Mills, Gabrielle Durepos and Elden Wiebe, 372–73. London: Sage.

Stepan, Alfred. 2011. "The Multiple Secularisms of Modern Democratic and Non-Democratic Regimes." In *Rethinking Secularism*, edited by Craig J. Calhoun, Mark Juergensmeyer and Jonathan VanAntwerpen, 114–44. New York: Oxford University Press.

Taylor, Charles. 1998. "Modes of Secularism." In *Secularism and its Critics*, edited by Rajeev Bhargava. New Delhi: Oxford University Press.

Taylor, Charles. 2007. *A Secular Age*. London: Harvard University Press.

Taylor, Charles. 2016. "Can Secularism Travel?" In *Beyond the Secular West*, edited by Akeel Bilgrami, 1–27. New York: Columbia University Press.

Temenos, Cristina, and Eugene McCann. 2013. "Geographies of Policy Mobilities." *Geography Compass* 7 (5): 344–57.
The Guardian. July 1, 2014. "France's burqa ban upheld by human rights court." https://www.theguardian.com/world/2014/jul/01/france-burqa-ban-upheld-human-rights-court.
The Independent. July 11, 2017. "European Court of Human Rights upholds Belgium's ban on burqas and full-face Islamic veils." Accessed February 10, 2021. https://www.independent.co.uk/news/world/europe/belgium-burqa-ban-upheld-european-court-of-human-rights-dakir-v-full-face-islamic-veils-headscarf-a7835156.html.
Theodore, Nik. 2019. "Policy Mobilities." Oxford Bibliographies: Geography. https://www.oxfordbibliographies.com/view/document/obo-9780199874002/obo-9780199874002-0205.xml.
The Washington Post. May 10, 2020. "France mandates masks to control the coronavirus. Burqas remain banned." Accessed October 11, 2020. https://www.washingtonpost.com/world/europe/france-face-masks-coronavirus/2020/05/09/6fbd50fc-8ae6-11ea-80df-d24b35a568ae_story.html.
Warner, Michael, Jonathan Van Antwerpen, and Craig Calhoun, eds. 2010. *Varieties of Secularism in a Secular Age*. Cambridge: Harvard University Press.
Wittgenstein, Ludwig. 2009. *Philiosophical Investigations*. Oxford: Wiley-Blackwell.
Wohlrab-Sahr, Monika, and Marian Burchardt. 2012. "Multiple Secularities: Toward a Cultural Sociology of Secular Modernities." *Comparative Sociology* 11 (6): 875–909.
Yin, Robert K. 2018. *Case Study Research and Applications: Design and Methods*. London: Sage.
Zubrzycki, Geneviève. 2016. *Beheading the Saint: Nationalism, Religion, and Secularism in Quebec*. Chicago: University of Chicago Press.

CHAPTER 2

Religious Freedom, Legal Activism, and Muslim Personal Law in Contemporary India: A Sociological Exploration of Secularism

Anindita Chakrabarti

1 Introduction[1]

Religion-specific family laws (referred to as personal laws in India) function under the constitutional guarantee of religious freedom — Articles 25–30 of the Indian Constitution. But they operate in a context where Article 44, part of the Directive Principles of the Indian Constitution, holds a tentative promise of a Uniform Civil Code (UCC)[2] that is supposed to replace these diverse religion-based family laws. The contradiction at the heart of religion-based family law of Indian Muslims can be summed up in the following way: the MPL exists due to the constitutional commitment to the principle of religious freedom but its archaic character symbolizes the antithesis of the very spirit of the Constitution. The question of personal law of Muslims (the largest religious minority) has, over the years, created distinct camps with those who want to protect what goes in the name of religion-based family laws and those who want to reject such obscurantist, gender unjust indulgences and arrive at a UCC at two ends of the spectrum.[3] The public as well as academic discussion on this question has centered around three key issues: gender justice, national integration, and the citizenship rights assured by the Constitution. Somewhat tautologically, they constitute the reason as well as outcome of the project of reforming/jettisoning religion-based family laws. The constitutionally backed promise of religious freedom loses much of its sure-footedness once tested

---

1 The ideas presented in this chapter took shape during my stay as a Senior Fellow at the "Multiple Secularities —Beyond the West, Beyond Modernities" project at Leipzig University in 2017. I would like to thank the group for a convivial academic home and opportunities for excellent discussions.
2 The idea of a UCC is based on the formulation of a single civil law for India, applicable to all the citizens in their family matters such as marriage, divorce, adoption, inheritance, and custody.
3 See Rajeswari Sunder Rajan (2003) for a nuanced discussion on the range of positions on this debate. For a discussion on the UCC as the 'new sacred' see Anindita Chakrabarti 2016.

© ANINDITA CHAKRABARTI, 2021 | DOI:10.1163/9789004468085_004

against the touchstone of these secular yardsticks. We argue that the idea of religious freedom in a secular democracy can be apprehended only when we pay attention to the forms of politics as well as cultural and epistemological assumptions that underlie these discourses and its longer history (Sullivan et al 2015, 1). It has been pointed out by scholars that in India, the idea of an ameliorative secularism, where "the Constitution seeks an amelioration of the social conditions of people long burdened by the inequities of religiously based hierarchies, but also embodies a vision of intergroup comity whose fulfillment necessitates cautious deliberation in the pursuit of abstract justice," (Jacobsohn 2003, 94) has led to incessant judicialization of religion. How has the idea of secularism as a commitment to social reform worked in the Indian context? Using a comparative lens, Yüksel Sezgin and Mirjam Künkler (2014) have argued how acting as a theological authority, the Indian judiciary's attempt to unify the Muslim fold, reform Islam, prepare Muslim public opinion for the eventual abolition and replacement of Muslim personal law with a UCC has "exacerbated identity politics and deepened ethno-religious schism" (Ibid., 451–57). This chapter traces the shifts in the idea of secularism and its tentative commitment to the ideal of religious freedom through two PIL landmark cases on MPL in a post-colonial constitutional democracy. But before that, we will revisit some of the key issues in the secularism debate in India.

In India, the secularism debate has, for a long time, revolved around the dualism of its absolute necessity on one hand and impossibility/irrelevance on the other. Both the advocates and the critics of secularism associate it primarily with the separation of religion from state/politics, and the concomitant idea of its privatization. The hopeful possibility of achieving a secular state in India backed by the Constitution was articulated by scholars writing in the 1960s and it has had a strong legacy (Smith 1963). For these scholars, since the separation can be a means to check communalism, religion must be restricted to the private domain of the social life, separated from the state and detached from politics (Panikkar 1991; Hassan 1991). But there have been many others who were quick to point out the difficulty of achieving this goal as the society remained "furiously religious." The critics of the separation theory (Madan 1987; Nandy 1985) uphold that religion cannot be separated from the polity in a society like India because a hierarchical relationship exists between religion and politics, the latter being encompassed by the former. For them, secularism in India is in crisis not because we are not trying hard enough but because of its deep conceptual flaw. Moving beyond the separation debate, scholars have drawn our academic attention to the ideal of religious nondiscrimination and equal liberty for all citizens as the guiding principle of the concept of secularism (Gurpreet Mahajan 2003). By focusing on its 'multi-value character',

Rajeev Bhargava (2007, 26) has argued for a distinctive and contextual variant of secularism in India with its policy of a principled distance between state and religion.

Drawing on the insights of the recent scholarship in cultural sociology that has argued for analyzing the secular as a culturally, symbolically as well as an institutionally anchored concept, we begin with the understanding that the meaning of secular in the idea of secularism alters with different social and political contexts and histories of social conflict (Wohlrab-Sahr and Burchardt 2012, 881). The question of MPL and the recent judicial activism around it as discussed in this chapter capture one such context where the conceptual anchoring of secularism shows prominent shifts. The cases show how the concept of secularism has come to be articulated in judicial activism by citizens as well as judges as subjection of religion to the rule of law as they questioned and initiated judicial intervention in MPL.

In this chapter we show that in the mid-1980s, in the wake of the Shah Bano judgment and its aftermath, the term secular acquired the conceptual vocabulary of minority appeasement backed by the idea of religious freedom. A constitutional promise turned into a partisan category (See Rochana Bajpai 2002). In this discourse, the ideal of a UCC, with its unclear idea of what a uniform code would look like in a multi-cultural nation-state where customs of marriage, divorce, and inheritance varied not only along the lines of religious communities but also within caste and region, curiously loomed large as a panacea to the problem of gender discrimination. The failure of the Indian state to enact a UCC is held against it; the underlying implication being that the state was protective of religious minorities as it indulged in identitarian or 'vote-bank' politics. The Indian National Congress — with brief periods, when it was out of power — the ruling party since 1947 till 2014, was accused of siding with the conservative forces among the religious minorities for electoral gains. In public perception, while a number of progressive legislations were brought about in the family laws of the Hindus, ranging from monogamy, divorce, and women's rights to property, MPL remained outside the ambit of judicial reform, thanks to the political exigency of minority appeasement. The appellate judiciary also has upheld this view in many of its judgments that in turn fed the public discourse.[4]

---

4 For example, in a judgment on the issue of personal law, the apex court stated that though the personal law of the Hindus had a sacramental origin in the same manner as in the case of the Muslims or the Christians, "the Hindus along with Sikhs, Buddhists and Jains have forsaken their sentiments in the cause of the national unity and integration, some other communities

This chapter is divided into four sections. The first section revisits the iconic Shah Bano judgment (1985) that has shaped the public discourse on MPL in India and still frames its everyday understanding. In this case, whereas the apex court directed divorced Muslim women to be covered by the religion-neutral Indian Code of Criminal Procedure (CrPc) 125,[5] under which the husband is supposed to maintain their divorced wife where she is unable to support herself, the judgment had to be repealed due to protest by conservative Muslim groups. The Muslim Women's (Protection of Rights on Divorce) Act (1986) was passed by the parliament to spell out the rights of Muslim women in divorces. Here, the concept of secularism was inflected with the idea of religious rights of minority communities. Next, I will explore how a unique jurisdictional innovation in the Indian judicial system, known as public interest litigation (PIL), has created a different trope to understand the issue of MPL and the scope of legal intervention in it. In the rest of the chapter, I will analyze two discrepant judgments on MPL, both brought to the apex court as PILs. In the first PIL, the *Vishwa Lochan Madan* petition, an appeal was made for banning sharia courts, or dar-ul-qazas, for delivering gender-unjust, arbitrary judgments. In July 2014, the Supreme Court dismissed the petition, arguing that the dar-ul-qazas functioned as ADR sites and were not in opposition to the secular judiciary. In the following year, a PIL petition was brought once again on the grounds of gender injustice in MPL. But unlike the previous PIL, this was a *suo-moto* ("the Court on its own Motion") PIL brought by the judges themselves. This case opened up a different discourse in the relation between state, civil society and the religious rights of Indian Muslims. The historic judgment came in August 2017. Framed in terms of constitutional morality and buttressed by justification from religion itself, it declared gender unjust instant divorce (triple talaq) as invalid. But within four months of the historic judgment, it became apparent that declaring triple talaq invalid did not end the age-old practice. Therefore, a bill was brought by the government to criminalize the practice. The parliament passed the bill in July 2019 that made arbitrary divorce by Muslim men a criminal offense with a three-year jail term. The Act, instead of making way

---

would not, though the Constitution enjoins the establishment of a 'common civil Code' for the whole of India". (Smt. Sarla Mudgal, President, Kalyani v. Union of India 1995).

5 The history of CrPC 125 goes back to 1898, when the revised Indian Penal Code used vagrancy to address the plight of impoverished women and children, making those without income and assets the responsibility of the male members of their families. Thereby the financial burden of maintaining women and children was unequivocally placed on the family and not on the state. Twenty-six years after Indian independence, the term "wife" was expanded to include all the women who had been divorced and not remarried. The responsibility for their maintenance was now placed on the husband (Sylvia Vatuk 2009).

for uniformity in civil code (a constitutional aspiration and hope of liberal politics in India) led to, for the first time, a non-uniform criminal law. In the concluding section, I will revisit the issue of judicial intervention in religion, especially the personal law of the minorities, and try to unpack how these recent interventions has led to a greater constitutional conundrum. By completely ignoring different provisions in religion-neutral criminal law through which the suffering of Muslim women could have been addressed, these PILs have (yet again) created a reified image of Muslim misogyny and Muslim women as victims who had to be saved from Muslim men. The concept of secularism was evoked to rectify the Shah Bano episode where secularism had become co-terminus with the idea of minority appeasement. It was now the corrective moment where secularism was evoked to bring about socio-religious reform buttressed by the ideal of constitutional morality and rule of law.

2 The Setting: From Shah Bano Judgment to PIL Petitions

Scholars commenting on the simultaneous emergence of the colonial categories of religion-based personal law and institutional structures of British rule of law have engaged at length with their historical and epistemological assumptions. The history of MPL goes back to the colonial power's creation of the legal category of religion-based personal laws where Hindus and Muslims were to be governed by their religious laws in matters of inheritance, marriage, divorce, adoption, and other religious usages (Anderson 1999; Kugle 2001). Yet, these personal laws had to be administered by colonial courts under the political authority of the state. Drawing on the insights of postcolonial theories, Rachel Sturman (2012) has shown the connections between the systems of personal law and the broader context of colonial civil law and administration. She argues that it was within this matrix of the legal discourse of personal laws and their necessary reform that womanhood emerged as an abstract universal category. Thus, the Hindu woman emerged at one stroke as a universal and particularistic category of colonial governance (Ibid., 5–14). While the liberal language of women's rights was equated with the Hindu-dominated ideal of Indian nationalism, the Indian Muslims were perceived as a community that attempted to subsume women's rights and autonomy to their religious identity (Newbigin 2018 [2013] 8–9). It was this discourse that gained a new life once the Shah Bano case unfolded in 1985.

In April 1978, driven out of her marital home in Indore (a city in Madhya Pradesh), Shah Bano, a 62-year-old Muslim wife, filed a petition in a local court demanding maintenance from her husband, Mohammed Ahmed Khan. When the local court ruled in favor of her but with a minimal amount of maintenance, she approached the High Court, in July 1980, for a higher amount. The High Court ordered her husband to pay INR 179.20 per month. Shortly after that, Mohammed Ahmed Khan divorced Shah Bano using the irrevocable divorce, or talaq, in one sitting. Mohammed Ahmed Khan, then, claimed that he had no obligation to support Shah Bano since she was no longer his wife and appealed to the Supreme Court of India to reverse the High Court order. The All India Muslim Personal Law Board (AIMPLB) sought and obtained permission to intervene on behalf of the husband. In the Supreme Court, counsel for Mohammed Ahmed Khan argued that he could not be ordered to pay maintenance to Shah Bano beyond the iddat period,[6] since to do so would be opposing the principles of Islam. The Supreme Court of India ruled in favor of Shah Bano. It dismissed Mohammed Ahmed Khan's appeal by upholding the High Court judgment awarding Shah Bano maintenance of INR 179.20 per month under CrPC 125 (*Mohd. Ahmed Khan v. Shah Bano Begum*). The judgment unleashed a nationwide protest from different sections of Indian Muslims. The orthodox Muslim leadership spearheaded by the AIMPLB were indignant that the judgment had quoted and misinterpreted the Quran and called for doing away altogether with MPL. In December 1985, the AIMPLB met with Rajiv Gandhi, the-then prime minister, to express their opposition to the Shah Bano judgment. The ruling government quickly bowed to the mounting pressure and introduced the Muslim Women (Protection of Rights on Divorce) Bill in the parliament. Women's organizations, secular political groups, human rights activists, and some independent Muslim organizations strongly opposed the bill's exclusion of Muslim women from the purview of CrPC 125. They also restated the demand for the long-promised UCC. The media framed the issue as a battle between "fundamentalist, orthodox, obscurantist male chauvinists" and "modern, secular, pro-women rationalists" (Vatuk 2009, 356–58).

Over the years, in the pitched battle between the "progressive" UCC versus the "regressive" MPL discourse, what has remained missing from public attention is how *The Muslim Women (Protection of Rights on Divorce) Act 1986* (MWA) is used as a legal instrument in actual practice. Though the MWA denied a Muslim woman the right to maintenance after divorce, it permitted her a one-off "reasonable and fair maintenance" payment from her husband. It also specified that a Muslim woman could approach a magistrate for a ruling directing

---

6 Iddat is the mandatory waiting period after Islamic divorce. During this period the divorced Muslim woman needs to refrain from sexual intercourse for three lunar cycles from the divorce pronouncement. This is to determine if she is pregnant with a child. If she is found bearing a child of her divorced husband, he has to maintain her till the child is born.

her adult children or any of her biological relatives to provide for maintenance. In the absence of a family member, the court could order the state Waqf Board[7] to provide her the amount. Quite counter-intuitively, the MWA, which was perceived as anti-women, was found to be used by the judges to give divorced Muslim women a "reasonable and fair" compensation[8] that was at times more than what they could have received under any other personal law as well as CrPC 125 (Agnes 2001; Solanki 2011). Despite these evidences of how the MWA is being used in the secular courts to the benefit of divorced Muslim women, it stands as a shorthand for the betrayal of Muslim women's citizenship rights and ideals of the secular nation-state. The fact that Indian Muslim women were forced to frame their marital rights within the frame of MPL is seen as a precipitous decline of the secular journey of the Indian nation-state. Over the years, the clamor for a UCC has brought odd bedfellows like feminists, liberals, and the Hindu-right on the same platform. We need to read the PIL cases discussed here in light of this changing political landscape since the Shah Bano judgment. The deflection in the discourse of MPL needs to understood in the context of the steady rise of the Bharatiya Janata Party (BJP) as a national level party committed to the ideology of Hindutva, in stark contrast to the Indian National Congress's secular identity. Interestingly, in contrast to the religious freedom argument of the Congress regime, it was constitutional morality and gender discrimination that framed the current judicial interventions into MPL.

Whereas the PILs in both the cases were brought on the same premise: gender oppression in MPL, the two contrasting judgments followed completely opposed judicial logic. In the first case, the judges chose not to evoke either the question of religion or gender and went on to understand how the religious institution in question functioned. In the second case, the majority judgment pitted unilateral instant divorce permitted in MPL against gender equality. In this case, the argument was that Muslim women could not be helped if oppressive practices within MPL were not done away with. It framed the question of sufferings caused by arbitrary, unilateral divorce as a uniquely Muslim problem

---

7 State Waqf Board manages, regulates, and protects the Waqf properties. Waqf is a permanent dedication of properties for religious, pious, or charitable reasons as recognized by Islamic law, given by community members.

8 The logic of "reasonable" amount under customary laws to prevent destitution and to provide the woman "wherewithal to maintain herself" was present in earlier apex court judgments as well. Ronojoy Sen had drawn attention to such judgments in 1979 and again in 1980 on the question of maintenance of divorced Muslim women (2010:140). For a discussion on the importance of the sources and modes of legal reasoning in the Shah Bano judgment and the Danial Latifi judgment that evoked very different public reception, see Narendra Subramanian (2017).

that called for judicial intervention. Revisiting the judgment and its aftermath, this chapter questions this assumption. The unfolding of the triple talaq case shows what happens when unjust practices are attributed to the particularism of a religious community to be brought under judicial scrutiny buttressed by civil society activism. I would argue that the PIL jurisdiction gave a sound justification and offered a perfect avenue for this intervention in the domain of religion, especially the religious practices of the "others."

To fully comprehend how the new form of judicial activism worked in the domain of MPL, we must first understand what PIL in the Indian context is and its applications. PIL, a writ petition that can be filed in the state High Courts or the Supreme Court of India, has been celebrated as India's unique contribution to contemporary jurisprudence. Why PILs are so important and what are its most innovative features? The answer lies in its procedural flexibility: the relaxation of the rules of *locus standi* of the petitioner and simplification of the formalities required during lodging of the petition. In a PIL case, the court could supervise and take follow-up actions regarding execution of the remedial orders. And most importantly, far-reaching remedial measures could be ordered by the court in the interest of the public (Bhuwania 2017, 2).

Bhuwania (2014), in a fine-grained analysis of the PIL regime, notes that the Indian form of PIL jurisdiction, born in the immediate aftermath of the Emergency[9] in India (1975–77), was right from its inception marked by impatience with technical formalities where arguments and justifications were made in the name of "the people" (Ibid., 314). Over the years, the PIL regime has led to the emergence of a judicial process that was initiated, led, managed, and implemented by the courts' own machinery (Bhuwania 2017, 8). As a result, the very same features that made PIL jurisdiction more participative and democratic, also had the troubling feature of being used by the judges to serve their own ideological predilections by relegating the role of the PIL petitioner to the background, bringing in *amicus curiae*[10] and *suo moto* cases. The PIL petitions on MPL analyzed here vindicate these concerns. These cases were not brought by the aggrieved party but by "concerned" citizens as well as the judiciary itself — in the name of the "victim", in this case, Muslim women. In the next section, I will discuss the *Vishwa Lochan Madan* case and show how the two-judge bench rejected the petition that was filed evoking the idea of

---

9   In June 1975, citing threat to national security, prime minister Indira Gandhi proclaimed a national emergency across the country that lasted for 21 months. The emergency limited democratic practices and citizenship rights and brought India's democracy to the brink.

10 Literally 'a friend of the court' who is supposed to be an expert, not a party to the case and assists the court.

secularism and Muslim women's victimhood. The judgment offered a possibility of addressing the issue of MPL by looking at local practices and pragmatic concerns and not inflect them into concerns of either secularism or religious freedom.

3   Institutions of Injustice: Dar-ul-qazas as Kangaroo Courts?

The *Vishwa Lochan Madan* case was a PIL brought by the petitioner, Vishwa Lochan Madan, a Hindu advocate. He alleged that all the fatwas supported by the AIMPLB show that they were striving for the establishment of a parallel Muslim judicial system in India. According to the petitioner, adjudication of disputes is essentially the function of the sovereign State, which it can never abdicate. The petition drew attention to a controversial fatwa given in a rape case where a Muslim woman was raped by her father-in-law. Saif Mahmood (2014) chronicles how the case unfolded in rural Uttar Pradesh. He writes:

> In 2005, a 28-year-old uneducated Muslim woman named Imrana was allegedly raped by her father-in-law in a village in Western Uttar Pradesh. A local Muzaffarnagar-based journalist approached the well-known Islamic seminary in nearby Deoband and, without disclosing the facts of this particular case, sought a general opinion (fatwa) on the status of the marriage of a woman who has been raped by her father-in-law in a hypothetical case. An ill-informed cleric who had no business to render opinions in such sensitive matters opined that, in such a case, the victim's marriage with her husband would stand dissolved. He founded his opinion on the Quranic edict which commands men to 'marry not the woman whom your father married.' It is needless to accentuate how bizarre the opinion was and how misplaced was the reliance on this salutary Quranic edict. The fatwa was, rightly, rubbished by scholars across the board. The matter rested there and was never taken to a Dar-ul-Qaza.[11]

Pivoting his writ petition on this fatwa and two other cases of rape by Muslim fathers-in-law around the same time, the petitioner Mr. Madan argued that the dar-ul-qazas were "absolutely illegal, illegitimate and unconstitutional" and urged the apex court to ban them. The writ petition, as Jeffry Redding (2013)

---

11   https://www.thehindu.com/todays-paper/tp-opinion/misunderstanding-a-good-judgment/article6226896.ece. Also see, Barbara D. Metcalf 2006.

points out, pegs its key arguments around the concept of the secular in the following way: "Interestingly in this respect, Mr. Madan views the Constitution of India as a social-reform document, applicable to all of India's religious communities, Muslims included. Writes Mr. Madan:

> [T]he Constitution of India seeks to synthesize religion, religious practice or matters of religion and secularism. In secularizing the matters of religion which are not essentially and integrally parts of religion, secularism [], therefore, consciously denounces all forms of super-naturalism or superstitious beliefs or actions and acts which are not essentially or integrally matters of religion or religious belief or faith or religious practices." (Ibid., 359)

Redding points out that according to Mr. Madan's petition, "Articles 25 and 26 ... [are] intended to be a guide to a community-life and ordain every religion to act according to its cultural and social demands to establish an egalitarian social order." By implication, inegalitarian social practices — including, non-state Muslim dispute resolution service providers — must be eradicated (Ibid., 360). By seeking a ban on these non-state adjudicating bodies, Mr. Madan sought to protect helpless Muslim women from authoritarian, patriarchal leadership of the community.

The judgment came in July 2014 and it unequivocally stated that dar-ul-qazas functioned as independent mediation centers and did not intervene in the functioning of the secular courts. The judgment thus legitimized the existence and functioning of extra-judicial dar-ul-qazas, or Islamic courts. The judges offered the following reasons for their decision:

> The stand of the Union of India is that Fatwas are advisory in nature, and no Muslim is bound to follow those. Further, Dar-ul-Qaza does not administer criminal justice and it really functions as an arbitrator, mediator, negotiator or conciliator in matters pertaining to family dispute or any other dispute of civil nature between the Muslims. According to the Union of India, Dar-ul-Qaza can be perceived as an alternative dispute resolution mechanism, which strives to settle disputes outside the courts expeditiously in an amicable and inexpensive manner and, in fact, have no power or authority to enforce its orders and hence, it cannot be termed as either in conflict with or parallel to the Indian Judicial System. The Union of India has not denied that Fatwas, as alleged by the petitioner, were not issued, but its plea is that they were not issued by any Dar-ul-Qaza. In any event, according to the Union of India, few bad

examples may not justify the abolition of the system, which otherwise is found useful and effective.

Vishwa Lochan Madan v. Union of India 2005

While giving the verdict that these adjudication structures were not an infringement on the constitutional rights of the citizens, the judges also made an important observation regarding the *locus standi* of the fatwa seeker. In the Imrana rape case, the fatwa was not sought by any family members of the victim or members of the community but by a Hindu journalist. The judgment rebukes the action. "In this way, victim has been punished. A country governed by the rule of law cannot fathom it." The judges were more worried about the morality of such fatwa-seeking behavior by those unconnected to a case than the legality of the dar-ul-qazas. The judgment pointed out:

> Fatwas touching upon the rights of an individual at the instance of rank strangers may cause irreparable damage and therefore, would be absolutely uncalled for. It shall be in violation of basic human rights ... In the light of what we have observed above, the prayer made by the petitioner in the terms sought for cannot be granted. However, we observe that no Dar-ul-Qazas or for that matter, anybody or institution by any name, shall give verdict or issue Fatwa touching upon the rights, status and obligation, of an individual unless such an individual has asked for it ... In any event, the decision or the Fatwa issued by whatever body being not emanating from any judicial system recognized by law, it is not binding on anyone including the person, who had asked for it. Further, such an adjudication or Fatwa does not have a force of law and, therefore, cannot be forced by any process using coercive method. Any person trying to enforce that by any method shall be illegal and has to be dealt with in accordance with law.
>
> *Vishwa Lochan Madan v. Union of India 2005*

The judgment neither evoked the concept of religious freedom/secularism nor the issue of gender justice. The most important point argued by the two-judge bench was that these bodies functioned as ADR units without any power to enforce their decisions. The legitimization of the dar-ul-qaza was done by the apex court on the basis of expediency and the fact that their opinion was sought by the community members. It also was argued that since the fatwas did not have any legal merit, they could not be declared as illegal.[12] The legal reasoning

---

12 This landmark judgment was evoked in 2016 when the Madras High Court had struck down the operation of dar-ul-qazas in the state. Abdur Rahman v. The Secretary to

of these arguments reflects Michael J. Broyde's (2018) views on the question of religious arbitration in the USA. According to Broyde, as long as certain checks and balances were observed, arbitration through contractual religious norms which are inherently customizable offered a good model for dispute resolution in family and financial matters in a secular democracy. A body of research in the recent years has described and documented how in India a plural judicial system operates through procedural and institutional cooperation and collocation between religious and civil institutions (Vatuk 2008, 2017; Solanki 2011; Ahmed 2016; Lemons 2019; Chakrabarti and Ghosh 2017; Ghosh and Chakrabarti 2019). But these findings have remained ignored in the public discourse on MPL.

The PIL case discussed in the next section offers a completely contrasting position to that offered in the *Vishwa Lochan Madan* judgment. Brought by *suo moto* action of the Supreme Court, for the cause of the oppressed Muslim women, it framed the question of women's suffering due to the unique religious practices of Muslims. I summarize the unfolding of what started as *Muslim Women's Quest for Equality* (2015), transformed into *Shayarah Bano v. Union of India* (2017), and came to be known in the popular media as the triple talaq case. This section tracks the legislative outcome of a PIL intervention.

4   Practices of Injustice: Arbitrary Divorce and the Legal Status of Personal Laws

One year after the *Vishwa Lochan Madan* judgment, a *suo moto* PIL case was brought by the Supreme Court of India on grounds of gender discrimination in MPL. Triple talaq (instant, unilateral divorce by a Muslim husband) permitted under MPL was flagged as one of the grounds of gender oppression. The case unfolded under the following circumstances. Two Supreme Court judges, while deciding on a case of the rights of Hindu women to ancestral property,[13] took note of comments by an advocate and relying upon some articles in the press, approached the chief justice to constitute a special bench to examine the discriminatory practices which violate the fundamental rights of Muslim women. After this, a number of writ petitions/intervener applications were filed by individual Muslim women. The Bharatiya Muslim Mahila Andolan (BMMA), an organization founded in 2007, was at the forefront of the campaign since 2015, when they came out with a report titled "Seeking Justice within Family."[14]

Government (2016) Writ Petition (Civil) No. 33059.
13   *Prakash v. Phulavati*, (2016) 2 SCC 36.
14   Niaz and Soman 2015.

The nationwide judicial activism also included the Rashtriya Swayamsevak Sangh (RSS)-affiliated Rashtrawadi Muslim Mahila Sangh, Lucknow, that filed an application asking for codification of MPL. The campaign was perceived and promoted as the Muslim women's fight for their rights as a community, not as individual sufferers (Punwani 2016). The Jamiat Ulama-i-Hind, the AIMPLB, and the Union of India were the respondents in the case.

The issue before the hand-picked, multicultural, five-judge bench, consisting of a Sikh Chief Justice, along with a Hindu, Parsi, Christian and Muslim, was whether instant triple talaq was constitutional. In other words, whether the practices granted under MPL violated the dignity and fundamental rights of Muslim women. On August 22, 2017, by a 3–2 majority, triple talaq was declared unconstitutional and therefore invalid.[15] In the 403-page document, the term secular/secularism appears 67 times. Locating the issue of gender justice and religious rights as absolute binaries, it proposed a mode of intervention to grasp the "levers of religious authority and to reformulate the religious tradition from within, as it were" (Galanter 1971, 480). This section summarizes the petitioners'/interveners' and the respondents' arguments and the legal reasoning of the landmark judgment.

5 The Petitioners' and Interveners' Arguments: Citizenship Rights of Muslim Women and a Unified Nation

The hearing began by drawing the apex court's attention to the violation of a fundamental right. Amit Singh Chadha, a senior advocate who initiated the litigation on behalf of petitioner Shayara Bano, argued that the petitioner's cause before the court was akin to a fundamental right justiciable by a court. The advocate argued that the practice of talaq-e-biddat, or instant talaq, which gives a Muslim husband the right to unilaterally divorce his wife, violated the right to equality and non-discrimination enshrined in Articles 14 and 15 of the Constitution. The discriminatory practice was also violative of human rights promised and protected under Article 21 of the Constitution (*Shayara Bano v Union of India* (2017) 9 SCC 1 (SC)). It was argued that the Court was obliged to perform its responsibility under Article 32 of the Constitution as a protector, enforcer, and guardian of citizens' rights.

---

15 *Shayara Bano v Union of India* (2017) 9 SCC 1 (SC). I present the petitioners, interveners and the defendant's arguments in this section based on this judgment.

In addition, the advocate contended that the practice should not be confused with the profession, exercise, and propagation of Islam as instant talaq was not sacrosanct to the profession of the Muslim religion. Articles 25, 26, and 29 of the Constitution that guaranteed religious freedom did not curb the jurisdiction of the Court to set right the breach of constitutional morality (Ibid., 69–70). The Court was asked to strike down the practice as violative of the fundamental rights and constitutional morality contemplated by the Constitution (Ibid., 71). The legal argument that the MPL could be "altered, repealed or amended by a competent legislature" was brought by lawyer activist Ms. Indira Jaising.[16] She argued that Article 372 of the Constitution mandated that all the laws in force in the territory of India immediately before the commencement of the Constitution shall continue to be in practice until altered, repealed, or amended by a competent legislature. Therefore, the *Muslim Personal Law (Shariat) Application Act, 1937* as law in force within the meaning of Article 13 (3) (b) was amenable to such alteration/reform (Ibid., 79). The attorney general of India, Mukul Rohatgi, argued that talaq-e-biddat was repugnant to the guarantee of secularism.[17] He designated the practice as regressive; anathema to a secular Constitution and cannot be allowed to be in force in a state which strives to achieve a social democracy (Ibid., 102–03). Thus, existing social inequalities should be removed by readjusting social order through the rule of law.[18] The attorney general also concurred that talaq-e-biddat was not an essential religious practice and therefore not entitled to protection under Article 25. Every sustainable (enforceable) religious practice must satisfy the Constitutional goal of gender equality, gender justice, and dignity.[19] Religion

---

16 Though she represented the Centre for Study of Society and Secularism, her position was closer to that of organizations like Bebaak Collective and the BMMA.

17 Attorney General Mukul Rohatgi submitted that it was a paradox that the Muslim women in secular India were more vulnerable in social status than those in the theocratic states with Islam as the State religion.

18 The attorney general cited the Valsamma Paul case where in the judge observed that various Hindu practices that are not in tune with the times had been abandoned in the interest of promoting equality and fraternity.

19 In this context, citing the judgment A.S. Narayana Deekshitulu v. the State of A.P 1996 AIR 1765, a constitutional perception of religion was offered. The judgment inferred that religion has its basis in a system of beliefs and doctrine which are regarded by those professing religion to be conducive to their spiritual well-being. Every religion must believe in conscience, ethical and moral precepts. Therefore, whatever binds a man to his own conscience and whatever moral or ethical principles regulate the lives of men believing i n that theistic, conscience or religious belief, can constitute religion as understood in the Constitution, which fosters a feeling of brotherhood, amity, fraternity, and equality of all persons who find their foot hold in the secular aspect of the Constitution.

must be confined to the practices that appertain to religion, and the rest of life must be regulated, unified, and modified to facilitate the evolution of the nation as a strong and a consolidated unit (Ibid., 105).

6 The Respondents' Arguments: Freedom of Religion Protected under the Constitution

To express the ambit and scope of personal law and demonstrate the contours of freedom of conscience and free profession, practice, and propagation of religion guaranteed in Article 25 of the Constitution, Kapil Sibal, the senior counsel for the AIMPLB, relied on the Constituent Assembly Debates. During the Constituent Assembly Debates, it emerged that the right of a group of people to follow their own personal law is within the purview of statutory and justiciable fundamental rights (Ibid., 153–54). It was also argued that the essential practices of a religion had to be ascertained with reference to the religion in question.[20] The respondents drew attention to the possibility of reforming the Islamic marriage contract (nikahnama) to a gender-just one, as well as for opting for a non-religious marriage law. The counsel for the Jamiat Ulema-i-Hind suggested that at the time of executing the nikahnama, the bride could incorporate the provision that the husband would not have the right to divorce his wife by declaring talaq-e-biddat. Further, since the enactment of *The Special Marriage Act, 1954*, all the citizens of India irrespective of their gender and faith (including Muslims) had the right to be governed by the Act instead of their personal law. Thus, it provided a legal exit option to Muslims from MPL and thereby practices such as talaq-e-biddat (Ibid., 161–62).

On the question of the practice of talaq-e-biddat being repudiated in many Muslim majority democratic countries as well as theocratic states, the counsel submitted that a constitutional right available to all the religious denominations as the fundamental right should not be negated merely because other countries have enacted certain legislations. The law of a state is based on the collective will of its residents and the will of the residents of a foreign country may not be thrust upon the residents of India (Ibid., 170).[21] Regarding the legal

---

20 The counsel referred to the *Sri Adi Visheshwara of Kashi Temple, Varanasi v. State of U.P. Judgment*. The judgment stated that what constituted the essential part of religion may be ascertained primarily from the doctrines of that religion itself — its tenets, historical background, and evolution (Ibid., 168).
21 It should be noted that though these Muslim majority countries have criminalized triple talaq, they do not deny its validity. The husband faces the legal consequences, but the divorce remains irrevocable.

technicality of whether personal laws were indeed *laws*, the counsel argued that even if Section 2 of the *Muslim Personal Law (Shariat) Application Act, 1937* was struck down, its mandate was protected in Article 25 of the Constitution. Therefore, a statutory enactment in the matter of personal law would not be justified. Finally, the question of personal laws and its significance in a secular democratic country needed to take cognizance of the fact that Islam was a minority religion.

7 The Judgment: Constitutional Morality versus Religious Freedom of a Minority

The bench pronounced the judgment in 3–2 verdict against the practice of triple talaq. Though three judges pronounced triple talaq as invalid, they differed in their reasoning for declaring it so. Justice Rohinton Fali Nariman who (for himself and Justice Uday U. Lalit) held that since the word "talaq" is mentioned in the *Shariat Application Act 1937*, it forms part of a statute and becomes a law in force. Therefore, it is amenable for being tested against the fundamental rights and declared unconstitutional. Justice Kurian Joseph, on the other hand, offered a more nuanced argument. He concurred with Justices Nariman and Lalit that the practice of triple talaq does not form the core of the Sunni Muslim religion. But at the same time, he also concurred with Chief Justice J. S. Khehar and Justice S. Abdul Nazeer that the personal laws of minorities are protected by the Constitution as a fundamental right, a clear statement against the enactment of a UCC, contained in Article 44 of the Constitution, which is merely a directive principle of state policy and not an enforceable fundamental right.[22]

In the judgment, Justice Joseph (Ibid., 284–85) held that the purpose of the *Shariat Application Act 1937* was to remove un-Islamic and oppressive customs and usages from MPL, and since triple divorce is not mentioned in the Quran, it is not a part of the Sharia — and thus cannot be enforced under the *Shariat Act*. But what is sinful in theology must be held bad in law and should be set aside, he concluded. Thus, Justice Joseph, staying within the realm of Islamic law, investigated whether instant triple talaq was an essential and core religious practice. It was pointed out that the Supreme Court in the landmark case of *Shamim Ara* (2002) had already declared instant triple talaq as invalid and had laid down the valid procedure for pronouncing talaq. Therefore, it was

---

22 See Flavia Agnes' (2019, 346) reading of the judgment.

concluded that triple talaq was not an essential core of Islamic law in India and could be declared as invalid.

The dissenting judges, Justice Khehar and Justice Nazeer, on the other hand, upheld freedom of religion (subjected to the restrictions given in Articles 25 and 26). After quoting from the Constituent Assembly Debates on Articles 25 and 44, they held that personal law is part of the freedom of religion, which courts are duty-bound to protect. They pointed out that the courts were not supposed to find fault with provisions of personal law, which were based on beliefs, not logic, and therefore beyond judicial scrutiny. Disagreeing with Justice Nariman, they observed that since the recognition of MPL by the *Shariat Act of 1937* does not give it statutory status, and it was not "law" as held by the Supreme Court, therefore, triple talaq cannot be held unconstitutional. They refused to strike it down as violative of public order, health, and morality, or for being contrary to other fundamental rights, such as the right to equality or human dignity.[23] They also drew attention to the fact that the issue at hand needed appropriate legislative intervention rather than a judicial one (Ibid., 280–81).

The legislative intervention did come two years later but it took a carceral turn that was not anticipated by the activism that led to it. After the apex court's invalidation of triple talaq, it was soon found that it did not deter the practice. A bill was brought in the parliament by the ruling government to make it a criminal offense. Thus, the *suo-moto* PIL led to legislative intervention whereby the civil issue of divorce was turned into a criminal offense. *The Muslim Women (Protection of Rights on Marriage) Bill 2017* was passed in July 2019 and since then arbitrary divorce by a Muslim man has become a cognizable offense for which the errant husband would serve a three-year jail term. In the concluding section, I argue that judicial activism articulated only in terms of particularistic, community-based identity, demanding state intervention in religion for addressing systemic social injustice can lead to serious unintended consequences as the unfolding of the triple talaq PIL amply demonstrates.[24]

---

23 The Indian Constitution guarantees the right to equal treatment before the law and against discrimination as mentioned in Article 14 and 15. It also ensures the right to life and liberty as in Article 21, which has been interpreted to mean the right to live with human dignity in all aspects of life that make a person's life meaningful.

24 A similar argument was made by Gregory C. Kozlowski when he showed how the British colonial rulers saw the question of endowment among Muslims solely in terms of an abstract notion of their faith (1985).

8   Conclusions: The Entangled Question of the Secular State, Religious Freedom and Religious Reform

If the connotation of secularism as the rights of the minorities to religious freedom had framed the debates in the Shah Bano case, it has been the conceptual vocabulary of "subjection of religion to rule of law" that has undergirded the idea of secularism in the recent public as well as judicial discourse. Scholars writing on the apex courts' intervention on religion have commented on the unintended consequences of the continuous judicialization of the religious domain. Ronojoy Sen's (2010) work shows how the Supreme Court's rulings have furthered the reformist agenda of the Indian state at the expense of religious freedom and neutrality and at the same time the Court became an inadvertent ally of the Hindu nationalists in their aggressive demands for homogenization and uniformity (Ibid., xxxi). Sen draws on Galanter's (1971) insight that in India it was the reformist judiciary that was called to decide what constituted religious rights and thereby religion itself.[25] This had led to two things: continuous judicialization of religion post 1950s and the judges' unmitigated power to decide *when* and *how* the boundaries between the religious and civil were to be drawn.[26]

This chapter shows how the triple talaq case unwittingly created a reified, homogeneous category of Islam and Muslim women who strangely and permanently reside outside the judicial reach of secular law. In this case, both civil society activism and the Supreme Court framed the question of arbitrary divorce as a particularistic religious problem without looking for ways to address it with existing secular law. During the course of the triple talaq case, grass-roots feminist activists like Flavia Agnes (Agnes 2016; Chopra 2016) had repeatedly argued that instead of a head-on intervention in MPL, a number of already existing gender-just secular law such as *The Protection of Women from Domestic Violence Act 2005* (PWDAV) that covers mental cruelty could have been evoked in cases of triple talaq.[27] Moreover, the media could have

---

[25] Marc Galanter (1971) had cautioned against the penchant of appellate courts in India in bringing about religious reform (and thereby social justice) by interpreting religion. He drew attention to the two alternative modes for the exercise of the state's "regulative oversight" in the domain of religion: the mode of "limitation" or that of "intervention." He considered the latter being undesirable in principle and of doubtful effect in practice.

[26] These writings stand in sharp contrast to the optimism around judicialization of religious freedom offered by James T. Richardson's (2015) analysis of court decisions on minority religions in America and Europe.

[27] Saptarshi Mandal (2019) in a recent article articulates this position as he argues for a possibility of harmonizing family law in India through the implementation of PWDAV that can address issues of gender discrimination overriding religion-based personal laws.

highlighted every Indian citizen's right to opt-out of personal law regime by marrying under *The Special Marriage Act 1954*. Legal scholar Faizan Mustafa also echoed this position in many of his writings, but these arguments fell on deaf ears as the clamor for banning oppressive Muslim laws and thereby reforming MPL, gained momentum in public discourse.[28]

The question of Muslim women's suffering emerged as a public concern; something to be ameliorated through PIL jurisdiction, curiously oblivious to existing legal remedies that were applicable to Indian women across religion. The PIL activism led to further homogenization of Muslims and reification of "Muslim misogyny." The apex court's *suo moto* PIL firmly framed the question of instant divorce as a religio-cultural evil, something that could not be addressed through existing legal measures and required judicial and legislative intervention in MPL. Civil society activism, supported by a media campaign, gave the *suo moto* PIL an unprecedented visibility in public discourse. The judicial campaign reminded us of Saba Mahmood's (2015, 2) caution against secular political rationality that paradoxically makes religion a more, rather than less, significant part of the lives and subjectivities of those who belong to both minority and majority communities.

While it has been argued that it is through the implementation of constitutional law and active judicial intervention in the question of religious affairs that the Indian nation-state deems its secular status, this chapter extends this argument and shows how the PIL jurisdictional innovation has brought a new dimension to judicial activism as cases were filed by the apex court itself. The concept of secularism in this context, deftly maneuvered through PIL jurisdictions, created the trope of "subjugation of religion to rule of law" as the necessary condition for addressing the oppression faced by Muslim women; the justification being suffering and the need to ameliorate the condition of the victims.[29] What is common to both the PIL petitions is that they were not brought to address a personal grievance (as did Shah Bano) but to

---

28 In public opinion as well as in academic writings, the participation by Muslim women's organizations as interveners was celebrated for offering a "decisive break from the past where Muslim women's interests used to be represented either by the state or the community within a discourse of protectionism" (Mandal 2018). What these celebratory writings miss is that even when it was led by Muslim women's organizations, by emphasizing rather than de-emphasizing religion and seeking state intervention, they reified particularistic identities. It led to religion-specific criminalization of a civil offense rather than seeking implementation of already existing legal rights of all women.

29 See Veena Das (1995) on the Supreme Court's use of the vocabulary of victimhood in the judicial discourse that emerged around the compensation for the victims of the Bhopal gas tragedy.

address the plight of Muslim women in general.[30] Once the campaign took off, it deterred any clear-headed analysis of the field of personal law and how it functioned.[31]

In contrast, the pragmatism of the *Vishwa Lochan Madan* judgment and its non-interventionist approach that did not pitch religion against citizenship rights but tacitly acknowledged that in a legal plural context, the litigants' right to approach whichever dispute resolution forum they considered as appropriate for the problem at hand is reminiscent of the "pragmatic multiple modernist" approach that Adam Possamai (2015, 300) has proposed. Field-based studies on procedural pluralism of family dispute in India and the voluntary nature of the religio-legal forum testify that they do not necessarily run the risk of creating enclave society. The latest *Consultation Paper on Reform of Family Law* (*2018*) by the Law Commission of India also echoes this position as it argues that instead of a UCC, each religious community needs to work toward reforming the gender-unjust practices specific to their community (Ibid., 7). By tracing two contrasting PIL cases, we observe that state intervention in matters of religion, be it delicate circumspection in minority religious practices captured in the guiding principle of balancing religious diversity or a strident demand for subjection of religion to the rule of law, needs to be attentive to the categories through which judicialization of religion takes place and the secular political rationality that animates it.[32] Unpacking the debate on secularism through a detailed scrutiny of the current judicial activism around the issue of religious freedom of minorities, personal law, social justice, and their boundaries would offer new insights into an otherwise old problematic.

---

30 Even the petitioner in the triple talaq case, Shayara Bano did not ask for any rights for herself. She was divorced by instant talaq and her contention was that such a divorce which abruptly, unilaterally and irrevocably terminates the ties of matrimony, purportedly under Section 2 of the Muslim *Personal Law (Shariat) Application Act,1937* be declared unconstitutional. At the same time, she did not want to continue with what she alleged was an abusive marriage. Sharaya Bano's marital discord was tagged with the Supreme Court PIL by her lawyer.

31 It also obliterated the fact that in practical terms, the consequences of arbitrary divorce and desertion/failed marriage did not have much difference for the women from certain socio-economic strata whether they were Hindu or Muslim (See Patricia Jeffery 2001).

32 The promissory quality of judicialization of religion reminds us of Judith Beyer's argument regarding the invocation of the constitution in Kyrgyzstan as an expression of people's hope for a peaceful and prosperous future, a just society, and a stable state (2015, 321).

References

Ahmed, Farrah. 2016. *Religious Freedom Under the Personal Law System*. New Delhi: Oxford University Press.

Agnes, Flavia. 2001. "Minority Identity and Gender Concerns." *Economic & Political Weekly* 36 (4): 3973–76.

Agnes, Flavia. 2016. "Uniform Rights, Not a Uniform Law." *Livemint*, August 27, 2016. https://www.livemint.com/Sundayapp/yXcMGdlDJymHN9p61ZNtLN/Uniform-rights-not-a-uniform-law.html.

Agnes, Flavia. 2019. "Aggressive Hindu Nationalism: Contextualizing the Triple Talaq Controversy." In *Majoritarian State: How Hindu Nationalism is Changing India*, edited by Angana P. Chatterji, Thomas Blom Hansen and Christophe Jaffrelot, 335–52. New York: Oxford University Press.

Anderson, Michael R. 1999. "Legal Scholarship and the Politics of Islam in British India." In *Perspectives on Islamic Law, Justice and Society*, edited by R. S. Khare, 65–92. Lanham: Rowmen and Littlefield.

Bajpai, Rochana. 2002. "The conceptual vocabularies of secularism and minority rights in India." *Journal of Political Ideologies* 7 (2): 179–98. https://doi.org/10.1080/13569310220137539.

Beyer, Judith. 2015. "Constitutional Faith: Law and Hope in Revolutionary Kyrgyzstan." *Ethnos* 80 (3): 320–45.

Bhargava, Rajeev. 2007. "The Distinctiveness of Indian Secularism." In *The Future of Secularism*, edited by T.N. Srinivasan, 908–34. New Delhi: Oxford University Press.

Bhuwania, Anuj. 2014. "Courting the People: The Rise of Public Interest Litigation in Post-Emergency India." *Comparative Studies of South Asia, Africa and the Middle East* 34: 314–35.

Bhuwania, Anuj. 2017. *Courting the People: Public Interest Litigation in Post-Emergency India*. United Kingdom: Cambridge University Press.

Broyde, Michael J. 2018. "Faith based Arbitration Evaluated: The Policy Arguments for and Against Religious Arbitration in America." *Journal of Law and Religion* 33 (3): 340–89. https://www.cambridge.org/core/terms. https://doi.org/10.1017/jlr.2018.44.

Chakrabarti, Anindita. 2016. "Democracy as Civil Religion: Reading Alexis de Tocqueville in India." *Journal of Human Values* 22: 1–12.

Chakrabarti, Anindita and Suchandra Ghosh. 2017. "Judicial reform vs Adjudication of Personal Law." *Economic and Political Weekly* 52 (49): 12–14.

Chopra, Mannika. 2016. "In Conversation: Gender Rights Lawyer Flavia Agnes On Why Triple Talaq Shouldn't Be Banned". *The Better India*, August 5, 2016. https://www.thebetterindia.com/63754/flavia-agnes-triple-talaq-muslim-women/.

Das, Veena. 1995. *Critical events: An Anthropological Perspective on Contemporary India*. Delhi: Oxford University Press.

Galanter, Marc. 1971. "Hinduism, secularism, and the Indian judiciary." *Philosophy East and West* 21: 467–87. https://doi.org/10.2307/1398174.

Ghosh, Suchandra, and Anindita Chakrabarti. 2019. "Religion-based 'Personal' Law, Legal Pluralism and Secularity: A Field View of Adjudication of Muslim Personal Law in India" *Working Paper Series of the HCAS "Multiple Secularities—Beyond the West, Beyond Modernities"* 16. Leipzig University.

Hasan, Zoya. 1991. "Changing Orientation of the State and the Emergence of Majoritarianism in the 1980s." In *Communalism in India: History, Politics, and Culture,* edited by K. N. Panikkar, 27–37. Delhi: Manohar Publishers.

Jacobsohn, Gary Jeffrey. 2003. *The Wheel of Law: India's Secularism in Comparative Constitutional Context*. Princeton: Princeton University Press.

Jeffery, Patricia. 2001. "A Uniform Customary Code? Marital Breakdown and Women's Economic Entitlements in Rural Bijnor." *Contributions to Indian Sociology* 35: 1–32.

Kozlowski, Gregory C. 1985. *Muslim Endowments and Society in British India*. London: Cambridge University Press.

Kugle, Alan Scott. 2001. "Framed, Blamed and Renamed: The Recasting of Islamic Jurisprudence in Colonial South Asia." *Modern Asian Studies* 35 (2): 257–313. https://www.jstor.org/stable/313119.

Law Commission of India. 2018. *Consultation Paper on Reform of Family Law*. New Delhi: Government of India.

Lemons, Katherine. 2019. *Divorcing Traditions: Islamic Marriage Law and the Making of Indian Secularism*. Ithaca: Cornell University Press.

Madan, T. N. 1987. "Secularism in its place." *Journal of Asian Studies* 46 (4): 747–59.

Mahajan, Gurpreet. 2003. "Secularism." In *The Oxford India Companion to Sociology and Social Anthropology,* edited by Veena Das, 908–34. New Delhi: Oxford University Press.

Mahmood, Saif. 2014. "Misunderstanding a Good Judgment." *The Hindu*, July 19, 2014. https://www.thehindu.com/todays-paper/tp-opinion/misunderstanding-a-good-judgment/article6226896.ece.

Mahmood, Saba. 2015. *Religious Difference in a Secular Age: A Minority Report*. Princeton: Princeton University Press.

Mandal, Saptarshi. 2018. "Out of Shah Bano's Shadow: Muslim Women's Rights and the Supreme Court's Triple Talaq Verdict." *Indian Law Review* 2: 89–107.

Mandal, Saptarshi. 2019. "Towards Uniformity of Rights: Muslim Personal Law, the Domestic Violence Act, and the Harmonization of Family Law in India." In *Conflict in the Shared Household: Domestic Violence and the Law in India,* edited by Indira Jaising and Pinki Mathur Anurag, 171–99. New Delhi: Oxford University Press.

Metcalf, Barbara D. 2006. "Imrana: Rape, Islam, and Law in India." *Islamic Research Institute* 45: 389–412.

Nandy, Ashish. 1985. "The Anti-Secularist Manifesto." *Seminar* 314: 14–24.

Newbigin, Eleanor. 2018 [2013]. *The Hindu Family and the Emergence of Modern India: Law, Citizenship and Community* (South Asia ed). Cambridge: Cambridge University Press.

Niaz, Noorjehan Safia and Zakia Soman. 2015. "Muslim Women's Views on the Muslim Personal Law." *Economic and Political Weekly* 50 (51): 83–86. https://www.epw.in/journal/2015/51/notes/muslim-womens-views-muslim-personal-law.html.

Panikkar, K. N (ed). 1991. *Communalism in India: History, Politics, and Culture*. Delhi: Manohar Publishers.

Possamai, Adam. 2015. "Shari'a and Multiple Modernities in Western Countries: Toward a Multi-faith Pragmatic Modern Approach Rather than a Legal Pluralist One?" In *The Sociololgy of Shari'a: Case Studies from around the World*, edited by Adam Possamai, James T Richardson and Bryan S Turner, 291–303. New York: Springer.

Punwani, Jyoti. 2016. "Muslim Women: Historic Demand for Change". *Economic and Political Weekly* 52 (34). https://www.epw.in/engage/article/muslim-women-historic-demand-change.

Richardson, James T. 2015. "Managing Religion and the Judicialization of Religious Freedom." *Journal for the Scientific Study of Religion* 54: 1–19. https://www.jstor.org/stable/24644243.

Rachel, Sturman. 2012. *The Government of Social Life in Colonial India: Liberalism, Religious Law and Women's Rights*. Cambridge: Cambridge University Press.

Rajan, Rajeswari Sunder. 2003. "Women Between Community and State: Some Implications of the Uniform." In *The Scandal of the State: Women, Law, and Citizenship in Postcolonial India*, edited by Rajeswari Sunder Rajan, 147–73. Durham: Duke University Press.

Redding, Jeffrey. 2013. "Secularism, The Rule of Law, and 'Sharia' Courts: An Ethnographic Examination of a Constitutional Controversy." *Saint Louis University Law Journal* 57, 339–76. https://papers.ssrn.com/sol3/papers.cfm?abstract_id=2221619.

Sen, Ronojoy. 2010: *Articles of Faith- Religion, Secularism, and the Indian Supreme Court*. New Delhi: Oxford University Press.

Sezgin, Yüksel, and Mirjam Künkler. 2014. "Regulation of 'Religion' and the 'Religious': The Politics of Judicialization and Bureaucratization in India and Indonesia." *Comparative Studies in Society and History* 56 (2): 448–78.

Smith, Donald Eugene, 1963. *India as a Secular State*. Princeton, N.J.: Princeton University Press.

Solanki, Gopika. 2011. *Adjudication in Religious Family Laws Cultural Accommodation, Legal Pluralism, and Gender Equality in India*. New Delhi: Cambridge University Press.

Subramanian, Narendra. 2017. "Islamic Norms, Common Law, and Legal Reasoning: Muslim Personal Law and the Economic Consequences of Divorce in India." *Islamic Law and Society*. 24: 254–86. https://www.jstor.org/stable/44634472.

Sullivan, Winnifred Fallers, Elizabeth Shakman Hurd, Saba Mahmood, and Peter G. Danchin, ed. 2015. *Politics of Religious Freedom*. Chicago: University of Chicago Press.

Vatuk, Sylvia. 2008. "Divorce at the Wife's Initiative in Muslim Personal Law: What are the Options and What are their Implications for Women's Welfare?" In *Redefining Family Law in India.*, edited by Archana Parashar and Amita Dhanda, 200–35. London: Routledge.

Vatuk, Sylvia. 2009. "A Rallying Cry for Muslim Personal Law: The Shah Bano Case and its Aftermath." In *Islam in South Asia in Practice*, edited by Barbara D. Metcalf, 352–69. Princeton: Princeton University Press.

Vatuk, Sylvia. 2017. *Marriage and its Discontents: Women, Islam and the Law in India*. New Delhi: Women Unlimited.

Wohlrab-Sahr, Monika and Marian Burchardt. 2012. "Multiple Secularities: Towards a Cultural Sociology of Secular Modernities." *Comparative Sociology* 11: 875–909.

Judgments

Abdur Rahman v. The Secretary to Government (2016) Writ Petition (Civil) No. 33059.
Prakash v. Phulavati, (2016) 2 SCC 36.
Smt. Sarla Mudgal, President, Kalyani v. Union of India 1995 AIR 1531, 1995 SCC (3) 635.
Shamim Ara v. State of UP (1992) Writ Petition (Civil) SCC 518.
Shayara Bano v Union of India (2017) 9 SCC 1 (SC).
Vishwa Lochan Madan v. Union of India (2005) Writ Petition (Civil)No. 386.
Mohd. Ahmed Khan v. Shah Bano Begum 1985 AIR 945, 1985 SCR (3) 844.
A.S. Narayana Deekshitulu v. the State of A.P 1996 AIR 1765.
Sri Adi Visheshwara of Kashi Temple, Varanasi v. State of U.P. Judgment 1997(2) SCR 1086.

Acts

Muslim Personal Law (Shariat) Application Act, 1937.
The Special Marriage Act 1954.
The Muslim Women (Protection of Rights on Divorce) Act 1986.
The Protection of Women from Domestic Violence Act 2005 (PWDAV).
The Muslim Women (Protection of Rights on Marriage) Act 2019.

CHAPTER 3

Religious Freedom and Secularism in Post-Revolutionary Tunisia

Anna Grasso

These days, religious freedom is a principle present in the constitutional texts of most countries. This principle defends the idea in which "no person shall be advantaged or penalized because of his/her beliefs, that all religious faiths are equally free before the law. This right is not only defended in secular countries but also those with a State religion" (De Naurois, n.d.). Tunisia is often defined as one of the models of a secular State in the Muslim world, a firmly modern State. This is especially the case because, following its independence, this country experienced a period of forceful secularism under the influence of Habib Bourguiba, the first president of Tunisia. Yet, it also is important to underline the fact that Bourguiba and his successor, Zine el Abidine Ben Ali, never made the choice of separating State and religion but rather chose to place religion under the State's power. As is the case for Tunisia, it is quite difficult to clearly define a secular State. Therefore, it is important to analyze the definitions of secularization and laïcité that have been forged by the scholars of such discipline.

In 1981, Karel Dobbelaere summarizes the contributions of the different authors that worked on the theory of secularization, which can be defined as a social process, and insisted on its multidimensional character. Secularization cannot be reduced to a disengagement from religion at solely an individual level but one also must take into account the relationship between religion and society, as well as within the various religions themselves. Therefore, he proposed to analyze this concept in a three-dimensional way: (1) at a societal/macro level, which has to do with the place of religion in society and the transformation of the relationship between State/religion; (2) at an institutional/meso level, which takes into account the evolution of religious organizations; (3) at an individual/micro level (3), which studies the religious participation, the development of practices and individual behavior (Dobbelaere 1981, 11–13). According to his analysis, Dobbelaere conceives laicization as a subcategory of societal/macro level secularization. He considers the concept of laicization as "a manifest process of secularization" (Dobbelaere 2004, 13), something conscious and intended. Manifest secularization aims at separating religion and other societal systems, such as education, medicine and law, through the implementation of legal measures granting the autonomy of each of these fields (Dobbelaere 2008, 179). On the other hand, he identifies latent laicization as an "unintended consequence of actions that promote (…) functional differentiation" (Dobbelaere 2004, 19). A similar distinction can be observed in the definition described by Ahmet T Kuru (2009) in the case of secularism, which refers to the State policy toward religion. Kuru makes the distinction between assertive secularism (laïcité de combat) and passive secularism (laïcité plurielle). Assertive secularism refers to a direct role of the State in an effort to "exclude religion from the public sphere and confine it to the private domain" (Kuru 2009, 11). On the other hand, passive secularism can be defined as a will of the State to play a more neutral role by accepting the presence of religion in the public sphere (Ibid., 11). Jean Baubérot (1991) and Micheline Milot (2002), instead of subdividing the concept of secularization/secularism, prefer distinguishing between secularization and laïcité. Secularization is defined as "a process of loss of social pertinence of religion" and laïcité as "explicit tensions between different social forces (religious, cultural, political) which can take the form of an open conflict" (Baubérot 1991, 460). According to Baubérot, empowering the notion of laicization allows us to examine the interrelation among different institutions (not only the religious ones) and to take into account the political and judicial role in such differentiation. Jean Baubérot and Micheline Milot do not consider the notion of laïcité as solely belonging to the French model.[1] Its definition resides in a universal set of principles that can be applied to all governments in spite of their histories and religious influences. They define this term through four interdependent principles: "Two principles tied to the notion of tolerance: freedom of conscience and religion and its necessary extension into equality. Two principles tied to political implementation, which contribute to the fulfillment of the two previous principles: separation and neutrality" (Baubérot and Milot 2011, 80). These two authors believe there is no such thing as a purely secular State, but rather there are different arrangements between State and religion (laïcités). In this sense, State policies toward religion can be considered as being "the result of ideological struggles" (Kuru 2009,10). Therefore, they analyze this relationship through different ideal types. We thus consider that religious freedom can be measured through the action of the government and its citizens to both avoid promoting one religion over another as well as influencing the internal affairs

---

[1] Nonetheless, it also is important to keep in mind the fact that the concept of laïcité is perceived as being tied to France and, in the case of Tunisia, to its colonial history.

of a given religion. Moreover, the issue of the separation between religion and State is also interpreted differently with regard to the religion of the majority, as is the case for Sunni Islam. In fact, the absence of a recognized hierarchy (such as Catholicism), pushes the State to play the role of organizing such religion (as in Tunisia through the Ministry of Religious Affairs).[2] Therefore, there can never be a complete State passiveness toward such religion. In this sense, religious freedom can be measured in the ways in which a State manages to organize a religion without controlling it.

In the Arab world, the issue of secularization and freedom of religion is often associated with two other terms: modernism and traditionalism. According to Alain Roussillon (2005), this division finds its roots in the *Nahda* (reformist phase that took place in the 19th century) in which different Arab thinkers conceived ways to catch up with the technological and social advances of the West. Two solutions stood out: "the first was to reform society through science and reason, employing exogenous, imported, ways of thinking and acting in order to speed up the course of history and modernize Muslim societies at a forced pace; the second option was to reform society though religion, by turning back toward what was considered as the original, the fundamentals of identity, in order to find the impetus for a fresh start" (Roussillon 2005, 13). The first solution is often associated to a "modernist" trend, while the second is closer to a "traditionalist" trend. Nonetheless, Roussillon also points to the presence of "multiple intersections between these two fields" (Roussillon 2015, 15–16). Within the context of the opposition between these two trends, three different stances were developed concerning laïcité in the Arab world: 1) Islam does not need laïcité; 2) Islam is opposed to laïcité; 3) Islam is compatible with laïcité. The first position considers that "Islam already possesses all the principles of modernity as it never had to deal with a Church from which to emancipate itself." Moreover, laïcité is seen as an "imposition to Muslim societies of a western conception of religion" (Roussillon 2015, 126). The second position assumes that the political field should be the one to submit itself to the principles of religious morality. It is up to the believers to ensure the project of establishing a religious society (Roussillon 2015, 127). Finally, the third position supports the idea of withdrawing the monopoly of religion from the political leaders who exploit it to consolidate their power. According to this vision, laïcité is seen as "a neutral and empty framework in which a new "Islamic conscience" can

---

2   We cannot therefore measure the second level of Dobbelaere's theory: the "secularization" of the religious organization.

emerge, more concerned with the internalization of such religion than with its historical tradition" (Roussillon 2015, 128).

By taking into account these different definitions, the aim of this chapter is to analyze the impact of the January 2011 revolution on the issue of religious freedom and secularism in Tunisia. To do so, we seek to develop a reflection on the concepts of secularization and laïcité, with regard to this specific context, and identify the main obstacles facing this country in terms of religious freedom. We chose to focus solely on Sunni Islam as it is considered to be the religion of the great majority of Tunisians[3] and can itself be identified as plural (we can include in this category non-practicing Muslims, Sufis, Islamists, Salafists, etc.). In order to do so, we have chosen to focus this chapter on three parts: the historical, socio-legal and socio-political context and factors that have influenced secularism and challenged religious freedom in post-revolution Tunisia.

This chapter is the result of a research project we accomplished between May 2011 and January 2018 on the topic of the relationship between the State and religion in post-revolution Tunisia, as well as literature on the sociology of religion and the issue of secularism and laïcité in the Arab world. As it is a contemporary issue, we also carried out online media monitoring on subjects related to this field.

1   The Impact of Authoritarian Rule on Religious and Political Fields (1956–2011)

Political scientist Abderrahim Lamchichi writes how:

> Muslim contemporary societies have endured, since the decolonization process, profound social and cultural mutations (…) they appear to be torn between an imported modernity—which, in some cases, transformed into authoritarian laïcité—and forms of contention which sometimes mobilized religious discourse.
>
> LAMCHICHI 2000, 35

Following the independence of the country in 1956, President Habib Bourguiba developed a policy close to what Dobbelaere calls manifest secularization or laicization by choosing to secularize the fields of education and law, as well as placing the religious field under State control. This forceful policy also can

---

3   Around 99% according to the Pew Research Centre (Pew Research Center 2014).

be associated to Baubérot and Milot's ideal type of authoritarian laïcité. This policy decision was interpreted by more "traditionalist" thinkers as an imposition that gave rise to religious opposition movements, mainly Islamism. Nonetheless, as Hamadi Redissi puts it, "even though secularization was imposed at the beginning, this process has been instilled in Tunisian society and has become a tradition. Tunisians have interiorized it. Yet, following the revolution, this model was under attack".[4]

2   The Need for a Nationalist Sentiment following the Independence of the Country

Baubérot and Milot (2011) define authoritarian laïcité as:

> [A] process in which a State decides to rid itself of the influence of religion which it sees as social menacing forces for political governance. In such case, the State will tend to resort to a surveillance position with regards to religion and interfere directly in religious affairs by limiting their freedom of expression, of demonstration or of advocacy. It has as an effect to downplay the principles of laïcité (freedom and equality), and reflects a will of control on religion by an authoritarian regime to avoid the emergence of any form of opposition.
>
> BAUBÉROT and MILOT 2011, 95

This form of laïcité in Muslim contemporary societies was implemented by Mustapha Kemal (1881–1938) in Turkey (Luizard 2008, 7).[5] With the independence of this State in 1923 and the end of the caliphate, the new president's mission was that of developing a strong nationalist sentiment (promoting race, history and language as unifying forces which would replace religious identities). In Tunisia, we can observe a similar situation with regard to the policies of President Bourguiba (1903–2000), who became the first president in 1957 following the independence from French protectorate and the end of the Beylical reign. The new keyword is that of tunisianité, which refers to the reinforcement of a nationalist sentiment against all other forms of allegiance. During the first part of his presidency, until 1969, Bourguiba promoted different projects to modernize Islam (Lamchichi 2000, 38–40), mainly through

---

4   Hamadi Redissi, in interview with the author, Tunis, August 2011.
5   For a more in-depth analysis of the Turkish case see Kuru 2009.

changes in its ritual expressions, such as softening of the daytime fasting during Ramadan (he believed the strict fasting hurt the State's productivity during the month-long observance); not requiring the wearing of the headscarf by women; abandoning the ritualistic sacrificing of lambs during Eid al-Adha; and, reducing the number of pilgrims going to Mecca (Kraiem 2011, 246).

Yet, authoritarian laïcité does not mean separation between State and Islam. For instance, even if Turkey's Mustafa Kemal is often depicted as a supporter of laïcité, he never declared to be against religion or Islam, but instead he opposed what he considered to be archaic expressions of this religion. He wished to modernize Islam instead of eradicating it. He considered the "real" Islam as being freed from all forms of ancient superstition,[6] which he considered to be part of the cause of the Ottoman decline and an Islam that could not be opposed to science and progress. To defend this vision, he promoted such decisions as the banning of Sufi brotherhoods[7] and the closing of their places of worship (Lamchichi 2000, 42). Since gaining its independence, we also can observe specific actions taken to free the State of the influence of religious institutions and their representatives. Political leaders positioned themselves as the only ones authorized to speak in the name of Islam. Bourguiba targeted *Ulemas* (religious scholars) by making them financially dependent from the State and by secularizing the fields of justice and education (where they were most influent) as well as placing numerous mosques under direct supervision of the State. Just like Mustafa Kemal in Turkey, he also pursued religious brotherhoods and their places of worship. Yet, Bourguiba never spoke against Islam itself and sought to give to each one of his reforms a religious justification by speaking of ijtihad (intellectual effort). Even in his decision targeting Ramadan, Bourguiba explained this decision as a form of jihad (struggle) against underdevelopment which he considered as being the priority, a religious obligation (Cherif 1994, 65). Nonetheless, this form of secularism was perceived by many as a top-down imposition, which did not match the people's will. This argument began to take root and gave birth to the Islamist movement.

---

6   Which can be associated to the process of rationalization/bureaucratization and demagnification of religion observed by Max Weber (Bobineau, n.d.).

7   Sufism "began in the seventh century as the quest for individual spiritual redemption, became by the late eighth century a collective religious movement. … Sufis gathered to recite the Quran and to sit in the presence of great masters. … Combining ascetic renunciation with spiritual growth leading toward union with God … a doctrine of the venerable and miraculous nature of saints" (Lapidus 2002, 94). As is the case with Islamism and Salafism, Sufism also is a concept that represents different groups of people, depending on the chronological and geographical context. (Zarcone 2009, 330–331).

3   Emergence of Islamism and its Vision of Secularism

The emergence of this movement began around the 1960s and reached its apex following the Iranian Revolution of 1979. These new actors sought to retrieve the control of the religious field by accusing official clerics of submitting themselves and their religion to the government. What is worth bearing in mind when observing the progression of Islamism in Tunisia is how this movement evolved. This proves the idea that the notion of Islamism is plural (Camau & Geisser 2003, 287) and does not have a clear definition as this phenomenon changes through time as well as through space (e.g., Islamists in Tunisia are not the same as those in Egypt). In fact, one could say that the evolution was symptomatic of the context in which it developed.

Islamists perceived secularism as being tied to French colonialism and thus associated it to the concept of laïcité. They believed that Islam did not need laïcité (the first case observed by Roussillon 2005, 126) as they considered it to be "the product of European history, which meets the specific needs of European societies at a given moment, and that it would be futile and dangerous to introduce it in Muslim countries" (Zakariya 1991, 31). By defending this position, they acquire a large support from the masses. This fight against laïcité allowed them to "hide behind a protective halo of sanctity and to present their opponent (the authoritarian State) as the one who is transgressing or defying the religious tradition of the country" (Zakariya 1991, 20). To motivate their position, they put forward two principal arguments: (1) secularism and laïcité were synonyms of atheism and (2) the imposition of these two processes corresponded to the loss of the Arab-Muslim identity and the westernization of society.

In this first argument, placing secularism/laïcité and Islam at two opposite ends effectively depicted anyone who spoke in favor of such principles to be non-Muslims. Therefore, anyone who was put into the position of choosing between one of the two options would identify with the latter, siding with the Islamists (Zakariya 1991, 20). The second argument, associating secularism/laïcité to "westernization and cultural colonization" (Zakariya 1991, 29), effectively depicted those supporters as being linked to the traumatic experiences under colonial rule (1881–1956). In fact, Islamists argued that, despite the independence, president Bourguiba kept carrying out policies that favored the West (as, for instance, backing upper-class and French-speaking civil servants) and betrayed the country's true cultural identity (rural and Arab speaking). The success of the Islamist discourse also was fostered by the "disenchantment which took place toward the end of the 1960s in Tunisia following the first phase of post-independence enthusiasm" (Burgat 2008, 203–204).

4 Government's Response: Return of Religion and Oppression of Islamist Opposition

The growing popularity of the Islamists convinced president Bourguiba and his successor Zine el-Abidine Ben Ali (1936–2019) to marginalize this movement by (1) developing a new Islam-friendly discourse and policies as well as (2) imprisoning and torturing its representatives. Toward the end of 1960s, Bourguiba modified his strategy concerning the practice of Islam. Different examples show this revised position: the month of Ramadan was promoted and the State institutions' or schools' schedules were adjusted to allow pious Muslims to be able to break the fast on time (Frégosi 2004, 98). This readjustment also was done for Eïd el-Adha (festival of sacrifice), the pilgrimage to Mecca, etc. Moreover, Bourguiba promoted the Arab-Muslim heritage by restoring mosques and monuments, reinstating religion courses in schools, etc. (Frégosi 2004, 96). The same strategy was adopted by his successor. We can cite different examples of Ben Ali's religious policy: each speech began with "Bismillah al-Rahman al-Rahim" (In the Name of God, the Compassionate, the Merciful) and was often concluded with verses from the Quran; large sums of funds were granted for mosques; the president was often filmed whilst praying or during pilgrimages in sacred places; and, the Friday prayer was broadcasted on national television, among other things (Burgat 2008, 265).

However, apart from developing these new Islam-friendly policies, both Tunisian presidents began to directly target the members of the Islamist movement. During the 1980s, the regime began "raids, searches and torture" of Islamists (Hermassi 1989, 299). In 1981,[8] a series of incidents (including clashes on university campuses; actions against non-fasting Tunisians during Ramadan; a fight over the nomination of a new imam in the city of M'saken) served as pretext for the regime to arrest around "one hundred and fifty militants and supporters of the Islamist party" (Burgat 2008, 232). Often these militants were condemned without just cause and at times the only belonging to this organization meant lengthy prison sentences (Burgat 2008, 119). For president Ben Ali, it was the elections on April 9, 1989, which triggered a repression strategy. In fact, although his party obtained the great majority of votes, the Islamists turned out to be the second political force, obtaining almost 18 percent of the votes (Hermassi 1989, 305). Therefore, in 1991, the regime took advantage of the civil war in Algeria to act against the Islamist movement. This resulted in the imprisonment and exile of these militants. A few of these actors managed to

---

8 Date in which the Islamist movement chose to become a political party.

function as dormant networks. Yet, the revolts, which began in December 2010, and the revolution that would take place in January 2011, changed the balance of power between these different actors and impacted both the judicial and political fields. This new phase can be associated to Baubérot and Milot's ideal type of civic faith laïcité:

> [T]his ideal type of laïcité requires allegiance toward common values of society. In secularized societies or in those where there is a majority religion, religious minorities (as well as atheists) could be suspected of secretly wanting to impose different values than those admitted and interiorized by the citizens. In this case, the State or segments of the population, can demand that those who adopt different religious practices from the majority soften this practice in order to 'prove' that such adhesion does not bring them to favor different values and undermine national unity.
> BAUBÉROT and MILOT 2011, 105–106

5 The Drafting of the "New" Constitution and its Impact on the Socio-Legal Context

In this second part of our work, we analyze how religious freedom is defended in the judicial texts, with a special focus on the old (dating back to 1959) and "new" constitutional text (approved in 2014). Two examples show the limitations to the principles of freedom of conscience and equality: the issue of the right of non-fasters during Ramadan as well as that of gender equality, which are a result of the persistence of some religiously inspired laws. The little modification concerning articles pertaining to the relationship between State and religion show how both secular and Islamist forces chose to maintain a status quo.

6 The Relationship between State and Religion and its Heterogeneous Legal Interpretations

In Tunisia, the issue concerning the relationship between State and religion as well as between Sharia[9] and positive law remains quite complex and

---

9 "Shari'a was not strictly speaking the revealed word of God, but it was widely taken by Muslims to be a divinely inspired extension of the teachings of the Quran and hadith.

open to different interpretations. Article 1 of the 1959 Tunisian Constitution states: "Tunisia is a free, independent, sovereign State; its religion is Islam, its language Arabic, and its system is republican" (Tunisia National Portal of Legal Information, n.d.). This article is quite fascinating for its ambiguity. In fact, the jurists had managed to avoid making Islam the State religion but rather the religion of the country and of the majority its people (Charfi 1998, 21). Nonetheless, this ambiguity also can be considered as quite dangerous for it can be interpreted in two completely opposite manners. The more rationalist readers interpreted this article as guaranteeing the neutrality of the authorities (especially in judicial affairs), yet, the more conservative thinkers considered that this article, as it mentioned the Muslim religion, implied that in all cases where other secular judicial documents don't explicitly state anything, a case can be judged according to Islamic law. Article 1 was kept the same in the 2014 Constitution. Yet, Article 2 was introduced, stating: "Tunisia is a civil State based on citizenship, the will of the people, and the supremacy of law" (Tunisia National Portal of Legal Information, n.d.). Jurist Yadh Ben Achour underlines how including both the mention of Islam and civil State creates confusion as to the real identity of the Tunisian State: is Islam the religion of State or is Tunisia a civil State? This issue contributes to causing an even greater misunderstanding concerning the legitimate source of law (Ben Achour 2016, 315–316). In analyzing the Tunisian case, French jurist Jean-Philippe Bras considers that the choice of defining Tunisia as a civil State also can be seen as a form of compromise. It works as a series of non-attributes of the State: "A Civil State cannot be military, nor violent, nor authoritarian, nor religious" (Bras 2016, 64).

The fact of mentioning Islam in the first article of the Constitution thus contributed to giving Islam a privileged position with regard to other beliefs. This advantage seemed to be in contradiction with other articles of the fundamental law as those promoting freedom of conscience and equality.

Muslim law has its origins in the efforts of seventeenth century judges and scholars to reform existing legal practice and inspire it with Islamic ethical standards. (...) The final corpus of the Shari'a thus represents custom and tradition transformed by Islamic ethical conviction." There are four surviving schools of law in Sunni Islam: Hanafi, Maliki, Shafi'i and Hanbali. (Lapidus 2002, 85).

7 The Limitations to the Principle of Freedom of Conscience and Equality

Although there have been cases of attacks by radical groups against religious minorities in Tunisia in the aftermath of the revolution,[10] it can be said that religions of the book are generally respected in this country. The greatest threat deals with the issue of freedom of conscience, which applies to non-practicing Muslims, converts and atheists.[11] Tunisian lawyer Yadh Ben Achour, observes how the traditionalist interpretation of Article 1 (considering Islam as the State religion) clashes with the principle of freedom of conscience (Ben Achour 2011, 55–56). He contends that a truly democratic country must recognize both "the active freedom of the religious believer and the negative freedom of the non-believer or of those who decide to abandon their religion" (Ben Achour 2011, 56). Freedom of conscience was granted in Article 5 of the old 1959 Tunisian Constitution, which stated: "The Republic of Tunisia shall guarantee the inviolability of the human person and freedom of conscience, and defends the free practice of religious beliefs provided this does not disturb public order" (Tunisia National Portal of Legal Information). Despite the fact of being omitted in previous drafts, freedom of conscience was finally granted in the official version of the new Tunisian Constitution of 2014. Article 6 of the new Constitution reads as follows: "The State is the guardian of religion. It guarantees freedom of conscience and belief, the free exercise of religious practices and the neutrality of mosques and places of worship from all partisan instrumentalization. The State undertakes to disseminate the values of moderation and tolerance and the protection of the sacred, and the prohibition of all violations thereof. It undertakes equally to prohibit and fight against calls for Takfir[12] and the incitement of violence and hatred" (Tunisia National Portal of Legal Information). Journalist Samy Ghorbal underlines how this text is the fruit of a compromise between Islamist and secular parties:[13] "Ennahda

---

10 As for examples, the attacks on an Orthodox church in the center of Tunis, which began in November 2011 (*Business News*, 2012) or that on a synagogue in the city of Gabès in southeast Tunisia in January 2011 (*Le Point & Reuters*, 2011).
11 This shows the similarity to Bauberot and Milot's (2011) ideal type of civic faith laïcité. These categories of actors are considered as a minority, which could put national unity in danger.
12 Accusation of apostasy/being an infidel. According to Mohamed Charfi the most disastrous idea which was forged by religious scholars (without any Quranic legitimacy) and associated to Sharia law is that apostasy is a crime that must be punished with death (Charfi 1998, 78).
13 Following the January 2011 revolution, a transition phase was followed by the first free elections held on October 23, 2011. These elections determined the number of seats/

obtained the mention concerning the protection of the sacred in exchange of the mention of freedom of conscience" (Ghorbal 2014). Tunisian specialist on Islam Abdelmajid Charfi declared his opposition to the introduction of the principle of "protection of the sacred" in the Constitution. He believed "this notion brings about all sorts of perverse interpretations as it is completely vague. Moreover, the concept of "sacred," as in the French version (sacré) is expressed in its singular form, which seems to solely refer to Islam whilst a State's role should be that of protecting ALL religions".[14]

This ambiguity can turn into a clash concerning appropriate behavior in the public sphere. Take, for example, the daytime fasting during Ramadan. During our fieldwork (Grasso 2011), we decided to focus on the issue of non-fasters' rights. We were able to observe the feelings of the population during this sacred month as well as interviewing different actors on their vision concerning this issue. Contrary to Algeria or Morocco, Tunisian law does not punish non-fasters and restaurants or cafés are not forced to shut down. Nonetheless, non-practicing Muslims still feel the social pressure not to eat or drink in public (Dahmani and Aït Akdim 2012). Political scientist Hamadi Redissi believes that "this period symbolizes the 'tyranny of the majority' as public space becomes somehow sacralized. Those who attempt to eat in public risk a fine for breaching public morality. The façades of the few cafés still serving food and drink are covered in wallpaper or cardboards" (Redissi 2011, 102). When asked whether religious minorities are respected in Tunisia, Redissi answered, "in dealing with the issue of freedom of religion and conscience, people tend to focus on religious minorities whilst, in the case of Tunisia, the true (and largest) minority is that made up of non-practicing Muslims and atheists."[15] Since the revolution, different issues appeared in the news during this sacred month. One such case came up in 2012 and included Adel Almi, a self-proclaimed defender of public morality and president of the centrist association of awareness and reform concerning non-fasting militants. These non-fasters were negatively labelled fatara (those who eat). Almi publicly demanded the government

---

party in the National Constituent Assembly, whose main role was that of redrafting a new Constitutional text. The Ennahda party won the majority of votes (obtaining 89 of the 217). They chose to set up a coalition with two other "secular" parties: Congress for the Republic (who had obtained 29 seats), party of historical opponent to the regime Moncef Marzouki which would be nominated President of the Republic, and Etakattol (with 20 seats), party of another historical opponent to the regime Mustapha Ben Jaafar, who would be nominated President of the National Constituent Assembly (ANC). Ennahda kept the post of Prime Minister.

14   Abdelmajid Charfi, in interview with the author, September 2013.
15   Hamadi Redissi, in interview with the author, Tunis, August 2011.

remove the license of those facilities who remained open during the sacred month and invited the fatara to avoid provoking Salafists[16] (Dahmani and Aït Akdim 2012). During Ramadan of the following year (2013), "non-fasters decided to use *Twitter* and the hashtag #fater to map the cafés and restaurants that were still serving food and drinks during the sacred month. Nonetheless, some feared this tool could backfire. Once again Adel Almi showed up in the media to demand the Ministry of Interior use this data to identify and punish non-fasters" (Olivier 2013). The ambiguity of Article 6 of the Constitution has a direct impact on the freedom of judges about whether to issue penalties to non-fasters. In 2017, in the town of Bizerte, "four people were condemned to one year in prison for 'indecent acts' after having eaten and smoked in a public park during Ramadan. NGOs and other associations mobilized against this decision in the name of 'liberty of conscience.' Nonetheless, jurists maintained this decision based on the principle of 'protection of the sacred' also mentioned in Article 6 of the Constitution" (Belaïd and AFP 2017).

Another principle that is defended in the new constitution is that of equality. Article 21 of the 2014 Constitution declares: "All citizens, male and female, have equal rights and duties, and are equal before the law without any discrimination" (Tunisia National Portal of Legal Information). Nonetheless, some exceptions persist. For instance, Article 74 states that to run for president of the republic, one must be a: "male and female voter who holds Tunisian nationality since birth, whose religion is Islam" (Tunisia National Portal of Legal Information, n.d.). Therefore, a Tunisian citizen who is not a Muslim cannot aspire to become president. Yet, the greatest obstacle is that of gender equality. This principle is defended and put forward as being part of Tunisian identity. For instance, Tunisian Personal Status Code (CSP), which was enacted

---

16   Shortly after the revolution, religious militants emerged seeking to impose their own moral vision on Tunisian society, which they considered as having been perverted by authoritarian (secular) rule. This movement finds its origins in the very beginning of Islam. The term Salaf refers to "the pious predecessors: three generations that represented the golden age of Islam. The Salaf were distinguished by their exemplary piety, and by their military conquests" (Amghar 2007, 42). This movement can be divided in three ideal types: revolutionary or jihadist Salafism (these emerged through the Islamist doctrine of the Muslim Brotherhood but broke away from them over participation in non-religious forms of government. They see violence as the sole efficient means of action to reestablish the Caliphate); conversion and predication Salafism (they are against political activism which they consider as polluting their spirituality. They consider that the only way to re-establish past glory is through purification and education); political Salafism (they consider that their mission is to convince the masses of the necessity to return to the past glory through political activism). This division is idealized as there is no clear frontier between these groups as well as between Salafists and Islamists (Ibid, 40–46).

in 1956, is often admired for being the most advanced in the Arab world as far as women's rights are concerned (abolishing polygamy, authorizing divorce, changing the legal marriage age for females to 18 years). Furthermore, Article 46 of the 2014 Constitution declares that: "The State commits to protect women's accrued rights and work to strengthen and develop those rights" (Tunisia National Portal of Legal Information, n.d.). Nonetheless, despite these advances, some exceptions remain as for the case of inheritance (where the female daughter inherits only half of what her brother does) or the case of the forbidding of marriage between a Muslim woman and a non-Muslim man. According to jurist Monia Ben Jémia, it is a simple government circular dating back from 1973 that imposed this second marriage limitation (Ben Jémia 2012, 161). This circular stated that:

> [A] Tunisian Muslim woman could not marry a non-Muslim unless he provided a conversion certificate. On September 17, 2017, this circular has been abolished. This was the result of the involvement of late president of the republic Béji Caïd Essebsi whom, on Tunisian Woman's Day (which commemorates the promulgation of the CSP on August 13), made such a commitment in the name of gender equality.
>
> VERDIER 2017

The issue is more complex with regard to the question of inheritance as this principle is clearly mentioned in chapter four, verse eleven, of the Quran (Belaïd and AFP August 2017). However, many consider this to be a meaningless debate as parents can chose to make a donation toward their daughter before their death in order for her to have the same amount as her brother (Ben Jémia 2012, 161). This is the position of Ajmi Lourimi, Ennahda's cofounder and member of the party's executive office.[17]

8 The Emergence of Religious Militancy and its Impact on Tunisian Post-Revolution Socio-Political Context (2011–2016)

The Tunisian Revolution can be seen as a new phase in Tunisian politics. With the reopening of the political field, different ideologies emerged in this arena to promote their own agenda. The threat to freedom of religion in this context mainly came from Salafi militants who sought to impose a

---

17 Ajmi Lourimi, in interview with the author, Tunis, August 2011.

"traditionalist" solution aiming at turning back toward the original message of Islam (Roussillon 2005, 13). These actors considered that Islam is opposed to the principle of laïcité, the political field should be the one to submit itself to religious morality and that it is up to the believers to ensure the project of establishing a religious society (Roussillon 2015, 127). These Salafist militants challenged the secular model, which had been maintained after the revolution and enshrined in the new Constitution.[18] Other political actors (especially the Nidaa Tounes party) put forward a more "modernist" approach, claiming to inherit the politics of late president Bourguiba, who were less controversial than Ben Ali. The Ennahda party seemed to defend a middle ground between these two visions, a stance which evolved and adapted to the changing context.

To analyze the position of these different actors, we chose to divide this third part of our chapter into two chronological phases: a first phase (2011–2013) where it is possible to observe the re-emergence and popularity of the Islamist movement and the impact on religious freedom in the country; followed by a second phase (2014–2016) in which we can witness the emergence of an anti-Islamist and anti-religious sentiment fostered by the ambiguous stance of Ennahda party as well as the violent actions committed in the name of Islam.

9 Re-emergence and Popularity of Political Islam (2011–2013)

Following the 2011 revolution, Tunisians interpreted this event in different manners. In the case of militants of political Islam, this transition meant giving new momentum to the true Islamic identity of the country. The main objectives were to set aside all those who had worked under the Ben Ali regime and to repair the authoritarian policies that had been carried out by both presidents for the sole purpose of weakening the religious institution. Nonetheless, there was a lack of consensus among these religious militants as to the type of reforms to carry out or the way in which to push their demands. The representatives of the Ennahda party chose a strategy of compromise with other ideologies, while the militants closer to the base as well as those who identify as Salafist reinforced the policies in favor of the re-Islamization of the country. This confirms the theory of a plural Islamist movement (Camau & Geisser 2003, 287).

---

18   By taking civic faith laïcité ideal type as a model we can define Salafis as another minority group which poses a threat to the vision of Islam of the majority of Tunisians and challenges national unity.

The Ennahda party won the majority of votes (obtaining 89 of the 217 seats of the National Constituent Assembly) during the first free elections of the country, held on October 23, 2011. Many voters were persuaded by the apparent unity and influence of this party, which in a short span of time had managed to reactivate all its dormant networks in the country. Moreover, Ennahda's moderate and conservative stance also reassured those voters who sought political and moral stability. According to Allani (2013), the five main factors that brought on this victory were:

> [T]he unique use of religious references; the fragmentation of the left, centre-left and liberal parties; the length of the period of persecution that the Islamists were subject to under Ben Ali's reign; the fear of voters to return to the Constitutional Rally (the ex-ruling party) on whom they placed financial and political blame; and Al-Nahda leaders' commitment during the election campaign to respect the Personal Status Code.
> ALLANI 2013, 133

Furthermore, in order to tackle left-wing opposition, Islamist party leaders also sought to win support by reactivating their rhetoric on laïcité as being both synonym of atheism and an ideology contrary to Arab-Muslim identity. The victory of the Islamist party was interpreted by the more conservative actors as the return of Islam in the country. Therefore, they expected Ennahda to promote this ideology at a political level. Nonetheless, their hopes were crushed with various decisions made by the Islamist party to compromise with other secular forces. This was especially the case with the refusal of Ennahda to impose a reference to Sharia law in the constitutional text. As mentioned by a study on the National Constitutional Assembly (ANC): "out of the 56 representatives of Ennahda, only 13 (less than a quarter) declared the need to mention the Sharia law in the constitution" (Redissi et al. 2014, 72).

Disappointed by Ennahda party, many Salafist militants chose to take it in their hands to apply this ideology within Tunisian society. These actors carried out violent actions to impose their own moral code in the name of the principle of protection of the sacred. Different incidents took place during this first phase (2011–2013), including the attack against legal brothels and their workers, (Dahmani 2014) as well as hotels and restaurants serving alcoholic beverages (*Franceinfo: Afrique* 2012). Cultural venues, such as a cinema (*Observateurs-France24* 2011) and a cultural centre, (Lafitte 2012) also were victims of attacks for having displayed "blasphemous" pieces. Universities and their presidents were targeted in both Sousse (Soudani 2011) and Tunis (*Le Point & AFP* 2012), because they refused to accept students wearing a niqab. Mosques were occupied and the official imams were expelled after being accused of collaborating with the authoritarian government (Verdier 2014). Political meetings were infiltrated (*Courrier de l'Atlas* 2011). Some of those violent actions also infringed the principle of freedom of religion as was the case with the attack on Sufi[19] zawiyas (saints' tombs). To justify the aggression against followers of the same Muslim religion, Salafists put forward the principle of tawhid (unitary nature of God). According to their vision, Sufis are not real Muslims and consider the cult of saints as well as the celebration of Mawlid (birth of prophet Muhammad) to be a form of idolatry. Since March 2012, around forty of the 2000 zawiyas of the country were the object of Salafist attacks (Rogers 2013). Among them was the famous mausoleum of Sidi Bou Saïd in the outskirts of Tunis. Contrary to Salafi accusations, Sufism has a long presence in Tunisia (Green 1978) and many representatives of the elite and Tunisian population are members of a tariqa. Therefore, these attacks fostered a great popular uprising. Following these actions, many opponents of the Islamist ideology accused the Ennahda party in power of permissiveness or even of a disguised support.

10 Growing Violence in the Country Lead to Distrust in Islamism and in the Religious Institution (2014–2016)

The anti-Islamist sentiment became increasingly hostile when violent actions turned into murderous ones, resulting in the deaths of Tunisian and foreign citizens. On September 14, 2012, the embassy of the United States was attacked by Salafi militants. This action was fostered by the release of an online video entitled "The Innocence of Muslims," which was produced in the USA and criticized Islam and the Prophet Muhammed.[20] Two militants died during the confrontation with security forces (Dahmani 2012). Moreover, soldiers were killed on Mount Chaambi at the border with Algeria. According to the media, an armed group close to Al Qaeda settled in this area (*Le Monde* & AFP 2013).

---

19 See note 7. In Tunisia, since the 19th century Nahda, Sufism was perceived as an irrational and backward practice. Nonetheless, when Ben Ali became the new president in 1987, among the decisions marking a break from the past, he chose to reconnect with this movement. "The new presidency attempted to appropriate religious symbols and chose to support zawiyas (saints' tombs) and the cult of saints, which he sought to control and exploit to obtain popular support and legitimacy. Ben Ali was aware of the power and influence of these institutions" (Zarcone 2009, 330–331).

20 On September 11, 2012, this same video caused the assault on the US Embassy in Libya, which resulted in the assassination of the ambassador as well as three of his collaborators.

Nonetheless, the events that mostly shocked the country were the murder of two left-wing politicians—Chokri Belaïd on February 6, 2013 and Mohamed Brahmi on July 25, 2013—as well as two terrorist attacks targeting foreign tourists in 2015, at the Bardo Museum of Tunis on March 18 and the beach in Sousse on June 26. These attacks were tied to radical extremists close to Daech.[21]

Following the murder of Mohamed Brahmi, a popular movement emerged demanding the resignation of the Ennahda-led government. The National Salvation Front was created on July 26. This front was made up of representatives of political parties (Nidaa Tounes[22] and Popular Front),[23] as well as civil society organizations. Starting on July 27, this front started a sit-in outside the National Constituent Assembly's headquarters demanding the finalization of the constitutional text and the substitution of the governing coalition with a national salvation government. A national dialogue was set up by four main organizations—the Tunisian General Labour Union (UGTT, Union Générale Tunisienne du Travail); the Tunisian Confederation of Industry, Trade and Handicrafts (UTICA, Union Tunisienne de l'Industrie, du Commerce et de l'Artisanat); the Tunisian Human Rights League (LTDH, La Ligue Tunisienne pour la Défense des Droits de l'Homme); the Tunisian Order of Lawyers (Ordre National des Avocats de Tunisie)—which finally managed to find a consensus and set up a technocratic government on January 2014. This government remained in power for about one year in charge of restoring order and organizing the legislative and presidential elections. These elections were won by Nidaa Tounes and its presidential candidate, Béji Caïd Essebsi, who campaigned on "the ability to block the Islamist danger" (Marzouki 2016, 89).

Popular distrust and the international context[24] impacted Ennahda's strategy. Having come second in the 2014 legislative elections, the "modernist" Nidaa Tounes party (with 86 out of 217 seats) was obliged to collaborate

---

21 Radical movement that taking advantage of the unrest of the "Arab Spring," started to emerge in 2012 and began conquering territories in Syria and Iraq between 2014 and 2019.
22 Nidaa Tounes party was created in June 2012 by Béji Caïd Essebsi (a well-respected politician who had served under Bourguiba and briefly under Ben Ali) with the ambition to reunite the "modernist" forces. This party reunited different types of actors: trade unionists, left-wing intellectuals, representatives of the bourgeoisie, businessmen, but also members of Ben Ali's party.
23 Popular Front is a coalition of left-wing and nationalist parties founded in October 2012. Chokri Belaïd and Mohamed Brahmi were both members of this coalition.
24 Apart from the apparition of Daech, the Ennahda party also was affected by the events in Egypt. On July 3, 2012, a coup d'Etat brought on by the military led by general Sissi removed from power democratically elected Muslim Brother Mohamed Morsi. Protesters were killed and Sissi became the new head of the State.

with the Islamist party (who had obtained 69 seats) to set up a government. Thus, despite opposing ideologies, both parties chose pragmatism. As a result, Ennahda was once again able to remain in power. Moreover, the Ennahda's 10th Congress, which took place between May 20–22, 2016, marked the "secularization" of the party. One of the decisions was to "rebrand" itself no longer as Islamist but as "Muslim Democrat" (Souli 2016). Moreover, leader Rachid Ghannouchi announced the decision to "separate [the party's] religious and political activities." This meant that representatives who held a position in the party could no longer simultaneously work in a religious institution (such as a mosque or an Islamic organization). These choices resulted in great mistrust of Ennahda by more conservative actors (within the party, among different types of Salafis, as well as their voter base).

The disillusionment with Islamism also was confirmed in a survey carried out by BBC Arabic using data collected by the Arab barometer.[25] Such phenomenon has been observed in all the Arab countries that were surveyed (Morocco, Algeria, Tunisia, Libya, Egypt, Palestine, Yemen, Jordan, Iraq, Sudan and Lebanon) except for Yemen. According to this study, trust in Ennahda party dropped by 24 percent between 2011 and 2019 (Khojji 2019). This survey also showed how factors such as Islamist parties' disappointing performance, the moralizing actions of Salafists, as well as the terrorist attacks perpetrated in the name of Islam, had contributed to an aversion toward religion. For instance, it is in Tunisia that the highest number of respondents declared themselves as being "non-religious." This trend has increased over time—more than 10 percent in 2013 and more than 30 percent in 2018–19 (*BBC* 2019). Some consider this to be the sign of a new secular wave in the Muslim world (Akyol 2019) and especially in Tunisia.

11   Conclusion

The aim of this chapter is to analyze the impact of the January 2011 revolution on the issue of religious freedom and secularism in Tunisia. To do so, we chose to develop a reflection on the concepts of secularization and laïcité with regard to this specific context and identify the main obstacles facing this country in terms of religious freedom.

---

25   A nonpartisan research network (uniting American and Middle Eastern research centers) that provides insight into the social, political and economic attitudes and values of ordinary citizens across the Arab world (Arab barometer).

The first part of our chapter was developed around a historical analysis from the independence of Tunisian republic up until 2011 and the policy of the two late presidents, Bourguiba and Ben Ali, with regard to the Muslim religion. Bourguiba adopted a policy of assertive secularism by separating religion and the fields of law and education. This secularization process remained a constant in Tunisian society. Nonetheless, religious freedom was not respected as the government carried out a policy of authoritarian laïcité, which meant interfering in the internal affairs of religion as a means to avoid emerging political opposition within the religious field — as was the case with Islamism.

The second part of this chapter focuses on the socio-legal factors that challenged religious freedom especially with regard to the new Tunisian Constitution. The absence of a clear separation between State and religion brought about some disagreement. This fostered the non-respect of religious freedom as some judges relied on religious-based reasons where law was undermined. This affected, for example, the freedom of non-fasters during the sacred month of Ramadan as well as the right to equal inheritance of Tunisian women.

In the third part of our chapter, we analyze the socio-political factors that have influenced religious freedom and the secular model in post revolution Tunisia. Religious freedom was mainly challenged by the action of Salafi militants who sought to promote Muslim religion above all others and impose their own vision of morality. Thus, they physically and symbolically targeted places and persons who did not respect their viewpoint. The emergence of this phenomenon pushed the "secularization" of Islamist party Ennahda as a means to distance themselves from such violence.

Taking into consideration these socio-legal and socio-political factors, we can question whether, as it has been the case for Ennahda and as some statistical data shows, the fear of radical Islam and the struggle for freedom of conscience and women's rights have fostered a will to go beyond the Tunisian secular model, especially among the youth.

References

Allani, Alaya. 2013. "The Post-Revolution Tunisian Constituent Assembly: Controversy over Powers and Prerogatives." *The Journal of North African Studies* 18(1): 131–40.

Amghar, Samir. 2007. « Le salafisme au Maghreb: menace pour la sécurité ou facteur de stabilité politique ? » *Revue internationale et stratégique* 67(3): 41–52.

Baubérot, Jean. 1991. « Conférence de M. Jean Baubérot. » *École pratique des hautes études, Section des sciences religieuses* 100: 459–66.

Baubérot, Jean, and Micheline Milot. 2011. *Laïcités sans frontières*. Paris: Seuil.

Ben Achour, Yadh. 2011. *La deuxième Fatiha*. Paris: Presses Universitaires de France.
Ben Achour, Yadh. 2016. *Tunisie: Une révolution en pays d'islam*. Tunis: Cérès.
Ben Jémia, Monia. 2012. « Le juge tunisien et la légitimation de l'ordre juridique positif par la charia. » Pp. 153–65 in *La charia aujourd'hui. Usages de la référence au droit islamique*, edited by Baudouin Dupret. Paris: La Découverte.
Bras, Jean-Philippe. 2016. « Un État 'Civil' peut-il être religieux? Débats tunisiens. » *Pouvoirs* 156: 55–70.
Burgat, François. 2008. *L'islamisme au Maghreb*. Paris: Payot & Rivages.
Camau, Michel et Geisser Vincent. 2003. *Le syndrome autoritaire: Politique en Tunisie de Bourguiba à Ben Ali*. Paris: Presses de Sciences Po.
Charfi, Mohamed. 1998. *Islam et liberté*. Paris: Albin Michel.
Cherif, Mohamed Hédi. 1994. « Réformes et islam chez Bourguiba. » *Annuaire de l'Afrique du Nord*, tome XXXIII: 59–67.
Dobbelaere, Karel. 1981. "Secularization: A Multi-Dimensional Concept." *Current Sociology* 29(2): 1–216.
Dobbelaere, Karel. 2004. *Secularization: An Analysis at Three Levels*. Brussels: Peter Lang.
Dobbelaere, Karel. 2008. « De la sécularisation. » *Revue théologique de Louvain* 2: 177–96.
Frégosi, Franck. 2004. « Habib Bourguiba et la régulation institutionnelle de l'islam: les contours audacieux d'un gallicanisme politique à la tunisienne. » Pp. xxx in *Habib Bourguiba, la trace et l'héritage*, edited by Camau, Michel and Geisser, Vincent. Aix-en-Provence: Karthala.
Grasso, Anna. 2011. « Quelle place pour la religion dans la Tunisie contemporaine? Religion et État au lendemain de la Révolution du Jasmin. » Master's Thesis, Institut d'Etudes Politiques d'Aix-en-Provence.
Grasso, Anna. 2018. « Les imâms dans la cité: politisation et syndicalisation des imâms dans la Tunisie contemporaine. » PhD diss., Institut d'Etudes Politiques d'Aix-en-Provence.
Green, Arnold H. 1978. *The Tunisian Ulama 1873–1915: Social Structure and Response to Ideological Currents*. Leiden: Brill.
Hermassi, Elbaki. 1989. « L'État tunisien et le mouvement islamiste. » *Annuaire de l'Afrique du Nord* XXVIII: 297–308.
Kraiem, Mustapha. 2011. *Etat et société dans la Tunisie Bourguibienne*. Tunis: MIP Livre.
Kuru, Ahmet T. 2009. *Secularism and State Policies toward Religion: The United States, France, and Turkey*. New York: Cambridge University Press.
Lamchichi, Abderrahim. 2000. « Laïcité autoritaire en Tunisie et en Turquie. » *Confluences Méditerranée* 33: 35–57.
Lapidus, Ira M. 2002. *A History of Islamic Societies*. New York: Cambridge University Press.
Luizard, Pierre-Jean. 2008. *Laïcités autoritaires en terres d'islam*. Paris: Fayard.
Marzouki, Nadia. 2016. « La Transition Tunisienne: du compromis démocratique à la réconciliation forcée. » *Pouvoirs* 156: 83–94.

Milot, Micheline. 2002. *La laïcité dans le nouveau monde, le cas du Québec*. Turnhout: Brepols.

Redissi, Hamadi. 2011. *La tragédie de l'islam moderne*. Paris: Seuil.

Redissi, Hamadi, Chekir, Hafedh, & Nouira, Asma. 2014. *La République des clercs: l'Assemblée Nationale Constituante Tunisienne*. Tunis: Diwen Editions.

Roussillon, Alain. 2005. *La pensée islamique contemporaine*. Paris: Téraèdre.

Zakariya, Fouad. 1991. *Laïcité ou islamisme*. Paris: La Découverte.

Zarcone, Thierry. 2009. « Confrérisme, maraboutisme et culte des saints face au réformisme. Le cas de la Turquie d'Atatürk et de la Tunisie de Bourguiba. » Pp. xxx in *Réforme de l'Etat et réformismes au Maghreb (XIXe-XXe siècles)*, edited by Moreau, Odile. Paris: L'Harmattan.

Websites & Online Newspapers:

Akyol, Mustafa. 2019. "A New Secularism Is Appearing in Islam.", *The New York Times*, December 13, 2019. https://www.nytimes.com/2019/12/23/opinion/islam-religion.html.

Arab barometer. n.d. "About Arab Barometer.", Accessed February 6, 2021. https://www.arabbarometer.org/about/.

BBC. 2019. "The Arab world in seven charts: Are Arabs turning their backs on religion?", June 24, 2019. https://www.bbc.com/news/world-middle-east-48703377.

Belaïd, Fethi & AFP. 2017. « Tunisie: un mois de prison pour avoir mangé en public lors du ramadan. », *France24*, June 1, 2017. https://www.france24.com/fr/20170601-tunisie-condamnes-prison-avoir-mange-fume-public-parc-ramadan-bizerte.

Belaïd, Fethi & AFP. 2017. « Égalité devant l'héritage: le débat enfle en Tunisie, les religieux s'en mêlent. », *France24*, August 18, 2017. https://www.france24.com/fr/20170817-tunisie-egalite-femmes-droits-heritage-debat-essebsi-mariage-ennahda.

Bobineau, Olivier. *Encyclopædia Universalis*, s.v. « Religion—Sociologie Religieuse. » Boulogne-Billancourt : Encyclopædia Universalis, 2021. http://www.universalis.fr/encyclopedie/religion-sociologie-religieuse/ (accessed February 6, 2021).

Business News. 2012. « Tunisie—Des « barbus » s'attaquent à l'église orthodoxe de l'avenue Mohamed V. », April 3, 2012. https://www.businessnews.com.tn/Tunisie---Des-%C2%AB-barbus-%C2%BB-s%E2%80%99attaquent-%C3%A0-la-l%E2%80%99%C3%A9glise-orthodoxe-de-l%E2%80%99avenue-Mohamed-V,520,30308,3.

Courrier de l'Atlas. 2011. « Tunisie—Attaque d'une réunion du PCOT par des salafistes à Tunis. », July 4, 2011. https://www.lecourrierdelatlas.com/-tunisie-attaque-d-une-reunion-du-pcot-par-des-salafistes-a-tunis--388.

Dahmani, Frida. 2012. « Tunisie: deux morts dans l'attaque de l'ambassade américaine par des islamistes. », *Jeune Afrique*, September 14, 2012. https://www.jeuneafrique.com/174278/politique/tunisie-deux-morts-dans-l-attaque-de-l-ambassade-am-ricaine-par-des-islamistes/.

Dahmani, Frida. 2014. « Prostitution: islamistes et maisons closes, le blues des filles de joie tunisiennes. », *Jeune Afrique*, April 25, 2014. https://www.jeuneafrique.com/133742/societe/prostitution-islamistes-et-maisons-closes-le-blues-des-filles-de-joie-tunisiennes/.

Dahmani, Frida & Aït Akdim, Youssef. 2012. « Ramadan: ceux qui le font, ceux qui ne le font pas. », *Jeune Afrique*, July 30, 2012. https://www.jeuneafrique.com/140601/societe/ramadan-ceux-qui-le-font-ceux-qui-ne-le-font-pas/.

De Naurois, Louis. *Encyclopædia Universalis*, s.v. « Religion et État. » Boulogne-Billancourt : Encyclopædia Universalis, 2021. https://www.universalis.fr/encyclopedie/religion-religion-et-etat/ (accessed February 6, 2021).

Franceinfo : Afrique. 2012. « Tunisie. Des salafistes attaquent le bar d'un hôtel à Sbeitla. », December 14, 2012. https://www.francetvinfo.fr/monde/afrique/tunisie-des-salafistes-attaquent-le-bar-d-un-hotel-a-sbeitla_186975.html.

Ghorbal, Samy. 2014. « Tunisie: Constitution, suite et fin. », *Jeune Afrique*, January 20, 2014. https://www.jeuneafrique.com/134846/politique/tunisie-constitution-suite-et-fin/.

Khojji, Zaynab. 2019. "Trust in Islamist parties plummets since Arab Spring.", *Arab News*, June 23, 2019. https://www.arabnews.com/node/1515091/middle-east.

Lafitte, Priscille. 2012. « Une exposition d'art contemporain à l'origine des heurts à Tunis? », *France24 & Reuters*, June 14, 2012. https://www.france24.com/fr/20120612-tunisie-heurts-tunis-exposition-art-contemporain-printemps-marsa-salafistes.

Le Monde & AFP. 2013. « Huit soldats tunisiens tués dans des heurts avec des "terroristes". », July 29, 2013. https://www.lemonde.fr/tunisie/article/2013/07/29/huit-soldats-tunisiens-tues-dans-des-heurts-avec-des-terroristes_3455135_1466522.html.

Le Point & Reuters. 2011. « Une synagogue et deux écoles attaquées en Tunisie. », February 1, 2011. https://www.lepoint.fr/monde/une-synagogue-et-deux-ecoles-attaquees-en-tunisie-01-02-2011-134372_24.php.

Le Point & AFP. 2012. « Tunisie: manifestation pour la réouverture d'une faculté à Tunis. », January 4, 2012. https://www.lepoint.fr/monde/tunisie-manifestation-pour-la-reouverture-d-une-faculte-a-tunis-04-01-2012-1415326_24.php.

Observateurs-France24. 2011. « Attaque du cinéma Africart par des islamistes: la vie culturelle tunisienne est-elle en danger? », June 28, 2011. https://observers.france24.com/fr/20110628-attaque-cinema-africart-islamistes-vie-culturelle-tunisienne-est-elle-danger.

Olivier, Mathieu. 2013. « Ramadan: avec #fater, les internautes tunisiens s'organisent pour ne pas jeûner. », *Jeune Afrique*, July 10, 2013. https://www.jeuneafrique.com/169743/politique/ramadan-avec-fater-les-internautes-tunisiens-s-organisent-pour-ne-pas-je-ner/.

Pew Research Center. 2014. "Tunisian Confidence in Democracy Wanes." Accessed February 6, 2021. https://www.pewresearch.org/global/2014/10/15/tunisian-confidence-in-democracy-wanes/.

Rogers, Benjamin. 2013. « Carte: les mausolées tunisiens en péril. », *Jeune Afrique*, February 7, 2013. https://www.jeuneafrique.com/172301/politique/carte-les-mausol-es-tunisiens-en-p-ril/.

Soudani, Seif. 2011. « Pour un refus d'inscrire deux étudiantes en Niqab, la Faculté de Sousse attaquée par des salafistes. », *Le Courrier de l'Atlas*, October 6, 2011. https://www.lecourrierdelatlas.com/no-data-pour-un-refus-d-inscrire-deux-etudiantes-en-niqab-la-faculte-de-sousse-attaquee-par-des-salafistes-911.

Souli, Sarah. 2016. "What is left of Tunisia's Ennahda Party?", *Al Jazeera*, May 27, 2016. https://www.aljazeera.com/news/2016/05/left-tunisia-ennahda-party-160526101937131.html.

Tunisia National Portal of Legal Information. n.d "Constitution of the Republic of Tunisia 1959." Accessed February 7, 2021. http://www.legislation.tn/sites/default/files/constitutionanglais.pdf; "Constitution of the Republic of Tunisia 2014." Accessed February 7, 2021. http://www.legislation.tn/fr/constitution/la-constitution-de-la-r%C3%A9publique-tunisienne.

Verdier, Marie. 2014. « La Tunisie essaie de reprendre le contrôle de ses mosquées. », *La Croix*, June 23, 2014. https://www.la-croix.com/Actualite/Monde/La-Tunisie-essaie-de-reprendre-le-controle-de-ses-mosquees-2014-06-23-1168792.

Verdier, Marie. 2017. « Les Tunisiennes libres d'épouser qui elles veulent. », *La Croix Africa*, February 18, 2017. https://africa.la-croix.com/tunisiennes-libres-depouser-veulent/.

CHAPTER 4

Religious Pluralism, Religious Freedom and the Secularization Process in the Greek Educational System

Alexandros Sakellariou

Greece is considered a predominantly Greek Orthodox society, while at the same time there are serious doubts expressed about the Greek state's secular character based on the Constitution and other laws and political decisions. In addition, despite the religious affiliation changes that have occurred during the last decade, the majority of the Greek population still self-identifies as Greek Orthodox. Religious pluralism, religious freedom, and secularization in the Greek educational system and the role of the Orthodox Church of Greece is one of the most important issues in the public sphere and the academia and it has been examined from political, theological, legal, and sociological perspectives (Sotirelis 1998; Zoumpoulakis 2002, 107–23; Karamouzis 2007; Perselis 2011; Karamouzis and Athanassiadis 2011). First, it should be noted that the Greek educational system is predominantly Greek Orthodox, based on a series of factors, such as everyday prayer, Orthodox symbols, church attendance, etc. But the education system also is religiously diverse with many immigrant children and people of no religion who have been very active in the last few years in the protection of their rights. Second, we should note that the Greek State constitutionally protects religious freedom and has validated the convention on the rights of the child which includes a special reference on religious freedom.

With this in mind, this chapter has three main goals: discuss the situation with regard to the place of religion in the Greek educational system; present the developments regarding the secularization process of the Greek society, in general, and the educational system, in particular; and, discuss the relation between a prevailing religion, religious pluralism, religious freedom, and secularization. Through a sociological perspective on human rights and religion (Breskaya, Giordan and Richardson 2018), this chapter will try to respond to the following questions: Is the Greek school secular? Does the Greek school and the Greek State respect the religious freedom of children and their religious or non-religious beliefs, especially during an era of religious diversity and the rise of non-religiosity? Does the school function as the Church's ideological mechanism reproducing the prevailing religion while this should be the Church's obligation? Which is the role of the Greek Constitution in the formation of this context? Could the inclusion of both provisions, i.e. the respect of religious freedom and a prevailing religion in the Greek Constitution, be considered as contradictory and what is the impact on education? Building on religious pluralism, religious freedom and secularization, this chapter will try to cast light on a difficult and burning issue in the contemporary Greek society that has created heated debates during the last years and has become a cornerstone of the secularization controversy. It also will try to explain why the secularization of the educational system is one of the most important aspects of the secularization process and how this relates to respecting children's rights. The main argument is that only if religious freedom is fully implemented and respected and religious pluralism becomes a central policy of the educational system, then the Greek school could be considered as secular.

1 Religious Pluralism, Religious Freedom and Their Impact on the Secularization Process

One crucial theoretical parameter that is very regularly discussed with regard to education and religious freedom is that of pluralism. According to Ammerman (2010, 20), religious pluralism is central to the human condition and the challenge for academics is to do their work with the full range of diversity before them. Pluralism, as a concept, needs to be differentiated from diversity. Pluralism belongs to the normative-regulatory level, while diversity in the descriptive one (Giordan and Pace 2014, 1). The term religious pluralism can refer to four different things: a) empirical forms of diversity in relation to religion, b) normative or ideological views about the positive value of religious diversity, c) the frameworks of public policy, law and social practices, which accommodate, regulate, and facilitate religious diversity, and d) relational contexts of everyday interactions between individuals and groups identified as religious (Beckford 2014, 16, 21–22).The descriptive dimension, diversity, or plurality describes the degree of religious heterogeneity within a society, whereas pluralism refers to the social arrangement favorable to a high or higher level of plurality. Pluralization, then, is the process of increasing plurality/diversity in a society (Yang 2014, 52). As a consequence, it is not fruitful to confuse normative pluralism with empirical diversity and for analytical purposes they should always be kept separate (Beckford 2014, 25–26). In addition, as it has been argued, religious diversity/plurality describes a state in a society and should be distinguished from pluralism, which refers to beliefs and attitudes about diversity/plurality. Societies are more or less religiously plural, but may or may not embrace pluralism and become a culture that favors diversity (Bouma and Ling 2011, 508). Based on the above, one could argue that in Greek society religious diversity is a fact that can be easily observed,[1] but when it comes to beliefs and attitudes about diversity, a series of questions are being raised especially with regard to the educational system.

For some scholars, to understand the scope of the category of pluralism it is necessary to place it outside the debate of secularization (Giordan and Pace 2014, 2). In this line of argument, the secularization thesis failed in its projection that religious diversity would lead to an overall decline in religion, because in the contemporary world religion persists, resurges and revives in almost all societies (Yang 2014, 50). However, I would argue that at least for the Greek society, this is not exactly the case. Indeed, the transition from the twentieth to the twentieth-first century has been characterized by a transnational migration process that has radically transformed the social and cultural landscape of wide areas around the world. Such a process of global mobility has caused a transformation from cultural and religious homogeneity either real or socially

---

[1] It should be noted that different religious communities (Muslims, Catholics, Jews, Protestants, and others) existed in Greek society for many years (Clogg 2002) but they were not visible and respected by the state (Christopoulos 1999). However, in the last 20–30 years, many religious groups succeeded in their legal fights on a European level in order to protect their religious freedom and at the same time there was a significant rise of Muslim immigrants. Although official data regarding religious affiliation are not collected in Greece, it is estimated that Muslims today are around more than 600,000 while unofficial estimations put this number at around one million (see, for example, Pew 2017). In addition, Greece has faced a rise of people who distance themselves from the Orthodox religion and become atheists, agnostics and religious indifferent leading to the founding of an Atheist Union of Greece (AUG) in 2012. This change is crystallized in several surveys during the last years. In one of them (Public Issue 2008), 7 percent stated that religion is not at all important in their lives, while 14 percent said that religion is not that important. More recently (Kapa Research 2015) 81.4 percent said they are Orthodox Christians, while 14.7 percent said that they are atheists, a number much higher than the 1.8 percent mentioned in the same company's opinion poll in 2006. In the most recent surveys on the issue conducted by Dianeosis (2020), it is mentioned that 15.4 percent don't believe in God, while in 2016 (Dianeosis 2016) this number was 15.8 percent. It is important to mention that these numbers are much higher among the ages 17–24. With regard to religiosity there seems to be also a significant shift between 2006 and 2015, based on the aforementioned poll (Kapa Research 2015). Those who attend the church weekly went from 22.7 percent in 2006 to 6.7 percent in 2015; those who go one to three times per month went from 24.6 percent to 10 percent; and those who never go went from 6.9 percent to 36.7 percent. Finally, people are more in favor of separation of church and state (from 59.2 percent to 74.5 percent) and the opinion that the religion class at schools should be compulsory for everyone and teach only Orthodoxy went down from 36.7 percent in 2006 to 13.8 percent in 2015.

constructed to the acknowledgment of diversity and an increasing focus on cultural and ideological pluralism (Giordan and Pace 2014, 7, 10; Sjoborg and Ziebertz 2017, 1). The inexorable processes of globalization, including the globalization of religious knowledge as well as migration, despite fostering uniform values in some areas of life, became increasingly diverse in matters of religion (Berglund, Shanneik and Bocking 2016, 1). This has been certainly the case for Greece, which was gradually transformed from a relatively homogenous Greek Orthodox society into a religiously diverse society during the last twenty to thirty years. According to Joppke (2015, 1–2) partially, but not exclusively, the revival of public religion is a result of international migration and the arrival of new religions into Western societies that challenge established arrangements between religion and the secular state. But the Greek State was not secular and it seems that this gradual change contributed to its secularization[2] and made the Greek society re-reconsider the place and role of religion in it. This development that started in Greek society since the 1990s initiated serious and heated debates about the secularization process of the state apparatus and further to that gave the space to secular people to demand the secularization of the state, including the educational system. Having said that, I would agree that pluralism is a fully modern concept arising in concert with the equally modern ideas of secularity and religion (Bender and Klassen 2010, 6). In addition, secularism is more than a conceptual partner of normative models of pluralism; it is one of its conceptual grounds. This view raises in a new

---

2 Secularization is the process that leads to the loss of power and influence that the sacred, in general, and religion, in particular, have on a society, meaning a process toward the establishment of a context of secularity. In that sense, secularity is the outcome of the secularization process, while secularism is the ideology that motivates people and activists or policy makers in order to pursue secularity (Demerath 2007, 65–66). Secularization, as defined by Dobbelaere (2011, 600), is the process by which overarching and transcendent religious systems of old are confined in modern functionally differentiated societies to a subsystem alongside other ones in this process, losing their overarching claims over these other subsystems. Such an approach focuses on the macro level and suggests that religious authorities have lost control over e.g. politics, economy, family, education, law, etc. Dobbelaere (1981; 2002, 165–195) has argued, though, that secularization is not found only on the macro, but on three levels: The societal, the institutional, and the individual, an argument also supported by other scholars (Casanova 2006). That means that religious institutions, societal sections and individuals could all face and undergo a process of secularization. As it has been proposed (Dobbelaere 2011, 606), individual secularization could, on the one hand, mean that religious authorities have lost control over the beliefs, practices, and moral principles of individual persons and, on the other hand, individual secularization is the secularization of the mind or compartmentalization. In this chapter, the main interest is, as expected, on the societal or institutional secularization focusing in particular on the secularization process of the educational system.

way a question about the relationships in our contemporary world between formations of the secular and formations of plural religions and religious plurality (Bender and Klassen 2010, 17). In relation to the Greek educational system, then, it could be argued that religious pluralism, or religious diversity to be more precise, opens the path for secularization and the implementation of religious freedom. In that sense, religious diversity and religious pluralism as a demand break the pre-existing homogeneity and create a fertile ground for secularization, but not the secularization as a linear and irreversible process. That said it is important to mention that serious debates in the Greek public sphere about secularization only appeared during the last twenty years or so together with the rise of religious diversity and the pluralization process.

Apart from religious pluralism that could have an impact on the secularization process, religious freedom is another important factor, which is directly related to religious pluralism as well. Religious freedom and the respect of the conventions of human rights together with any violation of the relative articles has become a cornerstone of such debates. This has been illustrated in many debates on the role of the European Convention of Human Rights (ECtHR) and the First Protocol of the Convention with regard to the right to education (Temperman 2019). When it comes to Greece and religious freedom more particularly, it has to be noted that Greece takes first place among European countries with the highest number of judgements for violations from the ECtHR with regard to religious freedom.[3] That is why a series of recent studies have focused on the role of the ECtHR and its rulings on the secularization process of the Greek State and society (Fokas 2012; Diamantopoulou 2012; Fokas 2015; Markoviti 2017). As it has been interestingly argued, the effects of ECtHR case law are significantly well beyond the direct legal changes they may instigate. ECtHR Article 9 (freedom of thought, conscience and religion) judgments become infiltrated in Greek society and influence, to different degrees, both the debates and the different types of mobilizations around actors' religious rights claims. Through such a "filtering effect" of its jurisprudence, the ECtHR thus becomes relevant to grassroots actors and contributes to the promotion of religious pluralism "on the ground" (Markoviti 2017, 279–280). As a consequence, both religious pluralism and religious freedom become crucial parameters of the secularization process of the Greek State and society. This relation and impact, however, is not deterministic and does not function both ways around. While religious pluralism and religious freedom could have an impact

---

3   https://www.echr.coe.int/Documents/Stats_violation_1959_2019_ENG.pdf (last accessed February 10, 2021).

on the secularization of the State and the society, a nominal secular state does not necessarily endorse inclusive religious policies and respect of religious freedom with the cases of China or former communist regimes being some illustrative examples.

2   The Secularization Process in Greek Society

Before moving into the educational system and in order to understand the whole context, it becomes crucial to briefly explain the role of religion in Greek society and the secularization process. The Orthodox Church of Greece continues to be a powerful and influential institution, with a significant impact upon the Greek political sphere, while its influence on the society diminishes during the last years without, though, being considered as insignificant. After the formation of the Greek State in 1830, the Orthodox Church was self-declared a national Church (1833) and became the state's ideological apparatus reproducing the national ideology.[4] This means that the Orthodox Church and the Greek State established close and collaborative relations, without any serious conflicts. On the one hand, the state supported the Church, considering it as the "mother of the nation" and the Church, on the other hand, always supported the national policies and ideology, e.g. the reproduction of Helleno-Christianism.[5] It could be argued that the Orthodox Church of Greece is actually a State Church and this is proved by the existing legal framework, which defines the relations between the two institutions and the legal status of the Church (Sakellariou 2013). According to Article 3 of the Constitution, the prevailing religion in Greece is the religion of the Eastern Orthodox Church of Christ. Moreover, the Constitution starts with the phrase: "In the name of the Holy and Consubstantial and Indivisible Trinity."[6] Some scholars argue that as long as there are such statements in the Constitution, talking about a secular state (Paparizos 1998; Dimitropoulos 2001, 70–80) is quite problematic, while

---

[4]   In Orthodox Christianity, despite the existence of the Ecumenical Patriarchate, almost all Churches are national, i.e. bureaucratically and organizationally independent and not officially belong to the Patriarchate, apart from some exceptions.
[5]   This ideology combines ancient Greece, the Byzantine Empire and Modern Greece, arguing that the Greek nation is unique, blessed by God, characterized by historical and biological continuity and that a true Greek must be Orthodox, implying that religion and nation are inseparable and that the real Greek identity consists necessarily of both these elements.
[6]   For an English translation of the Greek Constitution see https://www.hellenicparliament.gr/UserFiles/f3c70a23-7696-49db-9148-f24dce6a27c8/001-156%20aggliko.pdf (accessed February 10, 2021).

others contend that they are not substantial and have principally a symbolic and historical content (Venizelos 2000, 137–38; Manitakis 2000, 72–74).

It also should be added that in Article 2 of the first chapter of the law regarding the function of the Orthodox Church and its relation with the State (no 590/28.5.1977, Official Gazette A' 146), it is mentioned that the Church of Greece should cooperate with the State on themes of common interest, for example, the Christian education of the youth; the religious service in the army; the support of the institution of marriage and family; [...] the protection of the holy relics and Ecclesiastical and Christian monuments; the establishment of new religious holidays; and asks for the protection of the State whenever the Orthodox religion is insulted. Such a provision also exemplifies the close and privileged relation of the Greek State with the Orthodox Church. In addition, the crucial phrase for the theme discussed in this chapter is, of course, the one referring to both institutions' collaboration on "the Christian education of the youth."

To present and critically comment on every aspect and on all the historical and legal details of the relations between the State and the Orthodox Church is not an easy task and there are many illuminating studies examining this controversial relation from different academic disciplines (Zaharopoulos 1985; Stathopoulos 1993; Troianos and Dimakopoulou 1999; Dimitropoulos 2001; Paparizos 2007; Sakellariou 2008; Mitralexis 2019; Papageorgiou 2019). The above brief presentation of the Church-State relations background is critical in order to understand the impact they have upon the educational system, because this constructed homogeneity was dominant in Greek schools before the rise of religious diversity.[7]

Contrary to the legal and historical framework mentioned above after the restoration of democracy in 1974 and mainly after the socialist rule in 1981, there have been some initiatives to secularize the state and minimize the Church's role and influence on the state apparatus and society.[8] The most important developments, though, have been observed since the 2000s on a variety of issues. In 2000, after pressure from the European Union and the decision of

---

7 For many decades, the main narrative was that the Greek population was Greek Orthodox as of 95 to 98 or even 99 percent. However, since religious affiliation is not officially collected in the census, everyone could make assumptions on this number. According to the surveys mentioned above, it comes out that even if this number were true, now it has been reduced significantly.
8 It should be mentioned that the political declaration of the Socialist Party (PASOK) in 1974 stated, "The Church will be permanently separated from the state and the monastery property will be socialized." The proclamation was never implemented when the party came to power, http://pasok.gr/diakhryxh/ (in Greek) (accessed February 10, 2021).

the Hellenic Data Protection Authority,[9] the socialist government decided to remove religious affiliation from the identity card document (Dimitropoulos 2001, 151–158). This led to a huge reaction from the majority of the Orthodox Church, which organized massive rallies against this decision together with the right-wing opposition (Stavrakakis 2002; Anastassiadis 2004; Molokotos-Liederman 2007; Sakellariou 2014). Despite these reactions, the decision was not withdrawn, as the Church demanded, and it was recorded as one of the most important victories the State won against the powerful Church and a landmark case for the secularization endeavor. From one point of view, it could be argued that this "defeat" for the Church opened a Pandora's box for the establishment of strong secularization initiatives and led secular groups to ask for the further secularization of the Greek State.

Another example is that of civil marriage. Introduced as an option in 1982, five years ago civil wedding ceremonies surpassed religious ones.[10] Such data reveal that Greek people seem to prefer the civil options offered by the state and not the religious one and also suggest that there is a process of secularization happening on the individual and family level as well. Finally, other developments include the legislation in 2006 of cremation centers, the introduction in 2007 of the alternative option of a civil oath in the Greek army and the legislation in 2016 of civil funerals.[11] The impact of the secularization process also could be seen in the electoral success of the Coalition of Radical left (SYRIZA)

---

9   This was the decision 510/17 (May 15, 2000). The Council of State later verified this decision against those who appealed it (decision 2283/2001) and it was backed up by a ruling from the European Court for Human Rights in 2002.

10 According to the available data from 1991, out of 65,568 weddings, only 5,858 were civil. In ten years' time, in 2001, out of 58,491 weddings, 10,404 were civil. In 2016, out of 49,632 weddings, 25,854 were civil and 23,778 religious. After the introduction of the civil partnership option in 2013, the gap between religious and civil ceremony/partnership became even wider. For example, in 2018, the Hellenic Statistical Authority recorded 24,418 civil weddings, 23,010 religious weddings and 6,369 civil partnerships, compared to only 581 civil partnerships in 2013 (See: https://www.statistics.gr/documents/20181/1515741/GreeceInFigures_2020Q1_GR.pdf/fd8b6ddf-0ea2-9d56-e39f-b90671866336 (in Greek) (accessed, February 10, 2021). It should be noted that religious ceremonies taking place after civil wedding are not recorded. While there is the argument that because of the economic crisis of 2010 many couples decided not to make the much more costly religious service, it is not certain that this is the only, if even strong enough, reason for this significant shift.

11 For cremation, the original legislation was law 3448/2006 (Official Gazette, A 57), Article 57 and the new one 4277/2014 (Official Gazette, A 156) Articles 48–49. For the civil funeral, the legislation is law 4368/2016 (Official Gazette, A 21) Article 35A. The civil oath in the army was introduced via the fixed order 9-13/2007 of the Ministry of National Defense/Hellenic Army General Staff.

in 2015. Since most of the party's MPs and Ministers were predominantly not religious and openly in support of not intermingling religion and politics and of the separation of Church and state, it was the first time in the country's political history that the Prime Minister and the majority of the Ministers and MPs gave a civil and not a religious oath in front of the President of the Republic. The two main secular decisions of this government were the abolishment of the blasphemy legislation from the Greek penal code[12] and the Greek Parliament's successful vote to revise Article 3 of the Constitution which, as mentioned above, states that the prevailing religion in Greece is that of the Eastern Orthodox Church of Christ.[13] All the above briefly mentioned could be considered as important legislative measures toward the secularization of the Greek State during the last twenty years, but still many steps needs to be taken before one concludes that the Greek State is actually secular.[14]

---

12   Article 198 of the Penal Code stated, "1. One who publicly and maliciously and by any means blasphemes God shall be punished by imprisonment for not more than two years; 2. Anyone, except as described in paragraph 1, who displays publicly with blasphemy a lack of respect for things divine, is punished with up to three months in prison." Article 199 stated, "One who publicly and maliciously and by any means blasphemes the Greek Orthodox Church or any other religion tolerable in Greece shall be punished by imprisonment for not more than two years." In the new Penal Code, both these articles were abolished. The new penal code can be found here: https://www.e-nomothesia.gr/kat-kodikes-nomothesias/nomos-4619-2019-phek-95a-11-6-2019.html (in Greek) (accessed February 10, 2021).

13   The governmental suggestion was that Article 3 should clearly formulate the state's religious neutrality starting with the phrase: 'The Greek State is religiously neutral'. The reference to the prevailing religion would stay accompanied by an interpretive note arguing that such a statement does not lead to the recognition of a state religion and having no unfavorable consequences against other religions and overall on the exercise of the right of religious freedom. The proposal passed through both voting procedures in 2019 and was analytically discussed by the following Parliamentary synthesis after the national elections of 2019. However, since it needed a vast majority of 180 votes and not a simple majority of 151 in order to change, this suggestion was rejected by the new Parliament. In any case, even this process was considered a huge development for Greece. For this constitutional revision suggestion see https://www.hellenicparliament.gr/UserFiles/c8827c35-4399-4fbb-8ea6-aebdc768f4f7/%CE%88%CE%B3%CE%B3%CF%81%CE%B1%CF%86%CE%BF%20%CE%B1%CF%80%CF%8C%20%CE%A3%CE%B1%CF%81%CF%89%CF%84%CE%AE%20(215135).pdf (in Greek) (accessed February 10, 2021).

14   For example the Greek Constitution still includes the introductory phrase 'In the name of the Holy and Consubstantial and Indivisible Trinity'; Article 3 still stands strong and influential as it will be also clear in the following section on education; the President of the Republic can give only an Orthodox Christian oath before assuming the exercise of his/her duties, implying that no person of other religious beliefs or non-religious could be President, etc. Apart from that, each government maintains close relations with the Orthodox Church and tries to avoid conflicts because the Church can

3   Religious Pluralism and Religious Freedom in the Greek
     Educational System

As already mentioned, since the late 1990s and especially during the 2000s, Greek society gradually became more religiously diverse. This development was due primarily to two factors, the rise of immigration from Eastern Europe, Asia, Africa and the Middle East, and because a significant number of the Greek population started to disengage and distance itself from the Orthodox religion, identifying themselves as atheist, religiously indifferent, non-religious, etc., or in some cases, embracing other religions. This, as expected, started to have an impact upon the educational system and schools, which are far from what one could characterize as secular.[15] During the last decade, a large number of immigrant children, especially Muslims, were integrated into the educational system, while atheists and secularists initiated legal fights in order to be exempted from the religious class. Despite this obvious change, the Greek educational system did not become pluralist. Only two decisions can be described as secular and respecting religious freedom. The first one was taken in 2006 when the practice of exercising the sacrament of confession at schools by Orthodox priests was officially forbidden by the Ministry of Education and Religious Affairs. The second took place in 2008, when the Ministry decided that non-Orthodox pupils could ask for to be exempt from the religious class, which was based almost exclusively on the Orthodox religion and tradition.[16] This provision of exemption has caused heated debates and legal claims since then because the Ministry obliged pupils and their parents to reveal their religious beliefs in order to prove that they are not Orthodox Christians in order to be granted this exemption. In addition, such an official statement, according to

---

politically and ideologically influence people as it has been the case many times in the past (Sakellariou 2008).

15   Although religious affiliation data are not available for schools existing evidence show that immigrants consist around 10 percent of the school population, with a significant rise in the years 1995–96 to 2012–13 from 8,455 to 127,933 (Vitoraki 2015).

16   For the decision on confession see https://www.esos.gr/arthra/43311/ypoyrgos-i-k-giannakoy-apagoreyse-tis-exomologiseis-sta-sholeia, (in Greek) (accessed February 10, 2021) and for the exemption see http://union.atheia.gr/wp-content/uploads/2013/04/109744-2008.pdf, (in Greek) (accessed February 10, 2021). The exemption existed already from 1956 for evangelical pupils and then in the 1980s and 1990s for Jehovah's Witnesses. It was only in 2002 first and then in 2008 that this exemption started to be an option for all non-Orthodox pupils. It was only in 2008, when for the first time there was no need to reveal one's religious beliefs in order to be exempted. However, in 2015, this decision was overturned by the Minister and revealing one's religious convictions again became obligatory.

the ministerial instructions, should take place at the beginning of each school year within two weeks, meaning that if someone would change his/her religious beliefs or decided that the religious class is not compatible with his/her religious beliefs in the middle of the school year, he/she should continue to attend it without the option of being exempted.

The religious class has been one of the main issues of public debates when it comes to religious freedom and the secularization process in the Greek schools with a variety of opinions expressed (Zabeta 2003, 2018; Komninou 2018; Karamouzis 2018; Tsitselikis 2019). The common ground on which almost everyone agrees is that the religious class is Greek Orthodox-dominated in terms of its content, with very little information about other religions. In addition, almost no scientific and critical aspect with regard to religion is included. Even the so-called progressive effort implemented during the last years through the new curriculum and educational material was clearly Greek Orthodox oriented (Giagazoglou 2018). That is why there were many objections expressed arguing that pupils of other or no religion should be able to be exempted from this class.

To seek these exemptions, some parents appealed to the European Court for Human Rights and won the case (*Papageorgiou and others v Greece* 2020).[17] The Court argued that such had been the situation of the applicants who would have been forced into submitting a declaration from which it could have been inferred that they and their children held, or did not hold, a specific religious belief. Indeed, the current system in Greece for exempting children from religious education classes risked exposing sensitive aspects of the applicants' private lives. The system could moreover deter them from making such a request as it involved the school principal having to verify the information on the statement and alerting the public prosecutor in the event of a discrepancy. The potential for conflict was accentuated in the case of the applicants who lived on small islands and/or villages where the vast majority of the population owed allegiance to the Orthodox religion. There the risk of stigmatization is much higher than in the cities. Furthermore, as pointed out by the applicants and accepted by the Court, no other classes were offered to exempted pupils, meaning they would have lost hours of schooling just for their declared beliefs. Stressing that the authorities did not have the right to intervene in the sphere of individual conscience, to ascertain individuals' religious belief or to oblige them to reveal their beliefs, the Court held that there had been a violation of

---

17 For the decision see https://hudoc.echr.coe.int/fre#{%22itemid%22:[%22001-197254%22]} (accessed February 10, 2021).

Article 2 of Protocol 1, as interpreted in light of Article 9 of the Convention for human rights. After this decision, the Ministry of Education and Religious Affairs announced that these considerations would be incorporated into a new form of exemption for the following school year (2020–2021).

When it comes to the religious class content, though, there were some contradictory developments. After the production of the new curriculum and educational material in 2016–2017, mentioned above, a group of Orthodox priests and theologians appealed to the Council of State, arguing that the Greek Constitution says the religious class should be completely Greek Orthodox in content and does not include any kind of information on other religions, although this was certainly not the case (Giagazoglou 2018). Surprisingly, the court accepted their appeal, deciding that Article 3 of the Constitution is still valid, contrary to what some authors (Venizelos 2000) have superficially argued.[18] Article 16 of the Constitution, in paragraph 2, states that education constitutes a basic mission for the State and shall aim at the moral, intellectual, professional, and physical training of Greeks, as well as the development of national and religious consciousness. Although Article 16 doesn't refer specifically to the Orthodox Church, the judges ruled that it directly relates to Article 3, which names it as the dominant religion in Greece.

That ruling means the religious class should be almost exclusively Greek Orthodox, leaving no room for religious diversity and essentially excluding religious pluralism from the Greek schools. At the same time, the court ruled that in case a high number of school students exist, who, because of their religious beliefs, do not wish to attend the class, the Ministry of Education and Religious Affairs should prepare and introduce an alternative one to attend. In addition, the Council of State in another decision ruled that revealing one's religious beliefs in order to be exempted from the religious class is unconstitutional and

---

18   For the decisions of the Council of State see http://www.adjustice.gr/webcenter/portal/ste/ypiresies/nomologies?bltId=24495269&_afrLoop=4827323148425209#!%40%40%3F_afrLoop%3D4827323148425209%26bltId%3D24495269%26centerWidth%3D65%2525%26leftWidth%3D0%2525%26npath%3D%252Fwebcenter%252Fportal%252Fste%252Fypiresies%252Fnomologies%26rigthWidth%3D35%2525%26showFooter%3Dfalse%26showHeader%3Dtrue%26_adf.ctrl-state%3D17w5yaoh4w_197 (in Greek) and http://www.adjustice.gr/webcenter/portal/ste/ypiresies/nomologies?bltId=24495293&_afrLoop=4827361079669366#!%40%40%3F_afrLoop%3D4827361079669366%26bltId%3D24495293%26centerWidth%3D65%2525%26leftWidth%3D0%2525%26npath%3D%252Fwebcenter%252Fportal%252Fste%252Fypiresies%252Fnomologies%26rigthWidth%3D35%2525%26showFooter%3Dfalse%26showHeader%3Dtrue%26_adf.ctrl-state%3D17w5yaoh4w_222 (in Greek) (accessed February 10, 2021).

should be repealed. As a consequence, the situation seems to be as follows: The religious class will stay and become even more Greek Orthodox-orientated, while for those who wish, an exemption should be provided without the obligation to reveal their religious beliefs. This, of course, is a segregated, not inclusionary, approach, since it divides school students between Greek Orthodox and others and certainly doesn't move toward the school's secularization and pluralization.

Apart from the religious class, which mainly leads to the conclusion that the Greek school is not secular and pluralist, there are other issues that support this argument. First of all, until very recently, the Ministry included religious affiliation on the high school diploma.[19] After the appeal of the Atheist Union of Greece and the Hellenic League for Human Rights regarding the exemption from the religious class without revealing one's personal religious affiliation and on putting the student's religious affiliation on the high school diploma, the Hellenic Data Protection Authority published a very important decision.[20] The authority decided that both practices were against human rights (religious freedom) and unconstitutional, not respecting personal data protection, and urged the Ministry to take all the necessary measures to correct these practices. The Ministry omitted religious affiliation from the new diploma forms.[21] Although perhaps not the most important issue, the presence of religious symbols in Greek schools (e.g. religious icons and crucifixes) also is a topic of debate over religious freedom and pluralism. And there are three other religious practices that add to the argument of the non-secularity and lack of pluralism in the Greek schools, raising again questions about religious freedom. First, on the opening day of each school year a priest performs the religious ceremony

---

19 The decision can be found here https://www.dpa.gr/portal/page?_pageid=33,15453&_dad=portal&_schema=PORTAL (in Greek) (accessed February 10, 2021).
20 The decision can be found here https://www.dpa.gr/portal/page?_pageid=33%2C15453&_dad=portal&_schema=PORTAL&_piref33_15473_33_15453_15453.etos=2019&_piref33_15473_33_15453_15453.arithmosApofasis=28&_piref33_15473_33_15453_15453.thematikiEnotita=-1&_piref33_15473_33_15453_15453.ananeosi=%CE%91%CE%BD%CE%B1%CE%BD%CE%AD%CF%89%CF%83%CE%B7 (in Greek) (accessed February 10, 2021).
21 For the Ministry's reactions on those decisions one can see https://www.minedu.gov.gr/rss/42760-05-09-19-to-ypourgeio-paideias-kai-thriskevmaton-gia-tin-apofasi-tis-arxis-prostasias-dedomenon-prosopikoy-xaraktira-2, https://www.minedu.gov.gr/rss/42887-17-09-19-tropopoiisi-rythmiseon-anaforika-me-tin-anagrafi-tou-thriskeymatos-kai-tis-ithageneias-stous-titlous-kai-sta-pistopoiitika-spoudon, (in Greek) and https://www.minedu.gov.gr/rss/43389-01-10-19-dilosi-tis-ypourgoy-paideias-kai-thriskevmaton-me-aformi-tin-apofasi-tou-evropaikoy-dikastiriou-anthropinon-dikaiomaton, (in Greek) (accessed February 10, 2021).

of consecration in every school. In some cases, he even gives school students copies of the New Testament. Second, every morning before the start of school, pupils assemble for an obligatory collective prayer.[22] Third, with regard to the church attendance, which on average takes place three to five times per year, there is again the option of not attending for those who do not wish, and they can go to school one hour later, although such a provision is not made for the kindergarten. This again is not in any case an inclusionary policy and segregates children. In addition, there are other occasions showing the non-secular character of the Greek school, e.g. the celebration of the Three Holy Fathers, Great Hierarchs and Ecumenical Teachers, as they are called, Basil the Great, Gregory the Theologian, and John Chrysostom. This is a national school holiday. However, while in 2018 it was decided that pupils would just stay at home, the Ministry in 2020 decided to return to the status quo, meaning that during this day teachers should talk to children about the importance of these three Orthodox figures and/or also attend the church in the morning in order to celebrate them.

The above-described context signifies that religious freedom in the Greek educational system is at stake. For example, Article 2 of the First Protocol to the Convention for the Protection of Human Rights and Fundamental Freedoms says, "No person shall be denied the right to education. In the exercise of any functions which it assumes in relation to education and to teaching, the State shall respect the right of parents to ensure such education and teaching in conformity with their own religious and philosophical convictions." And in Article 9, paragraph 1, concerning freedom of thought, conscience and religion, it says, "everyone has the right to freedom of thought, conscience and religion; this right includes freedom to change his religion or belief and freedom, either alone or in community with others and in public or private, to manifest his religion or belief, in worship, teaching, practice and observance." Furthermore, according to the Convention on the Rights of the Child, which Greece has signed (1990, Article 14), 1) Parties shall respect the right of the child to freedom of thought, conscience and religion; 2) Parties shall respect

---

22 For both such practices (prayer and church attendance) parents and the Hellenic League for Human Rights have appealed to the Council of State, arguing that they are against religious freedom. In May 2020, the court decided (decision 942/2020) that both practices are constitutional and that within the framework of the educational process are considered as necessary means, together with the religious class, in order to fulfill the constitutional provision of Article 16, i.e. to develop the religious consciousness of the Greek population. However, the court decided that a provision of exemption from both religious practices should be made available for all those who do not belong in the Orthodox religion, following again a segregated model in education.

the rights and duties of the parents and, when applicable, legal guardians, to provide direction to the child in the exercise of his or her right in a manner consistent with the evolving capacities of the child; and that 3) Freedom to manifest one's religion or beliefs may be subject only to such limitations as are prescribed by law and are necessary to protect public safety, order, health or morals, or the fundamental rights and freedoms of others.

Looking into these legal provisions, there is no mention that the school is responsible for the religious upbringing of children. Instead, it is repeatedly mentioned that children's and parent's beliefs should be respected. But if religion is going to be taught in schools, the question still stands: Whose religion? And then the essential challenge would be how to include and teach religion in schools while protecting the right of an individual to freedom of thought, conscience and belief (Beaman and van Arragon 2015, 282). A solution could be if education about religion served two principle purposes: First, treating in theory all religions equally by subjecting them to the same rules of critical thought deployed in other subjects and, second, be seen as a way of teaching values considered essential for living in a modern, diverse and democratic society (Beaman and van Arragon 2015, 1). Beyond that it is up to the parents to decide together with their children if they wish to pray, attend the Mass or confession, but to do it outside of school. As it has been rightly argued, in a plural society the proclamation of a single, exclusive and particular religious truth is bound to cause offense, doubly so if this one truth is imposed on all children under the aegis of a state-sponsored education system (Wright 2004, 183) as it takes place in Greece.

4 Conclusion

There have been some efforts to respond to the dominance of secularism in the field of educational discourses around citizenship and civic education. Such responses argue that religious people and communities, as well as religious ideas, have much to offer to democratic societies (Arthur, Gearson and Sears 2010, 3–5) and that religion, particularly the Judeo-Christian religious tradition of the West, has played a substantial role in the development of contemporary ideas of human rights and democracy (Arthur, Gearson and Sears 2010, 139–40). On the other hand, others have argued that religion should never again be introduced into the common public school in a way that will make a secular child feel less welcome, but it should be vigorously introduced in ways in which children of all faith traditions will be equally at home (Frazer 1999, 6).

Questions of the role of religion in public schools do not occur in isolation, however, being a subset of wider questions on the role of religion in society since public schools are approached as microcosms of the societies in which they exist and develop (Beaman and van Arragon 2015, 1). This means that from the moment Greek society becomes more religiously diverse and to some degree secular (both on the individual and institutional levels), the educational system should accommodate these developments leading to an inclusionary neutrality as the most appropriate stance for public school religious education (Beaman and van Arragon 2015, 253) or what has been called a neutrality of understanding instead of a neutrality of indifference (Debray 2004, 44).

What then are the main conclusions with regard to the Greek educational system? A statement arguing that religious freedom is being violated probably would not be accurate. However, it is difficult to say that the Greek school system actually respects the religious beliefs and religious freedom of the children and their parents. More appropriate would be the argument that the school system merely tolerates religious diversity, without trying to incorporate it. This is definitely proved by the fact that the Ministry of Education and Religious Affairs proceeded to the vast majority of the changes mentioned in the above analysis only after court decisions and not from a genuine pluralist approach that would lead to such initiatives. With this in mind, it could be argued that the road to the full implementation and respect of religious freedom and pluralism in Greek schools is still long and relates to the secularization process of the broader state apparatus and legal system.

References

Ammerman, Nancy. 2010. "The Challenges of Pluralism: Locating Religion in a World of Diversity." *Social Compass* 57 (2): 154–67.

Anastassiadis, Anastassios. 2004. "Religion and Politics in Greece: The Greek Church's 'Conservative Modernization' in the 1990s." *Questions de recherché* 11: 1–35.

Arthur, James, Gearon, Liam, and Sears, Alan. 2010. *Education, Politics and Religion: Reconciling the Civil and the Sacred in Education*. Oxon: Routledge.

Beaman, Lori and van Arragon, Leon. 2015. *Issues in Religion and Education. Whose Religion?* Leiden: Brill.

Beckford, James. 2014. "Re-Thinking Religious Pluralism". In *Religious Pluralism: Framing Religious Diversity in the Contemporary World*, edited by Giuseppe Giordan and Enzo Pace, 15–29. Cham: Springer.

Bender, Courtney and Klassen, E. Pamela, eds. 2010. *After Pluralism: Reimagining Religious Engagement*. New York: Columbia University Press.

Berglund, Jenny, Shanneik, Yafa and Bocking, Brian, eds. 2016. *Religious Education in a Global-Local World*. Cham: Springer.

Bouma, D. Gary and Ling, Rod. 2011. "Religious Diversity." In *The Oxford Handbook of the Sociology of Religion*, edited by Peter Clarke, 507–22. New York: Oxford University Press.

Breskaya, Olga, Giordan, Giuseppe, and Richardson T. James. 2018. "Human Rights and Religion: A Sociological Perspective." *Journal for the Scientific Study of Religion* 57 (3): 419–31.

Casanova, José. 2006. "Rethinking Secularization: A Global Comparative Perspective." *Hedgehog Review*, 8 (1–2): 7–22.

Christopoulos, Dimitris, ed. 1999. *Legal Issues of Religious Diversity in Greece*. Athens: Kritiki (in Greek).

Clogg, Richard, ed. 2002. *Minorities in Greece: Aspects of a Plural Society*. London: Hurst and Co.

Debray, Régis. 2004. *Teaching Religion in a Religious Neutral School*. Athens: Hestia (in Greek).

Demerath, N. Jay III. 2007. "Secularization and Sacralization Deconstructed and Reconstructed." In *The Sage Handbook of the Sociology of Religion*, edited by James Beckford and Jay Demerath III, 58–80. London: Sage.

Diamantopoulou, Elisabeth. 2012. "Religious freedom in the light of the relationship between the Orthodox Church and the nation in contemporary Greece." *International Journal for the Study of the Christian Church*, 12 (2): 164–75.

Dianeosis. 2016. "What Greeks believe in." Accessed February 10, 2021. https://www.dianeosis.org/research/greek_values/ (in Greek).

Dianeosis. 2020. "What Greeks believe in." Accessed February 10, 2021. https://www.dianeosis.org/2020/03/ti-pistevoun-oi-ellines-to-2020/ (in Greek).

Dimitropoulos, Panagiotis. 2001. *Church and State: A Difficult Relation*. Athens: Kritiki (in Greek).

Dobbelaere, Karel. 1981. "Trend Report: Secularization: A Multi-dimensional Concept." *Current Sociology* 29 (2): 3–153.

Dobbelaere, Karel. 2002. *Secularization: An Analysis at Three Levels*. Brussels: P.I.E.-Peter Lang.

Dobbelaere, Karel. 2011. "The Meaning and Scope of Secularization." In *The Oxford Handbook of the Sociology of Religion*, edited by Peter Clarke, 599–615. New York: Oxford University Press.

Frazer, W. James. 1999. *Between Church and State: Religion and Public Education in a Multicultural America*. New York: Palgrave Macmillan.

Fokas, Effie. 2012. " 'Eastern' Orthodoxy and 'Western' Secularisation in Contemporary Europe (with Special Reference to the Case of Greece)." *Religion, State and Society*, 40 (3–4): 395–414.

Fokas, Effie. 2015. "Directions in Religious Pluralism in Europe: Mobilizations in the Shadow of European Court of Human Rights Religious Freedom Jurisprudence." *Oxford Journal of Law and Religion* 4 (1): 54–74.

Giagazoglou, Stavros. 2018. "Pluralism or Confessional Mentality in the Religious Class?" Accessed February, 10, 2020. http://ejournals.lib.auth.gr/religionteaching/article/view/6225 (in Greek).

Giordan, Giuseppe and Pace, Enzo, eds. 2014. *Religious Pluralism: Framing Religious Diversity in the Contemporary World.* Cham: Springer.

Joppke, Christian. 2015. *The Secular State under Siege. Religion and Politics in Europe and America.* Cambridge: Polity Press.

Kapa Research. 2015. *Easter, Faith and Religion in Greece.* Accessed February 10, 2021. https://kaparesearch.com/%CF%80%CE%AC%CF%83%CF%87%CE%B1-%CF%80%CE%AF%CF%83%CF%84%CE%B7-%CE%BA%CE%B1%CE%B9-%CE%B8%CF%81%CE%B7%CF%83%CE%BA%CE%B5%CE%AF%CE%B1-%CF%83%CF%84%CE%B7%CE%BD-%CE%B5%CE%BB%CE%BB%CE%AC%CE%B4%CE%B1/ (in Greek).

Karamouzis, Polykarpos. 2007. *Culture and Interreligious Education.* Athens: Ellinika Grammata (in Greek).

Karamouzis, Polykarmpos and Athanassiadis, Ilias. 2011. *Religion, Education and Post-Modernity.* Athens: Kritiki (in Greek).

Karamouzis, Polykarpos. 2018. "Religious Education Between Inter—School Function, Religious Perceptions and Social Practices of the Religious Field: A Case Study." *Social Cohesion and Development* 13 (1): 47–58.

Komninou, Ioanna. 2018. "The Changes of Religious Education since 2011 and the Impact to Religious Identities." *Social Cohesion and Development* 13 (1): 33–46.

Manitakis, Antonis. 2000. *The Relations of the Church with the Nation-State.* Athens: Nefeli (In Greek).

Markoviti, Margarita. 2017. "The 'filtering effects' of ECtHR case law on religious freedoms: legal recognition and places of worship for religious minorities in Greece." *Religion, State and Society,* 45 (3–4): 268–83.

Mitralexis, Sotiris. 2019. *State-Church Relations.* Athens: Armos (in Greek).

Molokotos-Liederman, Lina. 2007. "The Greek ID Card Controversy: A Case Study of Religion and National Identity in a Changing European Union." *Journal of Contemporary Religion,* 22 (2): 187–203.

Papageorgiou, Minas. 2019. *Church-State Separation.* Athens: iWrite (in Greek).

Paparizos, Antonis. 1998. "Du caractére religieux de l 'etat grec modern." *Revista de Ciencias de Las Religiones* 3, 183–207.

Paparizos, Antonis. 2007. "Religion and Politics, Church and State in Contemporary Reality." In *Politics and Religions,* edited by Konstantinos Zorbas, 101–60. Athens: Papazisis (in Greek).

Paparizos, Antonis 1998. "Du Caractére Religieux de l 'Etat Grec Modern." *Revista de Ciencias de Las Religiones*, 3: 183–207.

Perselis, Emmanouil. 2011. *Power and Religious Education in Greece during the 19th Century*. Athens: Grigoris (in Greek).

Pew. 2017. Europe's Growing Muslim Population. Accessed February 10, 2021. https://www.pewforum.org/2017/11/29/europes-growing-muslim-population/.

Public Issue. 2008. *Opinion Poll on Religion*. Accessed 21 May 2020. https://www.publicissue.gr/96/religion/ (in Greek).

Sakellariou, Alexandros. 2008. "Dictatorships and the Orthodox Church in Greece during the 20th century: Political, Economic and Ideological Relations under Regimes of Emergency." PhD diss., Panteion University of Athens (in Greek).

Sakellariou, Alexandros. 2013. "Religion and National Identity in Greece: The Identity Card Crisis and the Islamic Mosque Issue." In *Europe as a Multiple Modernity: Multiplicity of Religious and Identities and Belonging*, edited by Martina Topic and Srdjan Sremac, 194–211. Newcastle upon Tyne: Cambridge Scholars Publishing.

Sakellariou, Alexandros. 2014. "Religion in Greek Society: State, Public or Private?" In *Religion Beyond its Private Role in Modern Society*, edited by Wim Hofstee and Arie van der Kooij, 153–66. Leiden: Brill.

Sjöborg, Andres and Ziebertz, Hans-Georg, eds. 2017. *Religion, Education and Human Rights*. Cham: Springer.

Sotirelis, Giorgos. 1998. *Religion and Education*. Athens-Komotini: Ant. N.Sakkoulas (in Greek).

Stathopoulos, Michalis. 1993. *Church and State Relations*. Athens-Komotini: Sakkoulas (in Greek).

Stavrakakis, Giannis. 2002. "Religion and Populism: Reflections on the 'politicised' discourse of the Greek Church." Discussion Paper no 7. The Hellenic Observatory: LSE.

Temperman, Jeroen. 2019. "Education and Freedom of Religion or Belief under the European Convention on Human Rights and Protocol No. 1." In *The European Court of Human Rights and the Freedom of Religion or Belief: The 25 Years since Kokkinakis,* edited by Jeroen Temperman, Jeremy Gunn, Malcolm Evans, 178–208. Leiden: Brill.

Troianos, Spyros and Dimakopoulou, Charikleia. 1999. *Church and State: Their Relations during the 19th Century*. Athens-Komotini: Sakkoulas (in Greek).

Tsitselikis, Konstantinos. 2019. "Religion in Schools: Constitutional and International Boundaries." Accessed February 10, 2021. https://www.constitutionalism.gr/2019-12-tsitselikis-thriskeia-sholeio/ (in Greek).

Venizelos, Evangelos. 2000. *State-Church Relations*. Thessaloniki: Paratiritis (in Greek).

Vitoraki, Anastassia. 2015. *European Policies about the Education and Integration of Migrant Children*, Master Thesis. Athens: Harokopio University (in Greek).

Wright, Andrew. 2004. *Religion, Education and Post-Modernity*. London: Routledge.

Yang, Fenggang. 2014. "Oligopoly Is Not Pluralism." In *Religious Pluralism: Framing Religious Diversity in the Contemporary World,* edited by Giuseppe Giordan and Enzo Pace, 49–59. Cham: Springer.

Zaharopoulos, Nikos. 1985. *History of the Church-State Relations in Greece.* Thessaloniki: Pournaras (in Greek).

Zampeta, Evi. 2018. "Religion, Democracy and Education." *Social Cohesion and Development,* 13 (1): 19–31.

Zampeta, Evi. 2003. *School and Religion.* Athens: Themelio (in Greek).

Zoumpoulakis, Stavros. 2002. *God in the City: Essays on Religion and Politics.* Athens: Hestia (in Greek).

PART 2

Multi-level Study of Religious Freedom

∴

CHAPTER 5

Regulating Sincerity: Religion, Law, Public Policy, and the Ambivalence of Religious Freedom in Pluralist Societies

Zaheeda P. Alibhai

The sincerity of belief among Muslim women who wear the niqab and burqa[1] has increasingly become an issue under legal scrutiny in many countries around the globe. For instance, in the Canadian case *R. v N.S.* 2012, where the Supreme Court faced the decision between the right of a Muslim woman to wear her niqab while testifying as a victim in a sexual assault trial against her male Muslim relatives. During the preliminary inquiry, during which N.S. described wearing the niqab "as part of me," the presiding judge asserted that her belief was "not that strong" and "not sincerely held" since she had on several occasions removed her niqab during border checks and for taking her driver's license picture. This is the same argument the Federal Canadian Conservative government submitted to the court in *Zunera Ishaq v. Canada (Minister of Citizenship and Immigration)*, where Ms. Ishaq legally challenged the Canadian Conservative government's face-covering ban during the oath of Citizenship. In the French case of Mme. M., her citizenship request was denied by France's Conseil d'Etat on the primary basis that she adopted wearing the niqab after she immigrated to France from Morocco. The Conseil ruled that she wore the niqab not out of sincere religiosity but out of custom rather than conviction.[2] The implications of this becomes the marginalization and delimitation of a group's religious beliefs that become "defined out" (McGuire 2008, 74) as no longer legitimately religious and no longer worthy of a citizen's right to religious freedom. This chapter analyses the interlocking systems of power

---

1 Niqab is a face covering veil with the eyes showing and burqa is a full-covered body with netting in front of the eyes.
2 Muslim women who cover do so for a variety of reasons, including as a tool of empowerment or modesty, or a public expression of religious, ethnic, and cultural identity. For some, veiling is a religious obligation; these women interpret specific verses in the Qur'an (24:30–31; 33:59) as divine commands to cover as an embodiment of modesty and an integral step on their road to piety. These verses have been interpreted, debated, and argued amongst varying communities both inside and outside of Islam. Scholars, historians, and communities differ over this historically complex issue (Alibhai 2019, 126).

between the "judicialization of religious freedom" (Richardson 2015) and the regulation of sincerity of belief. Situated within a fraught political and social environment, I then critically examine how sociological understandings of lived religion as practice can conflict with state and legal definitions over what constitutes "religious freedom." I conclude by arguing that the judicialization of religious freedom has become instrumental for niqab-wearing Muslim women's legal claims.

This chapter unfolds in three sections. Section I sets out the analytical framework within which this chapter understands the "judicialization of religious freedom" and lived religion setting out of the context from which the cases are adjudicated. Section II of this chapter discusses the legal case, *Zunera Ishaq v. Canada* (Minister of Citizenship and Immigration), and critically analyzes the dimensions of normative intervention that formed the basis for the issuance of the 2011–2015 Canadian Conservative government's ban on the wearing of face coverings, specifically the niqab and burqa, during the Oath of Citizenship at Canadian citizenship ceremonies. I turn then to the *R. v N.S.* legal case and the French case of Mme. M. I conclude with a discussion of the Zunera Ishaq and the N.S. legal cases and raise several issues relating to the judicialization of religious freedom, lived practice of religion, and normative intervention.

1   The Politics of Religious Freedom

The judicialization of politics captures the increasing trend toward the expansion of the province of the courts and the judiciary to arbitrate and reflect on deep moral and political dilemmas, and public policy outcomes at the "expense of the politicians and/or the administrators, that is, the transfer of decision-making rights from the legislature, the cabinet or the civil service to the courts" (Vallinder 1994, 91). Hirschl Ran (2011) argues that one of the most problematic of this form of judicialization include formative collective identity and nation-building processes and struggles over the very definition — or raison d'etre — of the polity (Ran 2011, 257) that has become "inextricable from law's capture of social relationships, popular culture, and its expropriation of social conflicts" (Ran 2011, Teubner 1987, Habermas 1988). According to Ran, adjudicating such matters then, necessitates three critical requirements: the existence of a constitutional framework that promotes the judicialization of politics; a relatively autonomous judiciary that is easily enticed to dive into deep political waters; and above all, a political environment that is conducive to the judicialization of politics (Ran 2011, 258). On the basis of the previous discussion, it is important to keep the judicialization of politics in mind — since it leaves a formative imprint on how the judicialization of religious freedom intersects with, as Talal Asad argues, a distinctive feature of modern liberal governance, that is neither compulsion nor negotiation but statecraft that uses "self-discipline," "participation," and "law" as elements of political strategy (Asad 2003, 3).

In his influential article titled, "Managing Religion and the Judicialization of Religious Freedom" (2015), James T. Richardson draws from the term the "judicialization of politics" to argue that in many modern societies, courts rather than legislative or executive branches decide major political issues. In this way and in some societies, the courts have assumed the role of "ultimate decider," with the ability to rule against executive directives, legislation passed by legislators (Richardson 2015, 4) and as I discuss below, overrule ministerial directives. Richardson posits the conceptual model "judicialization of religious freedom" to shed light on the increased reliance on the courts to adjudicate in religious matters. The critical point here, Richardson argues, is that the courts in several Western countries are playing a principal role in defining and expanding the meaning of religious freedom and in this way, the courts are deeply involved in the social construction of religious freedom (13). Richardson (4) asserts that, "religious freedom is being interpreted in new and different ways." The meaning of religious freedom expands and in the process enables newer, smaller, and/or less popular faiths the freedom to practice their religion with less fear of being attacked in the legal arena (10). From this perspective, Richardson highlights a crucial feature of the judicialization of religious freedom — an autonomous judicial system that includes those occupying positions of authority in that system to share the values of tolerance and religious freedom (Richardson 2006). The autonomy of the courts and judiciary can serve to protect newer and minority religious groups from the impulses of political decision makers and legislative power majorities (Richardson 2006, Finke and Robert 2014). Finke and Martin (2014) caution that, "when the judiciary falls under the control of other religious or political institutions and leaders, this influence compromises the ability of the court to protect the promised freedoms, even when such freedoms are clearly promised in the constitution. In short, an independent judiciary holds the state accountable for the freedoms promised in the constitution" (Finke and Martin 2014, 701).

Richardson furthers that an autonomous judicial system can act as a protective measure against two variables that can limit the religious freedom of practitioners. First, newer and smaller religious groups usually have lower "status and prestige" than the group's opponents. Second, key decision makers may be unfamiliar with new and minority faiths and in the process share negative or ill-informed views of the groups and/or their practices, and those views can become influential and "hegemonic through negative media coverage" and the public statements and actions of societal opinion leaders and in our case, government officials and the former Canadian prime minister. For example, the Canadian Conservative government defended their ban against Muslim women from wearing the niqab and burqa during the oath of allegiance at Canadian citizenship ceremonies with similar arguments articulated by two Canadian Muslim organizations: The Muslim Canadian Congress (MCC) and the Coalition of Progressive Muslim Organizations (CPMO). Both social organizations claim to represent their idea of moderate Canadian Muslims. Although neither organization makes public the number of members they represent, instead they view their respective groups as umbrella organizations linked with other organizations. The MCC and the CPMO maintain positions that perceive the niqab and burqa as cultural products and not a religious obligation or right. The implications of this obstructs the historical and cultural assumptions that undergird the way that the "decision makers," such as government officials, collude with dominant religious groups and spokespeople to advance what Richardson terms "normative intervention" through public statements and the court to relegate some practices, behaviors, and beliefs as being unacceptable in "normal" society (Richardson 2006, 289). Indeed, to countermand these issues, I turn to lived religion as practice in my second section to explore the Zunera Ishaq legal case and demonstrate that an autonomous judicial system is crucial to maintaining religious freedom for niqab-wearing Muslim women.

2   Lived Religion

The study of lived religion as practice necessitates a revisioning, questioning, and rethinking of what religion is, where it is found, how it is practiced, and what it means to be religious (Hall 1997). Meredith McGuire (2008) argues that when we focus on religion-as-lived, we discover that religion is "made" and "unmade," shaped, reshaped, and experienced on the "secular" terrain of the "everyday." In this respect, Nancy Ammerman (2007) contends that to start from the everyday is to privilege the experience of non-experts. However, this does not mean that religion is completely decoupled from organized, religious institutions, and normative practices (Alibhai 2019, 52) but it does destabilize claims of religion operating solely behind the walls, theologically virtuous, or living in its assigned place (Asad 2011). Moreover the paradox and danger that emerges when the focus of religion as lived and practiced in everyday life then often stands in contrast to the prescribed beliefs and practices of official institutions (Ammerman 2016, 87) and becomes a subject for the courts.

Taking Asad's point as the basis for understanding lived religion in this chapter, I now turn to Nancy Ammerman's (2020) rethinking and broadening of the study of lived religion. Ammerman contends that one of the implications of three decades of scholarship on lived religion is that it has been largely defined by what it excludes. According to the now generally accepted framework by sociologists writing on lived religion, Ammerman argues that the study of lived religion has been constrained by the "tendency to define the subject *over against* the study of belief and doctrine, organizations and memberships, or elites and leaders" (Ammerman 2020, 10). The emphasis of which as Penny Edgell (2012) argues has most often been a focus on individual choice and agency and how the individual creates, shapes, and molds religious ideas and practices. What emerges from such an approach, Ammerman cautions, is that when the point of analysis begins from an "individualist" approach, the underemphasis of traditions and institutions permits the research to slip into dichotomies, hierarchies, and dualities that reduces the role and influence of anything "official," by erecting boundaries between organized religion as inauthentic in relation to lived religion (Ammerman 2020, 10). According to Ammerman this leaves unexplained the religion that takes organized form, including the religion that is located in other cultures, nations, and social settings (11). Ammerman furthers that if, "lived religion is about what people *do*, starting with an artificial line between organized religion and everyday life is not especially helpful" (Ammerman 2016, 89) and can as I argue, produce totalizing narratives that reduces religious practices to cultural innovations. The implications as Richardson (2015) cautions, can have an inhibiting effect on what constitutes religious freedom and who is worthy of its protections.

It is important to note that Ammerman's revisioning of the study of lived religion is not a critique of lived religion per se but as a means toward developing a deeper, expansive, and contemporary field of study that is more inclusive in geographic scope, institutional settings, and traditions. The nature of this then, can be brought into clearer focus as Ammerman argues for an additional set of layers of analysis to the study of lived religion (2016, 88) that encompasses the fruitful gains of over two decades of lived religion scholarship along with the substance of lived religious practice. Ammerman suggests that to broaden the scope includes a re-focused lens on the practices of lived religious communities that, "remind us that symbols, rituals and myths — no matter how individual or chosen they appear—are collective productions and travel beyond the places where they are originally produced" (Ammerman 2020, 95). This is not to say that the agency of the individual is simulated or insincere but that practices that are lived in everyday contexts may be taking root inside religious institutions (Ammerman 2020, 95). Asad (2006), Hurd (2015) and Mahmood (2005) make these epistemic points clear, religion does not exist in a vacuum separated or independent from institutional or organized religion (Hurd 2015, 13); rather, religious practices unfold, effectuate, and are entangled in all domains of the social, political, and economic spheres. What emerges from such an approach, as Ammerman points out, is to move toward understanding lived religion as "practice" that is inclusive to a wide and expansive range of human religious practices that can be constituted and reconstituted from religious institutions, texts, and cultural histories and habits.

3   Religion as Lived and Practiced: Normative Interventions Zunera Ishaq v. The Minister of Citizenship and Immigration 2015

On December 12, 2011, the former Canadian Immigration, Citizenship and Multiculturalism Minister, Jason Kenney, announced that the Conservative government was placing a ban on full and partial face coverings during the recitation of the oath of allegiance at Canadian citizenship ceremonies. The government's rationale was that an oath of citizenship is a "public declaration that you are joining the Canadian family, and it must be taken freely and openly — not with faces hidden" (Payton 2011). Indeed, the minister further elaborated using the language of the Canadian Charter of Rights and Freedoms that the Canadian family is undergirded by liberal, democratic values, including respect for freedom of religion, equality between men and women, as well as equality of all citizens before the law. To that end, the minister argued that covering one's face undermined those basic liberal values since he asserted the practice was a "tribal" and "cultural custom" and "not a religious obligation" (Payton 2011). Minister Kenney's statements highlight the power of normative intervention when used by the state. Normative intervention can be assessed in numerous ways, including in terms of inclusionary and exclusionary regimes that reify and legitimate representations and beliefs about people as a tenable argument that not only has a limiting effect on religious freedom but the "decision makers" draw the lines and boundaries between what are accepted forms of religion and unaccepted forms of religion in society. The danger of limiting religious freedom in this way is especially acute when constructing and assigning normative status to believers, individuals and groups of people since normalization establishes the measure and yardstick from which the newer, smaller religious group are defined, compared, and deemed worthy or unworthy of religious freedom. The crucial point here is that normative intervention contains messages and the rules of conduct — what Foucault refers to as the conduct of tacit rules that lay the framework for the structures of normalization (Foucault 1978). Moreover, structures of normalization convey messages about "what *is* (emphasis mine) the norm and what *is* not (emphasis mine). In effect — they establish the norm" (Carabine 2001, 277).

For example, the link between national values and religion adopted by the Canadian Conservative government became a signifier for real "old stock Canadians" and a technique of governance to enforce practices of a particular religion and indoctrinate citizens in particular beliefs and ways of being a Canadian. The danger and implications are especially acute and must be kept in sight since the power to define the object is a power that Foucault argues is mediated through a desired norm. Richardson (2006) argues that when assigning normative status to individuals and/or groups of people, in other words, normalization establishes the measure and political process by which all are judged, measured, compared, and deemed to conform to or not. Normative interventions by the state privileges some forms of religion over others and as Richardson argues, creates hierarchies of religious groups that serve as social control agents (278). Equally problematic, Talal Asad (2006) contends that the persistent tendency of the state to regulate religious life and practices should be understood as an exercise in sovereign power. Therefore, Richardson's concern is that the state's use of the legal system as a social control mechanism for normative intervention used against smaller religious groups and practices that are perceived as "unpopular" can embed a legally sanctioned diminution of their religious freedom (Richardson 2006, 287). The Conservative government implemented the new regulation on the same day as an immediate directive under Operation Bulletin 359, which expedited the ban and extracted it from the legislative process and Parliamentary debates.

On December 30, 2013, Zunera Ishaq's application for Canadian citizenship was approved by a citizenship judge. Ms. Ishaq, a former high school English teacher from Lahore, Pakistan, immigrated to Canada in 2008. She successfully completed all the necessary prerequisites (including taking the citizenship test) of the Citizenship Regulations; except for the final and mandatory requirement — the recitation of the oath of Canadian citizenship. Pursuant to subsection 5(1) of the Citizenship Act, RSC 1985, c C-29 [ACT], a prospective citizen must take the oath of citizenship in order to be considered a Canadian citizen. On January 14, 2014, Zunera Ishaq was due to recite her oath at the office Citizenship and Immigration Canada (CIC). Instead, on January 9, 2014, she filed an application for judicial review with the Federal Court of Canada. Ms. Ishaq agreed with the content of the oath. Her objection was with the Federal Conservative government's amendment to the Canadian Immigration

Citizenship's policy manual, *CP 15: Guide to Citizenship Ceremonies* section: 6.5.1: Candidates wearing face coverings are required to remove their face coverings for the oath taking portion of the ceremony (Ishaq 2015, 2–3). Ms. Ishaq believed that the amendment required her to temporarily abandon her religious beliefs. A devout Sunni Muslim who follows the Hanafi school of thought, her religious beliefs obligate her to wear a niqab in public and when in the presence of un-related males. Ms. Ishaq filed for judicial review.

Indeed, it is precisely here that Ms. Ishaq challenged the government's ban on face-coverings strategically seeking a declaration between two models of judicial review. First, an abstract model that enables legal challenges to a law/policy *before* (emphasis mine) it is applied and takes effect to determine whether it violates the law in the abstract, (Mayrl 2018, 521) and (2) concrete model that requires an actual case — and only then may be applied to determine whether the active law violates the constitution (521). She submitted to the court that the government's policy in the Canadian Charter of Rights and Freedoms, Part I of the Constitution Act, 1982 sections 2(a), affirms the fundamental freedom of conscience and religion and 15(1) every individual is equal before and under the law and has the right to the equal protection and equal benefit of the law without discrimination and, in particular, without discrimination based on race, national, or ethnic origin, color, religion, sex, age, or mental or physical disability. In a striking formulation in an affidavit to the court, Zunera Ishaq linked the government's policy, her religious beliefs and the denial of access to citizenship:

> My religious beliefs would compel me to refuse to take off my veil in the context of a citizenship oath ceremony, and I firmly believe that based on existing policies, I would therefore be denied Canadian citizenship. I feel the governmental policy regarding veils at citizenship oath ceremonies is a personal attack on me, my identity as a Muslim woman, and my religious beliefs.
> ISHAQ 2015

In stark contrast, court transcripts reveal that the Respondent (Minister of Citizenship and Immigration) argued that Ms. Ishaq "asserted nothing more than a subjective belief," since "she had removed her veil in the past," therefore, in the government's view the removal of her veil would be nothing more than "a trivial violation, as the oath takes less than a minute to recite." Moreover, the respondent noted since the Applicant had removed her veil for her driver's license, security and identity purposes, therefore "the effects are not onerous" as "wearing the niqab is just a personal choice" (Ishaq 2015). The minimization of Ishaq's religious belief as that which can be suspended — even for less than a minute — and then resumed, trivializes the harm and exclusion that Ms. Ishaq contended was the purpose of the government's policy to "compel her and others like her to temporarily abandon a religious practice" (Ishaq 2015). Nancy Ammerman (2020) argues that a practice-based study of religion provides the analytical space to shed light on what practitioners are doing when they say they are doing religion, more aptly what are practitioners doing when culture, law, or the state complicate the use of that term (9). Ms. Ishaq's legal argument was not that her religious practice conflicted or contradicted with Canadian values but that her religious *and* Canadian values were prevented from co-existing by the government's policy. When we study religion as practice, we shed light on the interweaving of religious identity with the emergence of new identities (new citizen) and how practitioners co-construct their experiences to reflect the suppleness of both.

On February 6, 2015, the presiding Federal Court judge, Keith Boswell, ruled in Ms. Ishaq's favor and deemed that the Government's ban against wearing the niqab during the oath of allegiance at the Canadian citizenship ceremony is unlawful. Judge Boswell ruled that there was a conflict between the ministerial directive and with current Citizenship Regulations that directed citizenship judges to administer the oath of citizenship with dignity and solemnity that allows for the greatest possible religious freedom in the religious solemnization or solemn affirmation of the oath (Ishaq 2015). Moreover, he asked, "How can a citizenship judge afford the greatest respect of the religious solemnization or solemn affirmation in taking the oath, if the policy requires the candidate to violate or renounce a basic tenet of their religion?" (Ishaq 2015).

The former Prime Minister of Canada Stephen Harper responded in the Canadian House of Commons that his government's ban on the wearing of the niqab during the oath of allegiance was not an issue of religious freedom, but one of defending Canadian identity, since Muslim women are not obligated, nor required to cover their faces in public and at any rate "most moderate Muslims support the ban" (Chase 2015). This became evident in two ways, through statements made by the Conservative government that highlighted strands from both the MCC and the CPMO. As the official website of this organization states, the CPMO is an umbrella for progressive Muslims across Canada who uphold Canadian values, especially separation of religion and politics, gender equality, one law for all, freedom of expression, and education against radicalization. Salma Siddiqui, the current chair of the organization, and past vice president of the MCC, has since 2007 lobbied the Canadian government to ban Muslim women from wearing the niqab and burqa in Canadian public spaces since they pose a "security risk" because they conceal the wearer's identity and are political symbols of Islamic extremism. The Coalition of Progressive Canadian Muslim Organizations (CPCMO) describes their organization as a think tank that provides a platform for diverse voices within the Muslim communities of Canada (Siddiqui 2017). The MCC is a self-proclaimed "moderate Muslim" organization formed in the aftermath of 9/11. The organization is founded on promoting a "progressive, liberal, pluralistic, democratic secular society where everyone has the freedom of religion" (Downie 2013, 30). In October 2009, the MCC lobbied the Canadian Federal Conservative government to introduce legislation to "ban the wearing of masks, burqas, and niqabs in public" (30). The MCC called veiling a practice that "reflects a mode of male control over women" and is a "vestige of medieval culture that has no place in Canada" (30). The MCC frames their arguments around orientalist perceptions that the niqab and burqa are "symbols of gender inequality, oppression and subordination" that prevent these Muslim women from participating and integrating into democratic society (Downie 2013, 40). Subsequently, the MCC declared that the burqa and niqab were not religious requirements and the practice was rooted in the tribal cultures of the desert and not Islam (40). There were, however, more reflective voices that situated the Conservative governments "niqab ban" as a defiance of Canadian Charter Rights, and as spokesperson for the Canadian Council on American-Islamic Relations Julia Williams stated, what could be "more damaging to women's equality and women's rights than removing their freedom of choice … to dress as she sees it" (Payton 2011).

Debates over "veiling," and "unveiling" Muslim women are complex and filled with tensions and contradictions that have existed since the early Muslim communities, the era of colonization, imperialism, de-colonization and Muslim state formation. It is important to note that the symbol of "the veil" as "oppressive," and "backward" is an enduring orientalist legacy of a perception of Islam as a medieval and backward religion that oppresses and subjugates "its" women (Kassam and Mustafa 2018). Contemporary views often reproduce this homogeneous colonial and imperial narrative that perceives the burqa and niqab as symbols of oppression and subordination that are seamlessly embedded in narratives replicated in political debates, legal arguments and social discourse (Alibhai 2020, 125).

Alarmingly, former Minister Kenney echoed the MCC when he made the media rounds introducing the Conservative government's new policy, Operation Bulletin 359. In an interview with the Canadian Broadcasting Corporation's *Power and Politics* (2011) with Evan Solomon, Minister Kenney defended the new policy by stating that the niqab "reflects a misogynistic culture — a treatment of women as property rather than people, which is anchored in medieval tribal customs as opposed to any religious obligation"

(Payton 2011). On January 23, 2012, the Muslim Canadian Congress held an event honoring former Minister Kenney (the keynote speaker) celebrating his "courageous" decision to ban the niqab during the oath of citizenship (Bell 2011). The disturbing circularity between the Conservative government, the Muslim Canadian Congress and the Coalition of Progressive Canadian Muslim Organizations is what Dressler and Mandair (2011) conceptualize as "religion-making from above" which refers to authoritative discourses and practices that define and confine things (symbols, languages, practices) as "religious" and "secular" through disciplining strategies of the state and its institutions (Dressler and Mandair 2011, 21). "Religion making from below" implicitly accepts the language from "above" and draws on a religionist discourse (theological evidence) to re-establish their identities as legitimate social formations (Dressler and Mandair 2011, 21).

Bringing attention to "religion making from above and below" can shed light on the way that power and agency are conceived when linked with religious and political identities that stand alongside each other in pluralist and diverse social, economic and political contexts. Ayelet Sachar argues that addressing with a clear moral voice the actual cases where conflicts between claims for equality and respect for diversity is imperative to shed light on the inequities of what is at stake when becomes excluded from the normative workings of society (Shachar 2015, 235). Many of these themes came to the forefront during the Zunera Ishaq case. I have argued elsewhere that more reflective voices countered the Conservative government's and the MCC and CPCMO's arguments — the loudest being the Canadian people who used various social media platforms to shift singular conceptions of religion and national identity. Similarly, "high status" individuals pushed back against the then-prime minister and his government, while the future prime minister of Canada, Justin Trudeau framed discourse in terms of Canada's acceptance of diversity as a value that strengthens the Canadian family. On September 15, 2015, the Federal Court of Appeals unanimously upheld Judge Boswell's ruling. Delivering the judgment from the bench, the three justices explained the swiftness (half-a-day) in dismissing the appeal was due in large part so that Ms. Ishaq could become a Canadian citizen in time to vote in the next month's election. On October 9, 2015, Zunera Ishaq finally took her oath of citizenship and became a Canadian citizen.

R. v. N.S.

The case of R. v. N.S. concerns the right of a Muslim woman (N.S.) to wear her niqab while testifying as a victim in a sexual assault trial against her male Muslim relatives. N.S. alleges that between 1982 to 1987, beginning when she was six years old, she was repeatedly sexually assaulted by two male family members (N.S. 2010). In 2007, N.S. brought charges of various sexual offenses against the two accused. As of the date of the court proceedings, N.S. had been wearing her niqab for about five years. The two men accused of sexually assaulting N.S. elected trial by judge and jury and both men sought an order requiring N.S. to remove her niqab when testifying at the preliminary inquiry. N.S. objected. The preliminary inquiry Judge, Norris Weisman, elected to informally question N.S. N.S. (wearing her niqab) testified that her objection to uncovering her face was "strong" and rooted in her religious beliefs that are premised on "modesty, respect, and honor" (N.S. 2010) that required her to cover her face in the presence of men who are not close relatives. Upon further questioning, N.S. disclosed that she did unveil in front of other women, children and very close, married male family members, but she does not appear in public without her veil. She described wearing her niqab "as part of me" (N.S. 2010) and that she would feel more "comfortable" wearing her niqab in the courtroom (N.S. 2010). Judge Weisman concluded that he was not convinced that her religious belief was "that strong" and therefore, "not sincerely held," since N.S. had been "content" (N.S. 2010) to remove her niqab when taking her driver's license picture by a female photographer — an identification piece that he argued can be required to show "all sorts of males," including "police officers and border guards" (N.S. 2010).

The presumption that a society's legal system has autonomy does not mean a system unfettered from the social world and external influence. To the contrary, Richardson argues that the courts "act within a cultural milieu, with its specific cultural values and beliefs, including ones concerning religion and religious groups" (Richardson 2006, 283). Benjamin Berger argues that when religion is put before the bar of law, law understands and casts its subject in accordance with its own symbolic and normative commitments (Berger 2008, 265). The paradox of which points to some of the coercive aspects of the residue of majoritarian religion (Beaman, Steele and Pringnitz 2018). Beaman cautions that it is pertinent to recognize that there remains a Protestant predisposition embedded in Canadian social and legal institutions (Beaman 2020). These shadows of Protestant affinities not only shape the ways religion is imagined and practiced but as Benjamin Berger argues, unfold within a social, political, and legal environment virtually unnoticed or unchallenged (Berger 2008). For instance, drawing the boundaries between legitimate religion, belief, and practice, the decision-makers seek to regulate Zunera Ishaq's and N.S.'s lived religious practices by creating and embedding hierarchal gauges — she uncovered her face *there*, then, she can do it *here*. However, the selectivity with which practitioners live, approach, negotiate, embody, and cultivate their religion should not undermine their claim to its sincerity or strength to become reduced to "got you" vindications (Alibhai 2019, 60).

N.S. objected to the preliminary court's ruling and pursued her case up to the Supreme Court of Canada, seeking an order permitting her to wear her niqab while testifying. On December 20, 2012, the Supreme Court dismissed N.S.'s appeal and remitted her case back to the preliminary judge. Although the court sent the case back to the preliminary judge, the majority emphasized that it had been "inappropriate" for Judge Weisman to conclude that N.S.'s religious beliefs "were not that strong" (N.S 2012). They wrote, "a sincere believer may occasionally lapse, her beliefs may change over time, or her belief may permit exceptions to the practice in particular situations" (N.S 2012). Ultimately, the court decided that whether a witness could testify while wearing a niqab for religious reasons during a criminal trial would be matter decided on a case-by-case basis in accordance with their newly devised balancing test. On April 24, 2013, Judge Weisman held to his original ruling, citing risks to trial's fairness, that N.S. must remove her niqab to testify in her sexual assault trial (Cader 2013, 91). N.S. appealed. In 2014, the Crown withdrew the sexual assault charges against the two men accused of sexually assaulting N.S., stating that there was no reasonable prospect for conviction (Cader 2013, 91).

Mme. M.

On June 27, 2008, the French Conseil d'Etat denied the citizenship request of Faiza Silmi, who the court alternatively identifies as Mme. Machbour or Mme M. Mme. Silmi was born in Morocco and in 2000 she married a French national and had four children. Since moving to France, Mme Silmi adopted the wearing of the niqab (voile integral), a dress style typical of "women of the Arabian Peninsula," because she found her traditional Moroccan djelaba, a long flowing garment with a head scarf, was not modest enough (Koussens 2011, 7). The Conseil ruled that she wore the niqab not out of sincere religiosity or "genuinely expressed religious modesty" but "out of custom (imposed by her husband) rather than conviction" (Koussens 2011, 8). The Conseil denied her citizenship request on the basis of her radical practice of Islam. In an interview with the *New York Times* (2008), the Silmis' stated that while they live by a literalist interpretation of the Koran, they do not like the term Salafism because it had come to mean political Islam; "people who don't like the government and who approve of violence call themselves Salafists" (Bennhold 2008). The co-creation of discourse, representation, and language is brought into clearer focus by unraveling the ways in which power operates in covert and overt forms that allow specific understandings of "religion," "citizenship," "national identity," and "gender" to become dominant, authoritative, and implicated in the production of emerging identities that are acceptable in public life.

Richardson argues that the legal system can be used by the State as a social control mechanism with religious groups and practices perceived as deviant within greater society (Richardson 2006, 287). The denial of citizenship sets the groundwork of normative intervention in two ways: first, as technologies of power, "which determine the conduct of individuals and submit them to certain ends or domination, an objectivizing of the subject" (Foucault 1988, 18) and, second, as technologies of the self, active practices of self as normative citizen formation.

4 Conclusion

The judicialization of religious freedom has become instrumental for niqab-wearing Muslim women's legal claims, access to the rights and privileges associated with citizenship and visibility in public space, while at the same time unsettling notions of agency and blurring the boundaries of lived religion and practice. The role that an autonomous judiciary plays in religious freedom claims are crucial for holding the state accountable to the rights and protections premised in the constitution for niqab-wearing Muslim women as both religious believers and equal citizens (Shachar 2015, 242). The Zunera Ishaq and the N.S. legal cases raise several interlocking issues relating to the judicialization of religious freedom and lived practice religion. As evidenced by the Zunera Ishaq case, an autonomous judiciary is crucial to countermand "high status" individuals who may want to exert control over a minority religious community (Richardson 2006, 285). More explicitly, when religious freedom claims are supported by an independent judiciary, restrictions on religion are reduced because "courts serve to uphold constitutional promises and protect minorities from the legislation of the majority as well as executive powers" (Finke and Martin 2014, 701). The religion-as-practice approach raises critical questions in the study of religion in contemporary society as to how religion is conceived and understood by reconfiguring definitions of what constitutes religious experience, practice, and space; and how these shape the ideological, legal and political landscape that influences and seeks to regulate religious identities. Yet, most often what is lost in the discussion is the recognition that it is the women themselves who are advancing the judicialization of religious freedom and deepening the ideals of the good society representative of diversity, social cohesion, citizenship, and belonging. Nilufer Göle (2013) argues that agency can be tricky for women and this becomes especially true for religious women who can be subjected to "agency override," (Beaman 2016, 7) particularly in matters concerning the state. Meredith McGuire (2008) argues that concepts defining traditional gender roles and moral constraints should not be taken for granted since religious and spiritual paths become avenues where for some people engaged in embodied and bodily practices embrace, transform, and re-create new gendered subjectivities. McGuire calls this "gendered spiritualities" since gender, sexuality, and gender identity play significant roles in many individuals' lived religion. Religious/spiritual communities and embodied practices are important ways that women negotiate new identities and forge new social relationships that have the potential to transcend boundaries established by sexist, racist, and classist social norms (McGuire 2008, 182). Identifying the dimensions of practice that are recognized by practitioners as specifically religious is more helpful and inclusive and broadens the field beyond the norms fixed by the state and religious institutions in order to bring into conversation a diversity of perspectives, beliefs, and practices.

References

Alibhai, Zaheeda. 2018. "Case Study: Zunera Ishaq v. Minister of Citizenship and Immigration." *EUREL: Sociological and Religious Data on Religions in Europe and Beyond.* February 15, 2018. http://www.eurel.info/spip.php?article3035.

Alibhai, Zaheeda P. 2019. "The Boundaries of Religious Pluralism." In *Emergent Religious Pluralisms*, edited by Bock, Fahy and Everett, 49–71. Switzerland: Palgrave Macmillan.

Alibhai, Zaheeda P. 2020. "Read Her Lips: The Ban on Wearing the Niqab and Burqa at the Canadian Citizenship Ceremonies 2011–2015." In *Migration and Stereotypes in Performance and Culture,* edited by Meerzon, Dean, McNeil, 121–40. Switzerland: Palgrave Macmillan.

Ammerman, Nancy T. 2007. *Everyday Religion: Observing Modern Religious Lives.* New York: Oxford University Press.

Ammerman, Nancy T. 2016. "Lived Religion as an Emerging Field: An Assessment of its Contours and Frontiers." *Nordic Journal of Religion and Society* 1(2): 89–99.

Ammerman, Nancy T. 2020. "Rethinking Religion: Toward a Practice Approach." *The American Journal of Sociology* 126 (1): 6–51.

Asad, Talal. 2003. *Formations of the Secular: Christianity, Islam, Modernity.* Stanford: Stanford University Press.

Asad, Talal. 2006. "Trying to Understand French Secularism." In *Political Theologies: Public Religions in a Post-Secular World*, edited by Hent de Vries and Lawrence E. Sullivan, 494–526. New York: Fordham University Press.

Asad, Talal. 2011. "Thinking about the Secular Body, Pain, and Liberal Politics." *Cultural Anthropology* 26 (4): 657–75.

Beaman, Lori G. 2008. *Defining Harm: Religious Freedom and the Limits of the Law.* Vancouver: University of British Columbia Press.

Beaman, Lori G. 2016. "Living Together v. Living Well Together: A Normative Examination of the SAS Case." *Social Inclusion*, 4 (2): 3–13.

Beaman, Lori G. 2020. *The Transition of Religion to Culture in Law and Public Discourse.* New York: Routledge.

Beaman, Lori G., Steele, Cory. Pringnitz, Keelin. 2018. "The Inclusion of Nonreligion in Religion and Human Rights." *Social Compass* 65 (1) 44–61.

Bell, Colleen. 2011. *The Freedom of Security: Governing Canada in the Age of Counter-Terrorism.* Vancouver: UBC Press.

Bennhold, Katrin. 2008. "A Veil Closes France's Door to Citizenship." *New York Times*, July 19, 2008. http://www.nytimes.com/2008/07/19/world/europe/19france.html.

Berger, Benjamin L. 2008. "Law's Religion: Rendering Culture." In *Law and Religious Pluralism in Canada*, edited by Richard Moon, 264–96. Vancouver: UBC Press.

Beyer, Peter. *Religion in Global Society.* 2006. New York: Routledge.

Cader, Fathima 2013. "Made You Look: Niqabs, The Muslim Canadian Congress, and R v N.S." *The Windsor Yearbook of Access to Justice* 31: (1) 67–93.

Canadian Broadcasting Corporation CBC News. 2011. "Face Veils Banned for Citizenship Oath." http://www.cbc.ca/news/canada/story/2011/12/12/pol-kenney-citizenship-rules.html. (retrieved February 27, 2021).

Carabine, Jean 2011. "Constituting Sexuality through Social Policy: The Case of Lone Motherhood 1834 and Today." *Social & Legal Studies* 10: (3) 291–314.

Chase, Steven. 2015. "Niqabs 'rooted in a culture that is anti-women,' Harper says", Globe and Mail (10March2015) <http://www.theglobeandmail.com/news/politics/niqabs-rooted-in-a-culture-that-is-anti-women-harper-says/article23395242/> (accessed February 27, 2021).

Downie, Caitlin. 2013. "Constructing Islamaphobia within the Muslim community: The Case of the Muslim Congress." *Amsterdam Social Science*, 5 (1) 25–46.

Dressler, Markus, and Arvind Mandair. 2011. *Secularism and Religion-Making.* New York: Oxford University Press.

Finke, Roger, and Robert R. Martin. 2014. "Ensuring Liberties: Understanding State Restrictions on Religious Freedoms." *Journal for the Scientific Study of Religion* 53 (4): 687–705.

Foucault, Michel et al. 1988. *Technologies of the Self: A Seminar with Michel Foucault.* Amherst: University of Massachusetts Press.

Foucault, Michel. 1978. *The History of Sexuality. Vol. 1, The Will to Knowledge.* New York: Pantheon Books.

Göle, Nilufer. 2013. *Islam and Public Controversy in Europe*. Surrey: Ashgate Publishing Limited.

Hall, David D. 1997. "Introduction." In *Lived Religion in America: Toward a History of Practice*, edited by David D. Hall, vii–xiii. Princeton: Princeton University Press.

Hirschl, Ran. 2011. "The Judicialization of Politics." In *The Oxford Handbook of Political Science*, edited by Robert E. Goodin, 253–74. Oxford: Oxford University Press. https://www.cbc.ca/news/politics/face-veils-banned-for-citizenship-oaths-1.1048750, (accessed February 27, 2021).

Hurd, Elizabeth S. 2015. *Beyond Religious Freedom: The New Global Politics of Religion*. Princeton: Princeton University Press.

Kassam, Shelina, and Naheed Mustafa. 2018. "Veiling Narratives: Discourses of Canadian Multiculturalism, Acceptability and Citizenship." In *The Routledge International Handbook to Veils and Veiling Practices*, edited by Anna-Mari Almila and David Inglis, 73–83. New York: Routledge.

Koussens, David. 2011. "Religious Diversity and the Divergence of Secular Trajectories: Comparing secularization practices in Quebec and France." http://hdl.handle.net/1814/19114 (accessed September 27, 2020).

Mahmood, Saba. 2005. *The Politics of Piety: The Islamic Revival and The Feminist Subject*. Princeton: Princeton University Press.

Mayrl, Damon. 2018. "The Judicialization of Religious Freedom: An Institutionalist Approach." *Sociology of Religion* 57 (3): 514–30.

McGuire, Meredith. 2008. *Lived Religion: Faith and Practice in Everyday Life*. New York: Oxford University Press.

Muslim Canadian Congress. "The Muslim Canadian Congress." Muslim Canadian Congress. http://www.muslimcanadiancongress.org.

Payton, Laura. 2011. "Face veils banned for citizenship oaths." Canadian Broadcasting Corporation, December 12, 2011.

R v NS, 2010 ONCA 670.

Richardson, James T. 2015. "Managing Religion and the Judicialization of Religious Freedom." *Journal for the Scientific Study of Religion* 54 (1): 1–19.

Richardson, James T. 2006. "The Sociology of Religious Freedom: A Structural and Socio-Legal Analysis." *Sociology of Religion* 67 (3): 271–94.

Shachar, Ayelet. 2015. "When Law Meets Diversity." In *Routledge International Handbook of Diversity Studies*, edited by Steven Vertovec, 234–44. New York: Routledge.

Siddiqui, Salma. 2017. "Muslim Reform Movement" https://muslimreformmovement.org/our-founders/Salma-Siddiqui/ (accessed February 27, 2021).

Teubner, Gunther. 1987. *Juridification of Social Spheres: A Comparative Analysis in The Areas of Labour, Corporate, Antitrust and Social Welfare Law*. Florence: European University Institute.

Vallinder, Torbjörn. 1994. "The Judicialization of Politics. A World-Wide Phenomenon: Introduction." *International Political Science Review / Revue Internationale De Science Politique.* 15 (2): 91–99.

Woodhead, Linda. 2011. "Five Concepts of Religion." *International Review of Sociology* 21 (1): 121–43.

Zunera Ishaq v. The Minister of Citizenship and Immigration 2015 FC 156.

CHAPTER 6

The Religionization in Alevi Culture: An Exploratory Study on Spiritual Leaders (*Dedes*)

Nuran Erol Işık

The multidimensionality of religious freedom and its rootedness in historical, socio-legal and socio-political contexts can be clearly exemplified through the phenomenon of the Islamic tradition of Alevism in Turkey. Since the 1980s, with the rise of identity politics worldwide, Alevi people in Turkey have become one of the intriguing groups on which a contested space of epistemological approaches revealed itself. Complicated and multilayered historical, political, and cultural markers have led to very different interpretations of Alevi identity, including: Heterodox/mystical Islamic Alevism, a new Shia-inclined Alevism, and a version of Liberation Theology. Alevis insist on their distinction from Sunni Islam, manifested historically in their social and political marginalization within Ottoman and Turkish societies, their ritual and social practices, and a worldview strongly shaped by Twelver Shiite mythology, Islamic mysticism, as well as various non-Islamic traditions.

The Alevi culture and its long-lasting historical traditional structure requires a thorough and a critical understanding of the ways in which ambivalences of ordinary religious belonging are transformed through formal structures, such as the European Courts of Human Rights (ECtHR). European Court's approach to Alevism as a "religious conviction distinct from Sunni Islam," manifests a tendency to erase the profound heterogeneity (and even inconsistency) of practices associated with Alevism, while reinforcing the Turkish state's capacity to classify and govern its citizens as *religious* subjects (Hurd 2014, 416). The tendency to define modern Alevism in such a process requires a focus on the ways in the legal processes are understood, mediated and negotiated by a diverse group of mystical/spiritual leaders (dedes), These legal processes are governed by supra-national agencies, as well as various forms of newly emerging institutions. Thus, this chapter will attempt to interrogate the ways in which dedes, who represent diverse groups within the Alevi community, position themselves with regard to such a process called the "religionization of Alevism." There have been institutional arrangements at different levels for various initiatives, including education programs for dedes; the formation of dede councils; and establishing Alevi schools. These practices are part of

© NURAN EROL IŞIK, 2021 | DOI:10.1163/9789004468085_008

a socio-political process, in which religious freedoms have been debated in relation to Sunni Islam. This chapter is based on the findings obtained from in-depth interviews with eight dedes in Turkey.

1 The Problem Statement

The area of religious freedoms in a society is highly contested, due to the ways in which social, historical and cultural forces reveal themselves in forms of identity-making practices, rituals, narratives, and ideologies. Differentiation of such an area presents itself in a conundrum, where voices of dissent and consent might be erroneously located.

The relation between sociological processes and micro level outcomes requires us to investigate theories on religious freedom in terms of moral, political, personal, social, and spiritual dimensions. The interstitial relationships of everyday life and social institutions represent a venue for understanding a wide variety of voices and paradoxes brought about by religious freedom in relation to modernity and post secularity. One of these paradoxes refers to the ways in which the tension between *regulation* and *autonomy* is acknowledged and resolved by local, national and supra-national agencies. Danchin highlights the causes of this paradox, on the one hand, religious freedom is said to be neutral toward religion, and indeed neutrality is the key leitmotif of modern religious liberty discourse, whether in moral, legal, or political contexts. On the other, he points out that religious freedom as a technology of the modern state and international governance is deeply implicated in the regulation of religion. This tension is internal to the concept of religious liberty itself, and serves to generate the distinctive antinomies and contradictions seen arising in struggles over its meaning, justification, and realization (Danchin 2015, 240). The ambivalences and tensions in reformulating a series formula for the community under investigation in this chapter, i.e., Alevi people in Turkey, are clearly historically linked to re-fashioning secularity and agency.

In the process of writing an Alevi historiography, politics of authenticity evolved into the formation of meta-discourses (Vande Kopple 2002, 92), which both Alevi and non-Alevi opinion leaders, writers, journalists, and others, defined freedoms and human dignity in relation to the question of agency. For the last thirty years, narratives on problems and issues derived from Alevism and Alevi culture served as an opportunity to legitimize different discursive instruments, which became a tool for re-defining the major fault lines in Turkish society (e.g. laicism vs Islamism). Religious freedoms, in this context, have been on the forefront of debates on Alevism, due to the variety of critical voices on a wide range of topics including the secularization process, the citizenship question, the judicialization of rights, the positioning of Alevi faith within Islam, supra-national legal solutions to rights, and statism in Turkey. Explorations on these entanglements have been extensively evaluated through the literature of fields including rights, international relations, and institutional decision-making processes. However, these macro level analyses have not been deeply complemented by micro-sociological inquiries, which would enlighten different sources of motivations.

Accordingly, one of the major objectives of this article aims at revealing the narratives of dedes on the question of agency within the contested sphere of Alevi civil organizations. Narratives, which are assumed to have an impact on identity markers (Somers 1993, 3–4), provide important indicators on how we understand our experiences. The ways in which Alevism is associated with its own cultural sphere, and religiosity, for example, constitute an area of highly controversial debate between Alevi organizations, which have different forms of organizational cultures exemplified through their narratives. Reading and interpreting these narratives, as well as strategies of formulating truth claims, a la Habermas, can enlighten the ways in which the Alevi community prioritize or delegitimize political will-making practices in certain areas of life. As is noted below, the views of spiritual leaders, in addition, are assumed to have an important reflection on the positioning of Alevi actors in a well-defined area of cultural divide between moral, sacralized, and religionized life worlds. In addition, their narratives about experiental, political, and cultural acts are assumed to be heuristic indicators of mediating morality, which have played a major role in defining acts of moralism.

Therefore, in this chapter, phenomenological interviews with eight Alevi dedes and two opinion leaders will be used to explore the question of religious freedoms in relation to agency and morality. The questions raised above also address the questions of dedes' capacity to act, and the ways they project their own values on to others' actions. How do they position themselves on the spectrum ranging from folkloric Alevi culture to modern Alevi culture? How do they negotiate between spiritual deeds and worldly duties? What are their ideas on the so called "Alevi openings?" How do they define their identity as dedes? How do they interpret the ways in which other opinion leaders, actors and dedes answer major questions on the politics of Alevism? The answers to the interview questions were designed to enlighten the contested nature of secularity and religiosity, which is an evolving duality in making sense of religionization as a highly visible process in various different societies. It is assumed that the means of regulating religion and constructing a harmonious ensemble of coalitions are mediated through macro level developments in reformulating identity markers. The mediated voices of Alevi dedes revealed here shed light on the nature of regulation and inviolability, which is evident in the history of all minorities.

This chapter, therefore, aims at amplifying the role of spiritual leaders in mediating, negotiating, and positioning the identity of dede in relation to the larger, macro affairs of politics, which become manifest in the highly narrativized language of meta-discourses. Dede's positioning on the spectrum between the markers of autonomy and regulation, noted above, constitute significant sociological indicators in understanding the issue of agency in Alevism in Turkish society, due to their roles, which are highly negotiated, in the everyday life of religious subjects. These leaders' own attitudes to specific acts, actors, values, ideologies, and processes also highlight their approach to certain actors' maneuvers aimed at influencing the politics of Alevism through powerful strategies, such as Sunnification. This chapter also aims at analyzing the narratives through which dedes configure their identities in relation to Alevi organizations, which is a mediated process vis-à-vis state-led policy-making practices, as well as institutionalized patterns stemming from intricate cultural value systems and highly debated codes of secularity. The methodological design followed in this study includes explicating an exploration on the demographics of the interviewees, and thematic analysis on their perceived roles of agency for resolving conflicts among relevant actors. These data provide a map which allows the detection of the plurality of themes and definitions as key argumentative markers in micro and macro processes.

2   Who Are Alevi People?

The historical narratives on Alevism refer to Muslims who are associated with the house of Ali, the son-in-law of Muhammad. Alevism is also used to describe the lineage of Muhammad and his siblings, Ehl-i Beyt.[1] The Alevi belief system interprets Islam from its own point of view, based on a series of important theological assumptions. Alevi faith is founded on the theme of a perfect human being (insan-ı kamil) under the guidance of spiritual leaders (dedes), and on the idea of lineage of Muhammad (Evlad-ı Resul). The

---

1   Ehl-I Beyt literally means "people of the household." When they asked Muhammad, he defined it as a group pf people under his coat: his daughter Fatima, his son in law Ali, and their sons St.Husain and St.Hasan. After this definition it has been believed that twelve imams of Ali descent from this family, who are affiliated with the lineage of dedes. See: Haydar Kaya, *Alevilik Tarihi* (History of Alevism), Ehl-I Beyt Publications, Izmir, 2011.

Alevi belief system also includes mystical mentors, who are accepted as dervishes, labeled as 'real' (people) (Işık 2011, 157). The Alevis of Turkey make up approximately 15 percent of Turkey's population, [and are not to be confused with the Arab Alawīs (Nusayris)]. In the Ottoman documents, they are called zındık, heretic, râfizi, schismatic, and also "shi'ite", mülhid, atheist. The beliefs of the Kızılbaş-Alevi are identical with those of the Bektashis. Both groups refer to Hacı Bektaş. But the Bektashis formed an organized group, whereas the Kızılbaş-Alevi, who lived in villages, remained more or less disorganized. The Bektashi follow an unchangeable ritual whereas the Kızılbaş-Alevi believe in myths in which legends are mingled with local folklore. The beliefs of both groups are syncretic (Melikoff 1998, 2).

The nature of Alevi history is complicated by different ways of contextualizing and interpreting the belief. The syncretic nature of Alevi mysticism and the humanist philosophy embedded in the basics of Alevi faith have been significant characteristics in delineating Alevi culture, and its reception by different regions. Studies on Alevism have heavily emphasized the core characteristics of rituals and faith practices, but without positioning these in a social context (Ocak 1999). The intertwined nature of social structures and theological characteristics led to different characterizations of Alevism. According to Işık (2011, 160), various approaches each carry their own presumptions on history and agency. Identity approaches based on Turkic discursive markers, Sunni evaluations, and narratives on "Alevism without Ali," all focus on different problematics, which derive their epistemological engines not only from ideological approaches, but also from contemporary themes and questions in social sciences. In addition, Alevi culture offers a rich area for investigation, due to its unique cultural characteristics, revealing formation of moral selves through strength of commitment among spiritual leaders (Pirs) and followers (talibs).

The system of holy lineage (ocak) is a formation which refers to strong ties between descendants of the medieval saints. Those dedes, who are the members of this hereditary sanctity, express their affiliation with their ocak in such ways that their sole source of moral identity derives its power from the lineage they inherited. Alevis, accordingly, take pride in being members of ocaks, whose purpose is to construct strong bonds between varying types of spiritual leaders (pirs, babas, dedes) and their followers. The ocak lineages are complemented by non-ocak lineages, whose members are called talibs. Ocaks as patrilinear organizations, such as Kureyshan, Baba Mansur, Dede Garkın, Ali Pir Cıvan, offer memberships defined as ocakzade. The interstitial institutions, such as ocaks, leaders, and followers have constituted an area of morality, where the followers receive and transmit normative claims to future generations. Offering consent to these claims is essential to their identity, which indicates a spiritual awakening. The more the followers accept, internalize and evaluate their own actions through a moral prism, the more they can evolve (into the level of spiritual ascension), which would also enlighten and revitalize their own surroundings (Işık 2017, 15).

Dedes, who are always male, are believed to be sayyids (Turkish: seyid) or Evlad-ı Resul. Intergenerational continuity of the status is realized through dedes' transmission of their roles to a close relative. They need consent from their predecessors to be allowed in this practice (Sökefeld 2002). The major role of a dede is to lead the Alevi rituals, especially cem, as the major form of communal Alevi worship. His descent grants him the religious charisma required for the performance of the rituals, as well as for instruction on the requirements and rules of the mystical path. In addition, the dede usually acts as mediator and judge (Dressler 2014). These mediations usually reveal themselves in the process of negotiating the normative order, e.g. for conflicts between couples, neighbors, friends. The institution of consent (rızalık) plays a major role in social interactions and the stability of moral order, which is the major core of equilibrium of the community. Such negotiations are offered by dedes in case of demands from talibs, who are assumed to reach a consensus before joining a ritual. Thus, the creation of unity is not possible by giving consent to dedes and their union, if (their) membership status would be threatened in case of persistent conflict.

The traditional dede roles have been transformed due to the rapid social change and urbanization in Turkish society since the 1950s. The migration from rural areas into big cities meant an increasing number of cemevis (houses where cem ceremonies take place). The status of newly urbanized dedes represented a transition from "dedes of traditional holy lineages" (ocaks) into "dedes of institutions." The authority of traditional dede institutions was intensively shaped by dedes themselves, and the urbanized Alevism has been characterized by associations and foundations (Yaman 2012). Dressler argues that "dedelik, the institution of the dede, is being secularized, i.e., the role of the dede is limited into ritual contexts, increasingly defined as religious, in opposition to non-religious functions such as representation of the community" (2012: 270). These transformations led to differentiations in the ways in which dedes have executed their traditional roles, and distancing themselves from talibs, who, in some regions, were very dispersed. As some of the interviewees expressed, earning a living through accessing talibs, and playing the roles of spiritual and moral guide became a real burden and source of tension for dedes. In some cities, ocaks started forming their own foundations due to the need for recognition, and the need to form a legal entity.

The politics of recognition led to new developments among Alevi people, who started to seek their rights by using judicial mechanisms. There have been significant developments in Alevi politics between 1992 and 2003, brought about by a series of historical grievances. Alevi organizations started negotiating their identity claims in the political and cultural sphere.[2] In 2009, the Alevi Initiative was introduced by the government (Justice and Development Party) to unite the Alevi leadership for negotiations over their claims on citizenship rights. Prior to the 2011 elections, the JDP showed an interest in promoting relationships with Alevis, particularly through seven joint workshops held from 2009 to 2010.[3]

Strategies in the politics of emancipation to improve and rebuild Alevi religious freedoms oscillated between the "inclusion of the Alevis into the fold of the nation on the one hand, and the non-recognition of them, assimilation, or outright discrimination against them on the other" (Dressler 2015: 449). The sociological transformations of Alevi groups have been strongly affected by these discursive acts of inclusionary policies, reflected by the relational structure of Sunni and Alevi sects. Different groups and leaders in Alevi organizations have been negotiating over the formulation of national and supra-national agencies' claims on Islam, Alevi-ness, the boundaries of actions, the definition of rituals, the role and the degree of sacralization and de-sacralization practices, re-invention of traditions, the representation and legitimacy issues of Alevi organizations, and the life-world of Alevi culture. As one of the interviewees argued, "a large majority of people started investing in Alevi politics, which led to the process of 'Alevization' in Turkey" (I#9),[4] referring to the adoption of the symbolic power of Alevism by several different actors. As is underlined in

---

[2] In 2007, 'The Cem Foundation filed a lawsuit against the Prime Ministry in order to force a change in the DRA (The Directorate of Religious Affairs) that provides no recognition of Alevi identity. The Sixth Administrative Court in Ankara decided that no cadres and no portion of the budget can be earmarked for Alevis, accepting the argument of the Prime Ministry that all sects and groups within Islam are embraced in Turkey under the single label of Islam' (Çarkoğlu and Bilgili 2011: 56).

[3] Erol (2015) evaluates the supra-national (the European Court of Human Rights -hereinafter the ECtHR) and national judicial processes including governmental strategies to navigate Alevi identity claims. Although the JDP government seemed concerned about Alevis' human rights and freedoms, the EU Commission criticized the state's official attitude toward Alevis, and the European Court of Human Rights (ECtHR) ruled that Turkey had violated those Alevi human rights and freedoms safeguarded under the European Convention on Human Rights (ECHR). In Doğan, et al. vs. Turkey Case, the Court stated that the different treatment of the Alevi followers had no objective or reasonable justification, and therefore represented a violation of Art. 14 ECHR in conjunction with Art. 9 ECHR. See: (Ferri 2017: 312).

[4] All interviewees are coded as I#1–I#10.

the following section, 'talk about talk,' i.e., meta-discourse, became one major discursive marker with regard to the Alevi world of politics and culture.

3 Conceptualizing Religious Freedom and Alevi People

The concept of religious freedom might be elucidated by adopting three approaches in succession: by examining cases which involve degrees of religious freedom, then the various types of religious freedom, and finally, constraints to religious freedom (Sharma 2011). The types of freedom are exemplified as follows: religious freedom of intellectual and spiritual inquiry, the freedom to speak and act — both individually and in community with others, the right — both individually and as part of a larger religious community — to express religious beliefs freely in civil society and political life, the right of religious individuals and groups to own and sell property, and the right to establish and run religious schools, charitable organizations, and other institutions of civil society (Shah, et.al.2012).

Accordingly, a complete conceptualization of religious freedoms throughout the history of Alevi people requires outlining a long and complex path beyond the scope of this chapter. The victimhood of Alevi people certainly made an impact of the historiography of minorities in Anatolia in terms of disclosing the actors playing major roles in the sphere of freedoms. The understanding of the exposure of Alevi people to varying degrees of discrimination at different institutions requires a nuanced interpretation of history. Nevertheless, certain key events, namely the massacres in Maraş in 1978, in Çorum in 1980 and in Sivas in 1993, had an especially strong impact on developing a discursive space regarding traumatizing collective identity-making practices. The politics of victimhood also derived its power from a series of institutionalized exclusion practices in different institutions. The nature of manifest and latent constraints on freedoms has been shaped by the ways in which processes of secularization and democratization have been re-negotiated by national and supra-national agencies.

The complicated nature of secularity,[5] revealed by the state's interference in certain practices, such as compulsory religious courses, for example, symbolized an area of tension where religious freedom for Alevis has been envisaged in terms of post-secularity and religionization. Post-secularity clearly refers to tendencies about the continuation of religious influence in a continually

---

5 For a thorough analysis on secularity, see (Bader 2010).

secularizing environment, and a more general rise in public consciousness of religious discourse and social action (Cloke, et. al. 2019). The evolution of the linkage between Turkish politics and society certainly paved the way for the increasing visibility of Islamic practices in everyday life, which facilitated the dissemination of religious rituals markers as to what was to be labeled as non-religious, if not secular. This process, whereby assemblages of knowledge (structures, practices, discourses) are interpreted through the modern concept of religion, is known as 'religionization' (Dressler 2019). This concept also influenced Alevi communities who, to some extent, started re-configuring their cultural identities through the rise of identity politics in 1990s. The visibility of Islam in public sphere and religionization has become an important discursive element of the religiosity/secularity debates. The veil issue, which became a symbol for emancipatory politics for Sunni Muslim women, the role of religiosity and piety in a highly differentiated and a polarized society, the transnational nature of minority groups and their religious rights, mediated nature of different faith practices, all made a contribution to the discussion, definition and negotiation of the role of religion. Decoupling secularism from modernity has been accompanied by discussion on multiple modernities in intellectual debates in which essentialized arguments on identity have been countered by constructivist approaches.

In this context, conceptualizing the theme of religious freedom in terms of positioning Alevi culture also results in opportunities to mediate how the concepts of regulation and inviolability emphasized by Danchin (2015) reveal themselves in cultural, political, and social spheres. Regulative practices about religiosity have been associated with a fixed notion of modernity. The notion of creating and imposing Alevi scripts, for example, have been seen as highly regulative, resulting from a homogeneous notion of modernity, which also is associated with religionization. Asad (2003) investigates the discourses and practices through which religion was first bounded and reified in the modern West. He aspires "to problematize 'the religious' and 'the secular' as clear-cut categories but also to search for the conditions in which they were clear-cut and were sustained as such" (Dressler 2019: 6) "What are the *conditions* in which these dichotomies, these binaries, do seem to make sense?" is a question posed by Dressler (2019: 6). The dedes interviewed for this chapter certainly mediated their understanding of being secular, religious, and pious within the framework of the politics of recognition, which led to them, in some cases, being employed as religious leaders by city municipalities. Alternatively, they mediated and re-negotiated their roles in their communities after the rulings of the ECtHR. Therefore, the concept of "religio-secularization" proposed by

Dressler (2019) clearly helps us to comprehend a world created by the intertwining of state-led institutionalization projects and their reception by Alevi people.

As the interviews below suggest, building a religious world in terms of organizing houses of faith (cemevi), employing spiritual leaders as officials, and developing standardized rituals for their ceremonies actually serve for a disenchantment for their spiritual world, contrary to the predictions of the modernist policy makers. The conditions produced when the government opts for defining a world of religiosity based on standard rules and regulations are thus reinforced by the dichotomy of the pre-modern and modern, which does very little to expand the area of religious freedoms. On the contrary, such practices as re-framing and re-contextualizing Alevi rituals in different settings are disavowed both by participants and by the dedes who lead these rituals; however, conforming to these expectations has become normalized by a large group of followers and religious leaders.

Religionization, which manifests itself through different discursive markers, is not limited to Alevism, but has also been studied in Israel, where the visibility of traditional religion surpassed new civil religion. The term hadata (religionizaton) defines this process of the ascending role of traditional religion in the social life of a society in which secularism has not been fully institutionalized (Peri Yoram et. al 2012). Such internal dynamics, triggered by the rise of nationalism, resemble the growth in Turkey of the prevalence of the national-religious culture since the 1980s. The sphere of religious freedoms has been historically a contested venue, where the state and other actors played major roles which were highly dynamic. This confirms that, as Laborde argues, "domination can be imposed not only by the institutions of the state, but also, more generally, by institutionalized patterns of cultural value that prevent individuals from participating as equals in social life" (Laborde 2008: 16). Thus, revealing and evaluating the narratives on freedom can enlighten the ways in which the role of the social, cultural and political forces constitute conditions under which sense can be made of the dichotomy of religio-secular. The theme of institutionalized patterns of cultural value emphasized above would certainly underline the vocabulary of religiosity, while the emphasis on constitutional rights would lead to a language on secularity. This study, therefore, also aims at understanding the representatives of Alevi people, and their constant re-negotiation and mediation of such an intertwined world of freedoms scripted at local, national, and global levels.

4 Methodology: Hermeneutic Interviews as a Tool for Narrative Markers

In this research, dedes were asked to express their alignment to faith and identity, their mediation strategies about the diversified world, and agency definitions on the Alevi community, which would indicate discursive indicators to evaluate the overall problems stated above. Instead of employing a question and answer session, the sensitivity and intensity of issues such as identity, religiosity, and piety required articulating a "philosophical hermeneutic interview."[6]

The subjects of the investigation, dedes and their own understandings of their lives, certainly falls under the category of hermeneutic methodology. The affirmations of tellers in defining their identity, their ways of negotiation with talibs, and their own subjective understanding of the macro-dynamics of Alevism would be an outcome of a complex array of interstitial arrangements. In order to explain the problems and interconnections between themes selected for this chapter, interviews with eight Alevi dedes were conducted between February 2020 and April 2020.[7] The sub-section of the hermeneutic inquiry for this study has been defined within the framework of narratives, due to their power in making and revealing identity markers. These narratives, which have sequential characteristics of different themes and meanings, convey significant answers to questions raised on religious freedoms in Alevi community.

---

6 According to Vandermause and Fleming (2011), it is crucial for the researcher to ask in a way that draws out the story without leading the participant into a set answer. Since Alevi culture is heavily based on non-written techniques of storytelling and dedes' duties as storytellers in cem ceremonies, the interviewers opted for using an in-depth interview which involved the cooperation of the researcher and the participant working together to generate an understanding as narrative text emerges and language is interpreted.

7 At the beginning of this research, ten interviews with the Alevi leaders were planned. However, the COVID-19 outbreak became a great obstacle to accessing all interviewees. The opinion leaders were added to the field research inventory due to their important roles in Alevi world. One of them (I#9) has been intensively working at one of the Alevi federations, and participated in negotiations with the government. The other interviewee was one of the most important figures in a project of an Alevi association to establish a school for Alevi youth in Istanbul (I#10). Their narratives were not included in the table, which summarizes the meta-discourses of dedes. However, their contributions in providing a picture about the social and cultural context were immense. The interviews in Istanbul were conducted by Ms. Satı Sarıaslan Atli, a Ph.D. student in folklore. I thank her for her delicate conduct and cooperation in this research.

4.1 Socio-Demographic Characteristics of Dedes

The socio-economic characteristics of dedes reveal variations in terms of age and occupation. One of the interviewees, I#1, although from the lineage of dedes, has not worked as a dede, but was included in this study due to his experiences and observations on Alevi dedes. The life story of dedes included a socialization process where the Alevi-ness revealed that they closely interacted with the elders of ocaks in different regions of Turkey.

TABLE 6.1 Socio-demographic characteristics of *Dedes*

Interviewee number	Age	City of residence	Education	Occupation	Duration of Dede status (year)
1	70	Istanbul	University graduate (B.A.)	Retired Instructor, Foundation Manager	N/A
2	65	Istanbul	Primary School	Retired Blue Collar Worker	20
3	45	Istanbul	High School	Trader/Businessman	15
4	55	Istanbul	Primary School	Blue Collar Worker, Artisan	20
5	34	İzmit	High School	Blue Collar Worker	15
6	39	İzmir	High School	Officer	13
7	64	İzmir	Primary School	Retired Worker	30
8	40	İzmir	Primary School	Worker	10

5 Thematic Analysis

After the answers to questions on selected themes were grouped into categories, the following issues in their narratives emerged clarified: As Table 6.2

shows, the role of dedes, problems of dedes, agency, major obstacles or major areas of contestation, Alevism, the role of supra-national institutions, and major argumentative markers enable us to form a conceptual map to position ideas on religious freedoms. The theme on the role of dedes defines the ways in which they position themselves in different spheres of life, as well as the nature of their identity, which may have religious, spiritual, or other connotations. The problems of dedes in everyday life refer to a multiplicity of tensions and struggles deriving from secular or non-secular grievances. The theme of major obstacles aims at revealing social, political or cultural boundaries which may limit their duties as dedes. Their understandings of Alevism were made possible through combining a series of themes and symbols, which have theological, historical, political and cultural markers. Dedes' level of awareness about the major supra-national institutions, such as the ECtHR, could help us to understand whether they navigate through the macro as well as the micro levels of reference points in the positioning religious freedoms. The major argumentative markers are derived from their overall rhetorical strategies in presenting their subjective meanings about the selected themes.

The following analysis will focus on evaluating the research questions in terms of explaining how dedes construct and negotiate their Alevi identities, the meanings they attach to their organizational and spiritual duties within Alevism, and their views on practices and actors which might be effective in configuring an agency for Alevi people.[8]

5.1 *The Role(s) of Dedes*

The majority of dedes referred to their self-understanding of their role(s) guides moral, spiritual mediators whose status are inherited from their ocaks. They refer to routinized duties and responsibilities at rituals such as cem, on the one hand, and recalled the theological qualifications derived from Alevi tradition on the other. In talking about their roles, they used rhetorical tones that tended to portray themselves as proud members of their communions and traditions.

I#3 A dede should be someone who can find out solutions, who can actively play roles in resolving problems, a person who would not be othering people and a person full of love.

---

8   All answers and themes derived from the data are not documented. The Table 6.2 summarizes coding results for each participant.

I#1 A dede is someone who descended from the genealogy of Muhammad's family (Ehl-i Beyit). Leaders of faith should be very careful in treating everybody equally; detaching themselves from politics, which is very fluid.

I#2 Dedes have many responsibilities about the society. Society has also responsibilities about them.
A dede is a person who has too many responsibilities. He must prevent deviancy. Is everybody giving his/her consent? What happens if they do not agree? A dede must form a consensus (rızalık) among people. One can say that if there is disagreement, you may go to a court. However, a dede must provide social solidarity. One day I observed a dede at a Cem ritual; he was trying to resolve a conflict between a man and his neighbor. The man was complaining about the behavior of his neighbor, who implied an accusation of stealing something. He told them to make an agreement in front of everybody, showing their consent. They agreed. After the ceremony I asked him: what if they did not have an agreement? He said: I would urge them to leave the Cem. Later, I asked: If they did not my follow orders, I would tell them to form a family council where they could discuss peacemaking.
A dede is someone who would not be discriminating against others due to their cultural roots and race. A dede should have one qualification, that is, consciousness and fairness. He should not loose his desire for justice.

The mediating position attached to dedes is narrated in such a way that collectivity of Alevis would be destroyed if a dede cannot perform his role. The role of dedes is defined as a vital precondition for being part of a society. The personal characteristics of a dede is also underlined in leading the communion, where, nonwritten cultural imaginaries have been transmitted from one generation to the other. "Deserving this position," refers to having such qualifications as being knowledgeable about the traditional rituals, having good rhetorical skills, and being highly committed to their faith. Dedes' roles are not only defined by their theological understanding of Alevism; the role talibs attach to them is also paramount. As the institutional differentiation required dedes to play different roles, people's interactions with dedes have created unforeseen tensions and problems.

I#2   Our genealogy allows us to have the identity of dede; however the ones who deserve this position are chosen by the people.

Dedes are like psychologists. People who come to us are very thirsty, you have to reply their needs. You have to do this in a Batıni way, not in a Zahiri way. You have to provide them some peace.

The theme of religio-secularity, emphasized earlier, seems to be a key to understanding the ways in which these men renegotiate their position as spiritual and religious at different instances. They are mediators, leaders of faith, and moralists, who, finding themselves in the unfamiliar territory of worldly affairs, are required to perform worldly duties and worldly deeds.

5.2   *The Problems of Dedes*

When asked about problems of being such a leader, they cite daily life struggles, their official status, the changing demands of their talibs, organizational role conflicts, and tensions on interpreting theological principles of their culture. The pressures they are experiencing at different associations, due to the legal procedures defining the Alevi associations, involve conflicts between the dedes and the leaders of the appointed management. It is claimed that these organizations tend to act in a corrupt way in their territorial games. All of these "immoral" acts are formulated as obstacles for keeping and transmitting their traditions.

I#2   There are not enough institutions which can provide education for prospective dedes. There are numerous theology schools; they are not very qualified in communicating people properly. There are too many variations (of faith), which may create problems.

"There are variations among Alevi people in different places. Alevism is being assimilated today. For example, there are some rituals being transformed and assimilated. We have not been informed or supported intellectually or theologically. Some people, our followers have not been expressing themselves because they were afraid. Serving the way (yol), serving God and serving people is our main principle."

> "The structure of Alevi organizations is very problematic: There have been some ex-leftists who occupied the management of these organizations; and our naive people went after them without knowing the danger. If they can get rid of these (people) we can re-establish places based on love and peace. The higher echelons of these organizations (federations, associations) are full of problems such as power games and nepotism. The followers are not aware of these corrosions, which, actually distort our moral order. Alevis are being used by some corrupt people."

I#3   There are pressures on dedes. For example they ask us the reason for not praying five times a day (which is a Sunni ritual). Some dedes cannot express themselves properly. We can see that it is getting harder for them. Some of them are getting away from their identities. This should not happen.

I#4   The real problems are not financial problems, income etc. Dedes must treat rich and poor equally. We come from a fair-minded tradition. But some people are abusing us by taking part in TV programs at Ramadan, or being part in conversation programs while using our tax money. We dedes should be given the same air time at least during our religious days.

I#5   Organizational structure of Alevi associations are the major obstacle for dedes who are exposed to the control of the managers (başkan) of these associations, which leads to the de-legitimation of dede roles as well as a loss of faith and trust for many Alevi people.

I#7   The Alevi movement has existed through velis, spiritual guides which all accepted the principle of consent (rıza) If people underline their material interests, there appears hypocricy (riya) You choose either consent or hypocrisy.

The last comment made by the seventh interviewee summarizes their apprehensiveness about losing control, being forced to de-emphasize their theological understanding of the rituals, and as one participant pointed out: "being forced to become an imam" (Sunni religious leader). As is noted earlier, imposition and enforcement of Islam on Alevis by state representatives reveal how these spiritual leaders are forbidden to define their identity as having a spiritual dimension. Instead, the process of "imamization" has become visible and normalized according to the validity claims of the Directory of Religious Affairs, as clearly described by interviewee no: #7. Such overlapping themes as Sunnification, delegitimization, resacralization, state-made Alevization, all refer to the same boundary issues, which also define the scope of will formation, which brings us to discern the patterns on their narratives about agency.

5.3   Agency

I#1 The major problem is to find out a legitimate organization, an institutional interlocutor, which would represent Alevis. The transmission of culture has been realized through the hearth system (ocak) in Turkey. There have been numerous ocaks, at least 200. However, in some regions there are other types of practices (sürek). These practices, which are more common and visible in some regions, should be included in the process too. Alevism accepts the principle of "The way (yol) is one, the roads one thousand and one!" This is why we should get in touch and bring these different roads together. This body will be an important interlocutor in making discussions with the state officials and its main purpose will be developing strategies for implementing the law.

I#2 The key to freedoms for Alevis is to lie in morality. Schools provide religion lessons in their curriculum. I think that (all) students learn morality lessons from Alevi sources.

I#3 Getting organized is very important. There are three Alevi Federations in Turkey. They try to find out solutions to our problems. Alevis are seen as Blacks of Turkey.
We are not somebody's back yard. All political parties instrumentalize us. Alevism is above all political parties.

I#10 We think that Alevi people should have chances to educate their children. The lawyers representing the government at the ECtRH claimed that Alevis can be granted rights to form schools where they can use a curriculum which includes well-designed classes about Alevi culture. This is why we tried hard to establish a school system which would not discriminate against Alevi children. All Alevis should be thinking about this problem.

The interviewees' answers to finding the most reasonable interlocutor, which could maneuver issues such as representation, negotiation, and leadership at the national and local level were expressed at different levels. They ranged from the formation of an encompassing a council, to being strongly committed to the trajectory (yol), and being moral actors. The increasing number of religious schools known as Imam Hatip Schools after the 1980 coup, as well as the allocated resources for these schools, forced Alevi people to integrate a language which refers the power of institutions instead of power of ideologies. The counter-institutionalization attempts in wanting to form Alevi schools clearly derives their own understand of secularity, which requires protecting their right to have a "cultural education," rather than following an abstract principle.

5.4 Major Constraints

Which actors are expressed as having an enforcement role on dedes? Who are the major actors defining and controlling their undefined sphere of action? Personal will to act through their moral capacity, as well as being part of an institution that could represent them are revealed as their priorities.

I#1   They are taking Islam into a non-peaceful track by emphasizing war (cihad). (The belief on) killing people on behalf of religion, and using these beliefs as a state religion on behalf of Islam has been an outcome of a long process starting from Emevi Empire. We can call this process as "statization" of religion.
Why is the state interested in personal faith of its own citizens? Why does it keep our state officials so busy? Its never easy to understand this. The mission of the state is to help citizens to implement their task of faith. Morally or legally, it's not the duty of the state not to implement the law regarding their rights.

I#2   (About Alevi openings): They did not offer any contribution. I joined one of these meetings where they were playing the ceremonial dance (semah) in a different way. I said that this is not real semah. You are turning it into a play. Semah is not a play. It is one of the core characteristics of Alevi faith and it cannot be separated from Cem ritual. Those who do not know anything about our faith presented and defined semah as part of the cultural heritage (to the UNESCO), which was a plot refused by our organization. The demand of those people who treat Alevism as culture, those who define Alevi faith without its own core values have been accepted. We totally refuse this (culturalization of religious ritual).

I#3 They have been discussing the salaries of dedes. Yes, they can receive their salaries from the Diyanet (DRA) however, in this case, they will be an official of the government, which is dangerous. They can inject Sunnism into our culture.

I#4 Some dedes tried to sell their faith. If you sell your religion you may as well sell your future.

I#5 The ways in which the representation issue of Alevi people are solved is totally wrong. Ocaks are being transformed into the foundations which has problems in their management, lack of qualified people in understanding and transmitting the Alevi tradition. This transformation led to a decay in our identity too, because ocaks are now competing with one another, which would not fit our theology or culture. Once I met someone from another ocak who was very condescending to me: He said, "Your ocak is much more smaller than ours," which shows a lack of maturity. This process of foundationalization (vakıflaşma) is at the core of all problems for Alevis in the cities right now. Some foundations, which derive their powers from ocaks, urged dedes to introduce our faith to society, to make it more visible and they said that "do good things for your faith." This led to a degeneration and demoralization. People are recklessly innovating new rituals, e.g. in the social media, saying that this is my cem ritual, trying to increase their followers in social media.
Some foundations have published small booklets called Erkanname, which are guidebooks about describing the basic duties for dedes. They include information and standards about leading a praying session at wedding ceremony, funeral services, etc. These booklets helped dedes in terms of guiding people, at least young dedes; however, the standardization led to loss of our faith in a sincere way. People join rituals for the sake of being there; they do not care about the meaning. This also leads to irresponsibility among dedes, loss of morality, and loss of spirituality. If these things are being lost, no one can act on anything.

The narratives on statization, Sunni injection, othering, the role of the DRA, and foundationalization of Alevi affairs emerge as the processes over which these *dedes* have actively crafted their own understandings. Their own interpretations, expressed by almost all interviewees in our study at some point, include ambivalent expressions of vicissitudes, affirmations on developing a series of strategies to enlarge the politics of recognition, and disappointments on the failed state of affairs in eliminating these obstacles.

5.5 The Role of National and Supra-National Judicial Organizations

The participants are all aware about the court cases in which some Alevi Foundations have sought their rights at national and international level. The line of questioning at the macro level is based on two different narratives: one is the representation and legitimation of Alevis; the second is the ways in which ECtRT rulings sparked the controversial issue of religionization. A large majority of dedes refused to accept the legitimacy of seeking justice at the ECtHR, declaring that the Court has no right to make legal rulings which indicate ideological and theological implications. For example:

I#2   There are many people who are unaware about the ECtRT rulings. Alevi organizations, debates on Alevi identity, etc did not have any impact on the government at all. All of these strategies called "openings" were just a way for distracting people.

I#4   These developments revealed that we are not recognized (by the government). If this is the case, what type of contribution can they offer us? Nothing. Some municipalities have recognized our status, granting us some rights. These are minor issues. They said that our electricity bills will be paid. So what? A complete solution did not emerge out of negotiations with the government.

I#6   I find it positive. The rulings (at the ECtRT) have not been implemented, unfortunately. It did not bring about any freedom. We could not develop a mechanism to implement these decisions. The Foundation aimed at designing a docile Alevism. Namely, they wanted to see people who go to their ceremonies, playing their saz (a folkloric instrument), not getting engaged in anything else, not seeking their rights, protesting. Whereas the essence of Alevism is the streets (protesting). Its essence is based on challenging. Playing saz does not mean Alevism. They (the Foundation) created a pro-state (statized) Alevism. I wish that the state and religion would be different, but it is not. We are being treated in the same manner with some other religious communities (cemaat).

I#7   The court (the ECtRH) asks you: To which religion you belong? Is it shamanism, materialism, etc. They force Alevis to define their religion. I. Doğan claims that we are the Turkish version of Islam. Is he a prophet descended into Turks? Islam already exists. There are too many variations among sects. We are one of them. Such an ignorant attitude! We are Islam, but have a different interpretation. Debating if we are Islam or not is not good. These kinds of actions cause polarization.

The law regarding the closure of all religious communities (The Law of Dervish Lodges and Retreats, no: 667) is already there; it's still valid. It negatively effected Alevis compared to Sunnis. Nobody mentions about this law, and they take their case to the European Court.

They want to mold Alevism, imposing their own rules and regulations: They created these rules for different rituals. Whereas there is diversity among Alevi rituals which cannot be unified. Its like different currents of water, which all come down and unite in a pool. There you see a saturation after a while, that's Alevism.

As is noted above, Prof. İzzettin Doğan, who is mentioned by I#7, is the head of the The Republican Education and Culture Centre Foundation (Cem Vafkı), which filed a suit against the Turkish Republic in 2013. In 2016, ECtHR ruled in favor of Turkish Alevi community leaders, and members in the case brought a case for the official recognition of Alevi houses of worship Cemevis (house of cem, the Alevi worship ritual) and employment of Alevi faith leaders (Turkish Daily Sabah). The bitterness and hostility toward the case is evident in the rhetorical style of some participants, and the majority believe that the problem of granting rights to Alevi citizens should have been left to the internal/national agencies.

The thematic analysis described above, can be outlined in the following table.

6   Conclusion

In an attempt to explore the example of dedelik, which is an institution in the sociology of Alevism, this chapter aimed at exploring Alevi dedes and their narratives on Alevi-ness, agency, identity, morality, and faith. In addition, the data presented here are assumed to have a symbolic power to explicate the constraints on religious freedom experienced by Alevi leaders known as dedes.

TABLE 6.2 The key themes in participants' answers

	The role of Dedes	Problems of Dedes	Agency	Major obstacles	Alevism	Supra-national institutions	Major argumentative marker
1	Major Actor; moral guidance; mediator; non-political	Lack of Recognition	A Council of Alevi Organizations; Ocak/Sürek Unity	Statization of Religion	A Religion	Yes	Legal-rational, ethos oriented
2	Moral Guidance, Moral Role Model	Lack of Education, De-traditionalizaiton	Conscious Alevis	History of Assimilation, Bias against Alevis, lack of identity awareness	Islam	Yes	Historicized understanding of identity, normative
3	Responsible for Followers (Talips)	Othering, Loss of Identity	All Alevis	Othering and Discrimination, oppression, Sunni Order	A Faith Based on Justice	No	Identity Recognition
4	Spiritual Counseling	Non-material, recognition	A Political Party	Instrumental relationship, extreme diversity	A Faith based on justice, followers of Ehl-i Beyt	No	Authenticty of Faith, self-representation

TABLE 6.2 The key themes in participants' answers (cont.)

	The role of Dedes	Problems of Dedes	Agency	Major obstacles	Alevism	Supra-national institutions	Major argumentative marker
5	Spiritual Counseling	Material and Non-Material	Ethical self	Foundationalization	A Spiritual Serving Practice	Yes/No	Ethos oriented, spiritual core
6	A member of an *ocak*	Lack of recognition	Citizenship Rights	Statization of Alevism; lack of legitimacy (for dedes); docile subjects	A Faith based on *Hak* (Justice)	No	Liberation, recognition
7	Moral Guidance	Non-material; lack of spiritual maturity	A Special and Independent Branch for Alevis	Assimilation, Oppression, Lack pf Recognition and Justice	A Religion/ Culture Based on Justice, Humanism,	No	Emancipatory, Laicism, Mysticism
8	Secular/ spiritual responsibility	Lack of wealth	Unity of *Ocaks* (Hearth)	Lack of Unity	A Faith based on *Hak* (Justice)	Yes	Spiritual empowerment as a precondition for action

These key narrative markers, it is argued, provided a way to enlighten the relationship between their reflexive pieties in everyday life, as well as their negotiations on rapidly changing status of their duties as part of multilayered modernization and religionization process in Turkish society. This presentation attempted to define their changing roles in relation to religio-secular world, which also is constructed by non-Alevi forces.

The status of dedes has been negatively affected by urbanization, migration, and other sociological processes to the extent that the divide between traditional and modern leaders visibly widened in the last twenty years. The institutionalization of dedelik in urban settings created a spiritual/moral vacuum, due to the lack of guides (pirs), which resulted in a weakening and delegitimized status. The findings explicated above clearly reveal how their narratives reflect such intricate negotiations so as to accommodate their understanding of freedom within the spectrum of worldly and spiritual markers. The apparently inherently spiritual status has been partially deemphasized, transforming it into an institutionalized one as an outcome of the differentiation between various Alevi organizations and foundations.

A large majority of the Alevi foundations, which had close ties with the holy lineage (ocak) system, intervened in this process of delegitimization and desacralization, requiring members to make Alevi-ness more visible and offer them educational opportunities. After the Alevi openings sparked an intense debate about Alevi culture in 2000s, various different actors developed their own approaches, leading to a multiplicity of discourses. The theme of "statization" emphasized by some interviewees has a connotation related to de-sacralization, which is formulated as an obstacle in the formation of their identities. In a similar vein, the theme of "foundationalization" manifests itself in the process of building Alevi organizations, which are no longer attached to the traditional ocak system, but rather, to higher levels of legitimacy. In addition, the scriptualizing of Alevi culture, noted by some interviewees, seems to have impacted Alevi dedes, leading to feelings of disorientation caused by the new formulae for their everyday duties. The highly regulative practices of DRA as well as attempts to open space for Alevi organizations in political sphere are not accepted as genuine maneuvers by dedes.

In this context, the participants in this study tended to express their narratives, which provide us a direction about their preferences and the degree of negotiations over the major principles, through a meta-discourse, that is, "discourse about discourse," which refers to the author's or speaker's linguistic text manifestation which interacts with receivers (Vande Kopple 1985: 83). Alevi dedes, in their narratives on the major themes and issues selected for this study, tended to construct their language in relation to other actors, which may be Sunnis, state officials, representatives of other associations and federations. The majority of dedes were highly critical and aware of the transformation from traditional into modern typologies of dedelik, which is argued to be crucial in understanding issues such as the lack of an agency, degeneration and corruption among some dedes, ranking and hierarchical ordering, the conflict between the organizational procedures of associations, and the need for political and spiritual recognition. When they described the pressure of their followers, they emphasized the vulnerability of dedes in replying to demands, due to the lack of a well defined ombudsman or strong leadership. The linguistic hegemony constructed by the social and political processes described in this chapter also enforced them to employ the modernist discourse on enlightenment, emancipation, liberation, and exploitation.

When asked about the differentiation in Alevi organizations, their narratives also focused on specific facts, such as common scripts (Erkanname) published by one of the Alevi foundations. These booklets define a common core of actions as reference points, e.g. used in rituals like cem, constituting an important part of a religionized language, which has been revealed through a series of concepts used above. As Dressler vividly evaluates, "while postcolonial studies have discussed the role of religion as a tool to legitimize and administer the hegemony of the nation-state, less attention has been directed to cases in which marginalized sociocultural communities have adopted the language of religion as a means of empowerment vis-à-vis assimilationist politics directed against them" (Dressler 2008: 41). The components of the dede narratives, with regard to their faith and roles, reflect a certain acceptance of such a vocabulary, where religionization (Dressler 2019) becomes more visible. In other words, "we can view religions, philosophies, paths, etc., as systems or frameworks for assessing, ranking, manipulating, and sometimes transcending things that matter (and, thus, are viewed as special)" (Taves 2010: 175). The process of de-sacralization, as well as the need to implement standardization, brought about a system of closure on experiencing and prioritizing their spiritual feature which are internalized in their own local organizations.

The wide variety of tensions and constraints expressed by the participants also displayed a conceptual network, in which the words and deeds are configured in relation to Sunni Islam. They felt that they could not re-claim their identities in a traditional sense, due to the boundaries set by the pressure of talibs or organizations. One of the participants (I#5) explained the tension in a clear way:

> The Alevi openings really created an excitement among people (at the beginning of 2000's). They organized numerous meetings, where they discussed the key to the problem of representation and institutionalization.

They ended up imitating the style of management used by the DRA. They debated about the formation of legitimate councils, and so on. None of these attempts could resolve our problem. These efforts failed, because they did not include the manifestation of God (tecelli). If they did, they could have been successful. But in this case, they could not find a position for themselves; because they separated themselves from Hakk (the essence of God). Alevis already have their own institutions, which are made of holy lineages (ocak, pir, babas, and dede), spiritual leaders with different roles and status. When you try to integrate this system into the other one where some corrupt, immoral people dominate everything, think about their own interests. This does not work. It can't. Our (ocak) system elevates the most moral, spiritual people up and makes them leaders, who have to have the highest energy and morality. Whereas, the structure we see in foundations and associations forbids everybody to their normal, moral (dedelik) duties. They give these duties to those who can speak well, advertise themselves. This cannot be accepted. One has to follow the trajectory (Yol) first, then start solving other problems. Dedes' own mistakes also caused this situation.

These comments, which have the power of self-reflexivity, clearly indicate the way in which the language of sacred/profane distinction leads to a form of alienation among dedes and their followers. This transition from an (I#1) "authentic," (I#7) "spiritual," and (I#8) "real" dedelik into something that "(I#5) nobody can recognize" presents itself through social and cultural obstacles, which prevent dedes re-claiming their identities. Comparing traditional dedes, who are heavily characterized by their telos of piety, and modern institutionalized dedes requires a "socio-theological understanding" (Juergensmeyer and Roof, 2011, 892), due to the ways in which the components of their narratives include storifications, emplotments, and metaphors, which necessitate referring to their folkloric and theological understandings.

Thus, the narratives of dedes on their subjective understanding of their statuses derive from a meta-discursive field where different actors are attached to their own formulae on religious freedoms. Social consequences of their sociotheological thinking have become one important source of "politics of deeming" (Taves 2010, 317). In addition, their views on the threat of the Sunnification through transformation of sacred practices illuminate the impossibility of re-negotiating their mediating powers. According to Durkheim, "la morale" combines the English words "moral" and "morale" into one concept. "It includes action and judgment, but it also includes aspects of worldview and the sense of purpose that undergirds a well-shaped human life" (Spickard 2017, 162). In forthcoming Alevi studies, cultivating the ability to position Alevi actors and their own understanding according to their judgment and sense of purpose, then, might foster the investigation of undiscovered themes and topics within the framework of relationality.

References

Asad, Talal. 2003. *Formations of the Secular: Christianity, Islam, Modernity.* Stanford University Press, 2003.
Bader, Veit. 2010. "Constitutionalizing Secularism, Alternative Secularisms or Liberal-Democratic Constitutionalism-A Critical Reading of Some Turkish, ECtHR and Indian Supreme Court Cases on Secularism." *Utrecht L. Rev.* 6, No.3 (November): 8–35.
Çarkoğlu, Ali and Nazlı Ç. Bilgili. 2011. "A Precarious Relationship: the Alevi Minority, the Turkish State and the EU." *South European Society and Politics* 16: 351–364. (Accessed June 3, 20019).
Cloke, Paul et al. 2019. Geographies of Postsecularity: Re-envisioning Politics, Subjectivity and Ethics. Routledge.
Danchin, Peter G. 2015. "Religious Freedom in Panopticon of Enlightenment Rationality." In *Politics of Religious Freedom*, edited by W. Sullivan et. al. 240–52. Chicago: University of Chicago Press.
Dressler, Markus. 2014. "The Modern Dede: Changing Parameters for Religious Authority in Contemporary Turkish Alevism." In *Speaking for Islam: Religious Authorities in Muslim Societies*, edited by G. Krämer, and S. Schmidtke, 269–95. Brill.
Dressler, Markus. 2008. "Religio-Secular Metamorphoses: The Re-making of Turkish Alevism." *Journal of the American Academy of Religion* 76(2): 280–311.. (Accessed February 6, 2009).
Dressler, Markus. 2015. "Turkish Politics of Doxa: Otherizing the Alevis as Heterodox." *Philosophy & Social Criticism* 41(4–5): 445–451. (Accessed March 1, 2017).
Dressler, Markus. 2019. "Modes of Religionization: A Constructivist Approach to Secularity." In "Multiple Secularities—Beyond the West, Beyond Modernities," edited by C. Kleine, and M. Wohlrab-Sahr. *Working Paper Series of the Centre for Advanced Studies Research Programme of the HCAS.* Leipzig.
Erol, Melih Uğraş. 2015. "Questioning Non-Discrimination, Equality, and Human Rights in Contemporary Turkey from the Perspective of the Alevi Religious Community." *Muslim World Journal of Human Rights* 12(1): 75–97. (Accessed 21 October, 2018).
Ferri, Marcella. 2017. "The Doğan et al. v. Turkey: a Missed Opportunity to Recognise Positive Obligations as Regards the Freedom of Religion." *European Papers* 2(1): 311–319. (Accessed 1 October, 2018).
Hurd, Elizabeth Shakman. 2014. "Alevis Under Law: The Politics of Religious Freedom in Turkey." *Journal of Law and Religion* 29(3): 416–35. https://doi:io.io17/jlr.zoI4.18. (Accessed 13 March, 2018).

Işık, Caner. 2017. *Erenlerin Süreği*. Istanbul: Tibyan.
Işık, Caner. 2011. "Anadolu Mistisizminde Gerçeklik ve Deneyim." *Alevililik Araştırmaları Dergisi* 2: 157–164.
Juergensmeyer, Mark and Wade Clark Roof. Edited. 2011. *Encyclopedia of Global Religion*. London: Sage.
Kaya, Haydar. 2011. *Alevilik Tarihi*. İzmir: Ehl-I Beyt.
Laborde, Cecile. 2008. *Critical Republicanism: The Hijab Controversy and Political Philosophy*. Oxford: Oxford University Press.
Melikoff, Irene. 1998. "Bektashi/Kızılbaş: Historical Bipartition and Its Consequences." *Alevi Identity: Cultural, Religious and Social Perspectives*: 1–7.
Ocak, Ahmet Yaşar. 1999. "Alevîliğin Tarihsel, Sosyal Tabanı ile Teolojisi Arasındaki İlişki Problemine Dair." In *Tarihî ve Kültürel Boyutlarıyla Türkiye'de Alevîler Bektaşîler Nusayrîler*, edited by M. Öz, 385–98. Istanbul: Ensar Neşriyat.
Peri, Yoram et al. 2012. "The 'Religionization' of Israeli Society." *Israel Studies Review* 27(1): 1–30. (Accessed 2 June, 2020).
Sharma, Arvind. 2011. Problematizing Religious Freedom" Canada: Springer Science & Business Media.
Shah, Timothy Samuel, Matthew J. Franck, and Thomas franklin Farr. 2012. *Religious Freedom: Why Now?: Defending an Embattled Human Right*. Princeton, CA: Witherspoon Institute.
Somers, Margaret R, and Gloria Gibson. 1993. "Reclaiming the Epistemological Other: Narrative and the Social Constitution of Identity." *CSST Working Paper Series*, 499.pdf (umich.edu).
Spickard, James V. 2017. *Alternative Sociologies of Religion: Through Non-Eastern Eyes*. NYU Press.
Sökefeld, Martin. 2002. "Alevi Dedes in the German Diaspora: The Transformation of a Religious Institution." *Zeitschrift für Ethnologie* 163–86. (Accessed 2 October, 2015).
Taves, Ann. 2010. "Experience as site of contested meaning and value: The attributional dog and its special tail." *Religion* 40 (4): 317–23. (Accessed 23 September, 2019).
Vande Kopple, William J. 1985. "Some exploratory discourse on metadiscourse." - College Composition and Communication 36, 82–93.
Vande Kopple, Willam J. 2002. "Metadiscourse, Discourse, and Issues in Composition and Rhetoric." *Discourse Studies in Composition:* 91–113.
Vandermause, Roxanne K. and Susan Fleming. 2011. "Philosophical Hermeneutic Interviewing." *International Journal of Qualitative Methods* 10(4), 367–77.. (Accessed 2 September, 2018).
Yaman, Ali. 2012. "Geçmişten Günümüze Alevi Ocaklarında Değişime Dair Sosyo-Antropolojik Gözlemler." *Turkish Culture & Haci Bektas Veli Research Quarterly* 63: 17–36.

CHAPTER 7

One, Many or None: Religious Truth-Claims and Social Perception of Religious Freedom

Olga Breskaya and Giuseppe Giordan

> Religious diversity involves not only differences in rituals and dress, but more significantly, basic differences in ways in which religions understand and respond to reality.
>
> HAROLD A. NETLAND "Inclusivism and Exclusivism" 2007, 226

∴

1 Introduction

As part of broader social-scientific concern with understanding how the meaning of religious freedom is constructed within societies, an ongoing scholarly debate has centered around agency and structural conditions of this freedom. Macro- and meso-theories of religious freedom offered explanatory arguments about the role of economic development, rise of modern liberal states, autonomy of judicial system, structural pluralism, disestablishment model of state-religion relations (Finke 1990, 2013; Richardson 2006, 2017; Gill 2008; Durham 2012; Fox 2015; Johnson and Koyama 2019) in advancement of religious freedom values and policies. A closer look at the sociological theories of religious freedom, however, emphasizes socioreligious conditions for a complete understanding of this concept. Among them are increasing religious pluralism of modern societies and multiplicity of individual responses to the quest for life meaning (Maclure and Taylor 2011; Richardson 2011; Berger 2014; Giordan 2014).

Introducing his definition of religious freedom, Peter Berger (2014) argued that pluralism of modern societies has to consider "the co-existence of different religions and the co-existence of religious and secular discourses" and "this co-existence occurs both in the minds of individuals and in social space" (Berger 2014, ix). Thus, the sociological levels of pluralism have to be designated together with the variety of forms which this phenomenon attains.

Moreover, Berger considered pluralism as a sociological condition of modern societies, which he described in terms of "social arrangement favorable for a high or relatively higher level of plurality" of society, i.e., its religious heterogeneity (Yang 2014, 136). Among various meanings of pluralism as a social arrangement, Berger highlighted the relevance of this concept to the idea of religious freedom by "granting and protecting for individuals the freedom to choose whatever religion they want, or no religion at all" (Yang 2014, 137).

James Beckford (2014) stated that it is a prerequisite of sociological study of religious pluralism to take into account its empirical and normative dimensions and analyze religious pluralism "in social settings and interactions" (Beckford 2014, 26). He designated three sociological levels of analyses of empirical diversity referring to a) a variety of distinct faith traditions, b) diversity within one faith traditions, and c) variety of individual ways of following religious traditions. With references to John Hick's theory of pluralism (1977), Beckford noted that normative religious pluralism "advocate[s] respect for the positive value of religious diversity in itself or as a means to the attainment of social and cultural cohesion and harmony" (Beckford 2014, 22). Among the wide array of factors that influence patterns of regulation of pluralistic societies, Beckford emphasized the role of human rights discourse, which emphasizes the principles of nondiscrimination and equality for religious groups and individuals. Thus, a balance between individual and social levels and empirical and normative dimensions of religious diversity was specified for sociological research of pluralism and religious freedom.

At the social level, the analysis of religious pluralism meant conceptualization among other issues, processes of establishing interfaith dialogue and religious truth-claims or theology of religions (Beckford 2014). Its analysis at the level of individual practices accounted the processes of strengthening freedom of individual choices in religious and secular spheres (Giordan 2007) which happened "obviously not without consequences for the relationship of the believer with the tradition" and "in tune with the needs of the 'inner self,' which pays more attention to subjective authenticity than to objective truth" (Giordan 2014, 5–6). The latter argument of Giuseppe Giordan emphasized the importance of analysis of normative pluralism and religious freedom at the individual level.

Accounting for the structural contexts supporting religious freedom, a micro-sociology of religious freedom initiated a search for correlates at the individual level by looking at individual religiosity, affiliation, practices of intercultural communication and interreligious learning, and religious truth-claims (Wuthnow and Lewis 2008; Van der Ven and Ziebertz 2012, 2013; Francis et al. 2018; Unser 2019). For instance, Anders Sjöborg (2012) showed that

importance of interreligious dialogue and pluralism and belief in a diversity of its forms and concepts (natural pantheism, Jesus liberation, Muhammad as a mystic, uniqueness of Muhammad, and inclusive and prophetic religious communities) together with views on politics, values of autonomy, and social critique predicted religious freedom views. In contrast, gender differences, religious saliency, contextual reading of the Bible or the Quran, interreligious exclusivism and inclusivism, and a variety of forms of belief[1] were not related to perceptions of religious freedom (Sjöborg 2012, 161–62).

Our previous research on religious freedom indicated variances in explanatory power of religious belonging, faith and spirituality experiences, religiosity, secularism, trust in governmental institutions (Breskaya and Botvar 2019; Breskaya and Giordan 2019; Breskaya and Rogobete 2020). It questioned the balance of socio-political and individual religious contexts which influence social perceptions of religious freedom in national society. However, it also raised the methodological problem in a modeling type of study on religious freedom, which can encompass such measures.

This chapter discusses a model of conceptualizing religious freedom as a multidimensional concept for its empirical research at the level of individual analysis. The previous research showed that this model allows exploring the constructed meaning of religious freedom by individual citizens controlling for religiosity, spiritual and religious identities, and socio-political practices together with the analysis of the role of political secularism and equal citizenship.

For the purposes of current research, we consider the relationship between perception of religious freedom and religious pluralism at the individual level of empirical analysis looking for a variety of truth-claims of individual conscience and positive and negative attitudes toward religious diversity. Considering the theoretical argument about the linkage between pluralism and religious freedom in modern societies, this chapter examines if and how religious pluralism can be considered as a correlate and predictor of perceptions of religious freedom. Along with pluralism, we explore how individual truth-claims, such as exclusivism, inclusivism, interreligious perspective, agnosticism, and atheism, are associated with religious freedom claims and views on religious diversity at the level of society.

---

1 Such as belief in God, individual pantheism, pantheism, deism, Jesus inspiration by spirit, Jesus in humanist view, Jesus solidarity, Muhammad in humanist view, and Muhammad as prophet (see Sjöborg 2012).

2   Religious Freedom and Variety of Religious Truth-Claims in Empirical Analysis

The social perception of religious freedom is a complex concept that holds many implications for public life. The adjective "social" refers to the process of construction of *shared* religious freedom meaning in society which "is produced by intergroup dynamics — by social actors with various civil, political, religious, and nonreligious identities — favoring one dimension of the concept more than the other" (Breskaya and Giordan 2019, 1).

In the process of establishing relationship between various aspects of religious freedom by citizens, the linkage between individual claims and meanings of religious freedom and condition of religious pluralism came to the center of research. Moreover, by taking into account socio-legal perspectives on "how people experience faith" by integrating "personal or subjective understanding of freedom of religion" (Maclure and Taylor 2011, 82) with normative principles of nondiscrimination and noncoercion, the socially constructed nature of religious freedom becomes more discernable. Despite the variety of connotations which religious freedom contains — making this concept challenging for sociological research — empirical research of social perceptions of its multidimensional nature provides possibilities for studying the process of establishing domains of its societal meaning.

In this research, we develop the idea of measuring religious freedom as a five-dimensional concept exploring its meaning as: (1) Individual and religious groups' autonomy; (2) Societal value; (3) Principle of state-religion governance; (4) International human rights standard; and (5) Impact of judicialization of religious freedom. Results of testing this theoretical model on a convenience sample of university students in 2018 in Northern Italy, suggested findings that primary, for young people, religious freedom is perceived through its meaning as a "Societal value," such as promotion of interreligious dialogue, cultural and religious diversity, tolerant and peaceful coexistence of religions, and connecting ideals of liberty with the principle of democratic citizenship (Breskaya and Giordan 2019). Second, it was perceived as an "International human rights standard;" thirdly, as a "Principle of state-religion governance;" fourthly, through the subjective meaning, such as an "Individual autonomy;" and, finally, as an "Impact of judicialization." We relied on the results of exploratory factor analysis in testing the latent factors of the SPRF measures (Breskaya and Giordan 2019).

Understanding the complex nature of religious freedom, its functionality for individuals and social order, we focus on sociological questions about the type of religious positioning that is more congruent with religious freedom claims.

In other words, what kind of predispositions toward religious truth endorse various aspects of religious freedom? To whom religious freedom-claims are more important: to the individuals who accept religious truth or those who "turn away" from religious perspectives? In answering this question, first we looked for self-assigned religious identities, such as Roman Catholicism, religious minorities and 'no religion' group and the modes they considered various dimensions of religious freedom, and second, for the patterns religious truth-claims and self-assigned religious affiliation produce differences in perceptions of religious freedom.

The pluralistic thesis (Hick 2007) emphasizes the conflicting nature between religious truth-claims and at the same time the "transformation of human existence from self-centredness to Reality-centredness" (Hick 1989, 240) within all traditions for individuals who share them. With references to Stephen Kaplan's ideas on "metaphysical democracy" (Kaplan 2002), John Hick noted that "individuals can choose for themselves between the different ultimate realities and paths of salvation/liberation" (Hick 2007, 217). His pluralistic thesis advocated for equality of religious truth-claims, stating that each position seems to be "equally effective (and of course also equally ineffective)" (Hick 2007, 221) in helping individuals in their search for the ultimate meanings. Western theologians started to share the pluralist thesis in the 1970s and 1980s, arguing that, "major religions should be regarded as more or less equally effective and legitimate alternatives for responding to the one divine reality" (Netland 2007, 227–28).

The pluralistic perspective taken together with other positions toward religious truth "as it is understood in respect to the *cognitive* claims of religion" (Astley and Francis 2016, 30) —exclusivism, inclusivism, interreligious perspective, agnosticism, and atheism — were operationalized in the Astley-Francis Theology of Religions Index (AFTRI) by suggesting seven statements for evaluation (see Table 7.1 below). Pluralism in AFTRI is measured by two perspectives: Pluralism A (All religions are equally true) and Pluralism B (All religions express the same truth in different ways). According to Jeff Astley and Leslie J. Francis, the "popularity of pluralism arguably reflects the dominance of postmodern thinking within advanced western society" (Astley and Francis 2016, 30), and it was also considered by the authors of the Index that pluralistic perspective would be the mostly privileged view among all options. In the AFTRI, two perspectives can be seen as opposite to pluralism: exclusivism and atheism. While the former establishes that, "Only one religion is really true and all others are totally false," the latter states that, "All religions are totally false." Against the background of theories of religious pluralism and recent empirical studies on religious freedom, we hypothesize that:

(H1) Perception of dimensions of religious freedom is sensitive to self-assigned religious identities (Catholic, religious minority, and 'no religion'), thus we expect to observe difference among the groups, specifically between religious minority and participants with "no religion."

(H2) Pluralism (Pluralism A and Pluralism B) as religious truth-claim is endorsed more in comparison with other perspectives (such as exclusivism, inclusivism, interreligious perspective, atheism, and agnosticism).

(H3) Pluralism oriented toward the idea that, "All religions express the same truth in different ways" (Pluralism B) is endorsed more than "All religions are equally true" (Pluralism A) by the participants.

(H4) Religious truth-claims contribute to differences in religious freedom perceptions. Specifically, we argue that there is a positive association between Pluralism (A and B), interreligious perspective, and various dimensions of the SPRF.

(H5) We argue that the more individuals endorse the pluralistic truth-claim (Pluralism A and Pluralism B), the more they are open toward religious diversity at the level of social life. That is also to say that the more individuals are leaning to the exclusivist and atheistic perspectives, the less inclusive they are regarding religious diversity and societal values of religious freedom.

3   Data and Measures

We use primary data from the survey Social Perception of Religious Freedom (SPRF). It was conducted in 2018 on a convenience sample of university students in Northern Italy (N= 1035). The aim of the SPRF survey was to verify the new measure of five-dimensional concept of religious freedom and explore the predictive power of socio-religious, human rights, and socio-political contexts of participants vis-à-vis perceptions of religious freedom. In terms of religious affiliation, two-thirds (64 percent) of participants identified themselves as Roman Catholics, near one-third (30 percent) as having "no religion," and six percent as belonging to religious minorities (including Muslim (2.4 percent), Christian-Orthodox (1.7 percent), and Protestants (0.2 percent)). Mean age in the sample was twenty-one years old, 32 percent grew up in the urban area, 30 percent in the rural area, 78 percent were females, 93 percent citizens of Italy, and 45 percent freshmen. Around 19 percent prayed at least weekly and more often, and 45 percent said they believe in God.

4   Dependent Variable

Previous research on the SPRF suggested that religious freedom can be measured with thirty-seven items covering multi-dimensional construct (Breskaya and Giordan 2019). For the purpose of keeping five theoretical dimensions together and aims of current research, we selected nineteen from those thirty-seven items. In doing that, we relied on the high internal consistency of the selected scales (Cronbach's Alpha (α)). Following the results of exploratory factor-analysis, we extracted the scales in the following order: "Societal value" (α = .83); "International human rights standard" (α = .70); "Principle of state-religion governance" (α = .74); "Individual autonomy" (α = .72); and "Impact of judicialization of religious freedom" (α = .60). All the items of the dependent variable of religious freedom were measured with Likert-type scales accounting from one (strong disagreement) to five (strong agreement). The individual items and scales — as developed for measuring the dependent variable and selected for this research — are listed in Table 7.3 below. For the purpose of this research, we present the answers of participants from the general sample and identify themselves with three groups (Catholics, "no religion," and religious minorities). Moreover, we examine the concepts of "Religious truth-claims" and "Religious diversity" to measure their predictive power vis-à-vis perceptions of religious freedom.

5   Independent Variables

Following the measurement model of Theology of Religions Index (AFTRI), as suggested by Astley and Francis (Astley and Francis 2016), we applied it in our research. Astley and Francis suggested a forced choice question with seven possible answers (Table 7.1) that cover six perspectives: exclusivism, inclusivism, pluralism, interreligious perspective, atheism, and agnosticism. The AFTRI was included in the SPRF questionnaire.

The scale "Religious diversity" was developed to measure positive and negative attitudes toward religious diversity in Italian society in the SPRF instrument (Table 7.2). This scale developed further the measure of "Cultural diversity" previously applied in the survey "Religion and Human Rights 2.0" (Van der Ven and Ziebertz 2012, 2013).

A Likert-type scale from one to five was used for the measurement of independent variable of "Religious diversity."

TABLE 7.1   The Astley-Francis Theology of Religions Index (AFTRI)

Theological position	Index statement
Exclusivism	Only one religion is really true and all others are totally false
Inclusivism	Only one religion is really true, but at least one other is partly true
Pluralism A	All religions are equally true
Pluralism B	All religions express the same truth in different ways
Interreligious persp.	Real truth comes from listening to all religions
Atheism	All religions are totally false
Agnosticism	I do not know what to believe about religions

Note: Interreligious persp. = Interreligious perspective

TABLE 7.2   Dimensions of the concept 'Religious Diversity'

Religious diversity (positive attitude)
  Having many different religious points of view is good for Italian society
  Having people from different religions in Italy is enriching
Religious diversity (negative attitude)
  Increasing numbers of religions groups in Italy cause unrest and tension
  In Italy it would be better to pay attention to one dominant religion and culture

6   Results

The starting point of our analysis is with the social perception of religious freedom, i.e., modes of constructing the meaning of religious freedom by participants belonging to majority religion, religious minority groups, and with "no religion" identity. The latter we call further "religious nones." Moreover, we examined predictive power of various perspectives toward religious truth-claims vis-à-vis religious freedom. Table 7.3 presents answers of participants about their perceptions of five dimensions of religious freedom. The data from the general sample and for participants with majority religion, "no religion," and religious minorities identities are provided separately.

The results about the dimension of religious freedom as "Societal value" (items 1–5), showed that all groups agreed with the suggested statements.[2] We observed total agreement with the statements "Religious freedom promotes religious and cultural diversity in society" ($M = 4.21$) for religious nones and "Religious freedom is important for tolerant and peaceful co-existence of religions" ($M = 4.20$ for religious nones, $M = 4.24$ for religious minorities). No statistically significant difference was observed for Catholics, religious nones, and religious minorities while performing a one-way ANOVA test.

The scale "Religious freedom as international human rights standard" (items 6–9) was perceived with unanimous agreement in all groups. Among the four statements of this scale, the one related to the freedom to write, issue and disseminate religious publications was valued with greater value of mean than other items ($M = 3.73$ for the general sample). A one-way ANOVA test revealed statistically significant difference in perceptions of the first [$F(2, 1001) = 6.05$, $p = .002$] and the third items [$F(2, 1006) = 3.54$, $p = .029$] at the $p < .05$. Post-hoc comparisons using the Tukey HSD test indicated that there was a statistically significant difference ($p = .002$ and $p = .032$) in perception of the statements "Freedom to establish religious group" and "Freedom to write, issue and disseminate religious publications" by Catholics ($M = 3.51$ and $M = 3.67$) and religious nones ($M = 3.73$ and $M = 3.83$).

The perception of religious freedom as a "Principle of state-religion governance" (items 10–13) accounts for the way young people evaluate the current policies of Italian state in managing religious groups. The participants from the general sample disagreed with the three first statements (items 10–12) and were positively ambivalent about the fact that Italian state provides equal conditions for the Catholics and non-religious people ($M = 3.22$). It is interesting to note that religious nones assessed more negatively the three first items ($M = 2.20$, $M = 2.32$, $M = 2.17$), while religious minority group was least supportive to the idea that "Italian state provides equal conditions for the Catholics and non-religious people" ($M = 2.96$). Further analysis of differences with one-way ANOVA statistics revealed the tendency of presence of statistically significant difference for all four statements between the groups at the $p < .05$ level. Post-hoc comparisons using the Tukey HSD test showed that those differences were between Catholics and religious nones.

Overview of perceptions of the scale of "Individual autonomy" (items 14–16) revealed agreement of participants with this dimension of religious freedom. Moreover, the greatest value of the mean ($M = 4.10$) was given to the statement

---

2   We rely on the following rule in interpreting the means: 1.00–1.79 = disagree totally; 1.80–2.59 = disagree; 2.60–2.99 = negative ambivalence; 3.00–3.39 = positive ambivalence; 3.40–4.19 = agree; 4.20–5.00 = agree totally.

TABLE 7.3   Means for dependent variable 'Religious Freedom'

		Gen	Cath	None	Min
SocVal	*Religious freedom ...*				
	1. Promotes inter-religious dialogue between religions	4.05	4.04	4.04	4.14
	2. Promotes non-discrimination on the basis of religion	4.01	3.97	4.09	4.10
	3. Promotes religious and cultural diversity in society	4.16	4.13	4.21	4.18
	4. Is important for tolerant and peaceful co-existence of religions	4.15	4.11	4.20	4.24
	5. Promotes liberty as a principle of democratic citizenship	3.94	3.93	3.94	4.09
	Composite mean	4.06	4.04	4.10	4.15
IHRS	*Religious freedom means ...*				
	6. Freedom to establish religious group	3.59	3.51	3.73	3.67
	7. Freedom to express religious views in the media	3.47	3.49	3.42	3.37
	8. Freedom to write, issue and disseminate religious publications	3.73	3.67	3.83	3.83
	9. Everyone should be free to teach their religion, either in public or in private	3.38	3.37	3.38	3.59
	Composite mean	3.54	3.51	3.59	3.61
PSRG	*According to me, Italian state ...*				
	10. Does not favor any religious group	2.45	2.57	2.20	2.51
	11. Provides equal conditions for the Catholic Church and religious minorities	2.56	2.69	2.32	2.67
	12. Manages religious issues very well	2.34	2.43	2.17	2.30
	13. Provides equal conditions for the Catholics and non-religious people	3.22	3.30	3.13	2.96
	Composite mean	2.65	2.75	2.46	2.61

TABLE 7.3 Means for dependent variable 'Religious Freedom' (*cont.*)

		Gen	Cath	None	Min
	Religious freedom ...				
IndAut	14. Is connected with search for individual truth	3.88	3.91	3.76	4.10
	15. Allows everyone to pursue their personal spiritual fulfillment	3.99	4.05	3.86	4.09
	16. Is connected with the idea of human dignity	3.74	3.78	3.66	3.86
	Composite mean	3.87	3.91	3.76	4.02
	Religious freedom means ...				
IJRF	17. In my country, people should be allowed to wear religious clothes and religious symbols at the workplace	3.59	3.56	3.63	3.74
	18. In my country, the state should not prevent female teachers from wearing a head scarf for religious reasons	3.38	3.31	3.48	3.51
	19. Freedom to wear religious clothes/symbols in public places	3.75	3.71	3.82	3.83
	Composite mean	3.57	3.52	3.63	3.69

Note: SocVal = Societal value, IHRS = International human rights standard, PSRG = Principle of state-religion governance, IndAut = Individual Autonomy, IJRF = Impact of judicialization of religious freedom; Gen = general sample, Cath = Catholics, None = religious nones, Min = religious minorities.

"Religious freedom is connected with search for individual truth" by the group of religious minorities. A one-way ANOVA for three groups confirmed statistically significant difference for the statement "Religious freedom is connected with search for individual truth" at the $p < .05$ level [$F(2, 1005) = 4.97, p = .01$] and "Religious freedom allows everyone to pursue their personal spiritual fulfillment" [$F(2, 1005) = 5.83, p = .003$]. Post-hoc comparisons using the Tukey HSD test indicated statistically significant difference between religious minorities ($M = 4.10$) and religious nones ($M = 3.91$) for the statement, "Religious freedom is connected with search for individual truth" ($p = .02$). The same test showed difference in the perceptions of that statement between Catholics and religious nones ($p = .04$). For the statement, "Religious freedom allows everyone to pursue their personal spiritual fulfillment," the results of post-hoc comparisons using the Tukey HSD test showed significant statistical difference between Catholics and religious nones ($p = .003$).

The dimension of "The impact of judicialization" (items 17–19) was perceived with agreement by all groups. There was no statistically significant difference as determined by one-way ANOVA. However, the values of the means were slightly greater in the group of religious minorities.

It is worth mentioning that the group of participants belonging to religious minorities endorsed four scales of the SPRF measure. Religious nones favored human right meaning of religious freedom and its societal value, while aspects of individual autonomy were less important for them (compared to Catholics and religious minorities). Catholic participants supported the way Italian state provides equal conditions for the Catholics and non-religious people more than the other groups ($M = 3.30$).

After presenting the descriptive statistics for the dependent variable of religious freedom, we report frequencies for AFTRI (Table 7.4) and means for the scales on "Religious diversity," their reliability, and suggest the analysis of the correlates of religious freedom.

Descriptive statistics for AFTRI presented in Table 7.4 show that Pluralism B, which claims that all religions express the same truth in different ways, prevailed in the general sample of Italian participants. Slightly less than a half of the sample expressed that claim (44 percent). One-fifth of the participants claimed the agnostic perspective (20 percent). Understanding that real truth

TABLE 7.4   Religious truth-claims AFTRI (frequencies (%))

	Gen	Cath	None	Min
Exclusivism	1.4	1.5	.0	6.9
Inclusivism	1.6	1.5	1.0	6.9
Pluralism A	11.7	14.4	6.9	5.2
Pluralism B	44.3	51.9	27.3	58.6
Interreligious perspective	12.1	11.6	13.5	10.3
Atheism	7.5	2.6	18.1	3.4
Agnosticism	19.7	15.1	31.9	3.4
No answer	1.7	1.4	2.3	5.3

Note: Gen = general sample, Cath = Catholics, None = religious nones, Min = religious minorities.

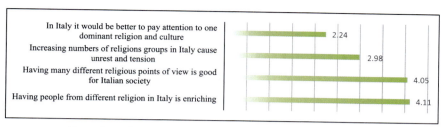

FIGURE 7.1 Means for 'Religious Diversity' (negative and positive attitudes)

comes from listening to all religions (interreligious perspective) was shared by 12 percent of participants, and nearly the same number claimed that all religions are equally true (Pluralism A). Atheistic claim was shared by eight percent of the participants. The exclusivist and inclusivist positions were supported by a small number of young people (three percent together).

If we consider the context of religious belonging of the participants, we find interesting differences in positioning on AFTRI. Among Catholics, there were 66 percent of pluralists (including 52 percent of participants who shared positions on Pluralist B and 14 percent on Pluralism A), 15 percent of agnostics, and 12 percent of those who shared interreligious perspective. For religious minority group, participants claimed pluralistic perspective (59 percent for Pluralism B), interreligious perspective (10 percent), exclusivism (seven percent), and inclusivism (seven percent). Religious nones identified themselves primarily with agnostic (32 percent) and pluralist perspectives (27 percent), and then with atheistic (18 percent) and interreligious positions (14 percent). Before discussing correlation results, means for the positive and negative views on religious diversity are presented (Figure 7.1).

Positive attitude toward religious diversity was privileged over the negative views on diversity. The importance of presence of religious diversity in the Italian society was endorsed with agreement (M = 4.05 and M = 4.11) and statements with negative connotations about religious diversity were evaluated negatively or with negative valence (M = 2.24 and M = 2.98). We computed two scales of "Religious diversity" relying on the internal consistency for the "Religious diversity" (positive views) (M = 4.08; α = .87) and for the "Religious diversity" (negative views) (M = 2.61; α = .54).

Pearson's correlation results (see Table 7.5) show that perceptions of religious freedom aspects were relevant to various religious truth-claims. Perceptions of religious freedom as "Individual autonomy" — subjective meaning of this freedom for participants — were associated more often with religious truth-claims than other dimensions of the SPRF instrument. Three out of seven perspectives of AFTRI were not relevant for the "Individual autonomy." The inclusivist (Only one religion is really true, but at least one other is partly true), interreligious (Real truth comes from listening to all religions), and "Pluralism A" (All religions are equally true) perspectives had no relevance to participants' perceptions of religious freedom as individual way of searching for truth and personal fulfillment. Meanwhile, exclusivist, pluralist ("Pluralism B" – all religions express the same truth in different ways), atheistic, and agnostic perspectives showed positive and negative correlations in this regard. That is to say, the claim of religious freedom at the individual level is to keep open the space for personal self-defining among the positions which not only suggest meaning about individual vision of religious truth but at the same time develop the patterns of relationships with other religious/nonreligious positions. Moreover, while religious freedom aims protecting a space for plurality of religious positions, our data highlight that "Pluralism A" (which emphasizes the equality mostly) is not associated with "Individual autonomy," while "Pluralism B" (which explains plurality as equality and difference) is better linked with the search of own spiritual perspective.

The most sensitive position to religious freedom is the one which claims that all religions are false, i.e., "Atheism." The results demonstrated a significant negative correlation between atheistic position and four of the five scales on

TABLE 7.5   Correlations (Pearson's r, 2-tailed) between AFTRI, SPRF and Religious Diversity

	SocVal	IHRS	PSRG	IndAut	IJRF	RD-pos	RD-neg
Exclusivism	.03	.00	.07*	.10**	-.09**	-.10**	.10**
Inclusivism	.00	.07*	.03	.06	-.01	-.10**	.06
Pluralism A	.05	.10**	.06	.01	.08*	.01	-.00
Pluralism B	.04	-.02	.04	.12**	.00	.04	.03
Interreligious persp.	.05	.06	-.07*	.05	.03	.10**	-.06*
Atheism	-.18**	-.12**	-.14**	-.21**	-.04	-.06	-.07*
Agnosticism	-.08*	-.05	.01	-.10**	-.04	-.05	.02

Note: Correlations are significant at $p < .00$ (**) or $p < .05$ (*) level (2-tailed); Interpretation of correlations: weak ($r < .15$), moderately strong ($.15 \leq r < .30$) and strong ($r \geq .30$) associations; Interreligious persp. = Interreligious perspective; SocVal = Societal value, IHRS = International human rights standard, PSRG = Principle of state-religion governance, IndAut = Individual Autonomy, IJRF = Impact of judicialization of religious freedom; RD-pos = Religious diversity (positive attitude); RD-neg = Religious diversity (negative attitude).

religious freedom. This is an interesting finding since it indicates that atheists in the sample are less favorable to religious freedom in comparison with other positions. The dimensions of "Societal value" ($r = -.18$), "International human rights standard" ($r = -.12$), "Individual autonomy" ($r = -.21$) were negatively correlated with atheistic perspective. Agnosticism was negatively correlated with "Societal value" of religious freedom ($r = -.08$), and dimension of "Individual autonomy" ($r = -.10$).

Pluralism A and Pluralism B together were positively associated with three dimensions of the SPRF related to human rights aspects, judicialization of religious freedom, and individual autonomy. Enforcement of the position that only one religion is really true, but at least one other is partly true (Exclusivism) was sensitive to the "Principle of state-religion governance" ($r = .07$) and "Individual autonomy" ($r = .10$) and negatively associated with "Impact of judicialization of religious freedom" ($r = -.09$). "Interreligious perspective" negatively correlated with the scale "Principle of state-religion governance."

The AFTRI measure is sensitive to the concept of normative pluralism. Specifically, exclusivist ($r = -.10$) and inclusivist ($r = -.10$) perspectives were negatively associated with endorsement of positive attitudes toward religious diversity, while interreligious position had positive correlation with this concept ($r = .10$). Moreover, atheistic position was negatively associated with negating the idea of diversity ($r = -.07$) as well as interreligious views ($r = -.06$). "Exclusivism" had a positive correlation with negative attitudes toward religious diversity ($r = .10$).

Table 7.6 below presents the results of logistic regression analyses predicting perception of five dimensions of religious freedom applying the SPRF measure and controlling for individual religious characteristics and attitudes toward religious diversity. In the first model, we included independent variables measuring positioning on the AFTRI, religious belonging, sex, and age. In order to explore if and how the predictive power of the AFTRI can vary if the attitudes toward religious diversity are considered, we run the second model of analysis.

The data from all regression models were statistically significant, and independent variables explained from two to 21 percent of the variance of religious freedom. Considering separately the results for each from five dimensions of religious freedom, it is important to highlight general observation concerning the scale of positive attitudes toward religious diversity. This is the only independent variable which had significant influence (mostly positive) on all dimensions of the SPRF. As far as a "Societal value" of religious freedom is concerned, participants who shared atheistic views favored less that dimension of the SPRF in comparison with other truth-claims positions.

TABLE 7.6 Regression analysis for Religious Freedom

	SocVal		IHRS		PSRG		IndAut		IJRF	
Exclusivism	.03	.07	.01	.03	.02	-.01	.12**	.14***	-.08	-.03
Inclusivism	-.01	.04	.07	.10*	-.02	-.04	.09*	.11**	-.01	.03
Pluralism A	.01	.01	.09	.09	-.09	-.09	.10	.09	.04	.06
Pluralism B	-.02	-.02	.01	.02	-.20	-.21	.21	.20	-.02	-.01
Interreligious p.	-.01	-.03	.05	.04	-.20*	-.20*	.13	.11	.02	.00
Atheism	-.15*	-.12	-.13	-.11	-.21**	-.21**	-.11	-.09	-.06	-.03
Agnosticism	-.13	-.08	-.05	-.02	-.13	-.16	.04	.05	-.08	-.03
Catholics (ref)	-.11**	-.04	-.11**	-.07	.16***	.12***	.02	.05	-.11**	-.02
Minorities (ref)	-.02	-.01	-.01	-.01	.03	.03	.03	.03	.01	.01
Sex	-.03	.01	-.01	.01	.05	.03	.02	.03	-.11***	-.08**
Age	-.04	-.01	-.05	-.03	-.07*	-.07*	.06	.07*	-.13***	-.11***
RD-pos		.37***		.20***		-.07*		.24***		.30***
RD-neg		-.10**		-.07*		.17***		.03		-.21***
Adj. R²	2%	18%	3%	8%	5%	9%	7%	11%	5%	21%
Significance	***	***	***	***	***	***	***	***	***	***

Note: N = 1035; $p < .05$, ** $p < .01$, *** $p < .001$; Reference: Interreligious p. = Interreligious perspective; SocVal = Societal value, IHRS = International human rights standard, PSRG = Principle of state-religion governance, IndAut = Individual Autonomy, IJRF = Impact of judicialization of religious freedom; RD-pos = Religious diversity (positive attitude); RD-neg = Religious diversity (negative attitude); Reference: Catholics (ref) = religious nones, Minorities = Religious minorities, Minorities (ref) = religious nones, sex = male.

Meanwhile, religious nones in comparison with participants who belonged to Roman Catholic Church endorsed in a greater degree societal meaning of religious freedom, which is associated with interreligious dialogue, non-discrimination, diversity, tolerance, co-existence of religions, and liberty, and democratic citizenship. Both effects disappear if we control for attitudes toward religious diversity. Moreover, the variable of "Religious diversity" (scale of positive views) had the strongest impact on that dimension of religious freedom ($\beta = .37$, $p < .001$) in comparison with other independent variables the models.

Regression results on perception of religious freedom as an "International human rights standard" showed the same tendency regarding religious nones: they endorse more the positive attitudes toward human rights aspects of this concept in comparison with Catholics. Moreover, sharing of inclusivist perspective (Only one religion is really true, but at least one other is partly true) had predictive power vis-à-vis religious freedom ($p < .05$) if we control for religious diversity attitudes.

For the dimension of religious freedom as a "Principle of state-religion governance," regression results suggested that participants who do not share the claim that "Real truth comes from listening to all religions" (Interreligious perspective) favor this dimension of religious freedom more in comparison with those who have interreligious positions (in both models: controlling and not-controlling for religious diversity views). Atheists, compared to non-atheists, are less supportive of the positive evaluation of state policies providing equal conditions for Catholics, religious minorities, and non-religious people. Catholics are much more supportive of state-religion governance outcomes in comparison with religious nones ($\beta = .16, p < .001$). In terms of age, the older the respondent becomes (even though the age range is from 19 to 24 years old), the less they favor policies of the state toward religions. Positive views toward religious diversity had a significant negative statistical impact on this dimension of religious freedom as well, while negative attitudes toward religious diversity increased the odds of favoring state-religion policies in Italy ($\beta = .17, p < .001$).

Table 7.6 further shows that for perception of religious freedom as "Individual autonomy," both exclusivist and inclusivism positions matter. The predictive power of exclusivist perspective grows, if to control for religious diversity views (from $\beta = .12, p < .01$ to $\beta = .14, p < .001$). The same tendency was observed for the inclusivist position; its predictive power increased from $\beta = .09, p < .05$ to $\beta = .11, p < .01$, if the scales on religious diversity were added to the model. Age has a statistical impact on "Individual autonomy:" with age, participants favor more the search for individual truth and spiritual fulfilment and endorse the idea of human dignity. Moreover, the more participants share the positive views toward diversity, the more they support "Individual autonomy" in the SPRF research.

As for the "Impact of judicialization of religious freedom," the AFTRI was not sensitive to it; none out of the seven items of the scale showed the predictive power for that dimension of the SPRF model. Catholic participants endorsed less that concept in comparison with religious nones. Meanwhile, sex and age impacted the perception of this dimension of the dependent variable. Females were more supportive to the presence of religious symbols in public space in comparison with males, and the older the respondents become the less they supported that concept.

7 Discussion and Conclusion

Building on theories of religious freedom, this research examines the predictive power of religious truth-claims and specifically focuses on the impact of pluralistic perspective on the SPRF measure. The linkage between pluralism and religious freedom was emphasized by sociologists of religion (Richardson 2006; Finke 2013; Berger 2014; Giordan and Pace 2014). We were looking for empirical evidence to confirm this hypothesis with statistical tests on the sample of university students, the group which is simultaneously characterized by intensive intercultural contacts, uncertainty of belief-system, and a high proportion of agnostics and atheists in comparison with their parents and grandparents (Garelli 2014).

The findings of this research provided empirical evidence for the arguments we introduced in the beginning. First, the SPRF measure allowed to depict that belonging to Catholic, religion minority, and religious nones groups matter for the perception of religious freedom in a variety of its dimensions. Descriptive statistics and one-way ANOVA tests confirmed that the SPRF measure is sensitive to self-assigned religious identities. Moreover, four out of five dimensions of religious freedom were assessed positively by participants from three groups. However, in contrast with previous research (Breskaya and Botvar 2019) — which revealed the main difference between religious minorities and participants who identified themselves with "no religion" in their perceptions of positive and negative obligations of the state related to religious freedom issues — current study in Italy showed that this difference exists between groups of Catholics and religious nones. Among the Italian youth in the sample, religious nones are more supportive to societal values of religious freedom and its human rights aspects in comparison with Catholics, while no difference in perceptions of religious freedom were depicted between religious minorities and nones. That fact can be explained by relatively comfortable conditions for religious minorities and absence of religious division in the Italian society, specifically if we consider the patterns of relationship within majority/minority nexus (Sarkissian 2015; Fox, Mataic, and Finke forthcoming). The first hypothesis (H1) was supported with some specifications.

Second, in terms of positioning toward religious truth-claims, we found that participants endorsed pluralistic perspective more than any other position. Together, the concepts of "Pluralism A" (12 percent) and "Pluralism B" (44 percent) composed 56 percent of the views regarding the religious truth-claims in the sample. The results of testing of AFTRI on the sample of Italian university students replicated the original results confirming that young people are more in favor of "Pluralism B" as "more religiously mature form of pluralism than "Pluralism A" (Astley and Francis 2014, 33). Thus, the second and third hypotheses (H2 and H3) were supported with empirical findings.

Third, we argued that religious truth-claims contribute to differences in perception of religious freedom, and that a positive association between pluralistic and interreligious perspectives and religious freedom can be observed. The correlation analysis revealed that all truth-claims perspectives were selectively sensitive to the SPRF dimensions. However, regression results were surprising. Exclusivist, inclusivist, interreligious perspective, and atheist positions had significant statistical effects on the SPRF, while pluralistic position in AFTRI had no causal relations with the religious freedom measure. The idea that "the major religions should be regarded as more or less equally effective and legitimate alternative ways of responding to the divine reality" (Netland 2007, 227) did not enforce the perception of religious freedom, according to the data. This result questions why opposite to pluralism positions, such as exclusivism, inclusivism, and atheism — perspectives that emphasize the truth of one, several, or no religion (as they were formulated in AFTRI) — were more sensitive to the SPRF. It seems that more antithetical to pluralistic views positions, which contain some tension with ideas of equality and diversity, held more linkage with values and claims of religious freedom for young people. This finding also replicated the results of recent research on pluralism/exclusivism nexus and religious freedom views among youth in Belarus and Norway; however, applying other measures of religious freedom (Breskaya and Rogobete 2020).

Moreover, participants who identified themselves with "no religion" were more in favor of three out of five suggested dimensions of religious freedom in comparison with Catholics. This statistical effect becomes weaker if we add to the model the concept of "Religious diversity" measured with the scales of positive and negative attitudes. That is to say, the role of religious affiliation in enforcing the SPRF decreases, when broader views on plurality of religious groups in society are taken into account. The fourth hypothesis (H4) is partly supported. Four truth-claims held significant statistical relationships with SPRF; however, neither Pluralism A nor Pluralism B were significant. The findings suggest considering the categories of religious nones and atheists with more detailed analysis.

Finally, we considered the effect of truth-claims controlling for positive and negative views toward religious diversity. The explanatory power of regression models increased (for some dimensions five times) if we added to the research model along with the AFTRI the concept of religious diversity. For the participants of this survey, positioning on theology of religion scale had less explanatory power for the SPRF measure, than their attitudes toward religious diversity in society. The scale on positive attitudes toward religious diversity had the strongest predictive power *vis-à-vis* four dimensions of the SPRF, while neglecting religious diversity led to the disrespect of religious freedom as a human right.

We hypothesized about the positive correlation and casual relationship between pluralistic truth-claim and religious diversity (H5). The Pearson's correlation results indicated that in AFTRI "Pluralism" (both A and B) did not show any association with positive and negative views toward religious diversity, while "Pluralism A" correlated with two dimensions of the SPRF that concern the human rights meaning of religious freedom, and "Pluralism B" was associated with "Individual autonomy" in the SPRF model. Exclusivism was negatively associated with positive views on religious diversity and positively correlated with negative views on religious diversity. Thus, the exclusivist position at the individual level was antithetical to the positive perception of religious diversity at the societal level. Moreover, atheism was negatively correlated with neglecting religious diversity in society and had no association with positive views on religious diversity, while agnosticism had no association with religious diversity at all. Only interreligious truth-claim showed a positive association with pluralistic perspective and a negative association with negative views on diversity of religious groups in Italian society. Thus, our findings did not support the first part of the fifth hypothesis (H5) about the linkage of pluralistic truth-claims with openness toward religious diversity at societal level and partially support the second part of H5. One exception, however, is that atheistic truth-claim is negatively associated with neglecting religious diversity at societal level.

Three limitations of current research have to be acknowledged. The first regards the SPRF measure and necessity to balance the dimensions strengthening some of them. Measure of "Impact of judicialization of religious freedom" requires more specification. Second, the results rely on a sample of young university students who are more critical and uncertain about religion than the general population. It is important to consider that among the participants belonging to Roman Catholicism, there were 15 percent of agnostics and three percent of atheists, while among religious nones there were 32 percent of agnostics and 18 percent of atheists. Thus, the replication of results about the relationship of religious pluralism and the SPRF is important in elder age-cohorts. Third, pluralism as a particular truth-claim is a specific feature of postmodern societies, and it is worth understanding in this regard the cultural background of participants of the survey. While 96 percent of participants from the general sample were born in Italy and Europe, of the seven percent of non-citizens surveyed, only 66 percent were born in Italy and Europe. That is to say that a small part of participants can have different general understanding of the value of pluralistic perspective. These three limitations of the current study have to be taken into account in the further research on pluralism and religious freedom.

Validating the SPRF measure by testing it with truth-claims, religious belonging, and views on religious diversity offers insights on how the meaning of religious freedom is constructed by a young generation. Why more closed positions in comparison with religious pluralism (exclusivism, inclusivism, or atheism) appeared to be more sensitive to the understanding of conception of religious freedom, meanwhile pluralistic one is less associated with a secular language of religious freedom. These empirical findings suggest considering the relevance and consensus between religious/theological concepts of truth-claims and secular rhetoric of religious freedom encompassing social, legal, and political connotations. The data brought the evidence about the fact that positive views on religious diversity in society hold greater statistical significance than the concept of truth-claims questioning further whether the meaning and language of religious freedom is more dependent on social dispositions than private conceptions of pluralistic truth-claims. While studies on the relationship between individual religious perspectives, liberty, and normative pluralism, argue that "religion is properly a private lifestyle option which must not threaten liberty and social harmony in a differentiated and pluralistic society" (Kosmin 2007), the problem of coherence of individual religious or secular position with the values and principles of religious freedom indicates important direction of further empirical research.

References

Astley, Jeff, and Leslie J. Francis. 2016. "Introducing the Astley-Francis Theology of Religions Index: Construct Validity Among 13- to 15-year-old Students." *Journal of Beliefs & Values* 37 (1): 29–39.

Beckford, James A. 2014. "Re-Thinking Religious Pluralism." In *Religious Pluralism. Framing Religious Diversity in the Contemporary World*, edited by Giuseppe Giordan and Enzo Pace, 15–30 Cham: Springer.

Berger, Peter L. 2014. *The Many Altars of Modernity: Toward a Paradigm for Religion in a Pluralist Age*. Boston and Berlin: De Gruyter.

Breskaya, Olga, and Pål K. Botvar. 2019. "Views on Religious Freedom Among Young People in Belarus and Norway: Similarities and Contrasts." *Religions* 10 (6), 361. https://doi.org/10.3390/rel10060361.

Breskaya, Olga, and Giuseppe Giordan. 2019. "Measuring the Social Perception of Religious Freedom: A Sociological Perspective." *Religions* 10 (4), 274. https://doi.org/10.3390/rel10040274.

Breskaya, Olga, and Silviu Rogobete. 2020. "Religious Freedom in Context: A Comparison between Belarus and Romania." In *Global Eastern Orthodoxy: Politics, Religion, and Human Rights*, edited by Giuseppe Giordan and Siniša Zrinščak, 125–48. Cham: Springer.

Durham, Cole W. 2012. "Patterns of Religion State Relations." In *Religion and Human Rights: An Introduction*, edited by John Jr. Witte and Christian M. Green, 360–78. Oxford: Oxford University Press.

Finke, Roger. 1990. "Religious Deregulation: Origins and Consequences." *Journal of Church and State* 32 (3): 609–26.

Finke, Roger. 2013. "Origins and Consequences of Religious Freedom: A Global Overview." *Sociology of Religion* 74: 297–313.

Fox, Jonathan. 2015. *Political Secularism, Religions, and the State. A Time Series Analysis of Worldwide Data*. New York: Cambridge University Press.

Fox, Jonathan, Dane R. Mataic, and Roger Finke. Forthcoming. "The Causes of Societal Discrimination against Religious Minorities in Christian-Majority Countries."

Francis, Leslie J., Andrew Village, Ursula McKenna, and Gemma Penny. 2018. "Freedom of Religion and Freedom of Religious Clothing and Symbols in School: Exploring the Impact of Church Schools in a Religiously Diverse Society." In *Religion and Civil Human Rights in Empirical Perspective*, edited by Hans-Georg Ziebertz and Carl Sterkens, 157–75. Cham: Springer.

Garelli, Franco. 2014. *Religion Italian Style: Continuities and Changes in a Catholic Country*. Burlington: Ashgate.

Gill, Anthony. 2008. *The Political Origins of Religious Liberty*. Cambridge: Cambridge University Press.

Giordan, Giordan. 2007. "Spirituality: From a Religious Concept to a Sociological Theory." In *A Sociology of Spirituality*, edited by Kieran Flanagan and Peter C. Jupp, 161–81. Aldershot: Ashgate.

Giordan, Giuseppe. 2014. "Introduction: Pluralism as Legitimization of Diversity." In *Religious Pluralism. Framing Religious Diversity in the Contemporary World*, edited by Giuseppe Giordan and Enzo Pace, 1–12. Cham: Springer.

Giordan, Giuseppe, and Enzo Pace, ed. 2014. *Religious Pluralism. Framing Religious Diversity in the Contemporary World*. Cham: Springer.

Hick, John, ed. 1977. *The Myth of God Incarnate*. London: SCM Press.

Hick, John. 1989. *An Interpretation of Religion*. Basingstoke: Macmillan.
Hick, John. 2007. "Religious Pluralism." In *The Routledge Companion to Philosophy of Religion*, edited by Chad Meister and Paul Copan, 216–25. London and New York: Routledge.
Johnson, Noel D., and Mark Koyama. 2019. *Persecution and Toleration: The Long Road to Religious Freedom*. Cambridge: Cambridge University Press.
Kaplan, Stephen. 2002. *Different Paths, Different Summits*. Oxford: Rowman & Littlefield.
Kosmin, Barry A. 2007. "Introduction." In *Secularism and Secularity: Contemporary International Perspectives*, edited by Barry A. Kosmin and Ariela Keysar, 1–13. Hartford, CT: Trinity College Institute.
Maclure, Jocelyn, and Charles Taylor. 2011. *Secularism and Freedom of Conscience*. Translated by Jane Marie Todd. Cambridge, MA: Harvard University Press.
Netland, Harold A. 2007. "Inclusivism and Exclusivism." In *The Routledge Companion to Philosophy of Religion*, edited by Chad Meister and Paul Copan, 226–36. London and New York: Routledge.
Richardson, James T. 2006. "The Sociology of Religious Freedom: A Structural and Socio-Legal Analysis." *Sociology of Religion* 67 (3): 271–94.
Richardson, James T. 2011. "The Social Construction of Legal Pluralism." *Democracy and Security* 7 (4): 390–405.
Richardson, James T. 2017. "Managing Religion: Courts as 'Partners' and 'Third Party Partisans' in the Social Construction of Religious Freedom." *Religioni e Società* 87: 17–23.
Sarkissian, Ani. 2015. *The Varieties of Religious Repression: Why Governments Restrict Religion*. Oxford-New York: Oxford University Press.
Sjöborg, Anders. 2012. "The Impact of Religion on Freedom of Religion and Freedom of Speech among Young Swedes." In *Tensions Within and Between Religions and Human Rights*, edited by Johannes Van der Ven and Hans-Georg Ziebertz, 147–77. Leiden-Boston: Brill.
Unser, Alexander. 2019. *Social Inequality and Interreligious Learning. An Empirical Analysis of Students' Agency to Cope with Interreligious Learning Tasks*. Zürich: Lit.
Van der Ven, Johannes A., and Hans-Georg Ziebertz, ed. 2012. *Tensions within and between Religions and Human Rights. Empirical Research in Religion and Human Rights*. Leiden: Brill.
Van der Ven, Johannes A., and Hans-Georg Ziebertz. 2013. *Human Rights and the Impact of Religion. Empirical Research in Religion and Human Rights*. Leiden-Boston: Brill.
Wuthnow, Robert, and Valerie Lewis. 2008. "Religion and Altruistic U.S. Foreign Policy Goals: Evidence from a National Survey of Church Members." *Journal for the Scientific Study of Religion* 47 (2): 191–209.

Yang, Fenggang. 2014. "Response by Fenggang Yang: Agency-Driven Secularization and Chinese Experiments in Multiple Modernities." In *The Many Altars of Modernity: Toward a Paradigm for Religion in a Pluralist Age*, edited by Peter L. Berger, 123–40. Boston-Berlin: De Gruyter.

CHAPTER 8

Religious Freedom in Prisons: A Case Study from the Czech Republic

Jan Váně and Lukáš Dirga

1   Introduction[1]

Freedom of religion is one of the traditional values of Western societies and is considered a fundamental human right. In the Czech context, this freedom is guaranteed by the Constitution of the Czech Republic.[2] However, the exercise of religious freedom may be restricted in specific institutional contexts that limit freedoms, such as prisons and refugee centers. This is because individuals who are serving prison sentences, for example, have been found guilty of breaking the laws of society. Therefore, some of their rights are legally restricted,[3] and so implicitly, some of their claims are automatically perceived to be less legitimate. In general, in the context of the Czech Republic, society is highly indifferent to religion and there is a long-term aversion to the presence of religious organizations in public spaces and institutions (Vido, Václavík and Paleček 2016; Váně et al. 2018).

It can therefore be expected that efforts to preserve religious freedom in the prison environment will not be a priority for most prison representatives, such as Czech prison guards (Váně and Dirga 2016). The aim of this chapter is to explain how religious freedoms are applied in Czech prisons. We present how, in this specific institution, even in a post-communist, repressive environment, religion is established, and then, via specific cases, we demonstrate the role of the conceptualization and promotion of religious freedom requirements in interactions between prisoners, prison staff and chaplains.

---

1   This study was supported by the project *"Professional training of prison chaplains in the context of prisons"* by the Technology Agency of the Czech Republic in the ÉTA program (no. TL02000390).
2   According to Article 15 of Constitutional Act No. 2/1993 Coll., on the Charter of Fundamental Rights and Freedoms.
3   The implementing act, which may restrict religious freedoms, is represented in the Czech Republic in particular by Act No. 169/1999 Coll., The Act on Imprisonment and on Amendments to Some Related Acts.

2   Theoretical Background. Total Institutions and Religious Freedom

The dispute[4] over the conceptualization of religious freedom and its role in the legal system of both secular and religious states (Brettschneider 2010) is significant. Its conceptualization foreshadows the nature of research responses to questions about the fulfillment or violation of religious freedom, especially when researchers turn their attention to a restrictive environment, such as the prison system. The problem, as Jonathan Fox points out, is that on closer examination, many formal legal documents do not define "religious freedom" (Fox 2015, 2). We are fully aware of the complications of conceptualizing religious freedom. For the purposes of this chapter, we have based our research on the following definition of religious freedom, which includes (a) the freedom of conscience associated with orthodoxy of faith and (b) the freedom of worship associated with religious practice. In particular, since we want to show the practical application of (dis-)respect for religious freedom (and the possibility of investigating its violation), we turn to the freedom of worship associated with religious practice. We examine the extent to which religious freedom can be put into practice in a prison environment. We do not address the freedom of conscience associated with orthodoxy of faith for several reasons. When the Prison Service or the courts deal with complaints, they are related to the practical exercise, not to the orthodoxy, of faith. Furthermore, it is very difficult to assess the authenticity of faith, as well as any obstacles to this faith (Becci 2012; Váně and Dirga 2016).

One of our initial assumptions was that the effort to preserve religious freedom in the prison environment would not be a priority for most prison representatives. This is because prisons are an environment typical of total institutions, i.e. they are governed by their own rules, and they are focused primarily on the role and exercise of power through the administration of discipline and punishment (Foucault 1977). By total institution, we mean the specific arrangement of space and the relations between the actors who share it. Since its inception, the prison has maintained a repressive character (Foucault 1977), one associated with a number of deprivations (Sykes 1958). The restrictive setting of the total institution encourages the emergence of prison subcultures that adopt their own value frameworks (prison code), which are often at odds with the official ideology and requirements of the institution (Jones and Schmid 2000). The role of religion in prisons is becoming ambivalent in this

---

4   For this discussion, cf. Spickard 1999; DeGirolami 2013; Fox and Flores 2012; Morgenstern 2012; Fox 2015; Tebbe 2016.

environment. Authors such as James A. Beckford have pointed to the threat of radicalization of some religious groups as a result of ignoring their religious demands (Beckford, Joly and Khosrokhavar 2005). In contrast, Winnifred Sullivan demonstrates the difficulties involved in applying government-funded, faith-based programs in US prisons, as well as the ability of prisoners to choose among these programs. This raises the question of the role of religious organizations and their connection to the state, and thereby the possibilities of preserving the religious freedoms of convicts on the one hand, and the separation of church and state on the other (Sullivan 2009). Despite the possible negative expectations associated with the world of prisons, the role of religion in prisons is attributed a mostly positive value: It is believed that religion can increase the chances of reforming a convict, either by accepting guilt or by increasing the likelihood of resocialization (Beckford 2015; Kerley 2018). These assumptions also are shared within the Czech Republic (Beláňová and Trejbalová 2020; Váně and Dirga 2020). Such assumptions are further supported by current legislation. Part of the Czech rule of law is the Charter of Fundamental Rights and Freedoms, which, according to the provisions of Article 15, guarantees "the right of the individual to freedom of thought, conscience and religion."[5] At the same time, the prison environment is strictly regulatory, with no separate, special regulation governing the exercise of religious freedoms. At the international level, various documents from key organizations are being developed to regulate the exercise of religious rights in the prison environment. It is expected that these recommendations will subsequently be implemented by each nation state. We rank, among the most important rules worldwide, the United Nations Standard Minimum Rules for the Treatment of Prisoners (UNODC 2020) and, in the context of Europe, the European Prison Rules. Both documents have a considerable influence on the Czech prison system (Ministry of Justice of the Czech Republic 2016). These rules entail three essential requirements: (1) a qualified representative should be appointed or approved if there is a sufficient number of prisoners of a certain religious affiliation; (2) the qualified representative may worship and provide pastoral services; and (3) no prisoner shall be denied access to this representative or to literature relating to religious rites and doctrines. However, security requirements arising from the specific environment of prisons are always taken into account. This also is reflected in the creation of individual

---

5 According to Article 15 of Constitutional Act No. 2/1993 Coll., on the Charter of Fundamental Rights and Freedoms.

regulations governing the conditions of imprisonment in Czech prisons,[6] in which normative formulations are conceived mainly on a general level, using the phrase "so far as is practicable." The role and position of prison chaplains is crucial for the protection and exercise of religious freedoms. In the Czech prison system since 1989, the process of institutionalizing the role of religion has followed a trajectory similar to that of other post-communist countries. Prison chaplains became part of the organizational structure of Czech prisons, which was made possible by the establishment and development of the Ecumenical Prison Chaplaincy, an organization of chaplains within the Prison Service of the Czech Republic. Institutionalization can be monitored both at the normative level and in everyday practice, where chaplains are increasingly involved in penitentiary care (Dirga and Váně 2020; Váně and Dirga 2020). At first glance, it may seem that the conditions for the observance of religious freedoms in prisons are adequately arranged. In order to better understand the results of our research, we consider it necessary to remind readers here that the following reality cannot be ignored when assessing set conditions. Key actors, such as prison management, prison guards, professional employees (civil servants or specialists—psychologists, educators, special educators, social workers, and sociologists), and chaplains apply different strategies in their approaches to convicts (Dirga and Hasmanová Marhánková 2014; Dirga 2020; Váně and Dirga 2020). These different strategies frame experiences of religious freedom and reflect different ideological visions in the approach to, and work with, prisoners. Without accepting this reality, the resulting findings regarding (dis-)respect for religious freedom would appear incomplete and interpretatively flat or misleading. Within the Czech prison system, we recognize three basic strategies for these three groups of actors. We call the prison guards' strategy a short-term strategy. Given the role of the guards, arising from their position in the prison's structure, it is logical that their primary objective is to prevent breaches of security and discipline (Dirga 2020). We call the strategy of professional staff medium-term, where their aim is to realize professional activities within so-called treatment programs. The efforts of professional staff are intended to maximize the likelihood that prisoners will successfully return to freedom ("successful re-entry"). Chaplains, finally, have a long-term strategy that seeks to change the value orientation of a prisoner, with the result that their effects may only be felt in the distant future (Váně

---

6 Within the framework of the Czech prison system, it is primarily an amendment at the level of the Act and its implementing regulations (internal regulations of the Prison Service of the Czech Republic), which include, in particular, the Regulation of the General Director of the Prison Service of the Czech Republic.

and Dirga 2020). Therefore, the chaplains do not place primary emphasis on the immediate effects of their work but instead believe in the so-called "seed method" (Váně and Stočes 2016)—that is, sowing the "seed of change" within an individual, which germinates at some point in time (Becci and Dubler 2017). Given the different strategies for treating convicts, we could intuitively expect that chaplains would be the primary guarantors of religious freedom. However, we will show that their situation is more complicated in this respect. In this chapter, we argue that the breadth of potential restrictions on religious freedom in the Czech prison system is considerable. Specifically, the state legally limits the rights and freedoms of convicts, regulating a number of personal and social aspects of their lives. Without some limitations, the enforcement of sentences would be de facto impossible. Within such a framework, it is easy to arrive at a situation in which a convicted person or outside observer would believe that the religious freedom of prisoners is not respected (the halal diet, the possibility of praying, participation in worship). This suppression, even in a secular environment, poses the potential risk of conflict that all parties are trying to prevent. We will discuss how this is occurring in the results section.

3   Research Design: Approach, Strategy and Methods

Restrictions in the prison environment that we have investigated are expected due to its nature. Our research question is whether these restrictions are imposed on religious institutions (organizations) or on group rights, or even on individual rights. In other words, we evaluated whether restrictions imposed on religious institutions and groups are more severe than those imposed on individual practices of religious freedom. As part of our research, we did not investigate disputes in which convicts complain about violations of religious freedom by legal means, primarily because this type of complaint occurs only rarely in the Czech prison environment. However, we came across cases in which it can be reasonably believed that some restrictions *were* imposed on religious freedom. These restrictions, the existence of which is admittedly not conclusive, can nevertheless illustrate how the position of institutionalized religion behind the walls of prisons is a repetitive subject of negotiation.

The arguments presented in this chapter are based on the realization of our ethnographic research on the environment of Czech male prisons.[7] During 2019 and 2020, we had the opportunity to conduct observations in medium-security

---

7   In the Czech context, this methodological approach has long been proven to be one of the most effective in examining the prison environment (see Nedbálková 2006; Dirga

male prisons.[8] Thanks to the permission of prison directors, we were able to visit three prisons and were allowed twenty-three hours of observation, during which we visited places related to religion, such as chapels, refectories, or a special department dedicated only to religious convicts. In the same period, we also interviewed thirty-five actors in five prisons. Specifically, we interviewed ten prison chaplains, thirteen convicts, four volunteers, two psychologists, one special educator, one educator, one guard, one deputy management representative and two church representatives.[9] The data gathered were analyzed according to the principles of thematic analysis (Ezzy 2002) and grounded theory (Charmaz 2006). All interviews were recorded with the informed consent of the interviewees and served as the basis for a separate analysis.[10]

4 Context of Religious Freedom in Czech Prisons

Our main finding was that there is no major struggle for religious freedom between guards and prisoners. The clash is rather between the chaplains and the guards. It should be noted that this is not a systematic struggle but instead a skirmish, one that is not waged in all prisons. Several factors have been shown to determine the probability of potential skirmishes. The first factor regards the region in which the prison is located. It makes a difference whether the prison is in an extremely secularized region (even for the conditions of the Czech Republic—for example, a borderland prison) or in a more religiously active region (for example, Moravia—part of the Czech Republic), as this factor influences the value frameworks of the guards. In addition, the ratio between believing and non-believing employees (most often prison guards) also is an important factor to consider. The attitudes of the prison management toward the activities of the prison chaplains also is significant. This individual level is based on the relationship between prison management and faith. It appears

---

2017; Dirga and Váně 2016; Dirga, Lochmannová and Juříček 2015; Dirga and Hasmanová Marhánková 2014; Beláňová and Trejbalová 2020; Lochmannová 2020).

8 Since 2017, the Czech prison system has recognized two basic types of prisons: with surveillance or medium security, and with increased surveillance or high security.

9 Among the 10 prison chaplains, there were seven representatives of the Catholic Church, one of the Methodist Church, one of the Orthodox Church, and one of the Evangelical Church. A total of two church representatives (not chaplains) were representatives of the Catholic Church.

10 With regard to the established limit on the length of the text, we present the basic methodological procedures here. However, we are prepared to provide more detailed information on the research methodology upon request.

that if a prison director is himself a believer, then he will largely support the activities of chaplains, or at least will not prevent the chaplains from doing their work (cf. Beláňová and Trejbalová 2020). Otherwise, it is often the case that prison directors only grudgingly allow chaplains in their prisons, as they are bound by the legislation in force, but do not actively improve the conditions for their activities. The age factor in the guard population, which can be divided into two basic groups, also is demonstrably important: the older generation, which was raised during the communist regime (including compulsory military service), and the younger generation, who did not have this experience. However, the chaplains themselves pointed out, across the board, that the situation has improved significantly in the last 10 years. According to their testimonies, this improvement was also influenced by changes on the part of the chaplains themselves, which is represented as generational change. Many of the older chaplains interviewed had personally experienced persecution during the communist period (often in the form of imprisonment), which, for some of them, led to a deepening distrust of prison guards. This in turn resulted in a disruption of their relationship and cooperation with guards. The number of chaplains who experienced imprisonment during the communist regime is declining, and, therefore, the influence of this factor is diminishing as well (Váně and Dirga 2020). Now we will look at some examples of disputes over the (im-)possibility of fulfilling religious freedoms while serving prison terms in Czech prisons. We do not intend to exhaustively list all of the possible cases. We will instead discuss a few selected examples that we encountered in our research.

5 Example 1. Popping into the Worship Service (When the Guards Allow It)

If a chaplain were to point out a violation of religious freedom, it would only be in connection with a restriction of the prisoners' ability to participate in worship. The chaplains emphasized that they fully respect the rule of security and the case-law prohibiting the participation of those prisoners who could pose a security risk to the group and to the whole service, and they do not perceive such a prohibition as a restriction on the prisoners' religious freedom. Such restrictions mainly apply to prisoners from special departments (e.g. for disciplinary punishment). Otherwise, prisoners from all divisions can practically attend church services. However, in the case of the less problematic prisoners, the chaplains mentioned cases in which participation in worship was indeed prevented. Let us offer one example shared by a chaplain:

> So I reported one hundred and one people for worship. And those people (the guards) are obliged to read the order or information report that the prisoners go to the doctor, psychologist, or worship, and be prepared for it. And twenty-three were brought, out of the hundred. A quarter of the people came. Others did not, either (the guards) did not look for them, or they just did not want to bring them, and so on. It sometimes happens that the guards do not bring the convicts in question for a set period of time. In some prisons, the chaplains accompany the convicts themselves. We just have it arranged to be accompanied by the guards. And sometimes they bring them to us, and sometimes they just fall asleep (in their offices), or they say they (the prisoners) did not want to come, or were not ready. What is true, what is not true, cannot be determined. If I complain about it, it will just lead them to say, 'Hey you're busting our balls here, so we'll cause problems for you, too.' And it just gets worse.

Not only on the basis of this description, but also due to other similar statements, we conclude that cases of this type of restriction of religious freedom of prisoners are more related to efforts to facilitate the work of the guards. In addition to disobeying the order to direct the prisoners to worship, the guards use other strategies that, aside from inconveniencing the chaplains or prisoners, also could be described as intimidation or harassment of convicts. According to some chaplains' testimonies, prisoners were subjected to forms of humiliation before worship: "The prison guards must inspect the prisoners, but the search method varies. So they wanted them to get naked and do five squats, or three at least. And then back to the same thing when they were coming back from worship, to get naked again, and do five squats." It can be concluded that this procedure (detention, intimidation) is directed toward the chaplains rather than the prisoners. In such cases, the humiliation and intimidation of prisoners led to a reduction in their interest in worship services, and as such their detention was aimed primarily at irritating chaplains in order to dispute or avoid the requirements to escort prisoners to religious ceremonies. Interestingly, in the situations described above, if someone complained, it was convicted persons, not chaplains. The respondents claimed that complaints were only occasional, especially because there was no redress. In most cases, the prison management's negative attitude to a complaint of non-observance of religious freedom was based on four basic points: (a) the purposefulness of the conviction/belief, (b) the financial cost of meeting convicts' requirements, (c) the need to protect public order and ensure security, and (d) the protection, rights and freedoms of other prisoners. The resulting comments on the complaints concluded that if prisoners needed an individual meeting with a chaplain, it should be allowed, because prisoners are not prevented from doing so. The complaints were primarily made by chaplains, and in our case, they concerned two prisons. The prisoners themselves did not mention in their interviews any limitation on their participation in the services. When they did speak about restrictions associated with religious freedom, it was always in relation to religious objects. Most often, they talked about the prohibition on using rosaries or possessing religious images. These statements by the convicts can be found in the second example presented below. In terms of worship, we still need to point out that in prisons, it is possible for staff (civilian staff and guards) to attend worship services unless obligations force them to engage in activities elsewhere. Probing the attendance of guards in these events has regularly shown that, although there are believing guards in prisons, they do not typically attend worship services (unless they are in charge of the event), even when the chaplains invite them to do so. They refused to do so even in two prisons in which whole sections were created for believer inmates. They attributed their lack of participation to the fact that doing so could reduce their authority in the eyes of convicts or colleagues: "Look, I just take them [inmates] through the yard here and go with them as an escort. I can't show that I am actually a believer." The environment enacted by the convict/guard relationship, where there are clear, defining lines (see Dirga and Hasmanová Marhánková 2014), does not provide room, in the minds of guards and civilian employees, for adopting or creating hybrid forms of participation in prison life, such as testifying to their religious affiliations by participating in worship services with convicts as guards/employees and also believers. This explicit barrier does not in any way limit the religious freedom of the convicts, but it does constitute an obstacle that the chaplains are trying to overcome: If a guard also could be involved as one of the worshippers, then in the case of guaranteeing the fulfillment of the right to worship, this right would more than likely not be restricted.

6 Example 2. Rosary, Prayer Rug and the Chaplain as a Supervisor

We found that when the convicts mentioned something that could be described as a violation of religious freedom, it was related to a ban on the possession and use of religious objects. The most frequently mentioned object was the rosary. The explanation for why this object was mentioned most often was related to two factors. Czech prisons are dominated by the Catholic faith, in terms of both the representation of denominations among chaplains (according to the Statistical Yearbook of the Prison Service of the Czech Republic for

2018) and the spectrum of services provided (Beláňová and Trejbalová 2020). Furthermore, a large portion of the convicts are Roma. There also is a significant number of members of the Roma minority from Slovakia. There is a strong family bond between Czechs and Slovak Roma. The Roma ethnic group, especially those with Slovak roots, is characterized by a specific, folkloric religiosity, for which religious objects (rosaries, the Madonna) play an important role (Podolinská and Hrustič 2010).

The ban on convicts wearing the rosary could lead to the assumption that some form of restriction of religious freedom is taking place. However, such an interpretation is strictly rejected by the chaplains. Conversely, they point out that the ban on wearing or using the rosary is justified, as there can be various motivations among complainants for securing or using them. Based on interviews with convicts and chaplains, we can distinguish four basic categories of prisoners who use the rosary: (a) prisoners who do actually pray with the rosary but do not need to have it physically because they care about its spiritual nature, (b) prisoners who perceive the rosary as a religious symbol, which occasionally reminds them of praying, and can then be borrowed during worship and prayer meetings, (c) prisoners who perceive the rosary as a symbol, not of a religious nature but as a reminder of the person who gave it to them (e.g. mother, wife, or grandmother) and therefore an embodiment of an emotional attachment to the person, and (d) prisoners who use the rosary as a fetish to serve as a defense against evil. Therefore, it is a security element. Last but not least, the rosary can serve as a tool of exchange. The chaplains repeatedly pointed out that, especially in the context of the Roma ethnic group, there is a demand to be able to carry the rosary with oneself, or to have it in the cell, in connection with points c and d. In this section, we present one specific case that illustrates the seizure of a rosary from an individual who, according to the testimony of his fellow prisoners and that of a chaplain, would belong to the first group. This case concerns a prisoner who converted and for whom the restriction of religious conscience and practice would represent the essence of the suppression of religious freedom. In this case, the rosary was seized on the grounds of protecting the prisoner and his fellow convicts. The convicted respondent explained (and from other sources, we could verify the truthfulness of the testimony) that the rosary had been confiscated by a prison guard from another prisoner. The rationale given for confiscating the rosary was that it contained a large wooden cross that could be used as a weapon. The convict disputed this rationale during his interview, claiming that prisoners can normally own cutlery (including knives). In his testimony and reflection on why the rosary was confiscated and how he perceived the situation, he pointed out that if he were to hang a knife and a rosary on the wall of his cell, and if someone were to breach his cell to attack him, the attacker would clearly reach for the knife and not the rosary. Asked if he could be suspected of using the rosary as a weapon, he refuted the idea, claiming that he was a born-again Christian. The question, then, of whether the guard confiscated the rosary as a form of revenge or as a means to restrain the prisoner's proselytical enthusiasm, or whether the prisoner perceived the confiscation as a restriction of his religious freedom, was asked, but the prisoner replied unequivocally: "Look, if it was an idol [rosary] for me, it would bother me that he took it from me. But for me, it was a test from the Lord. I hung it on the wall as a sign that I belong to Christ." He refused to interpret the confiscation as a violation of his religious freedom. This whole situation and its interpretation by the involved actors repeatedly returned us to the question of how to differentiate prisoners' so-called purposeful faith (faith demonstrated in order to achieve anticipated benefits) from inner faith. In other words, it is a question of how to determine when religious objects (in this case, the rosary) are used as a means of fulfilling one's own spirituality, and when they are, for example, employed as a symbolic declaration aimed at identifying oneself with a certain group, or declaring a non-religious purpose. If we study the guidelines for individual prisons, it is clear that religious images (or any pictures) are in many cases allowed only in private lockers, and only on the inside. In such circumstances, hanging a rosary on a cell wall would truly constitute a violation of prison rules. We are much more up-to-date with the recurring controversy over purposeful faith. In some of their dismissive grounds for complaints by convicts, prison guards, or prison management, use their objections, claiming that they are practicing a purpose faith (Váně and Dirga 2016). Another case that concerns issues related to religious subjects is that of the Muslim faith/community. Muslim prisoners are a minority in Czech prisons. Most are recruits from the former Soviet bloc who, in the environment of the Czech Republic, operate within post-Soviet gangs. Access to these prisoners is very complicated as a result of both their ethnic insularity and the language barrier. When they raise any objections that might reveal signs of a violation of religious freedom, these objections usually refer to the halal diet and/or to restrictions on the ability to pray five times a day (Demelová et al. 2015). Although the Muslim element is a minority in Czech prisons, it is such a sensitive issue that the prison management seeks to avoid it in the event of difficulties. Therefore, when addressing the requirements of Muslim convicts, they expect an evaluation opinion from prison chaplains (Demelová et al. 2015), among whom there is no Muslim cleric, or imam. The chaplains are therefore asked to state whether the prisoner in question is or is not a true Muslim believer and how the prison should respond to his requirements. Paradoxically, this creates a situation in which the prison chaplain becomes a participant in the possible restriction of religious freedom. The vast majority of chaplains resist being drawn into the role of arbitrator in the case of Muslim convicts, with one stating, "We are not cadres."[11] When there is a situation in which they are asked whether the halal diet requirement corresponds to the prisoner's religiosity, they always address the situation with regard to the capabilities of the prison kitchen. If the cooks are able to provide halal food, then chaplains recommend it. And in questions of purposefulness, they always point out that they do not distinguish between inner and purposeful faith because even special-purpose religiosity gives them the opportunity to engage prisoners in individual or community meetings.

Managing prisons to avoid problems with Muslim prisoners, where responsibility is transferred from management to chaplains through the gradual institutionalization of spiritual services (Váně and Dirga 2020), leads to a paradoxical situation. The effort to preserve the religious freedom of a convict who demanded to be able to pray, undisturbed, five times a day led to the following complication, according to a chaplain:

> With the prayer rug, which was actually a towel, one can kneel anywhere. The problem is with that place. Because we had, for example, an Uzbek, who was active. And we let him into the room where ping pong was played, and he sat there at the time he needed to pray and not be disturbed. But the others couldn't do sports, and at that moment it was quite a problem.

This example suggests that the pursuit of religious freedom may become a restriction on non-believers. Given the media reputation and hysteria associated with migration and Islam in the Czech Republic (cf. Topinka 2016; Rosůlek 2017), it is quite understandable that prison management seeks to relinquish responsibility for making decisions regarding Muslim convicts. The care given to them as unitary cases speaks more to a misunderstanding and ignorance of Islam than to a promotion of religious freedom. In the case of these convicts, this care is maintained even at the cost of "restrictions" on secular prisoners. The example demonstrates that, thanks to the successful institutionalization

---

11   This term is very important when the chaplains use it because it refers to the era of communism, when there were institutionally led individuals, "cadres," who examined the eligibility of people for advancement within the Communist Party or the potential opportunity for them to become members of the Communist Party. Their assessments and evaluations determined not only political advancement but also career and educational opportunities for individuals (and their families).

of the spiritual service in prisons, the chaplain can paradoxically become an instrument for limiting religious freedom, or at least a participant in disregarding some violations of religious freedom.

7   Example 3. Fight for an Icon—Who Fights Who?

The last example we present is used to illustrate the struggle for religious freedom between chaplains, civilian staff, and guards. In another text, we describe how the prison chaplains have been gradually incorporated into the functioning of prisons over the past 30 years (Váně and Dirga 2020). For the moment, we briefly state that there are chaplains in prisons within the territory of the Czech Republic who, at least, provide a spiritual service for convicts. However, this does not change the fact that, despite significant improvements, there is still some tension between the guards and the chaplains (Beláňová and Trejbalová 2020). We will now explain how an event that could be perceived as a restriction of religious freedom tested and redrew the boundaries of influence between the guards on the one hand and chaplains and civil staff believers on the other. We would like to point out here that we do not have records on the frequency of clashes, and that the following example serves as a symbol of the transformation of relationships and influence in the prison environment. In other words, we present an illustrative example to indicate the complexity of the problem and multi-layered thinking about the nature and forms of religious freedom and their enforcement in prison settings. One of the primary tasks of ensuring religious freedom (worship, individual conversation, prayer) is the need to create adequate space. In individual prisons, chapels have gradually emerged in designated areas. In addition, attempts have been made to extend the possibilities of care for convicts. One example of this is the establishment of departments in several prisons that are intended only for believers or for convicts who tend toward religiosity. In a few prisons, believers already have been actively involved in working with convicts in the position of not only chaplains but also educators and psychologists. Where they have managed to create more compact interaction with educators and psychologists, they also are able to systematically link medium- and long-term strategies of action to the extent that some prison guards may seem to be overstepping their powers and thereby leading to a conflict of positions for influence within the prison, especially in the form of symbols, which may not be understandable or evident to most. In one of the prisons where this systematic cooperation works, there has been an attempt to work more actively with believer prisoners—that is, to give them the opportunity to meet not only for worship or individual conversations but also, during the day, for morning or evening prayer or communal eating. The problem is that the creation of such a room contradicts, for example, hygienic standards. This group of employees, however, managed not only to acquire a room but also to ensure its legitimacy within the prison system. By implementing the use of the Latin term "refectory" for the room, the management, which supported the idea of more systematic work with believer prisoners, was able to avoid some regulations. "Refectory" sounded neutral enough for the standard administration but evoked the status of a sacral place. In addition to the standard objects, the room also was painted with the portraits of Maximilian Kolbe, Josef Toufar and Oskar Romero. The presence of the image of Franciscan monk Maximilian Kolbe is expected given his martyrdom in a concentration camp. His depiction refers not only to a specific, repressive regime, that of Nazism, but also to imprisonment as a repressive strategy in general and, above all, to the idea of Kolbe's sacrifice in favor of prisoners. The depiction of the Czech pastor Josef Toufar also is understandable. This is an obvious allusion to the brutality of the communist regime in Czechoslovakia. Toufar was brutally martyred by the communist secret police in the 1950s on charges of the so-called "Číhošť miracle."[12] All prisons in the Czech Republic, including the ones described by us, had political prisoners within their walls. Toufar is therefore, in not only a Catholic icon, he also is a symbol of the suppression of religious freedom during communist rule in Czechoslovakia. His depiction in the prison environment can be interpreted, among other things, as a message to local guards who still work in these prisons from the communist era. The choice of this depiction is an attempt to redesignate the chosen space, which should be a place of change and rectification for convicts who are motivated by references to personalities who opposed oppressive forces. The intention is permeated with profound symbolism, including a reference to the suppression of religious freedom in the church by the centuries-old method of pictorial expressions of the "Bible for the Poor"—that is, visual allusions. But the depiction of Toufar is more a message to those who work with convicts than to the convicts themselves, since almost none of the convicts we interviewed could describe the images depicted. Some were able to list the names of the depicted, but had difficulty explaining who the depicted individuals were. This does not, in our view, reduce the depth of symbolic expression. For example, in the already-mentioned allusion to pro-regime guards, we perceive this as a symbolic message to the former regime, one which is supported by

---

12 In the church in Číhošť, where Josef Toufar worked, there was a miracle: the movement of a half-meter-tall cross. The State Security Service accused Toufar of deliberate manipulation and tried to force him to confess. In 2019, Toufar's canonization process began.

the re-marking of a place of oppression as a space devoted to religion as an institutionalized form of working with convicts. This is evidenced by a statement made by one of the civil staff: "Now the cardinal will come to whom we will applaud here, but here are the people who imprisoned him. And they remember that. And they just know now that it must not be said out loud." The third depiction in the refectory is an interesting and intuitively unexpected figure — Oscar Romero, archbishop of San Salvador, who was murdered by a pro-government "death squad" as he was celebrating Mass. When asked why and how the Latin American saint was chosen, after a long discussion, the following answer was given by a member of the civil staff:

> We agreed that each of us would choose our own patron. For me, it was Maximilian Kolbe, for *** it was Toufar, and *** came up with Romero, saying that he was missing. And we didn't address it at all, why him? He is simply a martyr of the church.

After a long discussion, we were given clarification as to why Romero was selected: because he served as a reference to the alleged link of the murder squad with a drug cartel:

> So he was probably murdered by a drug cartel, wasn't he? And the drugs are in here, too. Romero was therefore associated with the drug issue, which is very typical of the prison environment in the selector's testimony.

This is the creation of a place for the fuller realization of religious freedom, as well as for the possibility of working more systematically with convicts in a friendlier environment than just cells and offices, although we see a small but gradual anchoring of the influence of religion in the environment of prisons. We illustrate the gradual increase in the influence of religion in another example, found in another of the prisons we visited. The staff there selected and hung the icon of the Madonna above the staircase of one of the cell blocks. This effort to visualize religion in the prison space was not merely an attempt to "test the limits of the possible" but a deep faith commitment to working with prisoners. This effort, however, repeatedly encountered resistance in the form of the icon's repeated removal from the wall by guards. According to one civil employee:

> It is an Orthodox, not a Catholic, icon. And we tended to put it at the entry to the main building, above the stairs. And it is probably the seventh time they have pulled it down. We'll put it there again. It is interesting to

us that these people tend to limit themselves to this symbol, destroy it and, for example, stuff it into a box of rat poison in every corridor. Which is interesting, they understand ideologically. That they perceive it as an important thing, as a battle for a flag.

This situation suggests to us some valuable insights. It is surprising that those guards who removed the symbol did so secretly. It would be sufficient to refer to the prison guidelines, which do not allow for the posting of any depictions in any part of the prison frequented by prisoners, with the exception of approved notice boards. Alternatively, it would be sufficient to raise the question of whether the posting of a religious image in the connecting corridor between the prison blocks was officially allowed by the prison management.

Instead, the icon, which hung at a height of a few meters, and which was thus very difficult to both hang up and take down, was nonetheless removed. This suggests that the opponents (prison guards) were not sure whether they would succeed with their complaint and actually admitted to the influence of the religious lobby, which is a very interesting phenomenon in the case of prisons and secular Czech society. The icon's removal and destruction is certainly not interpreted by those who placed it as a suppression of religious freedom, because they are well aware that hanging an icon has no legal support. The described situation is rather a testing of influence and struggle for symbols and values, along with advocated strategies of work with convicts.

8   Conclusion

With regard to the theoretical background, which we described in the section devoted to the theory based on our findings, it does not currently seem that, in Czech prisons as total institutions, there is an imminent threat of radicalization of some religious groups as a result of the disregard for or ignorance of their religious demands. Our findings do not give rise to the idea that some religious groups are being ignored. Even problems with the application of government-funded, faith-based programs, as Sullivan (2009) suggests, do not represent a fundamental problem in the environment we have examined. This is due to the sovereign secular environment in the Czech Republic. The findings can be used to address our research question, which was whether restrictions are being imposed on religious institutions (organizations) or whether they are instead being imposed on group rights, or even on certain individuals.

The examples in this chapter illustrate that there are indications of violations of religious freedom directed at convicts. We have, however, no record of their frequency. The individual examples illustrate the complexity of the situation as well as the contingent nature of the examples, which always depend on the circumstances. Our main conclusion is that rather than an explicit intention to limit the religious freedom of convicts, which could be seen as a structural problem, there exists a power struggle against the backdrop of a conflict of ideologies. At the heart of the struggle are different approaches to working with convicts and a latent dispute over the importance and role of religion in prison settings. These different strategies frame experiences of religious freedom. Without accepting this fact, the resulting findings regarding (dis-)respect for religious freedom will appear incomplete and interpretatively flat or misleading. The increasing degree of implementation and institutionalization of religion in the prison environment places demands on employees not only in terms of accepting value changes but also with respect to new work demands and requirements, including increasing the volume of their work. These factors then lead to a sense of inappropriateness and resentment on the part of the employees, especially prison guards, such as subtle sabotage when working with prisoners (e.g. the obligation for prison guards to accompany prisoners to worship).

The institutionalization of religion in the environment of Czech prisons therefore takes place against the background of a struggle for power (Foucault 1977), which seems to be liquid in the Czech prison system. But the successful institutionalization and strengthening of the emphasis on religious freedom has an unintended consequence in the form of a certain paradox of power. This manifests itself at those times when chaplains become part of the "repression" of the convicts (by participating in the rejection of prisoners' requests).[13] The reversal of the role of the guarantor of religious freedom of the convicted person to a potential violator of religious law results from successful incorporation into the organizational structure of the prison. It is important to consider whether the chaplains are better placed outside or inside the prison administration to perform spiritual ministry for prisons (in relation to the possibilities of protecting religious freedom).

---

13 The following is a link to a case in which a chaplain refused a prisoner's request to change his diet (source: Records of Ombudsman Opinions): http://eso.ochrance.cz/Nalezene/Edit/5312 Accessed March 26, 2020.

References

Becci, Irene, and Joshua Dubler. 2017. "Religion and religions in prisons: Observations from the United States and Europe." *Journal for the Scientific Study of Religion* 56 (2): 241–247. https://doi.org/10.1111/jssr.12352.

Beckford, James A. 2015. "Religious Diversity and Rehabilitation in Prisons: Management, Models and Mutations." In *Religious Diversity in European Prisons,* edited by Irene Becci and Olivier Roy, 15–30. Cham: Springer International Publishing. https://doi.org/10.1007/978-3-319-16778-7_2.

Beckford, James A., Danièle Joly and Farhad Khosrokhavar. 2005. *Muslims in Prison: Challenge and Change in Britain and France.* London: Palgrave Macmillan. https://doi.org/10.1057/9780230501300.

Beláňová, Andrea, and Tereza Trejbalová. 2020. "Prvních deset let jsem si s personálem netykal. Pozice kaplana v české věznici [In the First Ten Years no Staff Befriended me. The Position of a Chaplain in the Czech Prison System]." *Sociológia/Slovak Sociological Review* 52 (1): 5–23. https://doi.org/10.31577/sociologia.2020.52.1.1.

Brettschneider, Corey. 2010. "A Transformative Theory of Religious Freedom: Promoting the Reasons for Rights." *Political Theory* 38 (2): 187–213. https://doi.org/10.1177/0090591709354868.

DeGirolami, Marc O. 2013. *The Tragedy of Religious Freedom.* Harvard: Harvard University Press.

Demelová, Veronika, Eva Čermáková, Lenka Linhartová and Tomáš Janků. 2015. "Muslimové v českých věznicích [Muslims in Czech Prisons]." *České vězeňství* 1/2015: 10–11.

Dirga, Lukáš. 2017. "Body as a Project: The Relationship Czech Prisoners Have to Their Bodies." *Sociológia/Slovak Sociological Review* 49 (6): 636–56.

Dirga, Lukáš. 2020. *"Humanizace českého vězeňství očima jeho aktérů"* [*Humanization of the Czech Prison System from the Perspectives of its Actors*]. Pilsen: University of West Bohemia.

Dirga, Lukáš, and Jaroslava Hasmanová Marhánková. 2014. "Nejasné vztahy moci—vězení očima českých dozorců [Prison as a Place of Ambiguous Power Relations: The Perspectives of Czech Prison Guards]." *Sociologický časopis/Czech Sociological Review* 50 (1): 83–105. https://doi.org/10.13060/00380288.2014.50.1.31.

Dirga, Lukáš, Alena Lochmannová and Petr Juříček. 2015. "The Structure of the Inmate Population in Czech Prisons." *Sociológia/Slovak Sociological Review* 47 (6): 559–78.

Dirga, Lukáš, and Jan Váně. 2016. "Postpenitenciární péče z perspektivy nábožensky založených organizací" [Post-penitentiary Care from the Perspective of Religious Organizations]. In *Postpenitenciární péče: aktuální otázky* [*Post-penitentiary Care: Current Issues*], edited by Vratislava Černíková and Jana Firstová, 104–09. Hodonín: European Institute of Law and Forensic Engineering.

Dirga, Lukáš, and Jan Váně. 2020. "Czech Republic: Religion and Prison—The History of an Ambivalent Partnership". In *Religion and Prison: An Overview of Contemporary Europe. Boundaries of Religious Freedom: Regulating Religion in Diverse Societies,* edited by Julia Martínez-Ariño and Anne-Laure Zwilling, 91–111. Cham: Springer International Publishing. https://doi.org/10.1007/978-3-030-36834-0_7.

Ezzy, Douglas. 2002. *Qualitative Analysis.* London: Routledge.

Foucault, Michel. 1977. *"Discipline and Punish: the Birth of the Prison."* New York: Pantheon Books.

Fox, Jonathan. 2015. "Religious Freedom in Theory and Practice." *Human Rights Review* 16 (1): 1–22. https://doi.org/10.1007/s12142-014-0323-5.

Fox, Jonathan, and Deborah Flores. 2012. "Religious Freedom in Constitutions and Law: A Study in Discrepancies." In *Religion, Politics, Society, and the State,* edited by Jonathan Fox, 27–52. New York: Oxford University Press.

Charmaz, Kathy. 2006. *Constructing Grounded Theory: A Practical Guide through Qualitative Analysis.* London: Sage

Jones, Richard, and Thomas Schmid. 2000. *Doing Time: Prison Experience and Identity Among First-Time Inmates.* Stamford: Emerald Group Publishing Limited.

Kerley, Kent R. 2018. *Finding Freedom in Confinement: The Role of Religion in Prison Life.* Santa Barbara, California: Praeger.

Lochmannová, Alena. 2020. *Tělo za katrem* [*The Body Behind Bars*]. Prague: Academia.

Ministry of Justice of the Czech Republic. 2016. *Koncepce vězeňství do roku 2025* [*The Czech Prison System Conceptual Framework Until 2025*]. Prague: Ministry of Justice of the Czech Republic.

Morgenstern, Mira. 2012. "Religion and State: The View from Enlightenment." *Journal of Law Religion and State* 1 (2): 258–90. https://doi.org/10.1163/22124810-00103005.

Nedbálková, Kateřina. 2006. *Spoutaná Rozkoš: (re) produkce genderu a sexuality v ženské věznici* [*Chained Pleasure: (Re)production of Gender and Sexuality in Women's Prison*]. Prague: Sociologické nakladatelství.

Podolinská, Tatiana, and Tomáš Hrustič. 2010. *Boh medzi bariérami. Sociální inklúzia Rómov náboženskou cestou.* [*God between the barriers. Social inclusion of Roma with the aid of religion*]. Bratislava: SAV.

Rosůlek, Přemysl. 2017. *Sondy do studia (o) islámu v období migrační krize* [*Probes into the study of Islam in a period of migration crisis*]. Prague: Dokořán.

Spickard, James V. 1999. "Human Rights, Religious Conflict, and Globalization: Ultimate Values in a New World Order." *International Journal on Multicultural Societies* 1 (1): 2–19.

Sullivan, Winnifred. 2009. *Prison Religion: Faith-Based Reform and the Constitution.* Princeton: Princeton University Press.

Sykes, Gresham. 1958. *Society of Captives: A Study of Maximum Security Prison.* Princeton: Princeton University Press.

Tebbe, Nelson. 2016. "How to Think About Religious Freedom in an Egalitarian Age." *University of Detroit Mercy Law Review* 93: 353–67.

Topinka, Daniel. 2016. *Muslimové v Česku: Etablování muslimů a islámu na veřejnosti* [*Muslims in the Czech Republic Establishment Muslims and Islam in public*]. Brno: Barrister & Principal.

UNODC. 2020. *The United Nations Standard Minimum Rules for the Treatment of Prisoners (the Nelson Mandela Rules)*. Retrieved September 10, 2020 (http://www.unodc.org/documents/justice-and-prison-reform/GA-RESOLUTION/E_ebook.pdf).

Váně, Jan and Lukáš Dirga. 2016. "The Religiosity Behind Bars: Forms of Inmate's Religiosity in the Czech Prison System." *Sociológia/Slovak Sociological Review* 48 (6): 641–63.

Váně, Jan, and Lukáš Dirga. 2020. "The Prison Chaplain as a Part of Penitentiary Care? Transformation of the Czech Prison System after the Fall of Communism." *Archiwum Kryminologii/Archives of Criminology* XLII (1): 253–69. https://doi.org/10.7420/AK2020E.

Váně, Jan, Dušan Lužný, František Kalvas, Martina Štípková and Veronika Hásová. 2018. *Continuity and Discontinuities of Religious Memory in the Czech Republic*. Brno: Barrister & Principal.

Váně, Jan, and Jiří Stočes. 2016. "The Tachov Region and its Religious Memory: New Sudetenland or a Home of Failure?" *Pantheon* 11(1): 49–76.

Vido, Roman, David Václavík and Antonín Paleček. 2016. "Czech Republic: The Promised Land for Atheists?" In *Annual Review of the Sociology of Religion, Volume 7: Sociology of Atheism* edited by Roberto Cipriani and Franco Garelli, 201–32. Leiden: Brill. https://doi.org/10.1163/9789004319301_012.

PART 3

Politics and Policies on Religious Freedom

∴

CHAPTER 9

Organizations and Religious Restrictions: An International Overview of the Intersection of State and Non-Governmental Organizations and Religious Groups

Dane R. Mataic and Kerby Goff

Religious organizations along with governmental and non-government organizations operate in tandem navigating the extent of religious restrictions and attempts to protect religious freedoms. Religious organizations experience some of the most direct and restrictive practices by the state, impacting the ability of members to worship freely and openly. Similarly, governmental and non-governmental organizations have been both central in monitoring religious practice and freedoms, and in implementing the restrictions of religious practice. While numerous explanations abound for why countries regulate religious freedom (see Grim and Finke 2011; Finke and Martin 2014; Mataic 2018; Mataic and Finke 2018; Finke, Mataic, and Fox 2018), there is a substantial gap in the literature assessing the role and experiences of organizations. Exceptions exist, such as Dane R. Mataic and Roger Finke (2018) who identify the importance of an independent judiciary in maintaining promises of religious freedom, and George Thomas (2004) discusses the role of organizations as a potential actor in support of religious rights. Recently there also has been an effort to distinguish between restrictions on organizations versus restrictions on individual members (Finke et al. 2017; Fox and Finke 2020; Zhang 2020). Many others have brushed upon the topic of organizations and freedoms, such as the use of registration requirements for religious organizations without distinguishing between the types of restrictions (Sarkissian 2015; Finke, Mataic, and Fox 2018). In these cases, emphasis is made regarding the role of organizations, neglecting the specificity to determine organizations as the primary emphasis. Room exists for a comprehensive overview of the restrictions of organizations and role of organizations, both state and non-governmental, in promoting or restricting religious freedoms.

We provide this overview, addressing four intertwined components of the *organizations and religious restrictions* relationship. First, we address the "how" and "why" religious organizations themselves are restricted. Our second section addresses the role of governmental organizations and structures in the erosion and maintenance of religious organization's freedoms. The final two sections deviate from the first by addressing non-state actors, with an emphasis on international monitoring groups and international social movement organizations.

We reinforce the overview with original analyses and descriptions of religious restrictions and organizations. Data for these demonstrations are sourced from a variety of international collections (e.g. the Religion and State Project, the CIRI Human Rights Data Project, World Bank, Correlates of War, and the U.S. State Department). In section two, we argue and find that monitoring of the state through an independent judiciary and a free and open election are central to reducing state restrictions on religious organizations. Our third section builds upon an argument that international monitoring by states should reduce the state restrictions on religious organizations. In our descriptive analysis, however, we find the opposite, where sanctions made by U.S. *Office of International Religious Freedom* for violating religious freedoms did not impact subsequent levels of state restrictions on religious organizations. Finally, we document the extensive presence of international social movement organizations working toward religious freedom efforts, highlighting the role of religious freedom SMOs in working toward protecting religious practice.

1 Governmental Restrictions on Religious Organizations

Despite continued promises of religious freedom by 90 percent of countries with constitutions, almost all restrict religious minorities in some capacity (Finke and Martin 2014; Finke et al. 2017; Fox 2008; Grim and Finke 2011; Mataic and Finke 2018). Most generally, governmental restrictions on religion represent the denial or limitation of behaviors or actions by a religion. Such behaviors include restrictions to public religious speech, freedom to worship, and the operation of religious organizations. It is within the last component, the restrictions on the operation and presence of religious organizations that this section details.[1]

---

[1] There is extensive literature that provides overviews of restrictions more generally, including the assessment of the presence of general restrictions, potential causes, and spread between countries (see Grim and Finke 2011; Finke and Martin 2014; Finke et al. 2017; Mataic 2018; Fox 2015).

2 Defining Restrictions on Religious Organizations

Restrictions on religious organizations, while common, are routinely grouped with non-institutional restrictions together in a composite index. Recently, however, there has been a shift in this approach by assessing the relationship between certain government characteristics and institutional/non-institutional restrictions (see Finke, Martin, and Fox 2017; Fox and Finke 2020; Zhang 2020 for greater detail). The role this new avenue of research plays is vital in understanding the distinction between restrictions on institutional processes and non-institutional processes of religious practice. For instance, Roger Finke Robert R. Martin and, Jonathan Fox (2017) find a key difference where societal discrimination within a country is a prominent predictor of state restrictions directed at members of minority religions, yet is not related to state restrictions of institutions. The opposite pattern emerged when assessing the communist history of a country, which was positively related to state restrictions on minority institutions, but not members of the minority religion.

While Finke and colleagues (2017) constructed an initial distinction between institutions and members, Jonathan Fox and Roger Finke (2020) as well as Lihui Zhang (2020) offer a more comprehensive assessment and operationalization of these distinctions. Fox and Finke (2020) assert that one of the central motives for restricting a religious institution is because of a perceived threat by the state or religious majority. They argued that the perceived threat of religious institutions can take many forms, including potential threats to the majority religion and security risks. In some cases, the state will restrict a religious organization if it is perceived to be in opposition to the ruling party, such as during the Soviet era (Froese 2008) or the use of restrictions as a form of government control in China (Yang 2012; Finke et al. 2018). Other cases include fear of religious mobilization or group action (Finke and Harris 2012).

3 State Implementation of Restrictions on Religious Organizations

As for how these restrictions are implemented, Fox and Finke (2020) identified that around 72 percent of all countries restrict institutions for at least one religious minority group. Not only are these restrictions common throughout governments, the presence and amount of institutional discrimination has continued since 1990, with a significantly higher level of institutional restrictions in 2014 (Fox and Finke 2020).

With the continued increase and spread of restrictions on religious institutions, a question emerges: what form do these restrictions on religious institutions take? For Finke and colleagues (2017) as well as Fox and Finke (2020), the forms consist of a wide range of restrictions, including restricting the ability to build, lease, or repair places of worship to limitations on clergy access to jails, military, or hospitals. These past efforts routinely situate institutional restrictions into four categories: "Worship & Gatherings," "Religious Rites," "Related Institutional Operations," and "Clergy & Institutional Voice" (Fox and Finke 2020). By these definitions and forms, institutional restrictions are not necessarily restrictions to an organization exclusively, but also includes how a religious institution operates.

We focus on two categories that limit organizations directly or restrictions addressing the operations of a religious institution operations. In the first, which we consider explicitly organizational restrictions, includes the restrictions on the ability to build, lease or repair places of worship, registration requirements and limitations on formal religious organizations. The second category assesses the restrictions on institutional operations including the ability to import religious publications or write, publish, and disseminate religious publications within a country.[2] Figure 9.1 presents the scaled level of restrictions for these two categories by global regions in 2014. Not only does this explicitly demonstrate that the occurrence of these types of restrictions are global, but for most regions, are quite extensive. Turning to the necessity of registration requirements provides a good case for demonstrating how the state not only restricts organizations but uses restrictions as a tool for further restrictions of religious freedoms.

In the case of registration requirements, states often make the argument that the requirement is benign and simply a tool to maintain tax benefits for religious groups (Kolbe and Henne 2014). Researchers have documented that registration requirements is a tool of the state to monitor, restrict, and prevent worship by religious groups (Sarkissian 2015; Fox 2015; Grim and Finke 2011; Finke et al. 2018). In one of the most comprehensive assessments of registration requirements, Roger Finke and co-authors (2018) assessed the presence of registration requirements globally, finding a similar pattern as other organizational restrictions: their presence has increased from 1990 to 2008 and they are present throughout all global regions. More importantly, however, they confirmed that while registration requirements may appear benign by the state, the implementation of a registration requirement in one year is followed by an increase in other restrictions to minority religions in the following year.

---

[2] See Finke and colleagues (2017) and Fox and Finke (2020) for more detail about these categorizations and included measures.

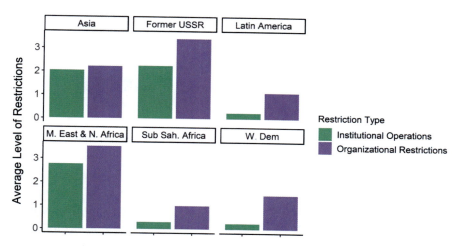

FIGURE 9.1 Distribution of restrictions on organizations of minority religions by global region in 2014
Average Level of Restrictions adjusted to the same scale ranging from 0 to 10.
Source: Religion and State Data

Regardless of the reason that states utilize to implement laws and requirements of religious minorities, these impact the freedom of religions within a country. In the specific case of registration requirements, their implementation predicts future restrictions on religious minorities. This should not be a surprise, however, as the registration requirements specifically provide a way for a state to monitor religious groups within a country. If a group is unable to register or simply does not, they may have to operate covertly or in some cases illegally, opening themselves up to further discrimination or mistreatment by a state. The global presence of these restrictions, and relative infancy in researching organizational restrictions, specifically introduces a new line of questions that should be addressed in future research.

One such question might be, how do other forms of restrictions on organizations impact future restrictions on minority religions? A second question might investigate the relationship between organizational restrictions and the presence of social conflict within a country. While an argument by states to utilize organizational restrictions is to protect against threats to the state, majority religion, and maintain civility, it appears that this justification is unfounded. In one case, Brian Grim and Roger Finke (2011) found that in the presence of state restrictions on religious minorities, there were more instances of social discrimination by the majority religion. Understanding these patterns in greater detail are necessary given the justification by states, but also the related pattern of additional societal conflict within a country.

4   Internal Maintenance of Freedoms for Minority Religious Organizations

Despite the presence of state originated restrictions on minority religious organizations as demonstrated above and the subsequent erosion of freedoms, other state organizations or structures within a country correspond with a maintenance of religious freedoms and lower levels of restrictions. Two structures most extensively researched are the presence of an independent judiciary as well as free and open elections (Finke and Martin 2014; Finke et al. 2017; Mataic and Finke 2018). In both, the organizational presence of an independent judiciary and the structure of open elections corresponds with active monitoring of a state, which in turn maintains levels of religious freedoms and a reduction in restrictions.

James T. Richardson (2015), utilized a number of examples documenting the success of autonomous courts within a country in the ability to protect minority religions from restrictive legislative and majority religion power. Thus, the independent judiciary acts as a distinct organization that can monitor and uphold promises of religious freedoms. This role is especially important in reducing the compliance gap between the number of promises of religious freedoms in a constitution and actions by the state through the extent of restrictions on religious practice (Mataic and Finke 2018).

Roger Finke and Dane R. Mataic (2019, 597) documented the level of restrictions within a country, finding that "in countries without an independent judiciary, 55 percent of the countries have medium to high levels of restrictions" using 2008 data. Further, Finke and colleagues (2017) demonstrated through statistical analyses that the presence of an independent judiciary was associated with a significantly lower odds of restrictions on minority religions measured in 2008.

Similar patterns emerge when assessing the presence of free and open elections within a country. Finke and colleagues (2018) found that the introduction of a free and open election in one year corresponded with a significant reduction in the presence of restrictions for minority religions in the following year. The distribution of countries with restrictions depending on the presence of free and open elections are also consistent with the presence of independent judiciaries, where lower levels of restrictions are present among countries with open elections (Finke and Mataic 2019).

Despite past patterns, only Finke and colleagues (2017) assessed the relationship between state organizations or structures and the presence of institutional restrictions. We build on this through an update of these patterns utilizing the most recent Religion and State dataset (Fox 2019) assessing the relationship between an independent judiciary, free and open elections, and the level of restrictions on minority religious organizations.[3]

5 The Protection of Organizational Freedoms

Table 9.1 demonstrates the patterns of an independent judiciary and government restrictions on minority religious organizations.[4] Restrictions are grouped into four categories: none, low, medium and high.[5] While 60 percent of the countries with an independent judiciary have zero to low levels of state restrictions on minority religious organizations, only about 42 percent of countries without an independent judiciary feature the same levels of restrictions on minority religious organizations. Even more drastic, however, is that 58 percent of countries without an independent judiciary restrict religious organizations at medium or high levels.

The patterns are even more clear with the presence of free and open elections. About 70 percent of countries with completely free and open elections have zero or low levels of restrictions on minority religious organizations. Conversely, over 70 percent of countries without a free and open election have medium or high levels of restrictions against religious organizations. As far as descriptive patterns go, the distinctions between countries without an independent judiciary or a free and open elections are evident: restrictions are

---

3 Finke and colleagues (2017) found consistent relationships between an independent judiciary and both institutional and non-institutional restrictions.
4 Reflecting the methods of Finke and colleagues (2017), we utilize the complete institutional restriction index (Finke et al. 2017; Fox and Finke 2020), not simply the two components discussed in the first section.
5 The categories of restrictions were calculated from the Religion and State Round 3 dataset, where countries with 0 restrictions were identified with the category "none." Countries with 1 to 5, 6 to 12, and 12 to 42 were marked as low, medium and high levels of restrictions respectively. This corresponds with about 25% of the country in each category of restrictions (none=22%; low=28%; medium=26%; high=24%). Independent Judiciary and Free and Open Elections were derived from the categories provided by the CIRI dataset. Table 9.1 was then derived taking a crosstabulation of the categories of restrictions on organizations and either the independent judiciary or the free and open elections.

TABLE 9.1 Internal organizations and structure and government restrictions on minority religious organizations in 2014

	None	Low	Medium	High
Free and Open Elections				
Free and open elections do not exist (*N*=39)	13%	15%	18%	54%
Free and open elections with some limitations (*N*=66)	26%	17%	32%	26%
Free and open elections in both law and practice (*N*=67)	24%	46%	24%	6%
Independent Judiciary				
Not independent (*N*=74)	16%	26%	28%	30%
Partially independent (*N*=48)	21%	23%	21%	35%
Generally independent (*N*=50)	32%	28%	26%	24%

Note: Data derived from the Religion and State, Round 3 Collection and the CIRI datasets. *N* = 172 countries.

highest in countries that do not contain organizations or structures that monitor the state's support of freedoms.

We would be remiss, however, if we did not include an analysis looking at these patterns while considering other country characteristics. Table 9.2 presents the results from these analyses, addressing the role of independent judiciaries and open elections in relation to levels of restrictions on minority religious organizations, holding other characteristics constant. Specifically, we find that both independent judiciary and free and open elections are significantly associated with lower levels of restrictions on minority religious organizations. A country with completely free and open elections, compared to a country without, is associated with an eight-point reduction in the level of restrictions on minority religious organizations comparing no open elections to countries with open elections in law and practice.[6] For each step increase in the independence of a judiciary, we expect a 1.92-point reduction in the level of restrictions, this suggests that the presence of an independent judiciary is

---

6 There are three categories for both independent judiciary and open elections (See Table 9.1).

TABLE 9.2   Regression modeling the sources of restrictions on religious minority organizations in 2014

	Coef.	Std. Err.
Free and Open Elections	-4.68***	.83
Independent Judiciary	-1.92*	.94
Societal Discrimination of Religious Groups	.24***	.05
Population in 2010	.00	.00
Log of GDP	2.45***	.69
Communism	6.13***	1.25
Government Effectiveness	-.71	1.16
Constant	-9.60	6.08

Note: *$p < .05$; **$p < .01$; ***$p < .001$. Data derived from the Religion and State, Round 3 Collection, the CIRI datasets, World Bank, InfoPlease collections. $N = 165$.

associated with an almost four-point lower score of restrictions compared to countries without an independent judiciary.

Not only are there patterns related to the presence of internal organizations and structures that monitor the state to maintain freedoms, but they are significantly related even when accounting for other country characteristics. These results do not completely erode the insignificant relationships found by other scholars or under other conditions (Mataic 2018; Finke et al. 2018). It is important to continue to explore the role of both independent judiciaries and open elections. This is especially true for one question that has been overlooked; what happens when an independent judiciary or open election is implemented in a country that did not have this previously. Finke and colleagues (2018) demonstrated that after such a change, the patterns were sometimes flipped, such as a positive relationship between the new presence of an independent judiciary in one year and higher restrictions in the following year. It is possible there is a lagged relationship between an organizational or structural implementation that is frequently overlooked by researchers and analyses.

6   International Monitoring Organizations and Religious Freedoms

Past research in explaining the presence of restrictions on religious minorities has routinely excluded external influence in modeling the relationships.

There are recent attempts such as the diffusion of restrictive practices between countries (Mataic 2018), but even these did not address the role of external organizations or structures. External influences are comparable to the internal influence discussed above, but may come about from different arenas. Within our brief overview we recount the role of three types of external influence: 1) foreign government organizations; 2) membership in international governmental organizations; and 3) human rights organizations.

7 Foreign Government Organizations and Religious Restrictions

One of the primary examples of a singular foreign government organization influencing or protecting religious freedoms of minorities globally is the United States' Office of International Religious Freedom. Following the passage of the 1998 International Religious Freedom Act (IRFA), the Office of IRF has been tasked with preparing a detailed report on the nature of global religious freedoms, including violations by international states (US Department of State 2020). These detailed reports are then utilized by the United States to shine light on abuses by international governments revolving around religious freedom.

The most direct influence the Office of IRF has in maintaining global religious freedoms is an annual declaration of "Countries of Particular Concern." Once designated as a country of concern, Congress is notified and then options are presented for how to cease the restrictions on religious freedom, including both non-economic and economic policy options (US Department of State 2020). Despite the presence of the Office of IRF and the annual reports of international religious freedom, global restrictions on religion have continued to rise since the passing of the 1998 IRFA. However, the IRF designations are limited in scope and only include a few countries annually. It is possible that the designation corresponds with reduced religious restrictions for only these specific countries.

Looking at the four years prior to the most recent Religion and State data of religious restrictions (2010–2013), there were eight countries continuously included as a "Country of Particular Concern" for each of the five years.[7] It should be expected that after being designated as a country of particular concern, the level of restrictions on religious minorities would decrease, especially

---

7 These countries are: Burma, China, Eritrea, Iran, North Korea, Saudi Arabia, Sudan, and Uzbekistan (US Department of State 2020).

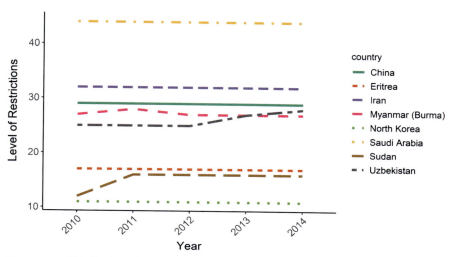

FIGURE 9.2 Distribution of restrictions on organizations of minority religions by countries of particular concern
Source: Religion and State Data, US Office of IRF

if designated multiple times by the Office of IRF. However, in the case of these eight countries, not a single one experienced a reduction in the level of restrictions on religious minority organizations despite consistent identification as a country of particular concern (Figure 9.2). The levels of restrictions actually remained relatively consistent between 2010 and 2014 and in the case of a couple countries, Sudan and Uzbekistan, the levels of restrictions increased while being designated a country of particular concern.

Another monitoring group, The United Nations' Special Rapporteur on the freedom of religion or belief, provides an overview of the state of global religious freedom and recommendations for protecting religious rights. Like the Office of IRF, the participation and impact seem particularly limited. For instance, in 2017, the Special Rapporteur noted that less than 10 percent of the Member States reported on their efforts for protecting religious freedoms during the previous five and half years (Special Rapporteur on Freedom of Religion or Belief 2017). While we document the lack of impact associated with sanctions provided by the US Office of IRF, given the continued increase in global religious restrictions, we expect similar patterns are present following the proposed actions outlined by the Special Rapporteur.

Thus, although the US Office of International Religious Freedoms and the UN's Special Rapporteur on the freedom of religion or belief offers attempts to reduce global restrictions on religious minorities, it seems the ability at least for organizations, is limited.

8 Membership in International Governmental Organizations

While sanctions by the United States or declarations by the UN may not directly impact the level of restrictions on religious minorities, it is possible that participation by states in international governmental organizations do impact restrictions. Among assessments of other human rights, researchers routinely demonstrate that membership in international organizations correspond with reduced levels of human rights violations, such as women's rights (Avdeyeva 2007, 2010; Hafner-Burton and Tsutsui 2005). However, unlike the relationship between membership and protection of women's rights, recent research exploring membership in international governmental organizations (IGO) and the protections of religious freedoms proved less convincing (Mataic and Finke 2018). Dane R. Mataic and Roger Finke (2018) modeled the relationship between total number of international memberships and the compliance gap between promises of religious freedoms and instances of restrictions on religious minorities, arguing that more membership will correspond with greater instances of monitoring of human rights. Despite the argument, the number of IGO memberships was not significantly related to a difference in restrictions or compliance gaps in any of their initial and expanded models. Thus, two of the organizational monitoring groups explored appear inconsistently related to the levels of religious restrictions, leaving only the influence of human rights organizations as a potential external organizational source of maintaining religious freedoms.

9 Domestic Presence of Human Rights Organizations

The presence of human rights organizations are vital components to monitoring and maintaining the protections of human rights broadly (DeMeritt 2012; Krain 2012; Murdie 2014). However, in a recent and extensive research project by Zhang (2020), the relationship between the presence of human rights organizations (HRO) within a country and the occurrence of restrictions on religious organizations was tested. Within the project, Zhang (2020) argued that HROs support religious freedoms by providing resources to religious organizations in order to change the restrictive practices. Unlike the two external organizations described above, and their limited relationship with religious restrictions, Zhang found clear evidence that the presence of HROs coincides with significantly lower levels of restrictions on religious organizations. Further, for each additional domestic HRO, the level of restrictions on religious organizations corresponds with even lower levels of restrictions on religious organizations within a country.

The findings by Zhang (2020) mirror expectations when looking at the history of human rights organizations efforts toward religious freedoms. Evelyn Bush (2007, 2017) documents 158 religious human rights organizations which focus on religious freedom. The United Nation's NGO Committees on Freedom of Religion or Belief in Geneva and New York identify 80 and 54 NGOs cooperating on advocacy for religious freedom (Union of International Associations 2020). Both religious and non-religious NGOs focus on the issue of religious freedom. Of the 36 organizations linked on the New York NGO Committee website, two-thirds are explicitly religious organizations—including the Baptist World Alliance and Muslims for Progressive Values—while the other third include humanist, atheist, and other organizations not tied to a specific religious tradition—such as the American Humanist Association and Religions for Peace. Many American religious freedom NGOs link together national and international human rights NGOs in advocacy for religious freedom. These efforts by HROs clearly emphasize the maintenance of religious freedoms globally, even when other external influences are not as effective.

The conflicting patterns of external influence on restrictions of religious organizations is interesting. On the one hand, it almost appears as though the results are in conflict, suggesting that external influence is inconsistent at best. Further examination about the types of external influence and how the influence is directed offers a stronger explanation for the distinctions described above. In the case of the US Office of IRF, the sanctions presented to countries are often blurred by actions that might not be directly related to religious freedoms. For example, in the case of China as a response from the 2010 report, the "Actions Taken Under IRFA" consist of the "Foreign Relations Authorization Act ... restriction of exports of crime control and detection instruments and equipment" (US Commission on International Religious Freedom 2010). This reported action was the same between 2010 and 2013. It is likely that in order to be effective in protecting religious freedoms, the actions should shift in response to continued violation of these religious freedoms rather than remaining consistent.

Membership in international governmental organizations as assessed by Mataic and Finke (2018) features the same problem as influence from the US Office of IRF, with little assessment of direct influence or efforts to maintain religious freedoms. In other words, membership in an IGO will likely only be related to protections of religious freedoms if the organizations themselves are dedicated to protecting human rights generally or religious freedoms specifically. Human rights organizations, as identified by Zhang (2020) addresses the premise of religious freedoms: the rights of individuals to practice their religious beliefs without restrictions or punishment. Consequently, their mission is directly related to the maintenance of human rights and their presence within a country represents their effort to protect human rights. Thus, it is logical that the HRO s identified by Zhang correspond with a reduction in restrictions on minority religions, while simple membership in IGO s does not.

The distinctions between different types of external influence on the maintenance of freedoms for religious minority organizations introduces additional questions to pursue in future research. First, while membership in international government organizations itself was unrelated in the reduction of religious restrictions, what happens if the type of IGO is assessed? Does membership in an organization dedicated to human rights initiatives feature the same effect as the presence of domestic human rights organizations? Additionally, the US Office of International Religious Freedoms designation of countries of particular concern may not be useful given organizational inertia, the tendency to continue with the same structure, and the duration that these countries have already existed on the IRF list. Tests could look instead at the role Tier 2 designations have on newly added countries. In other words, does the threat of potential sanctions for a country help reverse course from continued restrictions on religious minorities toward greater religious freedoms?

Wade Cole (2012) also offers some relevant conclusions about human rights treaties generally that may apply to the impact of external influence on maintaining religious freedoms. Cole (2012) found that countries with wholesale promises of human rights are inconsistently related to protections, but selective and precise commitments, even if reduced, have a direct relation to fewer human rights violations. It is possible that international monitoring of religious restrictions would follow a similar pattern, where active and serious commitments, even if they are less encompassing, are necessary before the participation will actually reduce the levels of restrictions. Ultimately, the impact of external influence is one still in need of the most direct and extensive assessments as interest in religious freedoms and restrictions of religious organizations continues.

10 International Social Movement Organizations and Religious Freedoms

Our last section addresses the role of social movements and a sometimes conflicting relationship with religious freedoms. While religious and secular social movements alike have resisted religious expression and practice, they have contributed to improving conditions for the free exercise of religion. We review the historical origins and contemporary network of social movement organizations (SMOs) focusing on religious freedom and discuss recent findings concerning SMOs impact on religious freedoms around the world, and finally produce potential questions and directions for continued exploration of the intersection of SMOs and religious freedoms.

Social movements coalesce around preferences and beliefs concerning how a society should change or resist change, and SMOs are organized to advance these preferences and beliefs (McCarthy and Zald 1977). Preferences for the free practice of one's religion, or the restriction of competing religions are documented widely throughout history, but religious freedom as a social movement goal emerged more recently. In the 19th century, transnational Protestant missionary SMOs diffused advocacy for religious freedoms around the world using a variety of techniques (Fields 1982; Woodberry 2012). The network of Protestant SMOs began shifting toward a Christian internationalism that emphasized a pluralistic concept of religious freedom (Hao 2001; Robert 2002).

After World War II, a specific type of SMO emerged within these transnational advocacy networks—non-governmental organizations (NGOs)—advancing religious freedom and other human rights (Keck and Sikkink 2014). NGO's were critical to the inclusion of human rights language, including the notion of religious freedom as a human right, in the charter of the United Nations in 1941 (Gaer 1995). In the United States, evangelical SMOs were important in collaborating with other religious groups to secure the passage of the International Religious Freedom Act in 1998, which ultimately led to the formation of the Office of IRF described above (Hertzke 2004, 2008). Today, religious and non-religious NGOs are active throughout the world advocating for religious freedom. In addition to the reports, the United Nation's committee on freedom of religion or belief, coordinates NGO activities in support of international agreements and declarations concerning religious freedoms (NGO Committee on Freedom of Religion and Belief 2012). Through securing international declarations and policies in support of religious freedom, SMOs concerned with religious freedom have generated the grounds for their own proliferation. Over the past 70 years, over 135 SMOs have emerged with a focus on religious freedom.[8]

---

8 This number is estimated based on available data. The Yearbook of International Associations (Union of International Associations 2020) documents 28 organizations founded since 1950 which focus on religious practice and human rights, and a supplementary data collection of religious human rights NGOs lists 107 founded since 1945 focusing on religious freedom (Bush 2007, 2017).

While many SMOs work to protect religious freedoms, they are not exclusive. Grim and Finke (2011) observed that religious and non-religious social movements often mobilize to suppress minority religions around the world. Religious social movements of dominant religions mobilize to restrict competing religious groups by taking advantage of gaps in state protections of religious minorities or moving the state to restrict religious minorities. Whether in conjunction with political parties—as in the case of the Hindu Nationalist Party BJP — or in opposition to a secular state — the Muslim Brotherhood in Egypt — SMOs mobilize social resistance and discrimination directed at religious minorities. Analyzing nearly a decade of International Religious Freedom (IRF) reports, Grim and Finke find that 45 percent of countries have assertive religious social movements restricting minority religions (Grim and Finke 2011). Non-religious social movements also seek to restrict religious freedoms. According to the 2005 IRF report, 40 percent of countries have non-religious social movements which harass religious groups. In 58 percent of countries, social movements and political groups threaten people based on their religion. Even more concerning, as demonstrated in Table 9.2 above, the societal discrimination corresponds with a significant increase in the number of state restrictions of minority religious organizations. Thus, not only are the groups themselves discriminating against minority religions, but they also have a direct influence on the states' treatment of the same minority groups.

But the negativity of religious SMOs should not overshadow their ability to advocate for openness in the religious market. Religious communities and congregations may function like SMOs in the public sphere (Beckford 2008; Casanova 1994), advocating for the freedom to worship and assemble even in authoritarian states (Koesel 2014). In authoritarian contexts like China, the tactics are non-confrontational, and the freedoms they gain depend on maintaining popular legitimacy, appeasing local and state authorities, and securing international support (Cheng 2003). In Latin America, networks of diverse religious communities and NGOs try to create social movements by advocating for human rights and independence (Loveman 1998). Following Vatican II, the Catholic Church encouraged and facilitated advocacy efforts for religious freedom and tolerance around the world (Casanova 2001). Additionally, throughout democratic states with open religious markets, religious SMOs advocacy for religious freedom moves beyond national borders to try and implement freedoms to worship and assemble elsewhere. In the U.S., religious SMOs move beyond freedom of practice and instead emphasize eroding restrictions on issues such as federal healthcare policies (Haberkorn and Gerstein 2014) and religiously based workplace discrimination (Liptak 2015).

Religious freedom SMOs have often been the initiators of political changes toward greater religious freedom. The advocacy and institution building of transnational Western Protestant missionary SMOs set the conditions for greater democracy and social movements for democracy (Kadivar 2018; Woodberry 2004, 2012), critical components of religious freedom. Through decades of advocacy, these organizations have also created thematic mechanisms or issue groups with the power to name specific countries who violated human rights including religious freedoms, including the UN Special Rapporteur on freedom of religion or belief (Gaer 1995). Further, in the early 2000s, organizations mobilized members at the UN to defeat "defamation of religion" resolutions—resolutions designed to allow states to prosecute "defamation" of state-sponsored religions, particularly Islam (Farris 2013).

While there is some research on the role of religious freedom SMOs on policy outcomes, there is very little on societal outcomes at the national level. Other questions that still remain include whether religious freedom SMOs help secure religious freedoms and improve conditions beyond the state level. Theoretical and empirical research on the role of civil society organizations suggests that societies with more SMOs promoting an open market for religious belief and practice should improve conditions (Putnam 2004; Thomas 2001). Data from the IRF reports provide little evidence that this is occurring, however. In 2005, only 13 country reports mentioned that the UN or NGO advocacy contributed to improvements in religious freedom, up from only six in 2001. Much more research is needed as SMOs with a stake in religious freedom are active in securing free exercise of religion through creative daily practices and strategic long-term activities (Cheng 2003).

In sum, the role of SMOs in the status of religious freedom is mixed. While religious freedom SMOs have helped to diffuse the ideal of universal religious freedom and secured significant policy changes, local and national SMOs often contribute to social restrictions of religious freedom. Whether in coordination with states or because of weak government enforcement of religious freedom, dominant or state-sponsored religious organizations can also suppress religious freedoms through SMO-like tactics.

11 Conclusions

Until recently, the efforts to described and assess the restrictions of religious organizations, and the role of organizations in maintaining religious freedoms, has received little exploration. As a result, the conclusions made about both have been limited at best, but at worst have generally been combined with other assessments blurring the lines between organizations and individuals. The new efforts are vital and represent a growing trend among researchers of religious restrictions: comprehensive assessments of the restrictions of religious organizations and role of organizations, in promoting or restricting religious freedoms. We added to these developing efforts through a broad overview of the relationship between religious organizations and restrictions on religious practice, organized into four key areas: 1) global regulation of religious organizations; 2) state agencies and the protection of religious freedoms; 3) international monitoring groups and religious freedoms; and 4) international social movement organizations and religious freedoms.

We began by reviewing the global regulation of religious organizations. This matches a growing effort among researchers to explore the intricacies of restrictions through the separation of restrictions directed at organizations and members. We detailed a few of the reasons why the state would restrict religious organizations as well as how restrictions of minority organizations are currently measured (Finke et al. 2017; Fox and Finke 2020). Then we provided a brief demonstration of the global spread of restrictions on religious organizations, detailing the presence of restrictions on the religious organization itself (e.g. the ability to build, lease, or repair places of worship or registration requirements for legal operation) and restrictions on institutional operations (e.g. ability to import religious publications or the dissemination of publications within a country) throughout six global regions. The end result is that not only are these two types of restrictions present in each of the six global regions, but they are quite common, with all regions featuring greater levels of organizational restrictions compared to restrictions on the institutional operations. This is logical, if a religious organization is unable to acquire a building or register to operate, it has a direct impact on the ability to operate through the dissemination of religious materials.

The second section dealt with the role of state organizations and structures in maintaining freedoms for religious minority organizations, outlining past research emphasizing the role of the independent judiciary as well as free and open elections (Finke and Martin 2014; Finke et al. 2017; Finke and Mataic 2019; Richardson 2015). Our update utilizes 2014 data from the Religion and State Round 3 dataset. The results were clear, states supporting both an independent judiciary and open elections contained significantly lower levels of restrictions on religious minority organizations. This pattern was documented through both descriptive tables showing a breakdown of the percent of countries with zero to high levels of restrictions and regression models controlling for other country characteristics. Independent judiciaries as well as free and open elections were most associated with none or low levels of restrictions on religious institutions (about 60 percent and 70 percent respectively). Taking these patterns one step further, we also found that both were significantly related to reduced levels of restrictions on minority religious organizations, suggesting that as a country has a more extensive independent judiciary or free and open elections, the lower the levels of restrictions for religious minorities. In addition to these patterns, we outlined the importance of addressing the possibility of a time lag between the implementation of a state organization or structure and a reduction in the number of restrictions on religious minority organizations.

In the third section, we turned to an assessment of three types of external organizations as a potential influence on the level of restrictions within a country. The first organization type was foreign government organizations, such as the U.S. Office of International Religious Freedom, that monitors levels of global religious freedom. Our second organization type was a measure of membership in international governmental organizations, depicted as a count of total memberships. Despite a logical expectation for both of these organization types as a potential influence in reducing restrictions, neither seem to provide relationship with a country's level of restrictions on religious minority organizations. The final organization type, presence of human rights organizations, was successful in reducing religious restrictions. We detailed the work of Zhang (2020) and the analysis of total number of human rights organizations within a country and subsequent pattern of lower levels of restrictions on religious minority organizations. Much like our second section, questions still remain, such as why certain external organizations have a significant relationship with a reduction on religious restrictions, while others even with a mission of monitoring and maintaining religious freedoms are possibly insufficient.

Our final section documents the rise, spread, and influence of social movement organizations in their relationship with global religious freedom. Not only are social movement organizations utilized to maintain religious freedoms such as evangelical SMOs in the United States pushing for the International Religious Freedom Act, but also the SMOs engaging in restrictive practices and efforts, including the Hindu Nationalist Party BJP. We conclude this section raising the question of whether SMOs can create change beyond the state level and whether the efforts can continue through long term efforts.

Ultimately, this paper highlights developments in research involving religious freedoms and restrictions by specifically addressing the intersection of organizations as both the target and actor. Continued efforts must be made to distinguish between restrictions on organizations versus a general assessment of restrictions. As Fox and Finke (2020) outline, organizations are the target of the state for reasons that do not always apply to members of a religious tradition. As such, the treatment, policies, and practices by the state may vary drastically. Moreover, the role of organizations in promoting religious freedoms or even eroding these freedoms necessitates greater emphasis. As of now, little work has been done to document how influential various organizations are in maintaining freedoms, but this dearth of research provides a direct avenue for continued efforts by researchers in order to document the intersection of organizations and religious restrictions.

References

Avdeyeva, Olga. 2007. "When do States Comply with International Treaties? Policies on Violence against Women in Post-Communist Countries." *International Studies Quarterly* 51: 877–900.

Avdeyeva, Olga. 2010. "States' Compliance with International Requirements: Gender Equity in EU Enlargement Countries." *Political Research Quarterly* 63, no. 1: 203–17.

Beckford, James A. 2008. "Social Movements as Free-floating Religious Phenomena." In *The Blackwell Companion to Sociology of Religion*, edited by Richard K. Fenn, 229–48. Malden. MA: Blackwell Publishing Ltd.

Bush, Evelyn L. 2007. "Measuring Religion in Global Civil Society." *Social Forces* 85, no. 4: 1645–65.

Bush, Evelyn L. 2017. "What is a Religious NGO?" In *The Faithful Measures: New Methods in the Measurement of Religion*, edited by Roger Finke and Christopher D. Bader, 260–86. New York, NY: New York University Press.

Casanova, Jose. 1994. *Public Religions in the Modern World.* Chicago, IL: University of Chicago Press.

Casanova, Jose. 2001. "Civil Society and Religion: Retrospective Reflections on Catholicism and Prospective Reflections on Islam." *Social Research* 68, no. 4: 1041–80.

Cheng, May M.C. 2003. "House Church Movements and Religious Freedom in China." *China: An International Journal* 1, no. 1: 16–45.

Cole, Wade M. 2012. "Human Rights as Myth and Ceremony? Reevaluating the Effectiveness of Human Rights Treaties, 1981–2007." *American Journal of Sociology* 117, no. 4: 1131–71.

DeMeritt, Jacqueline H.R. 2012. "International Organizations and Government Killings: Does Naming and Shaming Save Lives." *International Interactions* 38, no. 5: 597–621.

Farris, Virginia L. 2013. "Non-Governmental Organizations: Doing Their Share For International Religious Freedom." *The Review of Faith & International Affairs* 11, no. 1: 56–65.

Fields, Karen E. 1982. "Christian Missionaries as Anticolonial Militants." *Theory and Society* 11, no. 1: 95–108.

Finke, Roger and Jaime Harris. 2012. "Wars and Rumors of Wars: Explaining Religiously Motivated Violence." In *Religion, Politics, Society, and the State*, edited by Jonathan Fox, 51–71. New York, NY: Oxford University Press.

Finke, Roger and Robert R. Martin. 2014. "Ensuring Liberties: Understanding State Restrictions on Religious Freedoms." *Journal for the Scientific Study of Religion* 53, no. 4: 687–705.

Finke, Roger, Robert R. Martin, and Jonathan Fox. 2017. "Explaining Discrimination Against Religious Minorities." *Politics and Religion* 10: 389–416.

Finke, Roger and Dane R. Mataic. 2019. "Promises, Practices, and Consequences of Religious Freedom: A Global Overview." *University of St. Thomas Law Journal* 15, no. 3: 587–606.

Finke, Roger, Dane R. Mataic, and Jonathan Fox. 2018. "Assessing the Impact of Religious Registration." *Journal for the Scientific Study of Religion* 56, no. 4: 720–36.

Fox, Jonathan. 2008. *A World Survey of Religion and the State*. New York: Cambridge University Press.

Fox, Jonathan. 2015. *Political Secularism, Religion and the State: A Time Series Analysis of Worldwide Data*. New York: Cambridge University Press.

Fox, Jonathan. 2019. "A World Survey of Secular-Religious Competition: Government Religious Policy from 1990 to 2014." *Religion, State, and Society* 47, no. 1: 10–29.

Fox, Jonathan and Roger Finke. 2020. "Ensuring Individual Rights Through Institutional Freedoms: The Role of Religious Institutions in Securing Religious Rights." Paper presented at the Religious Freedom Roundtable.

Froese, Paul. 2008. *The Great Secularization Experiment: What Soviet Communism Taught us about Religion in the Modern Era*. Berkeley, CA: University of California Press.

Gaer, Felice D. 1995. "Reality Check: Human Rights Nongovernmental Organizations Confront Governments at the United Nations." *Third World Quarterly* 16, no. 3: 389–404.

Grim, Brian J. and Roger Finke. 2011. *The Price of Freedom Denied: Religious Persecution and Conflict in the Twenty-First Century*. New York: Cambridge University Press.

Hafner-Burton, Emilie M. and Kiyoteru Tsutsui. 2005. "Human Rights in a Globalizing World: The Paradox of Empty Promises." *American Journal of Sociology* 110, no. 5:1373–411.

Haberkorn, Jennifer and Josh Gerstein. 2014. "Court Sides with Hobby Lobby." *POLITICO*.

Hao, Yap Kim. 2001. "Ecumenical Movement." In *A Dictionary of Asian Christianity*, edited by S. W. Sunquist, D. C. S. Wu and J. C. H. Chea, 258–65. Grand Rapids, MI: Wm. B. Eerdmans Publishing Co.

Hertzke, Allen D. 2004. *Freeing God's Children: The Unlikely Alliance for Global Human Rights*. Lanham, Md: Rowman & Littlefield.

Hertzke, Allen D. 2008. "International Religious Freedom Policy: Taking Stock." *The Review of Faith & International Affairs* 6, no. 2: 17–23.

Kadivar, Mohammad Ali. 2018. "Mass Mobilization and the Durability of New Democracies." *American Sociological Review* 83, no. 2: 390–417.

Keck, Margaret E. and Kathryn Sikkink. 2014. *Activists beyond Borders: Advocacy Networks in International Politics*. New York, NY: Cornell University Press.

Koesel, Karrie J. 2014. *Religion and Authoritarianism: Cooperation, Conflict, and the Consequences*. New York: Cambridge University Press.

Kolbe, Melanie and Peter S. Henne. 2014. "The Effect of Religious Restrictions on Forced Migration." *Politics & Religion* 7: 665–83.

Krain, Matthew. 2012. "J'accuse! Does Naming and Shaming Perpetrators Reduce the Severity of Genocides or Politicides?" *International Studies Quarterly* 56, no. 3: 574–89.

Liptak, Adam. 2015. "Muslim Woman Denied Job Over Head Scarf Wins in Supreme Court." *The New York Times*.

Loveman, Mara. 1998. "High-Risk Collective Action: Defending Human Rights in Chile, Uruguay, and Argentina." *American Journal of Sociology* 104, no. 2: 477–525.

Mataic, Dane R. 2018. "Countries Mimicking Neighbors: The Spatial Diffusion of Governmental Restrictions on Religion." *Journal for the Scientific Study of Religion* 57, no. 2: 221–37.

Mataic, Dane R. and Roger Finke. 2018. "Compliance Gaps and the Failed Promises of Religious Freedoms." *Religion, State, & Society* 47, no. 1: 124–50.

McCarthy, John D. and Mayer N. Zald. 1977. "Resource Mobilization and Social Movements: A Partial Theory." *American Journal of Sociology* 82, no. 6: 1212–41.

Murdie, Amanda and Dursun Peksen. 2014. "The Impact of Human Rights INGO Shaming on Humanitarian Interventions." *The Journal of Politics* 76, no. 1: 215–28.

NGO Committee on Freedom of Religion or Belief. 2012. "About." *NGO Committee on Freedom of Religion or Belief*. Retrieved April 1, 2020 (https://www.unforb.org/about/).

Putnam, Robert D. 2004. *Democracies in Flux: The Evolution of Social Capital in Contemporary Society*. New York: Oxford University Press.

Richardson, James T. 2015. "Managing Religion and the Judicialization of Religious Freedom." *Journal for the Scientific Study of Religion* 54, no. 1: 1–19.

Robert, Dana L. 2002. "The First Globalization: The Internationalization of the Protestant Missionary Movement between the World Wars." *International Bulletin of Missionary Research* 26, no. 2: 50–66.

Sarkissian, Ani. 2015. *The Varieties of Religious Repression: Why Governments Restrict Religion*. New York: Oxford University Press.

Special Rapporteur on Freedom of Religion or Belief. 2017. "72nd Session of the General Assembly." Accessed 2020. Available at https://undocs.org/A/72/365.

Thomas, George. 2001. "Religions in Global Civil Society." *Sociology of Religion* 62, no. 4: 515–33.

Thomas, George. 2004. "Constructing World Civil Society Through Contentions over Religious Rights." *Journal of Human Rights* 3, no. 2: 239–51.

U.S. Commission on International Religious Freedom. 2010. *Annual Report 2010*. U.S. Department of State. Accessed 2020. https://www.uscirf.gov/sites/default/files/resources/annual%20report%202010.pdf.

U.S. Department of State. 2020. *Office of International Religious Freedom*. Accessed 2020. https://www.state.gov/bureaus-offices/under-secretary-for-civilian-security-democracy-and-human-rights/office-of-international-religious-freedom/.

Union of International Associations, ed. 2020. *Yearbook of International Organizations Online*. Leiden: Brill.

Woodberry, Robert D. 2004. "The Shadow of Empire: Christian Missions, Colonial Policy, and Democracy in Postcolonial Societies." PhD diss., University of North Carolina at Chapel Hill.

Woodberry, Robert D. 2012. "The Missionary Roots of Liberal Democracy." *American Political Science Review* 106, no. 2: 244–74.

Yang, Fenggang. 2012. *Religion in China: Survival and Revival under Communist Rule*. New York: Oxford University Press.

Zhang, Lihui. 2020. "Religious Freedom in an Age of Globalization, International Law, and Human Rights Activism." PhD diss., University of Oklahoma.

CHAPTER 10

Religious Freedom between Politics and Policies: Social and Legal Conflicts over Catholic Religious Education in Italy, 1984–1992

Guillaume Silhol

Religious freedom is a polysemic notion, operating both as a motive claimed by social movements and civil value in contemporary societies, value which is embedded in social practices, ideas, and rights. Individual and collective autonomy, areas of State administration and international standards are central to usual definitions of religious freedom, they also are strongly related to politics and public policies, and to the conflictual dynamics described by the concept of judicialization (Richardson 2015; Breskaya and Giordan 2019). Judicialization of an issue (public problem, political competition, policy program, etc.) refers to a process in which legal actions are taken by social actors, unfolding in institutional arenas where recourses to the law serve alternative visions of the "common good" as well as professional and strategic purposes (Sarat and Scheingold 2006). Definitions of "religious freedom," policy programs, and criteria of interpretation by administrators and street-level bureaucrats are a significant part of the social construction of this freedom. Courts can become sites of redefinition in the process of policy-making, but they always do so in connection with other arenas of decisions and conflicts, from parliaments to local agencies (Mayrl 2018). If inquiries on this theme are detached from the perspective of history of law, focused on norms and doctrines (Ferrari 2012), they can renew other research paths on "religious freedom." In relation to studies of symbolic and practical aspects, political perceptions and experiences, they can study how "religious freedom" becomes part of public problems in a specific society (Gusfield 1981), such as contemporary Italy. This chapter is an empirical contribution in political sociology to the research field on religion in public policies, with arguments from cause-lawyering and neo-institutional studies on State and religion (Mayrl 2011; Reeh 2013; Rota 2017, 114–37).

This analysis investigates a period of conflicts over the implementation of a reform of Catholic Religious Education (*Insegnamento della Religione Cattolica*, IRC) in Italian State schools, from the second half of the 1980s to the early 1990s, from a perspective in historical political sociology. Closely associated to the framework of State-Church relations, this reform was usually depicted as a shift from a compulsory school subject defined by the Catholic magisterium to a non-compulsory one with modernized curricula. Top-down negotiations between Catholic Church diplomats and government-backed delegations of legal experts in the previous decade were not the only impetus for this reform. It also was related to actions by other religious institutions and social movements, mainly teachers' unions and secular activists, to redefine the scope of the subject in terms of "religious culture" (Caimi 2014). On February 18, 1984, when Socialist President of the Council Bettino Craxi and Secretary of State Cardinal Agostino Casaroli signed the Agreement of Villa Madama to reform the Concordat between the Italian State and the Holy See, including the matter of IRC, most questions of the implementation process were still to be arranged in additional, "technical agreements" with the Italian Bishops Conference (*Conferenza Episcopale Italiana*, CEI). Nonetheless, the modalities of implementation became conflictual (teaching hours, alternative subjects, teachers' status, presence in school buildings for students who did not enroll, etc.). The process also led to long sequences of actions and resort to administrative courts, bringing about the definition of State secularism as a supreme constitutional principle in 1989.

While the aftermath of the reform of Italian ecclesiastical law is evaluated as a conflictual process, which triggered contradictory changes in Catholicism and on public debates, the case of IRC has served to assess the social bases and the limits of its democratizing aspects (Ventura 2014b, 77–80). The empirical research on the implementation of the reform of IRC in the 1980s and early 1990s is used in this chapter. It was based on a socio-historical inquiry on archives from the Presidency of the Council, political parties (PCI, DC and Socialist Party—PSI), and teachers' unions (CGIL-Scuola and SISM-CISL), along with an analysis of digitized press archives on IRC (in particular *Il Corriere della Sera, La Repubblica, La Stampa* and *L'Unità*). Twenty-three semi-structured interviews were conducted with politicians, representatives, and militants who were involved in the process in that period. Most of the research work took place between late 2014 and early 2017 in Rome, for most political documents, and in Turin, with local and unions archives, in order to develop an analysis of a complex diachronic redefinition. The analysis of these sources requires a critical perspective, in order to avoid both the "flattening" of conflicts by the institutional rhetoric of consensus, and militant memorial preoccupations that are foreign to a sociological analysis. Against this background, the following questions are addressed by the present chapter. What were the social conditions for the politicization and attempts of redefinition of "religious freedom" in the implementation process of a reformed IRC, rather than in previous periods? What role did courts play in the process?

What consequences did these conflicts bring to the bureaucratic management of "religious freedom?"

The main argument is that this definition of "religious freedom," as a set of individual rights in social life, arrangements, and collective guarantees justified by a notion of social pluralism, is socially constructed in a conflictual process. This process includes phases of judicialization, in which the courts are central spaces of interaction between political competitors, religious organizations, social movements, and State agents, yet not isolated from other institutional spaces (Agrikoliansky 2003, 63–66). It is relevant to assess not only the expansion (Richardson 2015) but also the relative decrease of use of law on some peculiar matters related to "religious freedom." Indeed, the definition of "religious freedom" also results from uneven social relations and from tensions between administrative regulation and social movements. Concerning IRC between 1984 and 1992, the judicialization of conflicts in the implementation of its reform brought about paradoxical changes. The process, marked by significant changes in policy contents, meant a strategical retreat for partisans of a pedagogic modernization, for a few militant secular actors and for Catholic bishops. Yet, it also produced lasting structural constraints favoring a depoliticized, local bureaucratic-based management of IRC from the 1990s, with a symbolic redefinition of "minority" statuses in schools.

After a short development on the case study, this chapter follows an analytic division in three parts: first on "religious freedom" as a conflictual object framed by various institutions and actors, then on collective actions and constraints for legal actions on IRC, and finally, on their contradictory symbolic and administrative effects, before concluding remarks.

1   Religious Freedom in Context: the Case of Catholic Religious Education in Contemporary Italy

Since the Italian unification, the relationship between religious institutions and the educational sector has retained a strong political significance even though it was marked by administrative discontinuities related to the latter's establishment as a markedly elitist school system. The liberal elites that dominated the political field in the Italian constitutional monarchy were in conflict with Catholics—both religious hierarchy and political leaders—until the early twentieth century on many issues, including Religious Education. The subject was controlled and defined by the Roman Catholic Church, based on catechetical texts, to be taught by schoolmasters in primary schools and by chaplains in secondary schools. Although the 1877 Coppino Law did not abolish Religious Education, it erased it from the official list of subjects in primary State schools. The implementation devolved its management to town councils, giving way to informal arrangements with very diverse local situations in terms of attendance. In spite of some controversies against the subject among the Italian Socialist and center-left parties, this broad configuration remained largely unchanged until the fascist regime and the Gentile Law in 1923 (Butturini 1987, 16–63). This reform sought to re-establish Religious Education, although still defined according to the Catholic tradition and taught by schoolmasters, as a compulsory subject in all primary State schools. It was defined in law as a "foundation and coronation of Public Instruction," but theorized by Minister Giovanni Gentile as a "minor philosophy", which hardly coincided with a traditional view of catechism. After years of negotiations, the new Concordat, signed by Benito Mussolini and Cardinal Gasparri on January 11, 1929, was supposed to symbolize a reconciliation between the totalitarian State and Catholic hierarchy by officializing in Article 36 the extension of this compulsory character of Religious Education in secondary schools (Pertici 2009,102–52). The downfall of fascism did not impact this legal framework, mainly due to the prestige and influence of the Church and Catholic networks. After World War II, the Italian Communist Party (PCI) brought a strategic political support for the inclusion of the Concordat in Article 7 of the 1948 Constitution of the Italian Republic and most provisions and curricula remained unchanged. Moreover, they were consolidated by Christian-Democrats' (DC) management of education in a favorable way to Catholic interests (Onida 2014).

Two long-term processes contributed toward putting the attempts of reforms of Religious Education on the political agenda in the early 1970s. Along with the consequences of the renewed pastoral practices encouraged by Catholic hierarchy after the Second Vatican Council, increased numbers of lay Catholics were recruited by dioceses to replace priests and chaplains as Religious Education teachers in secondary schools. Some of them took part in local movements and initiatives that renewed debates on the contents of the subject, including proposals of deconfessionalization by experts and intellectuals (Pietro Scoppola, Luciano Pazzaglia, Marcello Vigli ...) to teach "history of religions" or "religious culture" (Butturini 1987, 187–92). Meanwhile, the open conflicts between DC representatives and secular movements, which led to symbolic defeats for the Church (referenda on divorce in 1974 and on abortion in 1981), fueled the legitimization of a general revision of the Concordat. The legal revision process was mostly consolidated behind closed doors with the bilateral Gonella-Casaroli commission, producing several successive versions of the treaty according to political and institutional constraints. The later form of Article 9.2, in the text signed on January 18, 1984, added the "Catholic" adjective to Religious Education, now IRC, and described it as a subject "chosen" by parents and pupils, rather than a compulsory one. New modalities and justifications from government officials and Church diplomats, especially on "the value of religious culture" and on the inclusion of "the principles of Catholicism [as part of] the historical heritage of the Italian people" (Article 9.2), and guarantees for "religious freedom" were put forward in the treaty and in political rhetoric (Silhol 2017). A few movements, such as the Radical Party, could contest these definitions and criticize latent contradictions in the legitimization of this revision. These changes and a new agreement with Waldensian and Methodist churches, signed three days later — justified by the government on the basis of an improved protection of religious freedom — left some issues untouched. Far from closing a period of political conflicts on religion in the public space, the implementation of the reform led to their reconfiguration for a few years (Pazzaglia 2014, 271–73).

In that regard, the judicialization of "religious freedom" rested not only on conflictual perceptions of IRC, but also on resources, strategic shifts from opponents and supporters, and incorporation of the reform in bureaucratic practices. The analysis is unfolded successively on three aspects, frames used on "religious freedom," conditions of collective actions including judicialization, and contradictory effects of this process between 1984 and 1992.

2 Framing "Religious Freedom" and Claiming the Definition of Changes in Religious Education

The implementation of norms from the revision of the Concordat on the redefined IRC rested upon volatile relations in the five-party (*Pentapartito*) majority with the legitimization of the support of the PCI in a "concordatarian majority" claimed by the Craxi government. The claim of the making of a policy of reform on "religious liberty," together with the adoption of the revision of the Concordat and the agreement with Waldensian and Methodist churches, was constrained by bargains and internal tensions in the main parties, DC and PSI (Ginsborg 2007, 280–86). Thus, the official justifications of improvement of "religious freedom" were superposed over concurrent interests and conflicting frames. In the coalition government, the legitimization of the Concordat, as an improvement for individual and collective rights, outlined especially the case of IRC. Speaking in Senate on January, 25 1984, President of the Council Craxi argued that IRC:

[S]hould not be marginalized in the school system, and could be enriched by a perspective of religious culture and of historical reference of Italian Catholicism, which would however not infringe on the freedom of conscience of the persons concerned.
SENATO 1984, 9

While PSI leaders had to deal with internal discontents from their left-wing about perceived ambiguities in the implementation of the Concordat, the rival DC led by Ciriaco De Mita, despite a broader electoral support, appeared vulnerable in its privileged relationship with Catholic institutions and electorate. Despite their justification of Catholic control over Religious Education argued by Senator Antonio Bisaglia, in his direct reply to President Craxi on January 25 (Senato 1984, 14), the uncertainties about their role in the implementation process concerned margins of action left to Christian-Democrat Minister of Public Instruction Franca Falcucci and to bishops. For example, in a letter by the Italian ambassador to the Holy See addressed to the Minister of Foreign Affairs Giulio Andreotti—then a powerful right-wing leader in DC close to Vatican officials — IRC was described as a "painful question" for bishops, with the fear of dwindling numbers of enrolled students (Chelli 1984, 7–8). While the CEI representatives, mainly Bishop Attilio Nicora, were designated to discuss the modalities of implementation, the pontifical rhetoric of "complementarity and distinction" between traditional catechesis and IRC, urging Catholic parents to enroll their children to both, was maintained. In that frame, the autonomous finalities of schools were not incompatible with the duty to provide Italian youth with a "skillful and appropriate Religious Education", according to Pope John Paul II in his official letter to the CEI in May 1984 (Giovanni Paolo II 1984). Conversely, positions in the PCI were divided between the official endorsement of an improvement of religious freedom represented by direction members, such as Senator Paolo Bufalini, responsible for relations with the Catholic Church, and more skeptical members, such as the director of the party's Education Office, Senator Aureliana Alberici. Thus, the tacit tensions and visions of the expected effects of the Villa Madama Agreement among left-wing parties appeared to some observers, such as Catholic PSI Senator Gennaro Acquaviva, as remnants of old-fashioned anticlericalism caused by the uncertainties of the implementation and the behavior of Minister Falcucci (Acattoli, Acquaviva, and De Rita 1987, 89–90). A few small left-wing parties, such as Marco Pannella's Radical Party and the Independent Left, were still openly anti-Concordat, and they had supported previous motions to abolish Religious Education in State schools (Rodelli 1980). Finally, some other religious institutions, less endowed in resources and membership than the Roman Catholic Church, could express a peculiar prudence about IRC — for example in the agreement (*Intesa*) between the Waldensian and Methodist churches and the Italian government of February 1984. Indeed, Article 9 of this agreement, while not contesting its existence in State schools, asked for "in order to guarantee everyone's freedom of conscience, the right not to benefit from the practices and of [IRC] on the basis of their declaration, or those of their parents or tutors." As for Article 10, it theorized the possibility of organizing proper alternative classes on "the history of the religious fact and its implications" (sic) on request of students who would not enroll in IRC. Yet, requests from their representatives to put the schedule of IRC in the first or the last hours of schooldays, on the grounds of guaranteeing non-discrimination of non-Catholic students, had to be erased from the draft and replaced by a mere statement of principle in the final version, due to demands from DC components of the majority (Bouchard 2015).

Subsequently, the implementation process brought about significant changes on how these frames on "religious freedom" were formulated, and on how they were used to legitimize or criticize the official arrangements on IRC. Negotiations behind closed doors between representatives of the Ministry of Public Instruction and Catholic officials on the IRC were delayed until the ratification of the Concordat in 1985, raising criticism from left-wing parliamentarians. The main components of the specialized agreement on IRC, signed by Minister Falcucci and Cardinal Ugo Poletti, president of the CEI, on December 13, 1985, such as the validity of students' enrollment for whole school cycles, the discretionary aspect of IRC scheduling left to school principals, or the required degrees to teach IRC, gained visibility mostly through their denunciations by opponents in the following weeks (Giani 1990, 52–55). This publicity over the agreement as a problem resulted in various collective actions in political parties, teachers' unions, and media, and its extension to the parliamentary arena through a series of realignments. These included a hostile position from the direction of PCI to the agreement and the minister's "behavior," and a collective petition from left-wing intellectuals asking for extracurricular schedules for IRC, published by Communist newspaper *L'Unità* in January (Anon 1986). The broad disagreement over the definition of "religious freedom" inside the government majority quickly became more visible. DC leader Ciriaco De Mita demanded that Minister Falcucci would be protected by governmental solidarity from a threat of vote of no confidence supported by left-wing deputies, discussed on January 14, 1986, a move reluctantly approved in the Council of Ministers the following day according to the minutes of the meeting (Presidenza del Consiglio dei Ministri 1986). While DC representatives argued in favor of the enactment of "an agreement for freedom," the request of specific alternative subjects for students who did not enroll and the subsequent debate on their freedom of choice in high schools, created additional tensions. For example, DC Deputy Costante Portatadino — a member of the Catholic conservative group Communion and Liberation — sent a letter to the president of the parliamentary group and to the minister one week after the heated debate. Opposed to conceding a form of "religious majority" in high schools, he stressed that granting thirteen-and-a-half-year-old students the faculty of choice undermined parental authority (Portatadino 1986). Thus, the apparent consensus on the value of "religious freedom" carried by the new concordatarian norms on IRC was replaced by another configuration, which outlined divisions within and outside the majority, through the connection between social movements involved in protests and legal actions, and party politics.

3 Collective Actions on "Religious Freedom": Judicialization and its Conditions

Various groups investing the implementation of IRC's reform took the opportunities of judicialization as long as this ground was legitimately and successfully better for them than bureaucratic arrangements. This stated, we can examine social conditions for such material, symbolic, and effective investments by directing our study on these groups themselves and their actions, considered as the "demand-side" (McCann 2009, 837–38), not only on jurisprudence.

In the case of contesting actions directed at circulars from the Ministry of Instruction on the implementation of the reform of IRC, these legal actions rested upon differentiated practical knowledges of legal activism, which were not evenly distributed and used among representatives of religious institutions. Indeed, the personnel of the Waldensian and Methodist churches had a long history of contesting administrative coercive provisions with lawyers and experts, including Giorgio Peyrot who had defended individual cases of evangelicals and Pentecostals since the first decades of the Italian Republic (Mannucci 1994, xxi–xxix). Previous actions supported by Protestant officials had denounced the payment of fiscal stamps by pupils' parents to ask for exemption from Religious Education, for example in September 1980, with the request to withdraw this "tax" from the general assembly of a local section of secular teachers' union (UIL-Scuola) and parents' organizations in Turin (UIL-Scuola 1980). Meanwhile, Jewish lawyers had represented the Union of Italian Jewish Communities in negotiating an agreement with the government, signed in 1987, and this organization took part in legal actions against IRC, along with the main Protestant churches. Smaller religious communities, such as Italian Lutherans, although critical of IRC, did not hold enough resources to take part in legal actions (Bachrach 2010, 25–50). Conversely, the established relationships between DC and Italian Catholic institutions, which were gradually evolving from 1986 with the proactive political line endorsed by the new Secretary of CEI Bishop Camillo Ruini (Santagata 2014, 440–43), did not favor direct initiatives from the Catholic Church in courts. Christian Democrats in government were supposed to legitimize and counter-attack such criticism while negotiations between ministry personnel and Church officials happened behind closed doors. Recourses emanated mainly from ministers rather than from the CEI until 1990. Indeed, the structural constraints of the gradual end of a State religion status for Catholicism and opportunities for pluralistic recognition in the religious field meant that beliefs and ideas could explain the meanings given to the defense of rights and to "religious freedom," but not the actual sequences of judicialization (Hoover and den Dulk 2004, 21–26).

Other aspects of the legal actions against ministerial circulars on IRC, such as their relations to other modes of actions and to the making of cause coalitions in the implementation process, must be taken into account. Among the early actions undertaken by secular parents' organizations, lawyer Paolo Barile, a well-known secular activist and civil law professor in Florence, presented a case in December 1984, supported by the Waldensian and Methodist churches. The preliminary question of constitutionality of the very presence of Religious Education in schools was ineffective, however, and it was rejected by judges of the Constitutional Court (Tosatti 1985). Thus, changes in goals, framing and coordination of actions in legal arenas on IRC were brought about by strategic constraints, among which the support of significant parts of left-wing parties for actions against the implementation, rather than against the Concordat itself. On July 10, 1986, the National Committee School and Constitution (CNSC) was formed by claiming the opposition to circulars, especially on the obligation for unenrolled students to stay in schools during IRC hours and on the claim of an unambiguously facultative character of IRC. The CNSC was based on local committees mainly active in cities such as Rome, Bologna, Turin, and Milan, with support from left-wing teachers' unions (especially CGIL-Scuola and UIL-Scuola) and preexisting secular movements, such as the Association for Religious Freedom in Italy based in Milan, according to its manifesto against IRC published in the professional journal *Scuola e Città* in October 1986 (Comitato Nazionale Scuola e Costituzione 1986). The coalition operated as a legal information platform and militants' network, presenting a series of cases to regional administrative courts against the circulars, petitions to schedule IRC classes in extracurricular hours, and calls directed toward parents not to "choose" IRC for their children. While the implementation of reform produced additional tensions in the Catholic Church, the actions of CNSC did not end up in a united front against the Concordat. They did not prove consensual in all school contexts, due to other issues and disagreements. Indeed, some IRC teachers, who were often represented by teachers' union SISM-CISL and by autonomous unions, were active in organizing conferences to ask for a more secure regulation of their posts, which had been adapted from former part-time positions for clergy and through which dioceses controlled their working hours and careers. These groups of IRC teachers contested the arrangements sought by the Catholic hierarchy for their professional norms deemed too precarious, being uneasy with concordatarian and derived norms, and they gained the support of some left-leaning DC representatives and of SISM-CISL National Secretariat (Dolcetti 1991). Yet, they also had to face local opposition from other unions, some militant teachers, and potential colleagues.

In that regard, judicialization of "religious freedom" was inseparable from the use of specialized legal resources and from the ability of local teachers' collectives and religious institutions to argue about a general value for their claims against the modalities of policy implementation. It helped dramatize and politicize the issues of situations defined as discriminatory, based on frames critical of an "opaque" negotiation process and its effects. However, the specificities of the judicialization process also incurred bureaucratic arrangements and setbacks for opponents to the new regime of IRC, as well as issues about the sustainability of involvement in these recourses to the law.

4 Contradictory Effects, between Judicialization and Bureaucratization of Secular Motives

First of all, the visible judicialization of "religious freedom" in the case of IRC brought structural and symbolic effects on the policy contents, both at a local level and in national arenas. In local educational contexts, according to local strengths of teachers' unions, Catholic associations and State bureaucracies, the modalities of inserting IRC and "alternative subjects" could give way to some reactions from the early phase. For instance, in Turin, during the first school year with the new IRC, 1986–1987, local secular activists as well as collectives of teachers printed leaflets against the effects of the revised Concordat in schools. At least fifteen letters of protest against the vagueness of dispositions on IRC, on the contents of "alternative subjects" and their teaching staff, were sent by assemblies of secondary schoolteachers (*collegi dei docenti*) of Turin in fall 1986 to the provincial school administration and to teachers' unions. One such letter written by the council of teachers of the Matteotti middle school in Turin in September 1986, representative of such claims, indicted the ministry's circulars as a blow to secular principles of the State:

> The articles of [the ministerial circular] are a confirmation of the low esteem in which teaching staff's professionalism is held, to whom [the minister] considers adding aggravated responsibilities and broadened competences, without any prior consultation of adequate information. In addition to this, the implementation of articles proves to be discriminatory for youth who choose not to benefit from [IRC], in that the State considers as constitutional the presence in the school of a teacher chosen by the diocesan authority for Religious Education, and not the one of a teacher put in charge of alternative activities.
> COLLEGIO DEI DOCENTI SM MATTEOTTI DI TORINO 1986

Later actions led by secular activists and parents' associations related to the CNSC included legal support for students who resented being forced to attend "alternative subjects," or even the rejection of "pervasive" influence of Catholicism in textbooks, with a successful legal action taken by parents of kindergarten children in 1990 in Turin supported by the Turinese Committee for Secularism in Schools (Comitato Torinese per la Laicità della Scuola 2003, 34–37).

At the national level, some collective actions could reach higher effects and levels, leading to counter-actions from the coalition governments and new questions of constitutionality that formed jurisprudential references for later doctrines of State secularism. The following table was elaborated by listing the main decisions by the Constitutional Court on IRC between 1984 and 1992, inventoried in a report by the research office of the Italian Senate (Borsi 1999), and other significant decisions from lower courts described in a well-documented journalistic account (Giani 1990) and in contemporary press archives (mainly from Rome-based daily newspaper *La Repubblica*). It sums up the most important sentences in the process of judicialization of IRC from 1984 to 1992.

Before June 1987, the controversies over the implementation of IRC were politically dealt with by informal renewed negotiations between agents of the cabinet of the Ministry of Public Instruction, DC deputies, and CEI representatives. These talks included requests from the Secretary of the CEI, Bishop Ruini, toward the DC, to draft other norms on the contents and teaching staff of "alternative subjects," for which he proposed a curriculum on human rights (Martini 1987b). However, the results of the June 1987 general elections

TABLE 10.1 Main judicial sentences concerning IRC between 1984 and 1992

Jurisdiction and date	Complainants, subjects and institutions	Decision
Constitutional Court, December 11, 1984	*Coordinamento Genitori Democratici*, lawyer Paolo Barile	The Court judges ruled they were not able to assess the constitutionality of IRC.
Regional Administrative Court of Latium, June 26, 1987	CNSC, Waldensian and Methodist Churches	The Court halted the execution of Ministerial Circular 302-1986, which forced schools to provide lessons to students who did not enroll in IRC.
Regional Administrative Court of Latium, February 10, 1988	CGIL-Scuola	The Court stated that "alternative activities" were not compulsory for students who did not enroll in IRC.
Constitutional Court, April 11, 1989	Lawyers Paolo Barile, Andrea Proto Pisani, Elia Clarizia and Corrado Mauceri—related to CNSC	The Court confirmed the non-compulsory character of both IRC and "alternative activities".
Regional Administrative Court of Latium, February 2, 1990	Waldensian and Methodist, Evangelical Federation, Adventist and Pentecostal churches, the Union of Italian Jewish Communities, and pupils' parents from Cagliari	The Court canceled circulars and administrative provisions ordering students to stay in class even though they were not enrolled neither in IRC nor "alternative activities".
Council of State, May 5, 1990	Ministry of Public Instruction, CEI	The Council of State canceled the former decision of the Regional Administrative Court.
Constitutional Court, January 14, 1991	CNSC	The Court authorized students who enrolled in neither IRC nor "alternative activities" to leave secondary school premises during IRC hours.
Constitutional Court, June 22, 1992	Praetor (judge) of Trani, Puglia, and pupils' parents	Kindergarten directors were competent for the schedules of IRC hours.

reinvigorated right-wing currents of DC against its leadership, and showed gains for PSI at the expense of PCI (Ginsborg 2007, 293–309). In addition to these political constraints, the discussions between the Ministry and Catholic institutions were impacted by the first phase of judicialization, bringing about a more formal approach. On June 26, 1987, the Administrative Regional Court of Latium stated that the compulsory character of "alternative subjects" for students who did not enroll in IRC, as prescribed by Ministerial Circular 302–1986, was irregular. After a reversal of this decision by a sentence of the Council of State in August 1987, the new coalition government presided over by DC Deputy Giovanni Goria, still reliant on support from the PSI and three smaller allied parties, had to face an uncertain solution. In order to help the new DC Minister of Instruction Giovanni Galloni, who was being criticized by left-wing parties, members of the DC central offices, in particular the Deputy for Lucca and representative of DC for Catholic associations, Maria Eletta Martini, attempted to draft a consensual motion to obtain a minimal adjustment without a revision of the 1985 "technical" agreement (Martini 1987a). Yet, under the threat of hostile votes from the left, a diplomatic letter from the Vatican protested against the perspective of unilateral changes on the norms of IRC, giving way to renewed criticism of "clerical interference" (Tosatti 1987). After two days of intense debates in the Chamber of Deputies on October 9, and 10, 1987, a motion was approved by the majority, which forced the Goria cabinet to re-negotiate implementation modalities of IRC (Giani 1990, 64–67). The next three years saw both a return to talks behind closed doors with an emphasis on "technical" rather than "political" issues from DC officials, and increased difficulties to legitimize the enactment of the revision of the Concordat in schools. Following administrative-judicial decisions, particularly from the Council of State in 1988 and 1990 and from the Constitutional Court in 1989 and 1991, openly hostile stances appeared in parties that had previously supported the 1984 agreement. The new direction of PCI, that led to its gradual transformation into a social-democratic party between 1989 and 1991, adopted positions more akin to the criticism of the Concordat as outdated for secular modern, pluralistic Italy. Meanwhile, the "stop-and-go" logic of legal actions from the CNSC and counter-actions from Italian governments reached the constitutional level. The 203/1989 decision of the Constitutional Court (*Corte Costituzionale*), in April 1989, promoted a new definition of State secularism as a supreme principle of the constitutional order, and stated students' right to enroll neither in IRC nor alternative activities.

> One recalls, in matter of [IRC], the respect of freedom of conscience and parents' educational responsibility, which find a guarantee in the

Constitution of the Republic respectively in articles 19 and 30. Yet before the positive teaching of a religion made "in conformity with Church doctrine," according to provision of point 5, letter a, of additional protocol, the secular State has the duty to ensure that the liberties of article 19[...] and parents' educational responsibility do not end up undermined. Here comes the instrumental logic inherent to the State-community which welcomes and ensures citizens' self-determination, through the recognition of a subjective right to benefit or not from [IRC]. This right belongs to parents and, for high schools, directly to students, on the basis of article 1.1 of Law n°281 of June 18, 1986. Such a figure of subjective right has no precedent.
    CORTE COSTITUZIONALE 1989

These conclusions reinforced constraints for Catholic officials to use motives more acceptable for political counterparts, and to adapt their overall strategy to this jurisprudence. One particular way through which the CEI sought to use the rhetoric on students' needs of a "religious culture" in their formation became the regular use of official communications to students and parents before the deadline of choices every year. From a peripheral topic of bishops' communication, IRC became a central theme, reorganized with an explicit coordination of dioceses by the CEI and its National Office of Catechesis (Marzano and Urbinati 2013, 53–56). In the legal-administrative arena, the Catholic Church hierarchy finally sought to contain the effects of constitutional jurisprudence with its own statement of case presented by two lawyers before the Council of State in May 1990 (La Rocca 1990). The temporarily successful outcome of this action and the revision of the agreement on IRC on June 13, 1990, signed by Cardinal Poletti and Minister of Public Instruction Sergio Mattarella, stabilized some arrangements, among which provisions to avoid a pervasive Religious Education, strict limits on IRC teachers' votes in pedagogic commissions, and other "technical" aspects (Pazzaglia 2015, 70–78). However, the following year, decision n°13–1991 of the Constitutional Court outlined the non-compulsory character of both IRC and "alternative subjects" with students' right not to stay in school buildings in that schedule, confirming an ordinance from a judge in Arezzo, Tuscany. This was interpreted as a "defeat" in Catholic institutions, followed by the resignation of Cardinal Poletti from the Presidency of the CEI, as Pope John Paul II appointed former Secretary Cardinal Camillo Ruini in this position and as head of the Vicariate in Rome on March 7, 1991 (Galavotti 2011).

Hence, the publicizing of the issues of IRC was a critical factor in the redefinition of "religious freedom." When IRC was brought to the legal arenas by its opponents, activists, lawyers, teachers, and parents, dramatization helped its

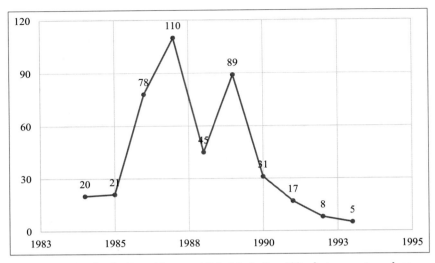

FIGURE 10.1 Articles dealing with IRC published in *La Repubblica* between 1984 and 1993

redefinition as a problem of school management, rather than on pedagogic grounds as expected previously. Figure 10.1 below gives a view on the coverage of the issue by a national left-wing daily newspaper based in Rome, *La Repubblica*, between 1984 and 1993, through 424 articles directly about IRC.[1]

Several peaks appear in the reporting of the judicialization of IRC, for example with 32 articles in the sole month of January 1986 with the first controversy on the agreement on IRC in Parliament, in Summer 1987, and between March and May 1989 after the first significant sentence from the Constitutional Court, before a steady decrease after 1990. While most articles on IRC were written by the "Vaticanist" reporters of *La Repubblica*, Domenico Del Rio and Orazio La Rocca, those published in "heated" phases of controversy were more likely to be categorized as education or political news.

The implications of this publicity have been ambiguous concerning the redefinition of "religious freedom" in Italian public spaces. Along with situations of pupils left alone in corridors covered by opponents, or classes of students made uneasy by a "default" IRC choice, reported in some secular and left-wing groups (Fotia and Mariconda 1987), the series of collective actions,

---

1 This graph was elaborated from the results of a research in the digitalized archives of *La Repubblica* with the keywords *"religione"* (religion) and *"scuola"* (school), based on articles published between January 1, 1984 and December 31, 1993. Readers' mails and unrelated contents were taken out of the 788 results, to establish a basis of 424 articles dealing with IRC. See *La Repubblica.it—Archivio*, accessed on 03/06/2019 on https://ricerca.repubblica.it/.

petitions and legal attempts contributed to the reshaping of political rhetoric on religion in Italian schools with normative and secular motives (de Galembert and Koenig 2014, 643). Paradoxically, Catholic representatives had to justify the presence of IRC in schools as a subject of "religious culture" open to all pupils independently from their beliefs, while opponents would argue against it on the basis of its confessional character in law. The sensibilization of the schools public and agents to these issues found nonetheless some limits with the gradual reduction of opportunities to contest features of the policy process. The last decision from the Constitutional Court to define IRC schedules as an autonomous competence of school directions in 1992 confirmed this shift from judicialization to an institutionalization of ordinary conflicts in schools' bureaucratic management (Mayrl 2011). The process also favored the rise of the CEI as a representation of interests for Italian Catholicism at the expense of DC representatives that were its traditional stakeholders, as the party was dissolved in 1994 after two years of anti-corruption inquiries and political upheavals (Scoppola 2006, 147–89). The CEI's routinized communication patterns on IRC legitimized its ownership over the problem of "religious culture," as a pedagogic matter less controversial than students' rights of opting-out. As the expected general dwindling of "choice" of IRC did not occur in official data, this rhetoric gradually stressed high rates of attendance of IRC over 90 percent until the 2010s, akin to the theme of a "national majority." The CEI's almost uncontested monopoly on national statistics of IRC contributed to the legitimization and continuation of this position. Moreover, the alliance of Cardinal Ruini's CEI with Silvio Berlusconi's center-right coalitions until the late 2000s followed through political exchanges, including the July 18, 2003 Law on IRC teachers' permanent posts. These recruitment norms ensured guarantees for diocesan control without completely homogenizing their status to the one of teachers of other subjects (Marzano and Urbinati 2013, 17–23). In brief, the social conditions of politicization of IRC became less favorable to its opponents and more to its promoters, using "religious freedom" as a general, consensual motive rather than a strategic claim.

5   Concluding Remarks

From 1984 to 1992, the enactment of the revision of the Concordat had to cope with contradictory conflicts and new patterns of regulation during a period of unstable power relations in politics. The first analytical part showed that "religious freedom" was politicized and redefined through a conflict of frames, referring to the ambiguous implementation of the reform of IRC after 1984.

While members of the "concordatarian majority" emphasized its value for "religious freedom," its new modalities proved to be controversial and received an unexpected publicity. In the second part, based on archival documents from parties, unions and newspapers, I argued that this process was continuously influenced by collective actions and various coalition causes between some political actors, teachers' unions, lawyers, and minority religious groups. Consequently, the judicialization of "religious freedom" was related to opposing social actors' interests and diverse resources and beliefs, who played a major part in the framing of "religious freedom," up to a jurisprudential definition of State secularism as a supreme constitutional principle that protects this freedom in schools. When these political and administrative configurations changed, along with established interinstitutional relationships exemplified by the demise of the DC and the rise of the CEI, the logic of local arrangements ultimately prevailed over the recourses to the law and to the courts. The request for "choice" of IRC, or Catholic hierarchy's voicing of "social demand" (Ventura 2014a, 71–73), did not entail a full democratization of IRC, but rather the institutionalization of an updated discretionary management that rarely favors alternative options (Bossi 2017). The management of "religious freedom" in Italy was produced through this peculiar conflict, even though its legal rationalization expanded later independently from this context. Since the mid-1990s, the social pluralization of the Italian religious field has been mostly disconnected from the production of new legal agreements of recognition (*intese*) between the State and religious institutions, stopped between 1994 and 2012. As for IRC, although a few legal actions and local controversies (often on account of some behavior deemed inappropriate from individual teachers or diocesan staff) have occurred since then, none has reached the degree of publicity of the previous period, or gained as much visibility as the controversies over the crucifix in classrooms or campaigns against construction of mosques led by right-wing movements (Ozzano and Giorgi 2016). In that regard, the case of IRC shows the relevance of the political context, as well as strategies of disruption and conservation of dominant positions in specific sectors, in studying the social fabric of "religious freedom."[2]

---

[2] This chapter is based on a part of my thesis presented on December 20, 2019 in Aix-en-Provence. My research benefited from a three-year funding by the French Ministry of Research and Higher Education (2013–2016), two research grants from the *Ecole française de Rome* (May 2015, March 2016) and the visiting researcher program of the *Culture, Politica e Società* Department of the University of Turin in Spring 2017. I thank Lorenzo Barrault-Stella, Olga Breskaya, Claire Dupuy, Alberta Giorgi, Alex Mahoudeau, Paul Michel, Luca Ozzano, Stefania Palmisano, Roberto Scalon, Sarah Tonsy, and the reviewers for their comments.

References

Acattoli, Luigi, Gennaro Acquaviva, and Giuseppe De Rita. 1987. *La Chiesa Galassia e l'Ultimo Concordato*. Milan: Rusconi.

Agrikoliansky, Éric. 2003. "Usages choisis du droit : le service juridique de la Ligue des droits de l'homme (1970–1990). Entre politique et raison humanitaire." *Sociétés contemporaines* 52, no. 4 (Winter): 61–84.

Anon. 1986. "Appello di Intellettuali contro l'Intesa." *L'Unità*, January 12, 1986. https://archivio.unita.news/assets/derived/1986/01/12/issue_full.pdf.

Bachrach, Riccardo. 2010. *L'intesa della Chiesa Evangelica Luterana in Italia. Un Evento Più Subito che Desiderato*. Turin: Claudiana.

Bossi, Luca. 2017. "L'Ora Invisibile. Le Alternative all'Insegnamento della Religione Cattolica in Italia." *Scuola Democratica* 8, no. 3 (Fall): 531–49.

Borsi, Luca. 1999. *L'insegnamento di religione cattolica nella giurisprudenza costituzionale*, Rome: Servizio Studi del Senato della Repubblica.

Bouchard, Giorgio. 2015. "Trent'anni Dopo. L'Avvincente Vicenda dell'Intesa tra le Chiese Rappresentate dalla Tavola Valdese e la Repubblica Italiana." *Quaderni del Circolo Rosselli* 35, no. 2 (Summer): 25–47.

Breskaya, Olga, and Giuseppe Giordan. 2019. "Measuring the Social Perception of Religious Freedom: A Sociological Perspective." *Religions* 10, no. 4 (April): 274.

Butturini, Emilio. 1987. *La Religione a Scuola. Dall'Unità Ad Oggi*. Brescia: Queriniana.

Caimi, Luciano. 2014. "L'insegnamento della Religione nel Quadro della Pastorale della Chiesa. Dalla Fine della Guerra alla Revisione del Concordato (1945–1984)." In *La Religione Istruita. Nella Scuola e nella Cultura dell'Italia Contemporanea*, edited by Luciano Caimi and Giovanni Vian, 215–49. Brescia: Morcelliana.

Chelli, Claudio. 1984. "Lettera Riservata dell'Ambasciatore Italiano presso la Santa Sede Claudio Chelli a Giulio Andreotti N°2025." Rome: Archivio Storico dell'Istituto Luigi Sturzo, f. Andreotti, Sottoserie 10–4, B. 163, fasc. 10.

Collegio dei docenti SM Matteotti di Torino. 1986. "Mozione del Collegio dei Docenti della Scuola Media Matteotti di Torino, 30 Settembre 1986." Turin: Fondazione Vera Nocentini, f. Federscuola CISL Torino, B. 10, f. 28, c. B.

Comitato Nazionale Scuola e Costituzione. 1986. "L'insegnamento della Religione. Materiali del Comitato Nazionale 'Scuola e Costituzione.'" *Scuola e Città* 37, no. 10 (October): 453–57.

Comitato Torinese per la Laicità della Scuola. 2003. *Laicità. Domande e Risposte in 38 Interviste*. Turin: Claudiana.

Corte Costituzionale. 1989. "Sentenza N°203–1989. Giudizio di Legittimità Costituzionale in via Incidentale". *Gazzetta Ufficiale*, April 19, 1989. Accessed April 3, 2013. https://www.cortecostituzionale.it/actionSchedaPronuncia.do?anno=1989&numero=203.

Dolcetti, Paolo. 1991. "Insegnanti di Religione. Dal Concordato al Contratto—Scuola Nuova, N°14–15, Aprile 1985." In *Chi vedrà vivrà. Scelta di scritti e disegni di Renzo Dolcetti*, edited by SISM-CISL, 49–52. Turin: SISM-CISL.

Ferrari, Alessandro. 2012. *La Libertà Religiosa in Italia. Un Percorso Incompiuto*. Rome: Carocci.

Fotia, Carmine, and Emma Mariconda. 1987. *L'Ora Illegale*. Rome: Il Manifesto—Sinistra Indipendente.

Galavotti, Enrico. 2011. "Il Ruinismo. Visione e Prassi Politica del Presidente della Conferenza Episcopale Italiana, 1991–2007." In *Cristiani d'Italia*, edited by Alberto Melloni, 1219–38. Rome: Treccani.

de Galembert, Claire, and Matthias Koenig. 2014. "Gouverner le religieux avec les juges. Introduction." *Revue française de science politique* 64, no. 4 (August): 631–45.

Giani, Anna Gloria. 1990. "L'intesa e la Contesa. Il Dibattito sull'Insegnamento della Religione dopo il Nuovo Concordato." In *L'insegnamento della religione nella scuola italiana*, edited by Enzo Catarsi, 49–67. Milan: Franco Angeli.

Ginsborg, Paul. 2007. *L'Italia del Tempo Presente. Famiglia, Società Civile, Stato. 1980–1996*. Turin: Einaudi.

Giovanni Paolo II. 1984. "Lettera alla CEI." *L'Osservatore Romano*, May 9, 1984.

Gusfield, Joseph R. 1981. *The Culture of Public Problems, Drinking Driving and the Symbolic Order*. Chicago: University of Chicago Press.

Hoover, Dennis R., and Kevin R. den Dulk. 2004. "Christian Conservatives Go to Court: Religion and Legal Mobilization in the United States and Canada." *International Political Science Review* 25, no. 1 (January): 9–34.

La Rocca, Orazio. 1990. "Dovrà Restare a Casa Chi Non Vuole Seguire l'insegnamento Religioso." *La Repubblica*, May 20, 1990.

Mannucci, Andrea. 1994. *I Protestanti e la Religione a Scuola. Analisi della Stampa Protestante dalla Revisione del Concordato ad Oggi*. Florence: Centro Editoriale Toscano.

Martini, Maria Eletta. 1987a. "Lettera di Maria Eletta Martini a Ciriaco De Mita del 3 Settembre 1987." Rome: Archivio Storico dell'Istituto Luigi Sturzo, f. Martini, B. 119, U.A. 3 prov.

Martini, Maria Eletta. 1987b. "Nota di Servizio di Maria Eletta Martini a Ciriaco De Mita del 27 Febbraio 1987. CEI Mons. Ruini." Rome: Archivio Storico dell'Istituto Luigi Sturzo, f. Martini, B. 119, U.A. 3 prov.

Marzano, Marco, and Nadia Urbinati. 2013. *Missione Impossibile. La Riconquista Cattolica Della Sfera Pubblica*. Bologna: Il Mulino.

Mayrl, Damon. 2011. "Administering Secularization: Religious Education in New South Wales since 1960." *European Journal of Sociology / Archives européennes de sociologie* 52, no. 1 (April): 111–42.

Mayrl, Damon. 2018. "The Judicialization of Religious Freedom: An Institutionalist Approach." *Journal for the Scientific Study of Religion* 57, no. 3 (September): 514–30.

McCann, Michael W. 2009. "Interests, Ideas, and Institutions in Comparative Analysis of Judicial Power." *Political Research Quarterly* 62, no. 4 (December): 834–39.

Onida, Valerio. 2014. "L'insegnamento della Religione Cattolica negli Atti dell'Assemblea Costituente. Una Cronaca Parlamentare." In *Rapporto sull'Analfabetismo Religioso in Italia*, edited by Alberto Melloni, 155–63. Bologna: Il Mulino.

Ozzano, Luca, and Alberta Giorgi. 2016. *European Culture Wars and the Italian Case. Which Side Are You On?* New York: Routledge.

Pazzaglia, Luciano. 2014. "I Tentativi di Riforma dell'Ora di Religione in Italia." In Rapporto sull'Analfabetismo Religioso in Italia, edited by Alberto Melloni, 259–81. Bologna: Il Mulino.

Pazzaglia, Luciano, 2015. "Scuola, Giovani e Società nell'Impegno Politico di Sergio Mattarella." In *Crescere Insieme. Scritti di Sergio Mattarella*, edited by Luciano Pazzaglia, 23–112. Brescia: La Scuola.

Pertici, Roberto. 2009. *Chiesa e Stato in Italia. Dalla Grande Guerra al Nuovo Concordato (1914–1984)*. Bologna: Il Mulino.

Portatadino, Costante. 1986. "Lettera di Costante Portatadino a Virginio Rognoni e Franca Falcucci del 22/01/1986." Rome: Archivio Storico dell'Istituto Luigi Sturzo, f. Martini, B. 54, u.a. prov. 20.

Presidenza del Consiglio dei Ministri. 1986. "Verbale della Riunione del Consiglio dei Ministri del 15 Gennaio 1986." Rome: Archivio Centrale dello Stato EUR, f. PCM Consiglio dei Ministri, 3/1/1986-15/4/1987 Craxi 3, B. 77.

Reeh, Niels. 2013. "Danish State Policy on the Teaching of Religion from 1900 to 2007." *Social Compass* 60, no. 2 (June): 236–50.

Richardson, James T. 2015. "Managing religion and the judicialization of religious freedom." *Journal for the Scientific Study of Religion* 54, no. 1 (March): 1–19.

Rodelli, Luigi. 1980. *Proposta di Riforma della Legislazione Scolastica in Materia di Religione in Base ai Principi della Costituzione della Repubblica*. Milan: Associazione per la Libertà Religiosa in Italia.

Rota, Andrea. 2017. *La Religion à l'École. Négociations autour de la Présence Publique des Communautés Religieuses*. Geneva: Seismo.

Santagata, Alessandro. 2014. "Ruinismo: The Catholic Church in Italy from 'Mediation Culture' to the Cultural Project." *Journal of Modern Italian Studies* 19, no. 4 (August): 438–52.

Sarat, Austin, and Stuart Scheingold. 2006. "What Cause Lawyers Do For, and To, Social Movements: An Introduction." In *Cause Lawyers and Social Movements*, edited by Austin Sarat and Stuart Scheingold, 1–34. Stanford: Stanford University Press.

Scoppola, Pietro. 2006. *La Democrazia dei Cristiani. Il Cattolicesimo Politico nell'Italia Unita*. Rome: Laterza.

Senato. 1984. "53° Seduta Pubblica. Resoconto Stenografico. Mercoledì 25 Gennaio 1984, Seduta Antimeridiana". *Atti Parlamentari. IXa Legislatura*, January 25, 1984. Accessed May 25, 2016. http://www.senato.it/service/PDF/PDFServer/BGT/317543.pdf.

Silhol, Guillaume. 2017. "Governing Catholic Religious Education in Italian State Schools: Between the Revision of the Concordat and Social Movements, 1974–1984." *Studia Z Prawa Wyznaniowego—Studies in Law on Religion* 20 (December): 167–84.

Tosatti, Marco. 1985. "La Religione a Scuola Incostituzionale o No?" *La Stampa*, December 24, 1985.

Tosatti, Marco. 1987. "Ora di Religione, anche il Papa contro la Protesta di Galloni." *La Stampa*, October 6, 1987.

UIL-Scuola. 1980. "Opponiamoci alla Religione Obbligatoria e all'Esonero Tassato. Foglio dell'Assemblea Pubblica della UIL-Scuola Torinese, 22 Settembre 1980." Turin: Fondazione dell'Istituto Gramsci, f. SNS-CGIL Segreteria Regionale, B. 92, fasc. 263.

Ventura, Marco. 2014a. *Creduli e Credenti. Il Declino di Stato e Chiesa come Questione di Fede*. Turin: Einaudi.

Ventura, Marco. 2014b. "L'eredità di Villa Madama: un Decalogo." *Quaderni di diritto e politica ecclesiastica* 17, no. 1 (April): 67–90.

CHAPTER 11

The Measure of CEDAW: Religion, Religious Freedom, and the Rights of Women

Barbara R. Walters

Studies of the United Nations Convention on the Elimination of All Forms of Discrimination Against Women (CEDAW 1979)[1] have thus far failed to include analyses of religious freedom as a social mechanism that conditions nation-state CEDAW support. An abundance of empirical research studies on dominant religion consistently reports lower levels of commitment to CEDAW and in gender parity among predominantly Muslim nations (Cole 2013; Fish 2011; Inglehart and Miller 2014; Inglehart and Norris 2002; Norris and Inglehart 2003; Tausch and Heshmati 2016; Walters 2014; Walters and Perez 2017; Wotipka and Ramirez 2008). However, the lacuna for studies that examine religious freedom as a qualifying or interacting factor persists. Moreover, few studies include level of commitment to CEDAW using the CEDAW Optional Protocol (CEDAW OP 1999) or other indicators for level of commitment rather than binary responses for countries as either CEDAW State Parties or non-State Parties.

This chapter's purpose is threefold. First, the chapter establishes the CEDAW Optional Protocol as a mechanism and one of two metrics of full commitment to the object and purpose of the convention. Second, CEDAW OP State Party status is then used as a metric to compare: (1) nation-states with different dominant religions, (2) predominantly Muslim nations with different levels of religious freedom. And third, predominantly Muslim nation-states with different levels of religious freedom are compared using critical indicators of the rights of women, such as the legal status of child marriage.

The United Nations Convention on the Elimination of All Forms of Discrimination Against Women (CEDAW, 1979) and its Optional Protocol (OP, 1999) represent perhaps the most important legal documents guaranteeing full economic, social, and political participation for women in the history of international law — on par with the Civil Rights Act in U.S. Constitutional law. CEDAW frames and legitimates international discourse on the rights of women; it provides a topical polis. A critical difference between CEDAW and the U.S. Constitution rests in the gap between rights embodied in CEDAW and

---

[1] Entered into force in 1981.

the legitimate authority of the CEDAW Committee to enforce these rights at the local level. The CEDAW OP partially bridges the gap. The OP amplifies the authority of the Committee by formalizing grievance communication structures and procedures for adjudicating cases (Cole 2005; 2012), which increases the frequency of communications on specific articles. The analysis therefore focuses on CEDAW and its Optional Protocol (CEDAW OP) during the first ten years after the CEDAW OP adoption by the United Nations General Assembly, that is, from 2000 to 2010, as one of two measures of commitment to CEDAW.

Key empirical questions in the chapter analyze CEDAW as a living document, which influences women's rights within and across diverse nation-state contexts through peaceful discourse. Three key factors emerge from the analysis as essential for understanding the sway of religion and religious freedom on the Convention's influence, given its limited enforcement provisions:

1. The secular international organizational field of the United Nations human rights "World Society" provides an exogenous source of support for the agency of women and women's organizations among both CEDAW State Parties and non-State Parties. Social interactions focused on the CEDAW articles through written and face-to-face oral communications among State Party representatives and the CEDAW Committee provide the potent social mechanism for changes in women's rights at the nation-state level. The CEDAW OP sharpens the focus and heightens the frequency of these communications for State Parties. Being an OP State Party also demonstrates a higher level of commitment to CEDAW. A second measure of commitment is ratification without reservations.

2. Endogenous nation-state cultural and religious factors may align with and fortify or contradict and challenge the object and purpose of CEDAW. These endogenous factors function to orient nation-states' official positions within the secular UN organizational field. Endogenous factors include existing gender inequality as measured by the Gender Inequality Index, but also religious traditions that fortify traditional gender roles. Past research consistently corroborates low levels of CEDAW support and high levels of gender inequality among predominantly Muslim nations.

3. Especially significant, religious freedom — the extent to which religious and political institutions are differentiated or fused (Philpott 2007, 505) — shapes the contours of religious and secular prescriptions and proscriptions regarding appropriate roles for women,

THE MEASURE OF CEDAW 243

discrimination against women, as well as support for CEDAW. Thus, here the analysis fruitfully telescopes Muslim nations with different religious freedom levels, especially those that have lagged compared to other nations in their full commitment to CEDAW.

The first data set examines differences between highly committed CEDAW State Parties and those with lower levels of investment on basic measures of endogenous gender inequality as measured by the Gender Inequality Index (GII). The data set also permits analysis of changes over time.

Hypotheses I
   H Ia: UN Member States with higher value-rational alignment, meaning endogenous cultural and structural support for gender equality as reflected in low Gender Inequality Index scores, have lower costs associated with ratifying CEDAW and especially the CEDAW OP, which connotes higher commitment. CEDAW OP State Parties have lower levels of gender inequality as measured by the GII.
   H Ib: Gender inequality as measured by the GII changes over time in an inverse relationship to the increasing number of parties by year for CEDAW OP State Parties.

The second data set examines the influence of nation-states' predominant religion on the degree of commitment to CEDAW and on endogenous gender inequality, or GII score. The operational definition refers specifically to Muslim, Catholic, or Protestant majority countries. In this instance, it does not permit distinctions between adherents and regimes, a topic taken up in the data set on religious freedom.

Hypotheses II
   H IIa: Fewer UN Member States that entered reservations on Article 2 and Article 16 upon becoming CEDAW State Parties are State Parties to the CEDAW OP.
   H IIb: Muslim majority countries more frequently enter reservations, often citing Sharia Law.
   H IIc: Muslim majority countries are less likely to be CEDAW OP State Parties.
   H IId: Muslim majority countries have cultural and structural values often at odds with CEDAW, that is, higher levels of gender inequality as measured by the GII.

The third data set examines the effects of religious freedom. The data provide evidence on differences in commitment to CEDAW and on the legal status of child marriage for forty-five predominantly Muslim countries based on (1) religious repression, (2) secular repression, and (3) religious freedom.

> *Hypotheses III*
> *H IIIa:* Secularly repressive Muslim countries are most likely to become CEDAW OP parties.
> *H IIIb*: Religiously repressive Muslim countries are least likely to become CEDAW OP parties.
> *H IIIc:* Religiously repressive Muslim countries are least likely to legislate against child marriage and polygamy.
>
> CEDAW, *the* CEDAW OP, *and the United Nations Organizational Field*

The United Nations General Assembly adopted the Convention on the Elimination of All Forms of Discrimination Against Women (CEDAW) on December 18, 1979, to address specific needs of women not covered in other United Nations documents, which emerged as part of the more general Post-WWII international human rights movement. CEDAW was entered into force on September 3, 1981, and within the first ten years, by 2010, 184 nation-states became State Parties; by 2019, this number increased to 189[2] (Cole 2005, 482; Wotipka and Ramirez 2008, 507; Zwingel 2018, 165).

The effects of CEDAW depart from the empirical pattern of other United Nations international human rights treaties. For the most part, a proliferation of treaties expanded the body of legislation aimed at increasing respect for human rights. However, the expansion of international law did not result in an equal measure of change in actual human rights conditions among State Parties to the treaties (Hathaway 2002; Hafner-Burton and Tsutsui 2005; Inglehart and Miller 2014, 22; Cole and Ramirez 2013; Hafner-Burton 2014, 279). By contrast, numerous studies report extensive expansions of women's rights in quantitatively measured outcomes among CEDAW State Parties after ratification with identifiable pockets of resistance (Wotipka and Ramirez 2008; Hill 2010; Cole 2013; Inglehart and Miller 2014).

---

2   The United Nations provide updated information via their CEDAW website: United Nations, Office of the High Commissioner, Human Rights Bodies, Status of Treaties (Map) http://indicators.ohchr.org/.

Inglehart and Miller (2014), using CIRI[3] indicators of women's social, political, and economic rights to measure change reported robust results on critical indicators for women's political rights, improvements in conditions among ratifying states, which occurred *after* rather than *before* ratification. These findings have been corroborated in other studies with other measures of women's political rights, such as representation in parliament (Hathaway 2002, 1976; Cole 2013; Inglehart and Miller 2014, 32; Walters and Perez 2017).

The expansion of women's rights occurred despite the weak enforcement provisions of the convention. As noted by Merry (2011, 52), "CEDAW is a law without sanctions." Rather, CEDAW and the CEDAW Committee "frame" and legitimate international discourse on the rights of women. The interactions function as a mechanism for cultural change at the nation-state and more local levels (Coleman 1986). "Framing" through the written text provides social agents with "cognitive distancing" and "emotional reasoning," which they deploy to solve practical problems and connect with like-minded persons and groups through social interaction around cultural objects that "resonate" (Goffman 1974; Wood, Stoltz, Van Ness and Taylor 2018; McDonnell 2014). Cultural objects, such United Nations conventions "work" because they "resonate; however, they resonate because they work" (McDonnell, Bail and Tavory 2017, 2; Hennion 2015). Cultural objects — here the text — draw attention to and reinforce shared beliefs and values through the ritualized interaction (Collins 2004).

Whereas for aesthetic cultural objects there is typically no real ethical sense of "right" versus "wrong," this is less true for international human rights treaties. These result from years of dialogue and consensus on ethical dilemmas across different contexts and diverse rational actors and audiences. Therefore, the process is perhaps more akin to what medievalist Brian Stark (1990) referred to as a "textual community." The latter privileges literate and value-rational discourse (Weber 1978) that may combine with an aesthetic dimension to produce group solidarity and desired ethical outcomes.

Stark (1990, 150) succinctly summarizes the distinctive features of textual communities. These provide communitarian social spaces in which texts are read aloud or silently and individuals in "groups of listeners can interpret, exchange, and profit from them." Parallel to the Deweyan natural and logical

---

3 The CIRI Scales for Women's Political Rights, Economic Rights, and Social Rights measure rights across these three factors (Cingranelli, Richards and Clay 2014): http://www.humanrightsdata.com/).

process of education outlined by McDonnell, new values and normative structures emerge, transform, and supersede the existing tribal or socio-economic allegiances of rational actors. Social exchanges within the textual community result in cognitive-emotional changes and thus propel the formation of both *gemeinschaft* and *gesellschaft* within the new social configurations. If members institutionalize the emerging norms and structural relationships, they provide capacity for a form of group perpetuation in which rules and not the text transcend pre-existing economic or social bonds. Modifications to the text may become the preserve of specialists, thus the idea of texts and textual communities give shape to an emergent layering of hierarchies, which privileges education and literacy as part of a normative "rationalizing" or "professionalization" process (Coleman 1986; DiMaggio and Powell 1983, 152–154; Weber 1978, 217–226).

The influence of the textual community for CEDAW and its cultural, educational, and emergent professional roles are borne out by the empirical evidence. By 2019, 7,147 journal articles, 12,567 newspaper articles, 765 book chapters, and 395 dissertations had been written on CEDAW since its inception, for a total of 21,645 items when books, conferences proceedings, government documents, and other sources are included (Walters 2019). This voluminous outpouring of texts contrasts sharply with the 139 cases adjudicated by the CEDAW Committee since 1999. The cases may be added to the 178 dialogues around reports submitted by CEDAW State Parties every four years over the thirty-two years between 1984 and 2014.[4] In tandem with the institutionalization process, human rights and the human rights documents have gained official status through their incorporation into social science curricula and textbooks (Meyer, Bromley, and Ramirez 2010).

1   CEDAW Optional Protocol

The United Nations General Assembly adopted the CEDAW Optional Protocol [CEDAW OP] on October 8, 1999. The OP was entered into force on December 22, 2000, per the provisions in Article 16:

---

4   STATUS OF COMMUNICATIONS REGISTERED BY CEDAW UNDER THE OPTIONAL PROTOCOL, information as of January 24, 2019, from: https://www.ohchr.org/en/hrbodies/cedaw/pages/cedawindex.aspx.

The present protocol shall enter into force three months after the date of the deposit with the Secretary-General of the United Nations of the tenth instrument of ratification or accession.

UNITED NATIONS 1999, 4[5]

Whereas nearly every United Nations Member State was by then a State Party to CEDAW, a little more than half, 104 nation-states or fifty-four percent, became parties to the CEDAW OP within the first decade; eighty-one CEDAW State Parties or forty-six percent did not[6] (Cole 2005, 482; Wotipka and Ramirez 2008, 507; Zwingel 2018, 165).

The CEDAW OP enhances the influence of CEDAW in three ways. Firstly, the Optional Protocol *amplifies the power of the CEDAW Committee* by granting authority to hear and adjudicate individual and group grievances. OP State Parties in signing commit to the possibility of external monitoring of their conduct concerning the provisions of CEDAW. Wade Cole (2005, 475), in his early sociological study of Human Rights Covenants, noted with respect to the International Covenant on Civil and Political Rights (ICCPR), the Optional Protocol provides "the most rigorous monitoring provisions available." CEDAW State Parties, likewise, in signing the Optional Protocol formally "recognize the competence of the [CEDAW] Committee to receive and consider communications ... by or on behalf of individuals or groups of individuals, under the jurisdiction of a State Party, claiming to be victims of a violation of any of the rights set forth in the Convention by that State Party" (CEDAW Article 1 and Article 2). By offering individuals a venue for filing grievances outside the state, the OP provides for this plausible instance of international monitoring (Cole 2005, 475; Cole 2009, 569), relinquishing, in Cole's words, a part of their sovereignty.

Secondly, by granting this enhanced power to the CEDAW Committee, OP State Parties *enact a more credible commitment* to adhere to the principles embodied in CEDAW. OP ratification may constitute an act less substantial than constitutional amendments or "credible commitments" as understood in Peace Studies (Nathan 2019); however, it nonetheless demonstrates a serious and convincing show of allegiance to the convention and its goal of eliminating discrimination against women. Zwingel (2018, 161–171) similarly notes the

---

5 As was the case for CEDAW, countries may become Contracting Parties by (a) signing without reservations, (b) ratifying after signing subject to reservations, (c) acceding to it. See the United Nations Treaty Handbook for more details.
6 See United Nations, Office of the High Commissioner, Human Rights Bodies, Status of Treaties (Map) http://indicators.ohchr.org/.

added weight of OP ratification, including the OP signing as one of her three components of "principled connectivity."

Third, the Optional Protocol *heightens the frequency and sharpens the focus of peaceful and strategic communication* between the CEDAW Committee and State Parties, albeit modestly due to time and budgetary constraints. The CEDAW Committee has reviewed 139 cases since 1999.[7] These formal communications add to the 564 reporting documents and constructive dialogues based on the country reports submitted by CEDAW parties every four years over the fifteen years between 1999 and 2014. Zwingel (2018, 174) identifies reporting habits and dialogue frequency as two components of "substantive connectivity." Reporting habits include both the number of reports and their timeliness. Time lags provide an important metric of commitment, meaning resources available and applied. For these three reasons, the CEDAW Optional Protocol represents a pivotal mechanism for enhancing the human development of women.

Wade Cole (2005) did not include the Optional Protocol as a critical predictor variable in his 2013 analysis of CEDAW, which is surprising given the significance of his findings on Optional Protocols in two earlier studies of different UN conventions (Cole 2005; 2009). However, other earlier and more preliminary work based on his work (Walters and Perez 2017) used the CEDAW OP with significant results. The findings corroborated the relationship Cole (2013) observed between the percentage of women in parliament and CEDAW State parties in a time-lag analysis.

Finally, nearly all United Nations Member States are parties to CEDAW, whereas this is not true for the CEDAW OP. Thus, in addition to the substantive rationale, as was the case in Cole's 2005 study of "sovereignty relinquished," the CEDAW OP shows variance among United Nation member nations. For these substantive and methodological reasons, the analysis that follows uses CEDAW OP State Party as an essential metric for analyzing commitments as well as pockets of resistance to the object and purpose of the convention.

2 Research Methods

2.1 *Data*

I created a data matrix on an Excel spreadsheet with all members of the United Nations listed in alphabetical order in the first column and then added columns

---

7 See STATUS OF COMMUNICATIONS REGISTERED BY CEDAW UNDER THE OPTIONAL PROTOCOL, information as of January 24, 2019, https://www.ohchr.org/.

with data for each on CEDAW and CEDAW OP status, predominant religion, Gender Inequality measures, indicators of religious freedom, and other indicators regarding the conditions of women, including the legal status of child marriage and polygamy. Data on the status of CEDAW and the CEDAW OP by country were obtained through the United Nations Treaty Status website[8] and the United Nations "Status of Ratification Interactive Dashboard."[9]

Codes were entered: "1" = State Party, and "0" = not a State Party for both CEDAW and the CEDAW OP alongside the year of ratification or accession. Data on the Gender Inequality Index (GII) were obtained for the years 2000, 2005, 2010, and 2015 from the United Nations Human Development Reports.[10] Data for reservations entered on Article #2 and Article #16 were coded as "1"= reservations entered; "0" = no reservations entered, based on information taken from the extensive information regarding reservations entered in the footnotes of the United Nations document on the Convention for the Elimination of All Forms of Discrimination Against Women.[11] The data were then checked against the tables found in Freeman (2009, 28–48). Data on predominant religion were taken from the website for the Association for Religion Data Archives (The ARDA), based on the work of Brown and James (2019). Predominant religion was operationalized as the religion for which the percent of adherents exceeded fifty percent and coded using the major religious groupings (Muslim, Roman Catholic, Protestant, Orthodox Christian, Hindu, and Buddhist) and categorial numbers for religion. In the absence of a predominant religion, the nation was coded as "8" for other.

Data on type and level of religious freedom were added using classifications created by Daniel Philpott (2019, 49–53; 12–13; 53–54; 79–80; 115–116).[12] Philpott based his initial classifications on the PEW (2009, 12–13) Global Restrictions on Religion report, which uses a Government Regulation of Religion Index (GRI) to classify countries as Very High, High, Moderate, and Low on their indices of religious freedom. Philpott's categories add regime characteristics and include religiously free (classified as "Low" in the PEW report), secular repressive, and religiously repressive. Data on Age of Marriage were added using Valerie

---

8 https://treaties.un.org/Pages/ViewDetails.aspx?src=TREATY&mtdsg_no=IV-8&chapter=4&clang=_en.
9 https://indicators.ohchr.org/.
10 http://hdr.undp.org/en/indicators/68606.
11 https://treaties.un.org/Pages/ViewDetails.aspx?src=TREATY&mtdsg_no=IV-8&chapter=4&clang=_en.
12 For a description of Philpott's measures, see pp. 49—53. For his list of Muslim countries, see pp. 12—13. For the list of Religiously Free countries, see p. 53. For the list of Secular Repressive Countries, see pp. 79—80.

M. Hudson's Age of Marriage Scale (AOM-3).[13] Data for the five categories in AOM-3 were combined to form three categories due to the small number of cases: "0" and "1" = Illegal; "2" = Parental Consent; "3" and "4" = Legal or Sanctioned by Law.

2.2　　Data Analysis

The data matrix described in the preceding section, including other variables not used in this chapter, was transferred to an SPSS file. Because the sample of UN Member States represents the entire population and nonetheless includes small number of cases, cross-tabulations, contingency tables, and chi-square to measure the level and significance of associations in bivariate distributions provided the tools for statistical analysis. Notes Cohen (1988, 215), these tools and chi-square are particularly appropriate for nominal scale (discrete) variables or other unordered categorial variables, especially in this case where the data represent an entire population rather than a sample. It is relatively free from constraining assumptions. For other variables, which have more than two values, Cramér's V was added to assess the significance of the relationship. Analysis of Variance is used when one variable is a ratio measure, such as GII. All results presented are statistically significant. The tables were transferred to Excel to create graphs as appropriate.

3　　Results I

Table 11.1 and Figure 11.1 show the mean GII by year and CEDAW OP status. The analysis corroborates the hypothesis linking endogenous cultural and structural support for CEDAW (value-rational alignment) as measured by the GII and CEDAW OP ratification status ($H\,Ia$ and $H\,Ib$). The data analysis partially replicates and expands earlier research (Walters and Perez 2017) and affirms the relationship between value-rational alignment (Weber 1978, 24) or substantive connectivity (Zwingel 2018) and CEDAW commitment level. CEDAW OP State Parties have lower levels of gender inequality with GII mean scores of .39, .37, .33. and .29 respectively for the years 2000, 2005, 2010, and 2015 as compared to GII mean scores of .54, .49, .47, and .44 for nation-states that are not CEDAW OP parties. The results using ANOVA are statistically significant for each year (**$p < .01$). The effects of the higher levels of focused communication precipitated by the CEDAW OP are perhaps revealed in the slightly higher rates of change over time for CEDAW OP State Parties.[14]

13　　WomanStats:http://www.womanstats.org.
14　　The specific effects of the CEDAW OP are explored in more depth in a forthcoming paper.

TABLE 11.1 GII by CEDAW OP state party and year

CEDAW OP Party	N	Yes		No			
ANOVA		Mean	S.D.	Mean	S.D.	df	F
GII2000	135	.39	.19	.54	.16	134	**23.03
GII2005	143	.37	.19	.49	.17	142	**15.29
GII2010	151	.33	.18	.47	.17	150	**24.93
GII2015	154	.29	.18	.44	.17	153	**15.29

**p <.01

Source: United Nations Treaty Collection; United Nations Office of the High Commissioner, Human Rights Bodies; United Nations Human Development Reports

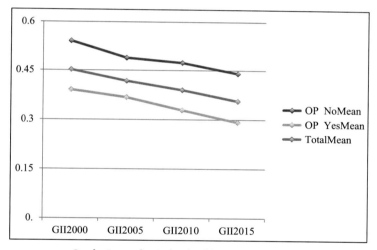

FIGURE 11.1 Gender Inequality Index (GII) by CEDAW OP state party and year
Source: See table 11.1

4   Religion

Religion in the contemporary world provides a significant but complex and often controversial variable given the onerous task of disaggregating religion from ethnicity and other meaningful indicators (Wilde 2018). Even defining what religion means across different national, regional, and ethnic contexts poses extraordinary challenges to sociologists of religion (Riesebrodt 2010, 72; Konieczny,

Lybarger and Chong 2012). It exists apart from our analytic concepts and exerts influence in ways not easily detected (Smith 2017; Gorski 2018), another contested idea (Asad 1993; 2018). Not surprisingly the capacious range for what constitutes religion at the United Nations leaves the task of defining boundaries in the hands of individual claimants and "a bewildering array of definitions" (Lerner 2012, 7–8). Lerner (2012, 185) further noted that the 1990 Cairo Declaration on Human Rights from the OIC (Organization of Islamic Cooperation) tended to "Islamize human rights at the cost of their universality." Moreover, he claims, OIC member nations more generally find the task of aligning Sharia with internationally recognized standards for human rights to be challenging.

The preceding notwithstanding, key empirical questions or hypotheses in the data analyses address value conflicts between the rights of women as embodied in CEDAW and institutional religions. The analysis telescopes the status of primarily Muslim but also other religious women within and across the economic, political, social, and cultural diversity of their nation-states (Fish 2011; Mahmood 2005; Blaydes and Linzer 2008). The diversity of values, attitudes and regarding CEDAW within the Muslim group in concert with reservations about CEDAW expressed by non-Muslim State Parties with and without official religions give pause to any stereotypes about Islam. Nonetheless, among other things, the pattern of gender exclusion and problems of equality in predominantly Muslim nation-states were acknowledged in the Ministerial Conference on the Role of Women in Development in Organization of Islamic Cooperation (OIC) Member States in December 2018.

Wade Cole (2013, 241–47) applied sophisticated time series models to expand the population size but also to capture the direct effects of CEDAW on Women's Rights Indices and the effects of CEDAW as mediated by a handful of cultural, legal, and political characteristics (Sharia law, percent Muslim, level of democracy, and linkages to INGOs). Generally, Cole's analysis revealed the overall positive effect of CEDAW, an effect that was more pronounced for political rights rather than others and some countries rather than others. However, with respect to religion, he noted: "Conversely, CEDAW proved ineffective in Muslim politics and societies, which reaffirms the widespread supposition that women's rights are culturally incommensurable with these countries' religious values" (Cole 2013, 247). His results corroborate results from earlier studies born in the wake of the events of 9/11 (Norris and Inglehart 2003) Tausch and Heshmati 2016).

5   Reservations

Many studies note that State Parties ratified CEDAW subject to reservations (Krivinko 2008) Freeman 2009; Bydoon 2011; Ariany 2013; Walters 2018; Zwingel

2018; Giordan and Breskaya 2018). Article 28 of the convention permits reservations per the Vienna Convention on the Law of Treaties "so long as these are not incompatible with the object and purpose of the Convention." Articles 2 mandates that State Parties pursue through all appropriate means and policies toward the elimination of discrimination against women, including national constitutions, legislation, and legal protections. Article 16 mandates that State Parties act to eliminate discrimination against women in all matters concerning marriage and family relations. These two articles are thus considered by the CEDAW Committee to be "core provisions" (Merry 2011, 50–51), central to the object and purpose of the Convention.

Ariany (2013, 530) examined the reservations and noted the possible contradictions with Sharia law in the Republic of Iraq but also observed inconsistencies in interpretations that highlight the significance of different socio-cultural contexts. Bydoon (2011) analyzed the case for Jordan with similar comments. Krivenko had earlier (2008, 116) observed that among the forty nation-states which incorporate some form of Islamic law, thirty-six are parties to CEDAW. She further notes that not all Islamic nation-states entered reservations, and not all reservations entered were entered to preserve Islamic laws and practices. Her legal examination provides a case-by-case analysis of twenty Muslim countries that entered reservations. While each author departs slightly in specific conclusions, a general and shared take-away rests in the contribution of socio-cultural context and the dynamic created by the reservations, which enable State Parties "to enter into real dialogue on the exact content of the reservation" (Krivenko 2008, 208).

More recent research by Susanne Zwingel (2018) corroborated both the endogenous cultural incompatibility and the ideas about the process noted initially by Krivenko (2008, 208). International norm translation and transmission via communications with the CEDAW Committee within the monitoring process proscribed in the CEDAW OP are "instrumental in thickening the relationship between the international women's rights framework and domestic contexts" (Zwingel 2018, 161). Zwingel included both the OP and the absence of reservations as one of her three indicators of "substantive connectivity," here referred to as *"commitment."*

6 Results II

Table 11.2 corroborates the hypothesis that nation-states that enter reservations on Article #2 and Article #16 are less likely to become State Parties to the CEDAW OP (*H IIa*). Sixty-one percent of the parties that did not enter reservations later became parties to the OP, compared to thirty-nine percent of parties

TABLE 11.2   CEDAW OP party by entered reservations

CEDAW OP Party	No (N=86)	Yes (N=108)	Total N
No Reservations Entered	39% (62)	61% (97)	159
Reservations Entered	69% (24)	31% (11)	35
Total	44% (86)	56% (108)	194
	x^2	df	Sig.
Chi-Square	10.790	1	***.001

*** p <.001
Source: See Table 11.1; Freeman (2009: 28–48)

that did enter reservations. Sixty-nine percent of the parties that entered reservations did not later become parties to the OP, compared to thirty-one percent who did not enter reservations and did not later become parties to the OP. The Chi-Square test, which evaluates the likelihood of frequency distributions for discrete nominal variables and has a value of 10.790 (***p < .001).

Table 11.3 evidences that a higher percentage of predominantly Muslim nations enter reservations on Articles #2 and #16, when compared to predominantly Catholic (Roman and Orthodox) and Protestant countries (*H IIb*). The full table provides valuable information. However, for the purposes of testing the significance of the results, the minimum expected cell count for seven cells violates the assumptions of Chi-Square (Hays 1963, 597). When the values are reduced to four categories (Muslim, Catholic, Protestant, and Other) the assumptions are met, and level of significance remains unchanged (***p < .001). Especially interesting are predominantly Roman Catholic countries, an extraordinarily complex issue given the history of ethnicity, regime, and colonialism (Valenzuela 1995). Ninety-one percent of the Roman Catholic countries entered no reservations on the two indicated articles.

Table 11.4 shows CEDAW OP parties by religion and corroborates the hypothesis linking predominant religion to enhanced commitment (*H IIc*). Thirty-seven percent of the Muslim majority countries are the CEDAW OP State Parties. Seventy-seven percent of the Roman Catholic and one hundred percent of the Orthodox Catholic countries are CEDAW OP State Parties. The contrast between predominantly Muslim and predominantly Catholic countries merits further examination to include political forms of secular repression, beyond the scope of this paper (Avdeyeva 2007, 887).

TABLE 11.3 Entered reservations by religion

Religion	Reservations		Total
	No (N=151)	Yes (N=36)	
Muslim	55% (24)	45% (20)	44
Roman Catholic	91% (52)	9% (5)	57
Protestant	92% (33)	8% (3)	36
Orthodox	92% (12)	8% (1)	13
Hindu	50% (1)	50% (1)	2
Buddhist	71% (5)	29% (2)	7
Jewish	0% (0)	100% (1)	1
Other	89% (24)	11% (3)	27
Total	151	36	187

	x^2	df	Sig.
Chi-Square	26.147	3	***.001

*** p<.001

Source: See Table 11.1 and Table 11.2; Association of Religion Data Archives; Brown and James (2019)

Table 11.5 and Figure 11.2 evidence statistically significant differences on mean GII scores by religion for years 2000 to 2015 (*H IId*). Muslim majority countries have the highest mean GII scores, .59, .52, .49, and .45 respectively for the years 2000, 2005, 2010, and 2015 as compared to .37, .35, .34, and .30 for predominantly Roman Catholic countries, bracketing the high scores for the two Hindu nations, which reaffim inequalities described by Mehra (1998). The results using ANOVA are statistically significant for each year (**p < .01).

7 Religious Freedom and Political Diversity within Muslim Majority Countries

The medieval Catholic hierocracy in France, which peaked in the twelfth to thirteenth centuries, provides a tempting analogy for the Organization of Islamic Cooperation (OIC). However, the individual countries within OIC are ethnically, culturally, economically, and most importantly here, politically diverse. As was the case in Western Europe, beginning with the French

TABLE 11.4 CEDAW OP party by religion

Religion	CEDAW OP Party		N
	No (N=82)	Yes (N=105)	
Muslim	63% (28)	37% (16)	44
Roman Catholic	23% (13)	77% (44)	57
Protestant	50% (18)	50% (18)	36
Orthodox	0	100% (13)	13
Hindu	50% (1)	50% (1)	2
Buddhist	57% (4)	43% (3)	7
Jewish	100% (1)	0	1
Other	63% (17)	37% (10)	27
Total	43% (82)	54% (105)	187
	x^2	df	Sig.
Chi-Square	31.29	3	***.001

*** p < .001

Source: See Table 11.1, Table 11.2, and Table 11.3

Revolution in 1789 and then later with the rise of Communism in Russia and the East, repressive monolithic power structures emerged in opposition to religion and traditional authority. These secular power structures and their laws often departed from the unique blend of principles in the English common law and the Occidental "natural law" tradition, which privileged reason and the legacy of constitutionalism in the transformation of natural rights to civil liberties (Walters and Perez 2017, 483; Arjomand 1992, 43; Perry 2013, 23).

In Turkey, the secular prototype, the Kemalists (named after Mustafa Kemal Ataturk) emerged victorious after the collapse of the Ottoman Empire at the end of World War I. Ataturk's goals "were a nation modeled on the West in pursuit of economic modernization, advancement in science and industry, and equality between the sexes. ... To achieve this vision, religion would have to be confined and privatized, first within the walls of the mosque and the household, then within the souls of humans, ever-shrinking, ultimately disappearing" (Philpott 2019, 86).

Kuru (2019, 36–37) perhaps best summarizes the changing contexts and political diversity across the Muslim world:

TABLE 11.5 Gender inequality index by religion and year

Religion		GII2000	GII2005	GII2010	GII2015
Muslim	Mean	.59	.52	.49	.45
	N	32	34	37	38
	Std. Deviation	.14	.17	.16	.17
Roman Catholic	Mean	.37	.35	.34	.30
	N	40	44	45	45
	Std. Deviation	.18	.18	.18	.18
Protestant	Mean	.43	.43	.39	.35
	N	27	28	27	27
	Std. Deviation	.23	.21	.23	.21
Orthodox	Mean	.37	.31	.27	.23
	N	8	9	12	13
	Std. Deviation	.09	.10	.10	.09
Hindu	Mean	.64	.64	.55	.51
	N	2	2	2	2
	Std. Deviation	.03	.02	.04	.03
Buddhist	Mean	.47	.44	.43	.42
	N	5	5	6	7
	Std. Deviation	.11	.11	.09	.06
Jewish	Mean	.20	.17	.14	.11
	N	1	1	1	1
	Std. Deviation				
Other	Mean	.44	.41	.38	.35
	N	20	20	21	21
	Std. Deviation	.19	.20	.20	.20
Total	Mean	.45	.42	.39	.36
	N	135	143	151	154
	Std. Deviation	.19	.19	.19	.19
ANOVA	df	134	142	150	153
	F	4.928	3.635	3.401	3.776
	Sig.	**.000	**.001	**.002	**.001

**p <.01

Source: See Table 11.1; Freeman (2009: 28–48)

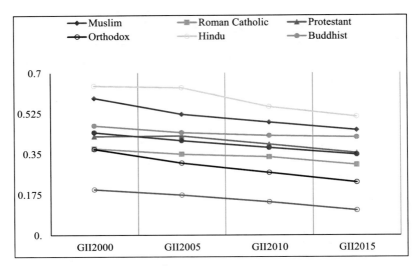

FIGURE 11.2 GIII by religion and year
Source: Table 11.5

In the first half of the twentieth century, Muslim supporters of women's rights took important steps forward. However, these supporters were largely associated with authoritarian secularist ideologies and state practices. Several secularist regimes, including those in Turkey and Tunisia, imposed headscarf bans, in addition to other restrictions on pious women and men. These authoritarian policies, together with secularist regimes' socioeconomic and foreign policy failures, helped Islamic actors gain popularity. In the second half of the century, Islamic actors have pushed Muslim-majority states and societies toward more conservative lines, which has resulted in the Islamization of constitutions and certain laws in several countries. This legal Islamization has severely affected women's rights.

Daniel Philpott, in his recent book (2019, 46–49), provides sharp focus with new categories he derived from the 2009 Pew Report, *Government Restrictions on Religion*. These decouple at the nation-state level religious adherents from regime types. Philpott utilizes both the GRI (Government Restrictions Index) and the SHI (Social Hostilities Index), developed by a team of sociologists led by Brian Grim and Roger Finke. In keeping with the time window in this study (2000 to 2010), he relied on data from the year 2009, "because the data for that year depict the Muslim-majority world before the changes of Arab Spring that began in 2011" (Philpott 2019, 46).

In creating his categories, Philpott carefully examined both the magnitude of government regulation and the manner of government restriction, what he calls the "regime's political theology." Here he refers to "a doctrine of political authority, justice, and the proper relationship between religion and state that is derived from more foundational theological and philosophical commitments" (Philpott 2019, 48). The modified classifications begin with dividing the PEW classifications into two parts: "religiously free" (the PEW category of "low restrictions") and "repressive" (the PEW categories of "very high," "high" and "moderate" restrictions). The "repressive" category is then further divided into two categories. "Secular repressive" identifies states that embrace a political theology of secularism, "holding that the public influence of Islam ought to be stifled so as to make way for nationalism, economic modernity, and modernity more generally" (Philpott 2019, 49). "Religiously repressive," by contrast, embrace the political theology of "Islamism," which promotes religion as the governing force in all areas of life.

8 Results III

Table 11.6 provides evidence on the relationships between types of "Religious Freedom" using Philpott's modified PEW categories: Religiously Repressive, Secular Repressive, and Religiously Free (*H IIIa and H IIIb*). Ninety percent of Muslim religiously repressive countries did not sign the CEDAW OP while fifty-three percent of the Muslim secularly repressive countries did. The results using Chi-Square are statistically significant (*$p < .05$). These results were replicated using the "Official Religion" scale (Fox and Flores 2008; Fox and Flores 2009). However, the results are not reported in this chapter.

Table 11.7 corroborates the relationship between types of Religious Freedom and child marriage (Hudson's Age of Marriage Scale—AOM-3) (*H IIIc*). Underage marriage (marriage under the age of 16) is legal in seventy-four percent of the predominantly Muslim religiously repressive countries compared to twenty percent of the Muslim secularly repressive countries. Underage marriage is illegal in sixteen percent of the predominantly religiously repressive countries compared to sixty percent of the secular repressive countries. These differences in the frequency of child marriage provide a critical benchmark for CEDAW compliance. In November of 2018, the United Nations passed a resolution to eliminate child, early, and forced marriage by 2030 to remove a major roadblock to human development for girls. The small N and five cells that fall below the minimum expected cell count pose challenges to the assumptions of the Chi-Square test, which are only partially

TABLE 11.6 CEDAW OP party by religious freedom for predominantly Muslim nations

CEDAW OP Party	CEDAW OP Party		
	No (N=29)	Yes (N=15)	
Religiously Free	50% (5)	50% (5)	100% (10)
Secular Repressive	47% (7)	53% (8)	100% (15)
Religiously Repressive	90% (17)	10% (2)	100% (19)
Total	66% (29)	34% (15)	100% (44)
	x^2	df	Sig.
Chi-Square	7.732	2	*.02
	Value	df	Sig.
Cramer's V	.424		*.02

*p <.05

Source: See Table 11.1 and Table 11.3; Philpott (2019: 49–53; 12–13; 53–54; 79–80) referencing PEW (2009: 12–13). The totals (N=44) depart from Philpott's (N=47) due to the exclusion of Kosovo and the coding here of Nigeria as "Other."

addressed by adding Cramer's v. Nonetheless, both the Chi-square test and Cramer's v are significant (*p < .05).

9 Conclusions

The results from the CEDAW research presented here answer some of the puzzles presented by the contradictory life-worlds drawn from experiential knowledge and ethnographic research (Swedberg 2002). They both support and challenge earlier studies reporting heightened gender inequality among Muslim majority nations. The latter are more likely to enter reservations on Article 2, which directs State Parties to implement policies, and Article 16, which directs State Parties to remedy inequality in marriage and family relations. Predominantly Muslim nations are less likely to be parties to the CEDAW Optional Protocol. The reservations often make specific reference to Sharia law, which predominantly Muslim nations may privilege over the international conventions, especially insofar as these concern marriage and family.

TABLE 11.7 Legal status of underage marriage in predominantly Muslim countries by religious and secular freedom

	Illegal (N=13)	Parental consent (N=8)	Legal or sanctioned by Law (N=23)	Total (N=44)
Religiously Free	10% (1)	30% (3)	60% (6)	100% (10)
Secular Repressive	60% (9)	20% (3)	20% (3)	100% (15)
Religiously Repressive	16% (3)	10% (2)	74% (14)	100% (19)
Total	30% (13)	18% (8)	52% (23)	100% (44)

	x^2	df	Sig.
Chi-Square	12.663	4	**.013

	Value	df	Sig.
Cramer's v	.384	4	**.013

**$p < .01$

Source: See Table 11.6; WomanStats, Hudson's Age of Marriage Scale (AOM 3): http://www.womanstats.org
http://www.womanstats.org/CodebookCurrent.htm#AOM

However, not all Muslim women view these laws as constraints rather than needed protections.

The higher levels of gender inequality for non CEDAW OP parties as measured by country scores on the Gender Inequality Index (GII) and, in an earlier study, on CIRI measures of Women's Political and Economic Rights increase the costs of implementing the convention for nation-states with high scores on the index. Thus, the findings corroborate the relationship between endogenous cultural and structural support for gender equality and the enhanced commitment for CEDAW OP State Parties. Based on earlier studies establishing this link, that predominantly Muslim nations have higher levels of gender inequality as measured by the Gender Inequality Index presents no surprise. Furthermore, correlatively, predominantly Muslim nations are less likely to be State Parties to the CEDAW Optional Protocol.

The pronounced inequalities on the GII in predominantly Muslim nations pertain primarily to the nineteen religiously repressive regimes, whereas predominantly Muslim nations identified as religiously free or secular repressive approximate the remainder of the world on measures of gender equality, including the GII. Moreover, all three groups show increasing parity between the years 2000 and 2015 with the religiously repressive and secular repressive in 2015 at .48 versus .39 respectively, moving closer on the GII. The differences between the latter two groups were not statistically significant for 2015.

The qualified empirical results point to the hazards of generalizing across dramatically different Muslim nation-states. The low level of consensus regarding how CEDAW might be interpreted differently across different national, ethnic, and socio-cultural contexts within the predominantly Muslim group indicates a need for further and more nuanced comparative work. The IMAGES-MENA study results strikingly illustrate some of the differences (El Feki, Heilman and Barker 2017). Ninety percent of Egyptian men compared to fourteen percent of Lebanese women agreed with "A woman should tolerate violence to keep the family together" (twenty-six percent of Lebanese men agreed). For the item, "When work opportunities are scarce, men should have access to jobs before women," ninety-eight percent of the Egyptian men agreed, compared to twelve percent of Lebanese women and thirty-two percent of Lebanese men. Thirty-one percent of Egyptian men compared to eight percent of Lebanese women and twelve percent of Lebanese men agreed with the honor killing item: "Men who kill their relatives for (so called) honour should not be punished."

NGOs and INGOs, a topic not taken up in the analysis, provide an essential mechanism for enhancing women's rights, a factor omitted in this analysis (Hafner-Burton 2014; Cole and Ramirez 2013, 712). However, religiously repressive Muslim nations' fusion of state and religious authorities amplifies traditional patriarchal constraints on women's spatial movement. The consequent limits on engagement in social interaction leading to political empowerment block the social mechanisms (Goertz 2020, 29) leading to emancipatory change. Representation in parliament as a potent factor in CEDAW ratification is perhaps the most robust and consistent finding across all research studies (Avdeyeva 2010, 211; Hathaway 2002, 1976).

The results also pose questions regarding how best to interpret the data on women's religious choices and outcomes. Is religion a factor or is it a right that conditions how gender parity comes to be defined and achieved? Assigning to religion a vital role in explaining differences in gender equality and what they mean for Muslim majority nations received some validation from the language of the Declaration and Resolutions from the 2018 OIC (Organization of Islamic Cooperation) Ministerial Conference on the Role of Women in the Development of Member States. The Declaration and Resolution acknowledge the problem but also offer some promise in bridging centuries of division over inclusion and parity issues for Islamic women, especially with its emphasis on refugees.

Nonetheless, the OIC documents make clear that the discussion and focus regarding women's rights in predominantly Muslim OIC Member States may take shape around a departure from the more secular values embedded in CEDAW (Mahmood 2005, 198; Blaydes 2014; Blaydes and Linzer 2008). Particularly the vision of family as "a divinely inspired and ordained institution, which consists of the marital union between a man and a woman" seems at odds with the secular international field from which CEDAW was inspired and thrived. Fundamental differences as expressed in Resolution #11, which ensures "an environment that allows the cultural and religious expression of Muslim women and girls" contrasts even more sharply in the latter context. The only safe conclusion is that women's rights in predominantly Muslim OIC Member States vary across cases but may follow a different trajectory with the compass oriented by complementary and conflicting values grounded in textual communities that depart from those propelling and propelled by CEDAW.

Acknowledgements

The author thanks Geoffrey Layman, Kraig Beyerlein, Christian Smith, Erin McDonnell, Ann Mische, Tamara Kay, Paolo Carozza, and the 2019 organizers of the Democracy Workshop at the Kellogg Institute for International Studies at the University of Notre Dame for opportunities to present this paper to different audiences; Joshua Weitz for added data set suggestions; Daniel Philpott for assistance in clarification of the coding; Gary Goetz and Laurie Nathan for inclusion in thought-provoking workshops; Mahan Mizrah for helpful readings on the Muslim world; Stephanie Perez for assistance with the data file; Feza Akova, Shanna Corner, Aníbal Pérez-Liñán, and Samuel Valenzuela for comments and suggestions on earlier written versions of the paper. Olga Breskaya and two anonymous reviewers helped bring focus and clarity to the arguments. Any errors of conceptualization or fact rest with the author.

Appendix

CEDAW STATE PARTIES—United Nations Member States
0= No
1= Yes

CEDAW PARTIES: Year Signed—United Nations

CEDAW OP PARTIES: Optional Protocol—United Nations
0=No
1=Yes

CEDAW OP Parties: Year Signed—United Nations

RESERVATIONS Entered on Articles #2 and #16 of CEDAW—United Nations
0=No Reservations Entered
1=Reservation Entered and not Removed

PREDOMINANT RELIGION—THEARDA
1=Muslim
2=Roman Catholic
3=Protestant
4=Orthodox
5=Hindu
6=Buddhist
7=Jewish
8=Other
Recoded by Religion: 1=yes; 2=no; 1 means >50 percent.
Also recoded variables for meaningful groups.

GII—United Nations Human Development Reports
2000, 2005, 2010, 2015

OIC: Organization of Islamic Cooperation Member
0=No
1=Yes

THEARDA National Profiles—Religious Indexes
Government Regulation of Religion (GRI)
Social Regulation of Religion (MSRI)

GRI: Government Regulation of Religion Index, averages from 2003, 2005, and 2008
0) No or virtually no regulation (GRI0308R=0)
1) Low level of regulation (GRI0308R=1–3)
2) Medium level of regulation (GRI0308R=4–6)
3) High level of regulation (GRI0308R=7–10)

I-GVTREG (SAX2010 below) PEW 2009 Forum on Religion and Public Life as modified by Daniel Philpott (2019)

SAX 2010: The Religion and State Project, Main Dataset and Societal Module, Round 3:
Official Religion, 2010 (SAX2010)
0) The state has no official religion.
1) The state has multiple established religions.
2) The state has one established religion.
Refer to: Fox and Flores (2009).

HUDSON'S AGE OF MARRIAGE SCALE—Women's Stats
This scale simply adds the scores from AOM SCALE 1 and AOM SCALE 2 to give an overall picture of the legal sanction and prevalence of underage marriage for girls in the nation. Underage marriage is defined as marriage at age 16 or younger. (Originally coded in 2011; look for updates in the database.)
0: Underage marriage (16 or younger) is illegal and there are very few exceptions with less than five percent of women married before age 16
1: Underage (16 or younger) marriage is illegal but there is little attempt to enforce the law, or five to 10 percent of women are married at age 16 or younger.
2: Underage (16 or younger) marriage can occur with parental consent and between five and ten percent of girls marry at age 16 or younger.
3: Underage (16 or younger) marriage for girls is generally sanctioned by law and is not uncommon
4: Underage marriage is legal and more than ten percent of girls are married at age 16 or younger.

References

Ariany, Bnar. 2013. "The Conflict between Women's Rights and Cultural Practices in Iraq." *The International Journal of Human Rights* 17 (4): 530–66.

Arjomand, Said Amir. 1992. "Constitutions and the Struggle for Political Order: A Study of the Modernization of Political Traditions." *European Journal of Sociology* 33 (1): 39–82.

Asad, Talal. 1993. "The Construction of Religion as an Anthropological Category," In *Genealogies of Religion: Discipline and Reasons of Power in Christianity and Islam*, 27–54. Baltimore, MD: Johns Hopkins University Press.

Asad, Talal. 2018. *Secular Translations: Nation-State, Modern Self, and Calculative Reason*. New York, NY: Columbia University Press.

Avdeyeva, Olga. 2007. "When Do States Comply with International Treaties? Policies on Violence against Women in Post-Communist Countries." *International Studies Quarterly* 51 (4): 877–900.

Avdeyeva, Olga. 2010. "States' Compliance with International Requirements: Gender Equality in EU Enlargement Countries." *Political Research Quarterly* 63 (1): 203–17.

Blaydes, Lisa, and Drew Linzer. 2008. "The Political Economy of Women's Support for Fundamentalist Islam." *World Politics* 60 (4): 576–609.

Blaydes, Lisa. 2014. "How Does Islamist Local Governance Affect the Lives of Women?" *Governance* 27 (3): 489–509.

Bydoon, Maysa. 2011. "Reservations on the "Convention on the Elimination of All Forms of Discrimination against Women (CEDAW)" Based on Islam and its Practical Application in Jordan: Legal Perspectives." *Arab Law Quarterly* 25 (1): 51–69.

Cohen, Jacob. 1988. "Chi-Square Tests for Goodness of Fit and Contingency Tables." In *Statistical Power Analysis for the Behavioral Science*, edited by Jacob Cohen, 215–73. Hillsdale, NJ: Lawrence Erlbaum Associates.

Cole, Wade. 2005. "Sovereignty Relinquished? Explaining Commitment to the International Human Rights Covenants, 1966–1999." *American Sociological Review* 70 (3): 472–95.

Cole, Wade. 2009. "Hard and Soft Commitments to Human Rights Treaties, 1966-2000." *Social Forces* 24 (3): 563–88.

Cole, Wade. 2012. "Human Rights as Myth and Ceremony? Reevaluating the Effectiveness of Human Rights Treaties, 1981–2007 1." *American Journal of Sociology* 117 (4): 1131–71.

Cole, Wade. 2013. "Government Respect for Gendered Rights: The Effect of the Convention on the Elimination of Discrimination against Women on Women's Rights Outcomes, 1981–2004" 1. *International Studies Quarterly* 57 (2): 233–49.

Cole, Wade, and Francisco Ramirez. 2013. "Conditional Decoupling: Assessing the Impact of National Human Rights Institutions, 1981 to 2004." *American Sociological Review* 78 (4): 702–25.

Coleman, James. 1986. "Social Theory, Social Research, and a Theory of Action." *American Journal of Sociology* 91 (6): 1309–35.

Collins, Randall. 2004. *Interaction Ritual Chains*. Princeton: Princeton University Press.

DiMaggio, Paul, and Walter Powell. 1983. "The Iron Cage Revisited: Institutional Isomorphism and Collective Rationality in Organizational Fields." *American Sociological Review* 48 (2): 147–60.

El Feki, Shereen, Gary Barker, and Brian Heilman. 2017. *Gender Equality Survey (IMAGES)—Middle East and North Africa*. Cairo and Washington, D.C.: UN Women

Fish, M. Steven. 2011. *Are Muslims Distinctive? A Look at the Evidence*. Oxford: Oxford University Press.

Fox, Jonathan, and Deborah Flores. 2008. The Religion and State Project, RAS Constitutions Main Dataset and Societal Module, Round 3. http://www.religionandstate.org

Fox, Jonathan, and Deborah Flores. 2009. "Religions, Constitutions, and the State: A Cross-National Study." *The Journal of Politics* 71 (4): 1499–513.

Freeman, Marsha A. 2009. *Reservations to CEDAW: An Analysis for UNICEF*. New York: United Nations Children's Fund (UNICEF), Gender, Rights and Civic Engagement Section, Division of Policy and Practice.

Giordan, Giuseppe, and Olga Breskaya. 2018. "Divided by Religion, United by Gender: A Socio-Religious Interpretation of the 'Convention on the Elimination of All Forms of Discrimination against Women.'" *Sociologia: Rivista Quadrimestrale di Scienze Storiche e Sociale* LII (1): 110–17.

Goertz, Gary. 2020. *Multimethod Research, Causal Mechanisms, and Case Studies: An Integrated Approach*. Princeton, NJ: Princeton University Press.

Goffman, Erving. 1974. *Frame Analysis: An Essay on the Organization of Experience*. New York: Harper and Row.

Gorski, Philip. 2018. "The Origin and Nature of Religion: A Critical Realist View." *Harvard Theological Review* 111 (2): 289–304.

Hafner-Burton, Emilie. 2014. "A Social Science of Human Rights." *Journal of Peace Research* 51 (2): 273–86.

Hafner-Burton, Emilie, and Kivoteru Tsutsu. 2005. "Human Rights in a Globalizing World: The Paradox of Empty Promises." *American Journal of Sociology* 110 (5): 1373–411.

Hathaway, Oona. 2002. "Do Human Rights Treaties Make a Difference?" *Yale Law Journal*, 111 (8): 1935–2042.

Hays, William L. 1963. *Statistics for the Social Sciences*. New York, NY: Holt, Rinehart, and Winston.

Hennion, Antoine. 2015. *The Passion for Music: A Sociology of Mediation*. Burlington, VT: Ashgate Publishers.

Inglehart, Ronald, and Melissa Miller. 2014. "The CEDAW Effect: International Law's Impact on Women's Rights." *Journal of Human Rights* 13 (1): 22–47.

Inglehart, Ronald, and Pippa Norris. 2002. "Islamic Culture and Democracy: Testing the 'Clash of Civilizations' Thesis." *Comparative Sociology* 1 (3–4): 235–63.

Konieczny, Mary Ellen, Loren D. Lybarger, and Kelly H. Chong. 2012. "Theory as a Tool in the Social Scientific Study of Religion and Martin Riesebrodt's *The Promise of Salvation. Journal for the Scientific Study of Religion*" 51 (3): 397–411.

Krivenko, Ekaterina Y. 2008. *Women, Islam and International law: Within the Context of the Convention on the Elimination of All Forms of Discrimination against Women* (Graduate Institute of International Studies (Series); v. 8). Leiden-Boston: Martinus Nijhoff Publishers.

Kuru, Ahmet T. 2019. *Islam, Authoritarianism, and Underdevelopment*. Cambridge, UK: Cambridge University Press.

Lerner, Natan. 2012. *Religion, Secular Beliefs and Human Rights*. Leiden, The Netherlands: Koninklijke Brill.

Mahmood, Saba. 2005. *Politics of Piety*. Princeton, NJ: Princeton University Press.

McDonnell, Terrence. 2014. "Drawing out Culture: Productive Methods to Measure Cognition and Resonance." *Theory and Society* 43 (3): 247–74.

McDonnell, Terrence, Christopher Bail, and Iddo Tavory. 2017. "A Theory of Resonance." *Sociological Theory* 35 (1): 1–14.

Mehra, Madhu. 1998. "And Miles to Go ... Challenges Facing Women's Human Rights." *Journal of the Indian Law Institute* 40 (1/4): 121–30.

Merry, Sally Engle. 2011. "Gender Justice and CEDAW: The Convention on the Elimination of All Forms of Discrimination Against Women." *Hawwa* 9 (1–2): 49–75.

Meyer, John, Patricia Bromley, and Francisco O. Ramirez. 2010. "Human Rights in Social Science Textbooks: Cross-national Analyses, 1970–2008." *Sociology of Education* (83) 2: 111–34.

Nathan, Laurence. 2019. "The Ties that Bind: Peace Negotiations, Credible Commitment and Constitutional Reform." Working Paper, Swiss Peace Foundation.

Norris, Pippa, and Ronald Inglehart. 2003. "The True Clash of Civilizations." *Foreign Policy* 135: 63–70.

Perry, Michael J. 2013. *Human Rights in the Constitutional Law of the United States*. Cambridge, UK: Cambridge University Press.

Philpott, Daniel. 2007. "Explaining the Political Ambivalence of Religion." The *American Political Science Review* 101 (3): 505–25.

Philpott, Daniel. 2019. *Religious Freedom and Islam: The Fate of a Universal Human Right in the Muslim World Today*. New York, NY: Oxford University Press.

Riesebrodt, Martin. 2010. *The Promise of Salvation: A Theory of Religion*. Chicago, IL: University of Chicago press.

Smith, Christian. 2017. *Religion: What It Is, How It Works, and Why It Matters*. Princeton, NJ: Princeton University Press.

Stark, Brian. 1990. *Listening for the Text: On the Uses of the Past*. Baltimore and London: The Johns Hopkins University Press.

Swedberg, Richard. 2002. "Theorizing in Sociology and Social Science: Turning to the Context of Discovery." *Theory and Society* 42: 1-40.

Tausch, Arno, and Almas Heshmati. 2016. "Islamism and Gender Relations in the Muslim World as Reflected in Recent World Values Survey Data." *Society and Economy* 38 (4): 427–53.

Valenzuela, Erika. 1995. "Catholicism, Anticlericalism, and the Quest for Women's Suffrage in Chile." Working Paper #214. University of Notre Dame: Kellogg Institute for International Studies.

Walters, Barbara R. 2014. "Normative Human Rights from a Sociological Point of View." Paper at the Annual Meeting of the Association for the Sociology of Religion. San Francisco, CA.

Walters, Barbara R. 2018. "CEDAW, Religiosity, and the Rights of Women." Annual Meeting of the Association for the Sociology of Religion. Philadelphia, PA.

Walters, Barbara R. 2019. CEDAW: Removing the Beam to View the Splinters. Center for the Study of Religion and Society.

Walters, Barbara R., and Stephanie Perez. 2017. "Cultural Commitments and Gender Parity: Human Rights and Implicit Religion." *Implicit Religion* 19 (4): 481–505.

Weber, Max. 1978. *Economy and Society*. Berkeley: University of California Press.

Wilde, Melissa J. 2018. "Complex Religion: Interrogating Assumptions of Independence in the Study of Religion." *Sociology of Religion* 79 (3): 287–98.

Wood, Michael, Dustin Stoltz, Justin Van Ness, and Marshall Taylor. 2018. "Schemas and Frames." *Sociological Theory* 36 (3): 244–61.

Wotipka, Christine M. and Francisco O. Ramirez. 2008. "World Society and Human Rights: An Event History Analysis of the Convention on the Elimination of All form of Discrimination against Women." In *The Global Diffusion of Markets and Democracy*, edited by Beth A, Simmons, Frank Dobbin, and Geoffrey Garrett, 303–342 Cambridge: Cambridge University Press.

Zwingel, Susanne. 2018. *Translating International Women's Rights: The CEDAW Convention in Context*. London: Palgrave McMillan.

Data Sources

Association of Religion Data Archives. Accessed February 28, 2021. www.TheARDA.com.

Brown, Davis, and Patrick James. 2019. Religious Characteristics of States Dataset Project—Demographics v. 2.0 (RCS-Dem 2.0), Countries Only.

Cingranelli, David L., David L. Richards, and K. Chad Clay. 2014. "The CIRI Human Rights Dataset." Accessed February 28, 2021. http://www.humanrightsdata.com. Version 2014.04.14.

Fox, Jonathan, and Deborah Flores. 2009. "Religions, Constitutions, and the State: A Cross-National Study." *The Journal of Politics* 71 (4): 1499–513.

Fox, Jonathan, and Deborah Flores. 2008. The Religion and State Project, RAS Constitutions Main Dataset and Societal Module, Round 3. http://www.religionandstate.org

Organization of Islamic Cooperation. Accessed February 28, 2021. https://www.oic-oci.org/home/?lan=en.

Pew Research Center. 2009. "Global Restrictions on Religion." Washington, D.C. Accessed on February 28, 2021. https://www.pewforum.org/2009/12/17/global-restrictions-on-religion/

UNICEF Data Sets. Accessed February 28, 2021. https://data.unicef.org/resources/resource-type/datasets/page/2/.

United Nations Homepage. Accessed February 28, 2021. http://www.un.org/en/.

United Nations Treaty Collection Database, Chapter IV: Human Rights (texts of the key documents). Accessed February 28, 2021. https://treaties.un.org/pages/CTCTreaties.

United Nations Treaty Collection, Chapter IV: Human Rights (Status of the key documents). 2019. Accessed February 28, 2021. https://treaties.un.org/Pages/ViewDetails.aspx?src=TREATY&mtdsg_no=IV-8&chapter=4&clang=_en.

United Nations, Office of the High Commissioner, Human Rights Bodies. Accessed February 28, 2021. https://www.ohchr.org/EN/HRBodies/Pages/HumanRightsBodies.aspx.

United Nations, Office of the High Commissioner, Human Rights Bodies, Status of Treaties (Map). Accessed February 28, 2021. http://indicators.ohchr.org/.

United Nations Human Development Reports. Accessed February 28, 2021. http://hdr.undp.org/en/content/table-4-gender-inequality-index.

United States Central Intelligence Agency. (2002) *Muslim distribution: Islamic countries.* [Washington, D.C.: Central Intelligence Agency] [Map] Retrieved from the Library of Congress. Accessed February 28, 2021. https://www.loc.gov/item/2005631747/.

US State Department: International Religious Freedom Report for 2013. Accessed February 28, 2021. http://www.state.gov/j/drl/rls/irf/religiousfreedom/index.htm#wrapper.

WomanStats Data Base. Accessed February 28, 2021. http://www.womanstats.org/.

The World Bank. Accessed February 28, 2021. http://www.worldbank.org/en/country.

CHAPTER 12

Religious Freedom and the Religionization of World Politics: Views of EU Political and Religious Representatives

Chrysa K. Almpani

1   Introduction

Over the last twenty years, real-world events have put religion front and center in the public discourse (Bellin 2008), leading to its "return from the exile" (Petito and Hatzopoulos 2003). In the aftermath of 9/11, the concept of religion has once again been included in political analysis and the geostrategic policy-making, in the defense of fundamental human rights and in mass media headlines, while religious communities themselves are interfering in a more prominent way in the public debate (Tsironis 2018, 94–95). This interest seems to be so intense, bringing into focus a discussion on the reawakening analysis of international relations theory toward this field.[1] Therefore, although up to the 2000's the religious factor had been out of the scope of the international affairs, it has since turned into one of the significant variables.

While the worldwide situation at international relations level has so far been regulated by international political agreements, the war conflicts and the major refugee waves of recent decades have illuminated "micro-politics", focusing on ethnicity and religion as the central factors (Tsironis and Almpani 2020, 4). Ulrich Beck's social theory recentered the research interest in the religious reference, not only in the context of personal identity but also in that of international developments. The religious field constitutes a dynamic social field that is in a continuous and two-way dialogue with the surrounding reality, as it intersects with the political, social, and ideological features of its epoch. The ever-growing interconnection and interaction of every social actor on a global level, one of the main characteristics of Second Modernity, brought religion to the fore as an image, a proposed way of life, a field of spirituality, a cause of terror, a fiction, etc. (Tsironis 2018, 157). Beck underlined though that

---

1 See works of Fox 2001, 2006; Philpott 2002, 2009; Thomas 2005; Haynes 2007; Sandal and James 2010; Snyder 2011; Toft, Philpott and Shah 2011; Toft 2012; Shah, Stepan and Toft 2012; Sandal and Fox 2013; Dawson 2015; Fox and Sandal 2016; Fahy and Haynes 2018.

this renewed interest in religion, in modern European democracies, does not indicate the "revival" of traditional religions, but it rather suggests the reconsideration of the religious factor dynamics within the European political context (Beck 2010, 33).

As Nelsen, Guth and Highsmith noted (2011, 1), "religion and politics may not mix well at dinner parties, but they undoubtedly interact in the real world of European governance." Religion is not a remnant of the past. The death of God and the age of secularization have not dispelled religion from Europe, its identity and its politics. Quite the opposite, religious reference continues to shape borders and boundaries within Europe and between Europe and "the others"; it continues to influence political identities, policies, symbolism, and international relations (Forlenza and Turner 2019, 18). The "religionization" of world politics indicates this reciprocal interaction and the simultaneous dependence of current social challenges on the realms of politics and religion, and it is depicted in the presence and influence that religion has in politics, both as a subject and object (see Ivanescu 2010; May et al. 2014).

The purpose of this chapter is three-fold. First, it illuminates the views of (EU) political and religious representatives on the intersection of religion with world politics. Second, it explores how the engagement with religion is mirrored in the policy-making of the EU, along with the way that the advancement of religious freedom at the EU external policy level may influence its relationship with third countries. Third, it identifies the challenges and prospects with regard to the contribution of religious actors and faith communities in the processes of conflict resolution and peacebuilding.

2 Has Religion Found its Way Back to International and European Politics?

Despite the prophecies about the ominous fate or even the "death of religion", representing an analytical trend up until the '70s–'80s, new analytical approaches emerged at the beginning of the new millennium. According to Jonathan Fox (2006), instead of collapsing under the weight of the modernization and secularization processes, the social and political dynamics of religion did not weaken as expected, but religion evolved to survive and thrive in the cultural context of modern societies. Fox (2006, 1059) claims that, although neglecting religion has been a tendency found in all of the Western social sciences, the international relations (IR) scholarship has more deeply rejected the religious factor as a variable of analysis. Until the end of the twentieth century, with few exceptions, academic journals on IR did not address religion as a serious influence on the international sphere. Religion also was off the radar of Western foreign policy-makers and diplomats. Two decades into the twenty-first century, though, "there is a growing realization that having a blind spot where religion is concerned is one of the greatest failings of IR theory" (Fox 2006, 1070).

Focusing on the multiple implications of religion on the IR and foreign policy, Fox and Sandler (2004) point out that religious reference influences the political leaders' worldview and decision-making, while it also can serve for them as a potential source of legitimacy. The traditional concept of "symbolic power" that nationalist movements try to derive from religious identity could be such a manifestation. Religious conflicts at the local level often transcend state borders and there is a number of phenomena related to religion (including religious fundamentalism, religious terrorism and the defense of religious rights as part of the HR agenda) that have become progressively transnational. Their central argument is that although religion may not be the driving force in world politics, it certainly needs to be incorporated into our understanding of international relations.

The intersection of religion and politics is at the core of the real world of human activity. Looking at world politics today, practitioners and analysts alike sense that religion, politics, and globalization need to be reconsidered, and to be reconsidered collectively. Wessels argues (2013) that there is a pressing need for a new theoretical approach to the relationship between religion and international politics. He finds that both these realities are often treated as selective variables, each of whom fills in the other's main analysis; the only question that arises is the direction of influence between the two dynamics within an interpretive model. But an integrated theory of global politics and particular religions must regard religion and globalization in tandem, as fundamental features of the lives of individuals and whole communities that converge and diverge in many ways (Wessels 2013, 323; see also Beyer 2013).

Beck chose the conceptual framework of Second Modernity to describe the contemporary social and cultural paradigm (Sørensen and Christiansen 2013). His theory emphasized the need of a paradigm shift in social sciences so that the analysis would take into consideration the continuous interaction and interchange between the individual and the global perspective (see Beck 2009; Beck and Grande 2010). According to him, the consolidation of globalization has reached such an extent that the experience of "a shared present and a universal proximity" (Beck 2010, 41) supplies the present-day context of all religious belief systems. The sociologist argued that this planet-wide interconnection leads to the "deterritorialization" of religions and therefore, the discussion is not about the vanishing of religion, but the weakening of Christianity in the historical centers of its political and symbolic power in Europe (Beck 2010, 23).

The long-standing exclusion of religion and religious actors from the systematic study of global politics has created a paradoxical situation. As Shah (2012, 3) notes, "religion has become one of the most influential factors in world affairs in the last generation but remains one of the least examined factors in the professional study and practice of world affairs." Referring to the EU perspective, Bilde (2015, 157) writes in that regard: "The fact that the global trend seems to suggest that religion (and religious identity) is on the rise sits uneasily with the very secular worldview of many Western officials and diplomats. It is more often than not considered intrinsically problematic for policy. Most diplomatic handbooks still largely hinge on realpolitik and interests, leaving little room for religion, identity, or culture. However, in parallel with that view, there has been a growing realization, within some European capitals and in the halls of the European Union in Brussels, that religion matters and that we need to, at minimum, understand when, where, and how."

In an attempt to approach the social role of religious reference in a world that is in a constant state of transformation, Beck focused on yet another changing condition: he claimed that religion has lost the justification to fully manage all life perspectives (Beck 2014, 83). As the old certainties of modern society are falling away, our connection with the grand collective narratives of the past is weakening, while the exposition of local and individual reality to global developments makes life in Second Modernity more vulnerable to the unpredictable and the uncontrollable (Tsironis and Almpani 2020, 10). In today's world risk societies, where the social reality is inextricably associated with the concepts of "ontological insecurity" and "manufactured uncertainty" (Beck 1987; 1992a; 1992b; 1996; 1999; 2009; 2014; Possamai-Inesedy 2002), the very concept of global risk could bring mankind closer (see anthropological shock), but it could also break it down on the basis of individual interests. In his book *A God of One's Own: Religion's Capacity for Peace and Potential for Violence*, Beck placed at the center of his analysis the ambiguous dynamics of religions to mobilize their adherents toward conflict or reconciliation and made significant effort to illuminate the conditions under which religion could contribute to the cosmopolitan vision of peace promoting the universal respect of human dignity.

Over the last few years, as the world witnessed a surge of acts of religious intolerance and discrimination, epitomized by violence and terrorist outbreaks in various countries, the European Union has been progressively dedicated to the promotion and protection of freedom of religion or belief (FoRB) and made an increased use of existing tools, both at bilateral and multilateral level, to more effectively promote and protect FoRB rights (Bolvin 2013, 48–49). From the 9/11 terrorist attacks to the Prophet cartoons crisis in Denmark in 2005–06, the EU has been obliged to take the religious factor into account. Before the Lisbon Treaty entered into force, at the end of 2009, there was no legal basis to develop mechanisms for analysis and dialogue with the religious actors and institutions. Therefore, the field is still quite new for the EU (Perchoc 2017). The Council of the European Union adopted the first Guidelines on the Promotion and Protection of Freedom of Religion or Belief in 2013 (Council of the EU 2013), while in 2015 a special Intergroup on FoRB and Religious Tolerance was founded within the European Parliament. A year later, the European Commission appointed a Special Envoy for the promotion of freedom of religion and belief rights outside the EU, who has been serving as special adviser to the Commissioner for International Cooperation and Development (Jenichen 2019). Nevertheless, "whereas religious freedom has traditionally been seen as the 'first entry point on religion', it has become increasingly clear that it is not possible to capture all the relevant aspects through this prism" (Bilde 2015, 159).

Chaplin and Wilton (2016) suggest that if religion has not quite "dramatically reemerged within European politics" (Foret 2015, 1), it does at least, with the words of Katzenstein (2006, 33), continue to "lurk underneath the veneer of European secularization." A growing literature is focusing on the multiple and overlapping avenues through which the religious perspective, the religious identities, and organizations relate to increasingly complex EU institutions and processes.[2] With the ongoing global geopolitical and social transformations, Foret (2015, 1–2) says that "the developing European political order can only be understood if gods fit somewhere in the picture, and religious beliefs and institutions cannot avoid coming to terms with the new political context." The present chapter discusses Ulrich Beck's thesis on the political impact of religion in our contemporary world and the way this impact is redefined in the context of Second Modernity. It also aims to explore whether reassessing the global religion-politics dynamics may influence our understanding of the relevant issues, including the way we approach the discourse on religious freedom.

---

2 See works of Bokern 2009; Leustean and Madeley 2010; Haynes and Hennig 2011; Bolvin 2013; De Jong 2013; Leustean 2013, 2016; Annicchino 2014; Haynes 2014; Nelsen and Guth 2015; Schirrmacher and Chaplin 2016; Foret 2017; Perchoc 2017; Forlenza and Turner 2019; Jenichen 2019.

3   Research Methodology

The qualitative research was conducted through semi-structured, in-depth interviews that were addressed to three different categories of participants. The first group of interviewees included political representatives at the EU level. These interviewees consisted of Members of the European Parliament (MEPS), some of whom were also members of the special European Parliament Intergroup on Freedom of Religion or Belief and Religious Tolerance (Intergroup on FoRB & RT), policy officers and advisors of the European Commission working in the fields of human rights, foreign affairs, security, and defense, representatives of the Commission's Agora on Religion and Development and Mr. Ján Figel's office, who had been appointed as the Special Envoy for the promotion of FoRB outside the European Union (2016-2019), foreign-policy practitioners from the European External Action Service (EEAS), and representatives of the Greek Deputy Ministry of Cultural and Religious Diplomacy.

The research also addressed the EU representation offices of religious organizations, which work in close cooperation with the policy-makers, providing expertise and advocacy on core European policies. Some of these organizations were the Commission of EU Catholic Bishops' Conferences (COMECE), the Conference of the European Churches (CEC), the Quaker Council of European Affairs (QCEA), the Baha'i International Community's (BIC) Brussels Office, the liaison-office of the Evangelical Church in Germany (EKD), also at the seat of EU institutions, and the Pax Christi International. The last group of interviewees was composed by social and humanitarian affairs officers and representatives of non-governmental European organizations working on social justice, sustainable development, mediation, and peacebuilding. Among these organizations were the European Institute of Peace, the Dialogue Advisory Group and the Sallux-ECPM Foundation in the Netherlands, the ASF Belgique Service de Paix, the Eurodiaconia, and the ACT Alliance EU.

Interviews were held between December 2018 and April 2019, during a research visit to Brussels (in person) or via Skype or telephone. The aim was to achieve a representative selection of key policy actors in the field. In that regard, there was an effort to address the head or the main policy advisors of each EU institutional unit and to build a comprehensive approach, by including representatives from both political, religious, and non-governmental European organizations in the research sample. Arguably, the greatest limitation within the research study was the low response rate, recorded mainly from the side of the political sphere. Eighty-seven representatives were approached in total, to secure the 30 interviews conducted.

The participants of the final sample represent different spheres of the political spectrum and diverse religious affiliations. The MEPs and policy advisors participating in the research belonged to different political parties of the European Parliament: the Group of the Alliance of Liberals and Democrats for Europe (ALDE), the Progressive Alliance of Socialists and Democrats (S&D), the Greens/European Free Alliance (Greens/EFA), the Europe of Nations and Freedom Group (ENF). The vast majority of the interviewees identified themselves as believers, belonging to different congregations and denominations (Orthodox, Catholic, Protestant, Anglican, Lutheran, Quaker, Muslim, Baha'i), while two out of the thirty participants in the research regard themselves as non-believers and another two as "not practicants" (believing without practicing). Interviews were audio recorded and subsequently transcribed by the researcher. Ethical protocols, anonymity, and consent were discussed with each participant.

4 Research Results

4.1 *Religion in the International Public Sphere*

Despite their different approaches on the way religious issues could be integrated in the field of international affairs, most of the interviewees recognize that religion becomes more prominent as a variable in global politics due to the urgency of current social challenges. "Insecure times always produce longing for sense and values," as pointed out by one MEP (Interview 5). According to the representatives of COMECE (Interviews 23–24),

> this current context highlights even more the importance of a deeper reflection that goes beyond purely material needs or short-term individual interests, and this is actually where religions can play an important role in today's society: to provide this long-term vision, to have this prophetic voice, to look beyond short-term horizons and to also help the policy-makers shaping policies that will be oriented to the common good.

The increasing visibility of religion in the international sphere is not conceived though as a "return" of religion to world politics. Religion is not coming back, it has always been part of the reality. "The difference is whether it gets the media headlines or not," a political representative noted (Interview 18). What is re-emerging is the realization that, whether for good or bad reasons, religion needs to be part of the conversation. As International Relations scholars move beyond the secularization thesis, religion is getting more respected in politics and in society, as a partner, than it was ten or twenty years ago. In the words of a humanitarian affairs officer: "Religions are hibernated. They are never dead, they are never in the back yard of our daily life. They need sometimes kind of an incitement to wake up" (Interview 16).

Some of the interviewees argue that religion comes to the fore in a broader discussion on "identity". Living in a time when nationality is decreasing in importance, especially in Europe, people seem to be in search of new ways to express and define their identity. Migration, climate change, social responsibility, sustainable consumption, they are all ethical questions that push people to confront their own belief system, and this is where their religious affiliation becomes relevant. One of the moral duties of faith communities is to counterbalance the emphasis that modern societies put on individualism with the ethic of communal responsibility. These remarks also are summarized by a representative of Pax Christi International (Interview 29):

> The fact that religion becomes more prominent is also due to the globalization of technology, globalization of movement, globalization of economy, globalization of ideas and values, that is already going on since decades. Migration is also part of this dynamic; people are moving all over the world, bringing their own values, their own faiths and religions to their new communities. Religion thus becomes more visible, and especially the 'other religion'. At the same time, this arises as a chance to work together, to collaborate, and to find new ways of dialogue and new ways of making religion important also in the political context.

Religion could be one way of eliminating or alleviating the underlying fear of a runaway world. As the representative of Eurodiaconia said (Interview 3), the "construction of fear" is emerging as one of the greatest international challenges, one that goes beyond the "traditional" geopolitical issues. It creates a transnational, invisible conflict that affects everybody. We live in a world where "there is so much "othering" going on: it's all about *the other*" (Interview 3). This leads to an endless struggle to accumulate power; social power, political power, economic power, trade power, and even "peace power". We don't work for peace without power. What if we could find different ways to quantify power? What about the power to compromise to embrace the other? "Religions contain insights without which humanity cannot progress and societies cannot advance in the long run," is one belief expressed by a Baha'i representative (Interview 26). These are not only the ecumenical, universal values, embedded in all world religious traditions, but also "leading by example" (Interview 3) and sharing the experience of living in a community.

The interviewees express different views regarding the way religious issues should be reflected at the international level. Some of them suggest that it should be an approach in terms of religious rights (i.e. the protection and respect to freedom of religion and belief). "I think it is always good to raise religious issues on international level as part of crucial human rights, but not beyond that," as one MEP stated (Interview 9). Religion, in that regard, has already been part of the international relations context, being explicitly integrated in international and European human rights treaties, such as the Universal Declaration of Human Rights, the European Convention on Human Rights, and the UN International Covenant on Civil and Political Rights. Another group of interviewees claim that the religious perspective should not be neglected in the discussion at the international arena, because the majority of the world population are believers, religion is generally accepted as a central aspect of society, and it is also a strong motivator for actions. One participant, an ideology analyst, depicted religion as a political trend: "We have to consider religion as a political belief, a trend, as there are people who believe that religions should be guiding the society. Religion, indeed, is like any other political party or organization. Sometimes they flourish, sometimes they are inclined to work between or behind the scenes" (Interview 14).

Religions also have a twofold dynamic. The first one is their universal dimension. All major religions have worldwide networks and religious institutions are regarded as influential actors in the international public fora. This strengthened global presence may be due to the rise of structures like the European Union and the understanding that national states are not the only powers, as described by a policy officer of the European Commission. "Religions are not a monolithic block, and in order to remain relevant — not only on society level, but also on an international level — they acknowledge the need to have a voice and to be represented toward these emergent powers (EU, UN, and intergovernmental organizations related to religion)" (Interview 4). The second dimension is the more vertical one. Religious actors are deeply rooted in the local context and they develop significant work at the grassroots level, by providing key social services, education, healthcare, and humanitarian assistance, to their communities. These initiatives on the ground are important since they are linked to international cooperation projects and they therefore contribute to the priorities made at higher political level. Religion can act as a "multiplicator" and support common social goals (e.g. Sustainable Development Goals), by spreading the knowledge with regard to these priorities, giving practical examples, and being a role model for faith communities. At the same time, religion can be a "social glue", a shared encounter that helps bind society together.

4.2 Religion at EU Policy Level

Responses from all three groups of interviewees converge on the need for a dialogue between political and religious institutions in managing the social transformations that modern pluralistic societies are witnessing. The need for such a dialogue also is reflected in the European Union's policy discourse. As an EU official put it (Interview 12): "It is very important that the two spheres connect and interact and that even difficult debates take place. For a long time, there were many areas where there was no dialogue, no confrontation. I think that now it's time to step into the gray area." The 1990's Balkans war was a major event that marked the need for religion to be part of the public agenda. However, extremism and migration were identified as the geopolitical and societal changes on a global scale that led the EU to integrate the religious dimension at its policy level. "The September 11 was certainly a "wake-up" call, but the Danish Cartoon Controversy in 2005 was for Europe the key point to engage more with religion. The realization of what a backlash the hurting of religious feelings can have in the world led to a series of initiatives toward the promotion of FoRB" (Interview 11), as expressed by a representative of DG Justice and Fundamental Rights policy.

Article 17 of the Treaty on the Functioning of the European Union (TFEU) represents the legal basis for an open, transparent and regular dialogue between the European institutions and churches, religious communities, and non-confessional, philosophical organizations. The initiative "A Soul for Europe", launched in 1994 by Jacques Delors, who was president of the European Commission at the time, established the first formal links between the EU institutions and those organizations, aiming to encompass the spiritual or ethical perspectives of European integration. Referring to Article 17, the interviewees emphasized that the clear idea is not to set up a dialogue *about/on* religion, but to assure an exchange with communities of faith and conviction on critical issues within the European agenda. As part of this, the EU institutions hold high-level meetings, dialogue sessions and seminars on an annual basis. In 2019, the Article 17 TFEU dialogue sessions focused on migration.

A faith-based network also has been developed at the EU level, an informal network of different religious organizations with headquarters in Brussels. The emphasis of this partnership is to reflect upon the way faith-based approaches can be promoted at EU policy level. Therefore, regular seminars are organized with a view to exploring the dynamics of religion in relation to certain policy areas (like the EU-Africa strategy, peacebuilding initiatives, etc.) and meetings with practitioners from the grassroots level and policy-makers are taking place on this direction. In the context of the European Development Days 2019, that network hosted an interactive and participatory lab debate about the role of faith-based approaches and actors in addressing inequalities in development.

Religious representatives clarified that there should be a distinction between the religious responsibility (in terms of moral leadership) and the political decision-making. The churches' and faith communities' engagement in a dialogue with politics, in a modern democratic society, should not be oriented toward political power seeking. Their contribution to the policy-making field should be about raising ethical concerns and developing a critical stance towards politics. "Especially when it comes to issues as it is the artificial intelligence, the aging population or the digitization, they are all ethical questions upon which the Church can communicate its concerns" (Interview 25), noted the EKD Brussel's office representative. This cooperation allows the decision-makers, as one MEP said, "to act quite safely even in the most complex ethical dilemmas (ethics committees/bioethical research)" (Interview 6).

The increasing awareness of religion's constructive role in EU political discourse is depicted in a series of European Parliament resolutions and Council conclusions, which were brought up by some of the interviewees. The European Parliament resolution of February 4, 2016, on the systematic mass murder of religious minorities by ISIS, recognized that political and religious leaders have a duty at all levels to combat extremism and to promote mutual respect among individuals and religious groups, while it also called for the EU to establish a permanent Special Representative for Freedom of Religion or Belief (European Parliament 2016). The Parliament's resolution of October 3, 2017, on addressing civil society space in developing countries, recalled the important role of religious actors in the development cooperation[3] and encouraged the EU to adopt specific guidelines on partnership with churches, faith-based organizations and religious actors on this field (European Parliament 2017). The Council's conclusions (January 2018), on the European Union's integrated approach to external conflicts and crises, called for the inclusion of religious (and cultural) representatives in joint conflict analyses that should be systematically carried out and updated for countries at risk of conflict or instability, having already recognized the crucial role of the Congolese Catholic Bishops Conference in mediating the crisis in the Democratic Republic of Congo in March 2017 (see Council of the EU 2017, 2018).[4]

---

3 "churches, religious communities and associations, together with other religion- or belief-based organizations are among the frontline and long-standing operational field actors in the provision of development and humanitarian assistance" (see European Parliament 2017).

4 "whose moral leadership, impartiality and legitimacy are indispensable for the success of the process" (see Council of the European Union 2017).

The religious perspective also is mirrored in the EU's external policies. According to a representative of the mediation policy field (Interview 13), "every single conflict mapping done in the EU is looking at what the religious groups and their interests are, and therefore what we need to consider in our communication with them. In every process that the EU is involved in the world, the analysis of the religious groupings, as well as the risks and opportunities that come along with that, is incorporated."

The European External Action Service (EEAS) has developed a two-pillar approach regarding the embodiment of the religious factor at the EU foreign-policy level.

The first one is aimed at enhancing the religious literacy of EU officials and encourage them to develop skills and mindset tools that will allow them "to navigate the world as is and not just as we see it through our predominantly secular worldview" (Interview 8). Since 2013, the EEAS has built an inclusive training program on the basis of four different reflection modules that focus on the areas of religion and foreign policy, Islam and politics, cultural and religious bias, as well as on radicalization and narratives. These training modules are not only addressed to the EEAS and Commission officials, but also to Member States' diplomats.

The second pillar is centered on the networking and the global exchange of best practices. Significant cooperation in terms of external capacity building has been developed, over the last five years, with the Transatlantic Policy Network on Religion and Diplomacy (TPNRD). Moreover, a task force on culture and religion, set up within the EEAS, has been hosting scholars and field experts from outside the European Union, with a view to stimulate and challenge the conventional way of thinking about the cross-section of religion and foreign politics at the EU level. Some of those key lecture-visits had a focus on the countering of violent extremism or on conflict transformation and the way(s) to positively engage religion, while "Culture and Religion" was discussed as a priority matter at the recent annual meetings of EU ambassadors.

Another initiative seeking to accommodate religion at the EU policy level is the establishment of the European Commission's Agora on Religion and Development, as part of the Directorate General for International Cooperation and Development (DG DEVCO), since 2018. Its aim is to foster the religious understanding of EU officials through a series of training sessions and seminars, particularly focusing on the nexus between religion and development policies. Despite the greater prominence of religion in the EU's public discourse, which the interviewees jointly acknowledged, some emphasized that there is still the need to advance the level of faith literacy among EU officials and to encourage a deeper understanding of religious specificities and religious dynamics. "I think there is a gap between the aspiration we have and the knowledge we built with regard to religious matters," a Commission official remarked (Interview 12). These initiatives are expected to help EU officers to regard religion as a strength in the policy-making process and to assist them in understanding and managing pluralistic societies and cultural diversity in a globalized world (Interview 8). "There is a movement within diplomacy to be less illiterate, more open, and informed on religion. This movement is growing fast and I think it's important to be supported" (Interview 7), said a policy advisor to the Special Envoy on the promotion of Freedom of Religion or Belief outside the EU.

4.3   Religion and Human Rights

Religious issues are broadly conceived by the interviewees as matters of human rights and rule of law that should be addressed either in diplomacy and political dialogue or in cooperation with the religious communities. It is their common view that a language of human rights and rule of law would highlight the universality of those issues, while the COMECE representatives posed a question of terminology in that regard; their comments included: "We noticed a tendency at EU level to insist referring to 'religious values', but we should rather focus on 'principles' and 'rights'. Values constitute a vaguer, less strong, and protective term that could undermine the rights-based approach, which from our point of view should guide the actions of the EU institutions" (Interviews 23–24). Some of the religious representatives clarified though that entrusting matters related to the core or to the internal workings of the faith communities to the political sphere would undermine the respect of their autonomy under freedom of religion.

Diverse remarks were expressed with reference to the intersection of religion and human rights at the policy level, and the EU initiatives for the promotion of Freedom of Religion or Belief (FoRB). A senior policy advisor indicated that religious freedom is often conceived as a collective right (i.e. protection of religious minorities) and that it is equally important to set freedom of thought as it brings back the matter to the individual level. He specifically suggested that it would be more comprehensive to use the European regulation of "freedom of thought, conscience and religion", instead of "freedom of religion or belief", and to respect the phrase as formulated in the Article 9.1 of the 1950 European Convention on Human Rights. "It is like the Russian dolls; freedom of religion is born out of freedom of thought," he said (Interview 2). On the other hand, some of the religious representatives said it is not uncommon for EU officials and their documents to emphasize the individual aspect of the right to freedom of religion or belief and to downplay, at least a little, the collective perspective.[5] "Therefore, it is important to keep all these elements of FoRB and its institutional dimension as well," they concluded (Interviews 20–21).

Another point that was given due consideration was the need to avoid the risk of creating hierarchy in terms of human rights. Many of the interviewees, both from the political and religious spheres, pointed out that religious freedom should be on the agenda as every other human right, but there should be an attention not to overemphasize on it. "We should be attentive not to create the impression that rights and freedoms can be put in a kind of ranking" (Interview 5). However, "undermining freedom of religion could also be regarded as an attack to the foundations of the human rights architecture, in the sense that to undermine *one* fundamental right is like putting into question the whole superstructure" (Interview 21).

The EU representatives' views diverge significantly when it comes to whether the incorporation of the religious factor at the policy level and the advancement of religious freedom could reinforce the union's position as a global actor. A policy advisor on security and defense particularly pointed out that the religious factor should be part of the EU politics but kept at a low profile, which means to be present but in an indirect way. "I really think that the Europeans are well-advised today to keep such an approach. We have had our past, the religious wars in Europe, so we should not give the impression that we are trying to export 'our' religion" (Interview 10). Instead, he suggested integrating the religious dimension in EU foreign policy-making in the context of "resilience versus fundamentalism". As he explained, "what we could do is to empower all those liberal religious people in fragile third countries who make an effort to stabilize their countries and

---

5 In the UN Report of the Special Rapporteur on freedom of religion and belief (UN General Assembly 2017), it is explicitly written in paragraph 24 that "Individuals, not religions, convictions, belief systems or truth claims, are the right-holders of the right to freedom of religion or belief. More specifically, this right is not designed to protect beliefs as such (religious or otherwise), but rather believers and their freedom to possess and express their beliefs either individually or in community with others in order to shape their lives in conformity with their own convictions (A/71/269, para.11)." However, in *Freedom of Religion or Belief: An International Law Commentary*, Bielefeldt et al. (2016) also stress the collective dimension of FoRB underlying that: "Moreover, States should facilitate the acquisition of a collective legal personality status which religious communities may need to undertake important collective functions, such as employing professional staff, purchasing real estate to build places of worship, or establishing institutions of religious learning. The obligation to fulfill also covers a broad range of promotional activities, such as education about religious and belief diversity as part of the mandatory school curriculum, interreligious dialogue initiatives, or ensuring an appropriate representation of religious minorities in public media, to mention just a few examples."

come up against all the fundamentalists, and we have the financial resources to do so."

On the same direction, a policy advisor of the EU Agora on Religion and Development emphasized that European policy-makers should be careful not to manipulate or instrumentalize religion. "I wouldn't say it is a golden rule to follow everywhere, sometimes you better step backwards" (Interview 30). With reference to the initiatives at the EU level for the promotion and protection of freedom of religion or belief rights, the view also was expressed that they were not articulated as a conscious EU policy, but as a response to US lobbies and their pressure toward that direction. This does not mean that those initiatives were against the European ideas and values, but rather that they are depicting a policy orientation that is not completely embodied within European countries.

Religious representatives argue, on the contrary, that engaging with religion at the policy-making level contributes positively and helps the European Union gain respect and credibility at the international level. Religion plays a role that cannot be neglected in most of the third countries with whom the EU is seeking to develop relations. Therefore, increasing its understanding in regard to the religious perspective would enhance the reliability of its foreign policy. This may be a longer process though in comparison to the UN, leaving further room for improvement. Some of the interviewees indicated, for example, that the mandate of the EU Special Envoy on the promotion of Freedom of Religion or Belief outside the European Union is not yet so strong, both institutionally and in terms of resources, compared with the relevant position of the Special Rapporteur on FoRB at UN level (Interviews 20–21).

From the European organizations' point of view, the concern was expressed that integrating the religious factor at the EU policy-making level might shut doors in the agnostic and atheist communities, however, most were positive about the impact it might have on the EU's position in the international scene. The representative of the Sallux-ECPM Foundation also added (Interview 15):

> The only way to liberate people from the oppressive structures creating all the current challenges (war, terrorism, migration streams) is by introducing fundamental freedoms in the mindset and in the reality of society, like freedom of religion and freedom of thought. If the existing oppressive mentalities were changing, that would cultivate a common attitude shared between the migrants and the host communities. Consequently, if the integration issue was less of a problem, then the populist movements would have no longer reason to exist and the European Union would be strengthened in the long run. With less external threats, there are fewer

internal threats and the EU has the chance to work on promoting inclusive societies.

Religious representatives also believe that the respect to freedom of religion or belief rights should be considered as an important parameter regarding trade negotiations and other agreements between the EU and third countries, while the political representatives seem to be more skeptical. A former Minister of Education & Religious Affairs stated that although this approach is right in theory, it could hardly stand as a precondition in practice. "As you realize, in foreign policy and economic exchanges, it is the realpolitik that prevails in the end," he emphasized (Interview 19). Several of the interviewees cited the example of EU's trading relationships with Pakistan, Saudi Arabia, and Iran, countries where severe violations of religious freedom are taking place, to support the argument that religious rights clauses are only used to justify political purposes. Advocacy on fair trade has been so far an approach on social rights. A policy officer at European Commission, working on justice and fundamental rights policies, noted (Interview 11):

> We know how politicized trade negotiations are — and that is for a good reason, when it comes to issues such as the protection of workers' rights, the protection of the environment, etc. Therefore, we should not exclude the aspect of the protection of religious rights, especially as we know that in many parts of the world, religious communities are under threat.

One of the interviewees made a reference to Brian Grim, a sociologist of religion focused on the socio-economic impact of restrictions on religious freedom, and his initiative on educating the global business community and the policy-makers about the economic value and social benefits of robust religious diversity and liberty (see Grim et al. 2014). The inclusivity of FoRB rights in trade partnerships, memorandums of understanding and other agreements with third countries is also a matter of policy coherence for the European Union. As a religious representative highlighted, "It would be certainly beneficial to ensure the coherence among human rights policies, trade policies, economic policies, and development policies. And of course, since the EU is a key economic actor globally, trade and economy can be regarded as significant tools or vehicles to promote peace and the human rights agenda" (Interview 17).

4.4 Religion in External Affairs, Conflict Resolution and Peacebuilding

Religions and faith communities are regarded by the interviewees as agents of universal values that can contribute to the social vision of a peaceful and more just world order. A 75-year-old MEP said that those common values, having their roots in universality and respect for others, express an embodied Western culture even for those who have no belief at all, and that is where the real "power" of Europe is hidden. One of the religious representatives noted in that regard (Interview 28):

> If we agree on the basic presumption that the European Union is *a community of values*, these values have to be developed and cultivated in society. They should not only be declared in a Treaty and then forgotten. Religions, churches, and faith communities can contribute in the living of values and in stimulating ethical reflection in a society; and that is something that the EU would expect from them, I think. Building common values (respect, tolerance) has a continuation and goes hand in hand with building inclusive societies of justice and solidarity. It is just expressed with different language.

According to the interviewees, it is the instrumentalization or the misinterpretation of religion that leads to controversy and conflict. They claim that the lust for power — ideological or political — has been making religion "a kind of flag", a potential resource or framing of violence. In countries like Iraq, Syria, or Yemen, religion can be seen as a driver; there is always a religious narrative justification for people to mobilize. Even when religion is associated with political violence though, it is very difficult to judge which is the independent and which is the dependent variable. "Does religion constitute the only motive? Is it the root cause? It is hard to distinguish whether it is the religious agenda or the fact that religion is used as an argument among others to gain control of resources. We have to look at each case separately and to collect a lot of data," suggested a policy advisor on foreign affairs (Interview 1). The representative of Eurodiaconia noted that, during the last decade, it has been "an abusive form of religion" that came to the fore through a series of traumatic events, leading to the misconception of religions as agents of violence.

Religious actors are considered among these actors that are present at all stages of a conflict resolution. Being familiar with the local reality, they are aware of any developments on the ground that might lead to conflict situations and, therefore, they have a pivotal role in developing early warning mechanisms in terms of conflict prevention. Their inclusivity in the consultation analysis procedure could enhance "pre-emptive peacebuilding" (Interview 23), which derives from a universal ethical imperative to avoid the use of force in the resolution of a conflict whenever possible. The second level of their contribution to peacebuilding processes is the direct provision of humanitarian assistance, development assistance, and social services (education, healthcare), while the third level is consisted of their mediation efforts and their subsequent work in post-conflict reconstruction and reconciliation.

Religion also can be used, potentially, in healing of memories or past divisions, while religious leaders always have played an important role in transitional justice transformation. On the one hand, the major world religions promote the principles of mercy, forgiveness, and justice, which are facilitating elements in the process of reconciliation. On the other hand, from a more pragmatic point of view, religious communities are usually communities of trust and confidence that have long-term experiences in bridge-building. The reunification of Germany and the role that religion played in South Africa's Truth and Reconciliation Commission are examples that "there is a phase into reconciliation, transition into peace, that would necessitate all actors to be involved" (Interview 14). The interviewees emphasized the need of religious actors to be included in the political dialogue even in cases where a conflict lacks a religious dimension, since they can contribute constructively as "peace-building initiators" (Interview 17) or "middle players in mediation" (Interview 3), with the mute advantage to be regarded as "useful arbiters without invested interest" (Interview 27) or neutral actors that are equally respected by both conflicting parties.

Churches had been a crucial component regarding the alleviation of oppression from authoritarian regimes in the past. The Baha'i representatives pointed out, though, that peace-making is not just about putting the democratic structures back in place. It is a much more profound process in which religion has a central role to play with reference to the change of attitudes and behavioral patterns, both at individual and societal level. Religious representatives agree on the fact that *peace* should be conceived and addressed as a positive, comprehensive concept that encompasses more than the absence of war and violence. As the EKD interviewee mentioned, "the promotion of freedom, the elimination of needs, and the respect of cultural diversity, along with the prevention of use of violence, are critical aspects in that regard" (Interview 25). An "authentic" peace policy thus presupposes: 1) developing a people-centered approach, based on the idea of human dignity, and 2) recognizing the need for a broader approach to sustainable peace and human security that is not only limited to military responses, but goes beyond that. This is the link to promoting *justice,* which is another key principle; there should be an integral approach of human justice, socio-economic justice and environmental-ecological justice (Interviews 23–24).

Religions have both dynamics as the vast majority of interviewees claimed — they can either play a part in fueling conflict or in influencing those concepts of justice and leading to renewed relations on the basis of mutual understanding and respect. They therefore need to fulfill certain criteria in order to form a common ground for "a cosmopolitan vision of peace" and that is to acknowledge that any claims of exclusivity need to be avoided and liberate themselves from blind imitation and superstition. The societal changes bring about great responsibility on religious leaders at global level. A Commission official indicated that "it has taken us hundreds of years and a lot of violence to acknowledge that religious texts are not set in stone; for it also means that we need religious actors putting those texts into a context of people nowadays" (Interview 4), and outlined the importance not to neglect the training and education of future religious leaders. The representatives of Pax Christi International noted, in addition, that in many conflicts, like in Northern Ireland or the Balkans, religious leaders are called to speak out not only to defend their people, but at the same time to help them overcome the divisions that might separate them with "the others".

"Religion should be part of the solution and not part of the problem" (Interview 29), and that is why it needs to get integrated into the EU external policy framework. The policy advisor on foreign affairs put it this way (Interview 1):

> There are strong conflicts currently taking place in some of our neighborhood countries (Middle East, Northern Africa) and, whether we want it or not, the religious factor should be put on the table. From the EU perspective, there is not much to do at strategic level. However, we could contribute in pacifying and stabilizing our neighborhood through financial support and capacity-building, with a view to empowering the people on the local level who are working on mediation and bridge-building.

One of the participating MEPs, with sixteen years of Parliamentary experience, added that developing a religious understanding is translated into getting greater credibility, especially with reference to the external policies. As she explained, religious literacy is helpful in world affairs as a tool for understanding ourselves and understanding the others. The engagement with religious actors and faith-based organizations, as part of the civil society fabric, at the EU external policy level also is depicted in their cooperation with the EEAS in the fields of relief and development work. Religious representatives acknowledged that it is not rare for the EU officials, before visiting a country, to try to get in contact with the religious authorities of that country and exchange views on the local situation, showing trust on their observations. However, some of the EU policy advisors on foreign affairs, security, and defense, cautioned that there should be a distinction about how involved the religious actors actually should be on a diplomatic mission. "Religions could have a complementary, advisory role, but I see no need to include religious representatives in a diplomatic delegation, it could be seen as rather provocative—like a 'crusade'" (Interview 10).

5 Concluding Remarks and Discussion

In a world transforming rapidly into a global neighborhood, the ever-growing awareness that all people share in common the worldwide risks and opportunities, without time-bound constraints, makes "both politics and religion act in the same place: that of human uncertainty" (Bauman 2014, 72). Ulrich Beck argued that what differentiates the social experience in the fragile times of Second Modernity is that there are no longer any given normative responses to address the anxiety that the unknown is causing (Tsironis 2018, 174). His social theory approaches religions as value systems of reference that give meaning and context to the social action and interplay, both at the local and the global level, and that can mobilize people to jointly address the global challenges.

Most of the interviewees conceive the renewed visibility of religion within the European political context as the result of the global geopolitical and social transformations of recent decades. As Fox points out, it is not that religion has become increasingly important as an influential factor in international relations since the new millennium, but there is definitely a "tectonic shift" in how we think about religion in IR ever since (Fox 2020). In a globally interconnected world, where people are called to "deal with the otherness of the other" (Beck et al. 2014, 210) and individuals are expected to seek biographical solutions to systemic contradictions (Beck 1992a, 137), religious actors are called to remind politicians about the need of assuring *organized* transformations. Both the EU political and religious representatives acknowledge that religion has the task to be constructive in the society and within the world context; it is important to raise ethical questions and to stimulate open-minded discussions on the basis of "metamorphosis of European politics" (see Beck 2016).

There is no doubt that, over the last twenty years, the voice of religions in world affairs is not only heard in the sphere of noble partnerships. The association of religion with extremism, the escalating violence in the name of faith at global level and the instrumentalization of the religious factor in political debates, they have all indicated the ambiguous participation of religions on global politics. Even when religion is associated with political violence, though, it is difficult to identify the causal relationship between the two variables, as some of the interviewees underlined. Korzec, in 1993, recognized human rights as a "global religion" that one would be free to either adopt or reject, focusing primarily on their institutional dimension. In today's turbulent world, however, the continuing human rights violations in the name of religion reveal that the real challenge remains the global faith in a dignified, well-protected life for everyone (De Gaay Fortman 2011).

Religious freedom has been one of the most distinctive hallmarks of the identity of contemporary Europe and EU institutions offer collectively a robust political affirmation of, and formal framework of legal protection for, freedom of religion or belief rights (Schirrmacher and Chaplin 2016). Foret (2017, 4) says that "freedom of religion and belief is the dominant repertoire of action in the contemporary political handling of religion under the aegis of human rights." Political and religious representatives jointly admit that there is a very close relationship between the concerns expressed in world religions and the human rights agenda, and that is important for the years to come to connect human rights officers and religious actors around this agenda, and particularly in articulating freedom of religion or belief. In that regard, they suggest that EU officials should be more aware and develop a deeper understanding of the tensions around religious freedom, and not speak blindly a human rights and rule of law language, while religious actors should be more self-introspective and open to reassessing their contribution to this area.

The European Parliament has adopted numerous resolutions in defense of the principles of religious diversity and pluralism, and stressed the significance of a constant, comprehensive dialogue with churches, faith communities, non-confessional and philosophical organizations (Pasikowska-Schnass 2018). Some of the interviewees remarked that it is crucial "not to box the Article 17 just in the corner of freedom of religion or belief." This dialogue with the European institutions is not on the issue of religion per se, but a consultation from religious and humanist actors on priority EU policies. Religious representatives expressed the belief that enhancing religious freedom and embodying the religious perspective at the EU policy level could reinforce the European Union's credibility as a global actor and the reliability of its external policies. Political representatives, on the contrary, keep a realpolitik perspective and suggest that religion should be part of the equation but maintain a subsidiary, complementary role and not being directly integrated in the EU policy-making process. Mandaville and Silvestri (2015) note that encouraging the engagement with the religious factor in diplomacy and foreign policy would include, among else, two developments: 1) moving away from a model whereby religion is viewed as being relevant only to certain specialized objectives, such as the international advancement of religious freedom, and 2) becoming more conscious of its broader significance as a societal force in world affairs.

Regarding the religion-diplomacy nexus, Bilde (2015, 158) states that religion constitutes "a central policy challenge that is simultaneously difficult to handle and impossible to ignore." As Germain explains: "Religion has become a rather 'exotic' element in the mind of many of our senior civil servants [...] For highly secularized people who have downplayed religion for a very long time, there is now a danger in *over*stating the role of religion. The strategic imperative is 'fine-tuning' our understanding of this subtle-reality" (Germain 2014, 72; 2020). The interviewees emphasized the need of strengthening the religious literacy of EU officials and cultivating the skills that will help them escape the narrative trap of "us versus them" in situations where the religious component matters. Religion is not any more considered "outdated" for international politics; the engagement with religion and the whole spectrum of civil society, cultural, religious actors is rather seen as a "diplomatic must" (see also Perchoc 2017; Foret 2017).

Religion also is seen by many of the EU representatives as an important part of developing societal dynamics. Beckford (2008, 24) writes that "religion is 'real' in the sense that it affects the lives of people and societies," while Thomas (2005, 24) argues that religion is not just "a body of beliefs", but a "community of believers". Considering the changing religious landscape worldwide and the rising number of people for whom religion is an integral part of their identity, there is a greater acknowledgement that the religious factor should be put on the table. The vast majority of the interviewees admit that religions have both dynamics; they can either lead to controversy and conflict or play a critical role from mediation to reconciliation processes and healing of traumas. Most of the EU representatives recognize that religious actors could really have a considerable added-value being part of peacebuilding negotiations, based on the religious background of people, the moral authority and prominence that religious communities have and their reliability as partners on the ground. Either depicting religion as a political trend, a fundamental human right, a driver of bridging gaps in modern pluralistic societies or a potential agent of violence, the results show that the majority of the interviewees emphasize the need for "inclusivity" of the religious actors to the EU political dialogue. Religious communities are identified as important civil society players that have the dynamics to mobilize people to address common social challenges (i.e. refugee crisis, fear of the other, social inequality, climate change, sustainable development) and therefore, faith-based institutions are seen as important future partners for the EU's action on the international scene.

The present research study is coordinated with the international discourse on the renewed interest of political science to religion, and it aims to enhance an interdisciplinary, long-term, and thorough research on the field.

Acknowledgements

This project has received funding from the Hellenic Foundation for Research and Innovation (HFRI) and the General Secretariat for Research and Technology (GSRT), under the PhD Fellowship Grant No 2401.

References

Annicchino, Pasquale. 2014. "Is the European Union going deep on democracy and religious freedom?" *The Review of Faith & International Affairs* 12 (3): 33–40.
Bauman, Zygmunt. 2014. "Jerusalem Versus Athens Revisited." In *Ulrich Beck: Pioneer in Cosmopolitan Sociology and Risk Society*, edited by Ulrich Beck, 71–75. Heidelberg: Springer Cham.
Beck, Ulrich. 1987. "The Anthropological Shock: Chernobyl and the Contours of the Risk Society." *Berkeley Journal of Sociology* 32: 153–65.
Beck, Ulrich. 1992a. *Risk Society: Towards a New Modernity*. London: Sage.
Beck, Ulrich. 1992b. "From Industrial Society to the Risk Society: Questions of Survival, Social Structure and Ecological Enlightenment." *Theory, Culture & Society* 9 (1): 97–123.
Beck, Ulrich. 1996. "World Risk Society as Cosmopolitan Society? Ecological Questions in a Framework of Manufactured Uncertainties." *Theory, Culture & Society* 13 (4): 1–32.
Beck, Ulrich. 1999. *World Risk Society*. Cambridge/Malden, MA: Polity Press.
Beck, Ulrich. 2009. "Critical Theory of World Risk Society: A Cosmopolitan Vision." *Constellations* 16 (1): 3–22.
Beck, Ulrich. 2010. *A God of One's Own: Religion's Capacity for Peace and Potential for Violence*. Cambridge/Malden, MA: Polity Press.
Beck, Ulrich. 2014. "Incalculable Futures: World Risk Society and Its Social and Political Implications." In *Ulrich Beck: Pioneer in Cosmopolitan Sociology and Risk Society*, edited by Ulrich Beck, 79–89. Heidelberg: Springer.
Beck, Ulrich. 2016. *The Metamorphosis of the World*. Cambridge/Malden, MA: Polity Press.

Beck, Ulrich, and Edgar Grande. 2010. "Varieties of Second Modernity: The Cosmopolitan Turn in Social and Political Theory and Research." *British Journal of Sociology* 61 (3): 409–43.

Beck, Ulrich, Johannes Wilms, and Michael Pollak. 2014. *Conversations with Ulrich Beck*. Cambridge/Malden, MA: Polity Press.

Beckford, James A. 2008. *Social Theory and Religion*. Cambridge: Cambridge University Press.

Bellin, Eva. 2008. "Faith in Politics: New Trends in the Study of Religion and Politics." *World Politics* 60 (2): 315–47.

Beyer, Peter. 2013. *Religion in the Context of Globalization: Essays on Concept, Form and Political Implication*, 1st ed. Oxon/N.Y.: Routledge.

Bielefeldt, Heiner, Nazila Ghanea, and Michael Wiener. 2016. *Freedom of Religion or Belief: An International Law Commentary*. Oxford: Oxford University Press.

Bilde, Merete. 2015. "Religion and Foreign Policy: A Brussels Perspective." In *Faith, Freedom, and Foreign Policy: Challenges for the Transatlantic Community*, edited by Michael Barnett, Clifford Bob, Nora Fisher Onar, Anne Jenichen, Michael Leigh, and Lucian N. Leustean, 156–60. Washington, DC: Transatlantic Academy.

Bokern, Friedrich. 2009. "Interreligious Peacebuilding: A New Engagement of Religious Actors in European Politics?" *European View* 8 (1): 107–15.

Bolvin, Jean B. 2013. "The European External Action Service and Freedom of Religion or Belief." In *Freedom of Religion or Belief in Foreign Policy: Which One?*, edited by Pasquale Annicchino, 48–51. San Domenico di Fiesole, Italy: European University Institute.

Chaplin, Jonathan, and Gary Wilton, eds. 2016. *God and the EU: Faith in the European Project*. Oxon/N.Y.: Routledge.

Council of the European Union. 2013. "EU Guidelines on the Promotion and Protection of Freedom of Religion or Belief." https://eeas.europa.eu/sites/eeas/files/137585.pdf, retrieved 16 April 2020.

Dawson, Stephen. 2015. "The Religious Resurgence: Problems and Opportunities for International Relations Theory". In *Nations Under God: The Geopolitics of Faith in the Twenty-First Century*, edited by Luke M. Herrington, Alasdair McKay, and Jeffrey Haynes, 23–29. Bristol: E-International Relations Publishing.

De Gaay Fortman, Bas. 2011. "Religion and human rights: A dialectical relationship." http://www.e-ir.info/2011/12/05/religion-and-human-rights-a-dialectical-relationship/, retrieved 16 October 2020.

De Jong, Dennis. 2013. "The Role of the European Parliament in Helping to Protect Freedom of Religion or Belief via the EU's External Relations." In *Freedom of Religion or Belief in Foreign Policy: Which One?*, edited by Pasquale Annicchino, 43–47. San Domenico di Fiesole, Italy: European University Institute.

European Union: Council of the European Union. 2017. *Council Conclusions on the Democratic Republic of Congo*, December 11, 2017, 15633/17, https://data.consilium.europa.eu/doc/document/ST-15633-2017-INIT/en/pdf, retrieved 19 July 2020.

European Union: Council of the European Union. 2018. *Council Conclusions on the Integrated Approach to External Conflicts and Crises*, January 22, 2018, 5413/18, https://data.consilium.europa.eu/doc/document/ST-5413-2018-INIT/en/pdf, retrieved 19 July 2020.

European Union: European Parliament. 2016. *European Parliament Resolution on the Systematic Mass Murder of Religious Minorities by the so-called "ISIS/Daesh"*, February 4, 2016, P8_TA(2016)0051, https://www.europarl.europa.eu/doceo/document/TA-8-2016-0051_EN.html, retrieved 19 July 2020.

European Union: European Parliament 2017. *European Parliament Resolution on Addressing Shrinking Civil Society Space in Developing Countries*, October 3, 2017, P8_TA(2017)0365, https://www.europarl.europa.eu/doceo/document/TA-8-2017-0365_EN.html, retrieved 19 July 2020.

Fahy, John, and Jeffrey Haynes. 2018. "Introduction: Interfaith on the World Stage." *The Review of Faith & International Affairs* 16 (3): 1–8.

Foret, François. 2015. *Religion and Politics in the European Union: The Secular Canopy* (Series: Cambridge Studies in Social Theory, Religion and Politics). Cambridge: Cambridge University Press.

Foret, François. 2017. "How the European External Action Service Deals with Religion through Religious Freedom." *EU diplomacy paper* 07/2017. College of Europe: Department of EU International Relations and Diplomacy Studies.

Forlenza, Rosario, and S. Bryan Turner. 2019. "Das Abendland: The Politics of Europe's Religious Borders." *Critical Research on Religion* 7 (1): 6–23.

Fox, Jonathan. 2001. "Religion as an Overlooked Element in International Relations." *International Studies Review* 3 (3): 53–74.

Fox, Jonathan. 2006. "The Multiple Impacts of Religion on International Relations: Perceptions and Reality." *Politique étrangère* 4: 1059–71.

Fox, Jonathan. 2020. "Understanding Global Trends in Religion and Politics: An Interview with Jonathan Fox." Interview by Robert Joustra. *Religion & Diplomacy*, November 16, 2020. https://religionanddiplomacy.org.uk/2020/11/16/understanding-global-trends-in-religion-and-politics-an-interview-with-jonathan-fox/, retrieved 16 November 2020.

Fox, Jonathan, and Shmuel Sandler. 2004. *Bringing Religion into International Relations*. (Series: Culture and Religion in International Relations). Oxon/N.Y.: Routledge.

Fox, Jonathan, and A. Nukhet Sandal. 2016. "Integrating Religion into International Relations Theory." In *Routledge Handbook of Religion and Politics*, 2nd ed., edited by Jeffrey Haynes, 270–83. Oxon/N.Y.: Routledge.

Germain, Eric. 2014. "On French Foreign Policy and Religion: Interview by Judd Birdsall." *The Review of Faith and International Affairs* 12 (3): 72–4.

Germain, Eric. 2020. "Is French Laïcité State Atheism or Religious Freedom? An Interview with Eric Germain." Interview by Tobias Cremer. *Religion & Diplomacy*, March 17, 2020. https://religionanddiplomacy.org.uk/2020/03/17/is-french-laicite-state-atheism-or-religious-freedom-an-interview-with-eric-germain/, retrieved 30 March 2020.

Grim, Brian J., Greg Clark, and E. Robert Snyder. 2014. "Is Religious Freedom Good for Business?: A Conceptual and Empirical Analysis." *Interdisciplinary Journal of Research on Religion* 10 (4), article 4.

Haynes, Jeffrey. 2007. *An Introduction to International Relations and Religion*, 1st ed. Harlow, Essex: Pearson Longman.

Haynes, Jeffrey. 2014. "Faith-Based Organizations at the European Union and United Nations: From Marginalization to Significance." In *Towards a Postsecular International Politics: New Forms of Community, Identity and Power*, edited by Luca Mavelli, and Fabio Petito, 197–217. New York: Palgrave Macmillan.

Haynes, Jeffrey, and Anja Hennig. eds. 2011. *Religious Actors in the Public Sphere: Means, Objectives and Effects*, 1st ed. Oxon/N.Y.: Routledge.

Ivanescu, Carolina. 2010. "Politicised religion and the religionisation of politics." *Culture and Religion: An Inter-disciplinary Journal* 11 (4): 309–25.

Jenichen, Anne. 2019. "A Transatlantic Secular Divide? The Representation of Religion in EU and US Foreign Policy." *Foreign Policy Analysis* 15: 451–69.

Katzenstein, Peter J. 2006. "Multiple modernities as limits to European secularization?" In *Religion in an expanding Europe*, edited by Timothy A. Byrnes, and Peter J. Katzenstein, 1–33. Cambridge: Cambridge University Press.

Leustean, Lucian N. eds. 2013. *Representing Religion in the European Union. Does God Matter?* Oxon/ N.Y.: Routledge.

Leustean, Lucian N. 2016. "The Representation of Religion in the European Union." In *God and the EU: Faith in the European Project*, edited by Jonathan Chaplin, and Gary Wilton, 175–90. Oxon/ N.Y.: Routledge.

Leustean, Lucian N., and T.S. John Madeley. eds. 2010. *Religion, Politics and Law in the European Union*, 1st ed. Oxon/N.Y.: Routledge.

Mandaville, Peter, and Sara Silvestri. 2015. "Integrating Religious Engagement into Diplomacy: Challenges and Opportunities." *Issues in Governance Studies* 67, Washington, DC: Brookings Institution.

May, Samantha, K. Erin Wilson, Claudia Baumgart-Ochse, and Faiz Sheikh. 2014. "The Religious as Political and the Political as Religious: Globalisation, Post-Secularism and the Shifting Boundaries of the Sacred." *Politics, Religion & Ideology* 15 (3): 331–46.

Nelsen, Brent F., L. James Guth, and Brian Highsmith. 2011. "Does Religion Still Matter? Religion and Public Attitudes toward Integration in Europe." *Politics and Religion* 4: 1–26.

Nelsen, Brent F., and L. James Guth. 2015. "Religion in the European Union: The Forgotten Factor." In *Nations Under God: The Geopolitics of Faith in the Twenty-First Century*, edited by Luke M. Herrington, Alasdair McKay, and Jeffrey Haynes, 203–10. Bristol: E-International Relations Publishing.

Pasikowska-Schnass, Magdalena. 2018. "Article 17 TFEU: The EU Institutions' Dialogue with Churches, Religious and Philosophical Organizations." EPRS | European Parliamentary Research Service, November 2018.

Perchoc, Philippe. 2017. "Religion and the EU's External Policies: Increasing Engagement". (In-Depth Analysis). EPRS | European Parliamentary Research Service, December 2017.

Petito, Fabio, and Pavlos Hatzopoulos. 2003. *Religion in International Relations: The Return from Exile*. New York: Palgrave Macmillan.

Philpott, Daniel. 2002. "The Challenge of September 11 to Secularism in International Relations." *World Politics* 55: 66–95.

Philpott, Daniel. 2009. "Has the Study of Global Politics Found Religion?" *Annual Review of Political Science* 12: 183–202.

Possamai-Inesedy, Alphia. 2002. "Beck's Risk Society and Giddens' Search for Ontological Security: A Comparative Analysis between the Anthroposophical Society and the Assemblies of God." *Australian Religion Studies Review* 15 (1): 44–56.

Sandal, Nukhet A., and Patrick James. 2010. "Religion and International Relations Theory: Towards a Mutual Understanding." *European Journal of International Relations* 17 (1): 3–25.

Sandal, Nukhet A., and Jonathan Fox. 2013. *Religion in International Relations Theory: Interactions and possibilities*. Oxon/N.Y.: Routledge.

Schirrmacher, Thomas, and Jonathan Chaplin. 2016. "European Religious Freedom and the EU." In *God and the EU: Faith in the European Project*, edited by Jonathan Chaplin, and Gary Wilton, 151–74. Oxon/N.Y.: Routledge.

Shah, Timothy S. 2012. "Introduction: Religion and World Affairs: Blurring the Boundaries." In *Rethinking Religion and World Affairs*, 1st ed., edited by Timothy S. Shah, Alfred Stepan, and D. Monica Toft, 1–12. Oxford: Oxford University Press.

Shah, Timothy S., Alfred Stepan, and D. Monica Toft, eds. 2012. *Rethinking Religion and World Affairs*, 1st ed. Oxford: Oxford University Press.

Snyder, Jack, eds. 2011. *Religion and International Relations Theory*.(Series: Religion, Culture, and Public Life). New York: Columbia University Press.

Sørensen, Mads P., and Allan Christiansen. 2013. *Ulrich Beck: An Introduction to the Theory of Second Modernity and the Risk Society*, 1st ed. Oxon/NY: Routledge.

Thomas, Scott M. 2005. *The Global Resurgence of Religion and the Transformation of International Relations: The Struggle for the Soul of the Twenty-First Century*. New York: Palgrave Macmillan.

Toft, Monica D. 2012. "Religion and International Relations Theory." In *Handbook of International Relations*, edited by Walter Carlsnaes, Thomas Risse, and Beth A Simmons, 673–91. Oxford: Oxford University Press.

Toft, Monica D., Daniel Philpott, and S. Timothy Shah, eds. 2011. *God's Century: Resurgent Religion and Global Politics*. New York: W.W. Norton & Company, Inc.

Tsironis, Christos N. 2018. *Religion and Society in Second Modernity*. Arguments and Debates in Ulrich Beck's Theory. Thessaloniki: Barbounakis.

Tsironis, Christos N., and Chrysa Almpani. 2020. " 'Uprooted' Religion in a Cosmopolitan World: A "Second Round" for Religion in Second Modernity?" *Sociology and Society* 5 (1): 2–18.

UN General Assembly: Human Rights Council. 2017. *Report of the Special Rapporteur on freedom of religion and belief*, January 17, 2017, A/HRC/34/50, https://undocs.org/A/HRC/34/50, retrieved 19 July 2020.

Wessels, David. 2013. "Religion and Globalization." In *An Introduction to International Relations and Religion*, 2nd ed., edited by Jeffrey Haynes, 323–39. Oxon/N.Y.: Routledge.

Index

A.S. Narayana Deekshitulu v. the State of A.P 48
Abdur Rahman v. The Secretary to Government 45
administrator 106, 220
advocacy for religious freedom 63, 209, 211–213
affiliation 21, 83, 85, 89, 90, 92, 95, 107, 139, 152, 155, 156, 169, 177, 183, 277, 278
Africa 15, 92, 280, 288, 289
agency 5, 6, 109, 115, 118, 124, 125–127, 133, 135, 139, 143, 144, 147, 151, 242
agreements of recognition (*intese*) 236
Alevi community 123, 125, 133, 143
Alevi culture 6, 124–127, 129, 131, 133, 139, 146
Alevi *dedes* 6, 125, 126, 133, 134, 143, 146
Alevi organization 125, 126, 129, 138, 142, 144, 146, 147
Alevism 6, 123–129, 132, 133, 135–137, 139, 140, 142, 144, 145
Algeria 66, 70, 75, 89
All India Muslim Personal Law Board (AIMPLB) 40, 43, 47, 49
Ammerman, Nancy 5, 6, 84, 108, 109, 110, 113
anti-religious sentiment 73
Arab-Muslim identity 74, 65
Article 9 of the European Convention on Human Rights (ECHR) 87, 94, 96, 224, 226, 283
Asad, Talal 107–110, 123, 131, 252
Asia 15, 92
assemblages 13, 16, 17, 19, 27, 28, 131
assertive secularism 60, 78
assimilation 129, 144, 145, 147
Association for Religion Data Archives 249
Astley, Jeff 6, 155, 157, 158, 169
atheism 6, 65, 74, 153, 155–158, 162, 164, 166, 169–171
Atheist Union of Greece 85, 95
Austria 4, 9, 14, 23, 25, 27
authoritarian *laïcité* 5, 62–64, 78
autonomy 6, 39, 60, 107, 116, 124, 126, 151, 153, 154, 157, 159, 162, 164–167, 170, 220, 283

Baha'i International Community 276
ban on religious garments and symbols 21, 22

Baptist World Alliance 209
Bauman, Zygmunt 8, 290
Beck, Ulrich 8, 271–275, 290
Beckford, James A 1, 3, 5, 84, 152, 177, 212, 292
Belgium 4, 9, 14, 23–27
Berger, Peter L. 14, 116, 151, 152, 168
Bible 153, 188
Bruce, Steve 14
Bulgaria 4, 9, 14, 23–25, 27
Burchardt, Marian 4, 13, 15, 16, 24, 37
bureaucratization 8, 64, 229
burqa ban 4, 14, 19, 23, 25, 27

Canada 9, 27, 111, 113–115, 117
Canadian Muslim organization 108, 114, 115
Casanova, José 15, 19, 86, 212
Catholic Church 20, 160, 166, 212, 221, 222, 225, 228, 229, 233
chaplain 7, 175, 178–187, 191, 222, 223
Charter of Fundamental Rights and Freedoms 175, 177
child marriage 241, 244, 249, 259
China 88, 199, 206, 209, 212
Christian-Democrats' (DC) 223, 224, 226–230, 232, 235, 236
citizens' right 53, 105
Citizenship and Immigration Canada (CIC) 111
citizenship 4, 35, 42, 47, 54, 59, 68, 97, 105, 106, 108, 110–113, 115, 117, 118, 145, 153, 160, 166
civic education 97
Coalition of Progressive Canadian Muslim Organizations (CPCMO) 114, 115
Coalition of Progressive Muslim Organizations (CPMO) 108, 113
collective right 224, 283
Commission of EU Catholic Bishops' Conferences (COMECE) 276, 277, 283
concordat 221, 223–229, 232, 235
Conference of the European Churches (CEC) 276
conflict resolution 272, 286, 287
conflict 2, 4, 7, 8, 37, 44, 60, 88, 91, 106, 113, 115, 126, 128, 136, 137, 147, 167, 191, 187, 191, 201, 202, 220, 221–224, 235, 236, 252, 263, 271–274, 278, 281, 282, 286, 287, 289, 292

constitutional law   4, 53, 241
Convention for the Elimination of All Forms of Discrimination Against Women (CEDAW)   8, 241–257, 259, 261, 262
converts   69, 184
convict   7, 177, 178–180, 182–191
couple   90, 128, 207
COVID-19 context   25, 133
cross-national analysis   3, 7, 8
cultural marker   123, 135
curtailing religious freedoms   16
Czech prison system   177–180
Czech Republic   9, 175, 177, 178, 180, 183, 185–188, 190

democratic society   97, 114, 281
Denmark   4, 9, 14, 23, 25, 27, 275
developing countries   9, 281
dignity   24, 47, 48, 51, 113, 124, 161, 167, 274, 288
diplomacy   276, 282, 283, 291, 292
discrimination   2, 3, 5, 37, 41, 46, 51, 52, 71, 112, 129, 130, 144, 199, 201, 205, 212, 243, 247, 253, 274
disestablishment   151
disrespect to human rights   7, 170
diversity management   21
divorce   35, 37–41, 46, 49–54, 72, 223
Dobbelaere, Karel   1, 5, 59–62, 86
Dressler, Markus   6, 115, 128, 129, 131, 132, 147
Durham, Cole W.   151

Eastern Europe   92
economic development   151
educational context   5, 229
Egypt   65, 76, 77, 212, 262
empirical analysis   9, 153
empowerment   05, 145, 147, 262
Ennahda party   73–77
equal citizenship   153
equality   5, 15, 41, 47, 48, 51, 60, 63, 67, 69, 71, 72, 110, 113, 115, 152, 155, 164, 243, 252, 256, 261, 262
ethnicity   251, 254, 271
ethnographic observation   18, 179, 260
EU policy-making   285, 291
EU political dialogue   8, 292
European Commission   275, 276, 279, 280, 282, 286

European Convention on Human Rights   129, 283, 279
European Court of Human Rights   1, 23, 25, 26, 129
European institution   280, 291
European Parliament   276, 277, 281, 291
European Union (EU)   8, 14, 281, 282, 285–287, 291
European Union external policy   272, 289
European Union policy-making   272, 283, 284, 285, 291,
exclusivism   20, 153, 155, 156, 158, 162, 163, 164, 166, 169
exercise of power   7, 176
exercise of religious freedoms   13, 18, 175, 177, 178
experiences of religious freedom   178, 191

Finke, Roger   2, 3, 14, 15, 107, 118, 151, 168, 197–203, 209, 212, 214, 215, 258
Foucault, Michel   7, 111, 118, 176, 191
Fox, Jonathan   1, 3, 15, 151, 168, 176, 197, 198n, 199, 200, 203, 214, 218, 271, 272, 273, 290
France   4, 9, 14, 20, 21–28, 60n, 105, 117, 255
Francis, Leslie   6, 152, 154, 157, 158, 169
freedom of conscience   49, 60, 67, 68, 69, 70, 78, 112, 176, 226, 233
functional differentiation   5, 18, 60

gender equality   8, 41, 48, 57, 67, 71, 72, 113, 243, 261, 262
gender inequality   8, 114, 242, 243, 249, 250, 251, 257, 260, 261
gendered spiritualities   119
geography   4, 13, 14, 16
Gill, Anthony   2, 15, 151
Giordan, Giuseppe   1, 5, 83–86, 152, 153, 157, 168, 220, 253
global actor   9, 284, 291
global religious freedom   3, 7, 206, 207, 215
global restrictions on religion   206, 208, 249
globalization   273, 278
Gonella-Casaroli commission   223
Government Regulation of Religion Index (GRI)   249, 258, 264
government restrictions   203, 204, 258
Greece   1, 5, 9, 83, 85–88, 88n, 89–91, 91n, 93–97

INDEX

Greek educational system 5, 83, 87, 92, 96, 98
Greek Orthodox Church 5, 90, 94, 96
Grim, Brian 201, 258, 286
Guidelines on the Promotion and Protection of Freedom of Religion or Belief 275

harassment 182, 212
Hick, John 6, 152, 155
Hindu 37, 39, 41, 43, 45–48, 54n, 212, 215, 249, 255–258, 264
human rights organizations 206, 208, 210, 215, 221
human rights regime 16
human rights 8, 23, 25, 45, 83, 87, 95, 97n, 129n, 152, 154, 157, 159, 164–168, 170, 206, 208–211, 244, 252, 271, 276, 279, 283, 284, 286, 291
humiliation 182

identity marker 21, 125, 126, 133
identity politics 36, 123, 131
imprisonment 66, 91n, 175n, 178n, 181, 188
inclusivism 6, 151, 153, 155, 156, 158, 162–164, 169
independent judiciary 7, 107, 118, 197, 198, 202–205, 214, 215
India 4, 9, 35–54
Indian Supreme Court 4, 40, 42, 51, 52
inequality 8, 114, 242, 243, 249–251, 257, 261, 292
Insegnamento della Religione Cattolica (IRC) 220–236
institutionalization 132, 140, 146, 147, 178, 186, 191, 235, 236, 246
interfaith dialogue 152
Intergroup on FoRB and Religious Tolerance 275, 276
internal secularization 2
international relations 1, 125, 271–273, 277, 279, 290
International Religious Freedom Act 1, 16, 206, 211, 215
interreligious learning 152
interreligious perspective 6, 153–158, 162–170
Iraq 76n, 77, 253, 287
Islamist movement 64, 65, 73
Islamist party 5, 75, 77, 78

Italy 6, 8, 9, 23, 24, 154, 156, 158, 163, 167, 168, 171, 220, 222, 228, 232, 236

jihad(struggle) 64, 71
judgment 25, 26, 37, 39–47, 48n, 50, 54, 87, 115, 149
judicial system 3, 38, 43, 108, 151
judicialization of politics 106, 107
judicialization of religion 4, 36, 52, 54
judicialization of religious freedom 6, 52n, 106, 107, 118, 157, 161, 165–167
judicialization 4, 6, 8, 10, 36, 52, 52n, 54, 54n, 106, 107, 118, 125, 154, 157, 161, 162, 164, 165, 167, 170, 220, 222, 224, 227, 229, 230, 232, 234, 247, 236

Kemal, Mustafa 63, 64, 256
Kosmin, Barry A. 171
Kuru, Ahmet 3, 5, 15, 60, 63n, 256

laïcité 4, 5, 14, 19–23, 25, 27, 59–65, 67, 73, 74, 77, 78
law 1–5, 14, 18, 18n, 19–25, 27, 35, 35n, 37, 37n, 39, 40, 41, 41n, 45, 46, 48–54, 59, 60, 62, 67, 68, 68n, 69–71, 74, 78, 83, 86, 87, 89, 90, 97, 107, 110, 112, 113, 116, 139, 140, 143, 175, 177, 191, 201, 204, 220–223, 228, 229, 233, 235, 236, 241, 244, 245, 250, 252, 253, 256, 258, 260, 261, 265, 283, 284n, 291
Lebanon 77
legal pluralism 54
Libya 75n, 77
limitation of religious freedom 1, 52n, 69, 97, 198, 200
lived religion 6, 106, 108, 109, 110

Mahmood, Saba 43, 53, 110, 252, 263
McGuire, Meredith 6, 105, 108, 119
meaning of religious freedom 6, 7, 107, 124, 133, 151–154, 158, 162, 164, 166, 170, 171, 228
Middle East 15n, 92, 289
Mme. M. 105, 106, 117
mobilities 4, 13, 14, 16–20, 23, 26, 27
Mohd. Ahmed Khan v. Shah Bano Begum1985 AIR 945, 1985 SCR (3) 844.
Morocco 1, 70, 77, 105, 117
mosque 64, 66, 69, 74n, 77, 236, 256

multiculturalism   21, 110
multidimensionality of religious freedom   123, 153, 154
multiple modernities   15, 131
multiple secularities   15, 35
Muslim Canadian Congress (MCC)   108, 113–115
Muslim Personal Law   4, 35, 36, 40, 48, 50, 54
Muslim women   6, 20, 22, 25, 38–41, 41n, 43, 44, 46, 47, 47n, 51–53, 53n, 54, 105n, 106, 108, 113, 114, 118, 131, 261, 263

narrative identity   133, 133n, 134, 139, 141–143, 146, 147, 148
national identity   115, 117
niqab   6, 20, 23, 25, 74, 105, 105n, 106, 108, 112–118
no religion   83, 93, 152, 155–158, 168, 169
non-believing employee   180
non-confessional   280, 291
nondiscrimination   36, 152, 154
non-governmental organization (NGO)   17, 18, 26, 71, 209, 211–213, 252, 262
non-practicing Muslims   62, 70
normative intervention   106, 108, 110, 111, 118
normative order   128

Office of IRF   206, 207, 209, 211
open election   198, 202, 203, 205
oppression   41, 46, 53, 66, 114, 144, 189, 288
Optional Protocol (CEDAWOP)   241, 242, 246, 247, 248, 260, 261, 263
organization   2, 7, 8, 16, 17, 20, 22, 23, 40, 46, 48n, 53, 59, 61n, 66, 76, 77, 88n, 108, 109, 113–115, 125, 126, 129, 130, 135, 137–140, 142, 144, 146, 147, 175, 177–179, 191, 197–203, 203n, 204–216, 222, 227, 228, 242, 244, 252, 255, 262, 264, 275, 276, 279, 280, 281, 285, 289, 291
Orthodox Christian   88n, 91, 249
Orthodox Church   5, 69, 83, 89, 90, 91, 94, 249

Pace, Enzo   5, 84–86, 168
Palestine   77
passive secularism   5, 60, 61
peacebuilding   272, 276, 280, 286–288, 292
penitential system   7

perception   6, 7, 18, 37, 48, 114, 153, 154, 156–160, 163–170, 220, 224
personal choice   112
philosophical organization   280, 291
pilgrimage   66
pluralist society   6, 114, 152, 163
policy implementation   17, 229
policy-making   8, 126, 220, 271, 272, 281, 283–285, 291
policy-mobilities approach   4, 13, 14, 16–20, 23, 26, 27
political debate   114, 290
political rights   245, 252
political secularism   4, 153
politicization   x, 8, 221, 235
politics of religious freedom   106
politics   5, 8, 16, 18n, 36, 37, 39, 72, 73, 86n, 106, 107, 113, 123–126, 129–131, 136, 147, 153, 220, 227, 235, 252, 271–275, 277, 281, 282, 284, 290, 292
populism   19
post-communist countries   7, 175, 178
post-conflict condition   8, 288
Prakash v. Phulavati   46n
prayer   45, 66, 83, 96, 97, 138, 141, 156, 179, 183–188
prison   7, 20, 66, 71, 175–191
privatization of religion   14, 36
privilege   5, 111, 118, 245, 246
protecting religious freedoms   6, 70, 97, 140, 152, 164, 191, 198, 206, 207, 209, 210
Protection of Women from Domestic Violence Act (PWDAV)   52, 58
Public interest Litigation (PIL)   38, 39, 41–43, 46, 49, 51, 53, 54, 54n
public policy   84, 105, 106
public spaces   26, 70, 118, 167, 224
punishment   7, 27, 176, 181, 210

Quaker Council of European Affairs (QCEA)   276
Québec   4, 14, 20–23, 28
Québec's Council of Intercultural Relations   21
Quran   40, 43, 50, 64, 66, 67, 69n, 71, 105, 153

R. v.N.S.   105, 106
radicalization   113, 177, 190, 282

INDEX

rational choice theory   2
religion and human rights   8, 157, 283
Religion and State Project   3, 7, 198, 264
religion   2, 3, 4n, 6, 14, 18, 19, 26, 27, 36, 39, 41, 42, 44, 49, 49n, 54, 59–63, 64n, 65, 67–72, 75, 77, 78, 83, 84, 85n, 86, 88, 91, 91n, 93, 96, 97, 106, 108, 109, 116, 117, 125, 140, 143, 147, 155, 158, 162–165, 167–170, 175–177, 189, 191, 198–202, 206, 207, 210–213, 220, 224, 234n, 235, 243, 249, 251, 252, 254, 255, 257, 259, 262, 264, 271–273, 275–283, 284n, 285–293
religionization   6, 8, 123, 125, 130–133, 142, 146, 147, 271–293
religiosity   14, 83, 85n, 105, 117, 125, 131–133, 152, 153, 186, 187
religious communities   85, 114, 119, 131, 142, 143, 153, 228, 271, 278, 288
religious diversity   5, 7, 54, 83–85, 87, 89, 94, 98, 151–154, 156–158, 163–167, 169–171, 286
religious economy   2, 16
religious freedom measure   61, 153, 165, 168, 170, 201, 204–207, 249
religious freedom of a minority   50, 54
religious freedom   1–9, 13–16, 18, 19, 22, 26–28, 35–37, 41, 43, 45, 48, 52, 52n, 54, 59–62, 67, 73, 77, 78, 83, 84, 85n, 87, 88, 92, 93, 95, 96, 96n, 98, 105–108, 110, 111, 113, 118, 123–125, 129–133, 135, 143, 148, 151–172, 175–191, 197, 198, 202, 205–215, 220–229, 233–236, 241–244, 249, 259, 260, 272, 275, 283–286, 291, 292
religious militancy   72
religious minority   1, 3, 20, 21, 37, 67, 69, 70, 155, 157–162, 167, 168, 198, 201, 205, 206, 208, 210, 212, 215, 281, 283, 284n
religious pluralism   5, 6, 83, 84, 87, 92, 94, 151–155, 170, 171
religious practice   2, 6, 28, 46, 48, 66, 67, 69, 86, 92, 96, 106–111, 113–119, 124, 127, 129, 131, 132, 139, 145, 152, 179, 198, 199, 202, 210, 211, 214
religious truth-claim   6, 152–156, 162, 163, 165, 168–171
revolution   20, 59, 62, 63, 65, 67, 69–78
Richardson, James T.   1–4, 5, 8, 83, 106, 107, 108, 109, 111, 116, 118, 151, 168, 202, 220

Roman Catholicism   155, 170
rosary   183–185
rule of law   37, 39, 45, 52–54, 177, 283, 291

Sandberg, Russell   1, 2
Sarkissian, Ani   3, 168, 197, 200
Sarkozy government   23
Second Vatican Council   212, 223, 234
secular diffusion   16, 28
secular flows   18, 19
secular repression   244, 254
secular state   2, 4, 36, 52, 59, 60, 88, 212, 233
secularism   4, 5, 14, 15, 20, 22, 23, 36–39, 43, 45, 47, 48, 48n, 52–54, 59–62, 64, 65, 78, 86, 86n, 132, 153, 221, 230, 232, 236, 259
secularity   2, 4, 13–16, 18, 20n, 25, 26, 28, 86, 124–126, 130–132, 140
secularization   1–5, 13–15, 18, 20, 59–61, 61n, 62, 63, 77, 78, 83–86, 86n, 90, 91, 93, 98, 130, 131, 272, 275, 277
secular-religious divide   5, 8
security   24, 42n, 75, 112, 113, 177, 178, 179, 180, 182, 184, 188n, 199, 276, 284, 288, 289
Shamim Ara v. State of UP   50
sharia courts (Dar-ul-Qazas)   38, 43, 44, 45n
Shayarah Bano v. Union of India   46, 47, 54
sincerity of belief   105, 106, 117
Smt. Sarla Mudgal, President, Kalyani v. Union of India   38n
social construction of religious freedom   2, 3, 107, 220
Social Hostilities Index (SHI)   258
social movement organization   7, 198, 210, 211, 214, 215
sociology of religion   13, 16, 18, 27, 28, 62
Special Rapporteur on the freedom of religion or belief   207, 213, 284n, 285
Spickard, James V.   148, 176n
spiritual leader   6, 123, 125–127, 132, 138, 148
Stepan, Alfred   15, 271n
Sudan   77, 206, 207
Sullivan, Winnifred F.   1, 36, 177, 190

Taylor, Charles   13, 15, 18, 21, 151, 154, 245
total institution   7, 176, 190
Tunisia   4, 5, 9, 59–78
Turkey   6, 9, 28, 63, 64, 123–125, 127, 129, 132–134, 256, 258

unconstitutional   43, 47, 50, 51, 54, 94, 95
Uniform Civil Code   35, 35n, 36, 37, 40, 41, 50, 54
United Nation's Committees on Freedom of Religion or Belief   211
United Nations Standard Minimum Rules for the Treatment of Prisoners   177
United Nations   8, 177, 207, 223, 241, 242, 244, 244n, 245–247, 247n, 248, 249, 251, 252, 259, 264
Universal Declaration of Human Rights   279

veiling   21, 28, 114
Vishwa Lochan Madan v. Union of India   38

Waldensian church   224, 226–228, 231
Wohlrab-Sahr, Monika   1, 15, 37

Yang, Fenggang   3, 5, 84, 85, 152, 199
Yemen   77, 287

Zunera Ishaq v. Canada   105, 106, 108, 110–112, 115, 118

Printed in the United States
by Baker & Taylor Publisher Services